This volume of essays by the distinguished musicologist Charles Hamm focuses on the context of popular music: the interrelationships between popular music and other styles and genres, including classical music, the meaning of popular music for audiences, and the institutional appropriation of this music for hegemonic purposes. Specific topics include the use of popular song to rouse antislavery sentiment in mid-nineteenth-century America, the reception of such African-American styles and genres as rock 'n' roll and soul music by the black population of South Africa, the question of genre in the early songs of Irving Berlin, the attempts by the governments of South Africa and China to impose specific bodies of music on their populations, the persistence of the minstrel show in rural twentieth-century America, and the impact of modernist modes of thought on writing about popular music, with specific engagement with the work of John Cage.

PUTTING POPULAR MUSIC IN ITS PLACE

PUTTING POPULAR MUSIC
IN ITS PLACE

CHARLES HAMM

Emeritus Professor of Music,
Dartmouth College

CAMBRIDGE
UNIVERSITY PRESS

Published by the Press Syndicate of the University of Cambridge
The Pitt Building, Trumpington Street, Cambridge CB2 1RP
40 West 20th Street, New York, NY 10011-4211, USA
10 Stamford Road, Oakleigh, Melbourne 3166, Australia

Cambridge University Press 1995

First published 1995

Printed in Great Britain at the University Press, Cambridge

A catalogue record for this book is available from the British Library

Library of Congress cataloguing in publication data

Hamm, Charles.
Putting popular music in its place / Charles Hamm.
p.   cm.
Essays previously published between 1970 and 1993.
ISBN 0 521 47198 2 (hardback)
1. Popular music – History and criticism. I. Title.
ML3470.H35 1995
781.64'09–dc20 94-9191 CIP MN

ISBN 0 521 47198 2 hardback

CONTENTS

CONTENTS

ACKNOWLEDGEMENTS

Permission has kindly been granted to reprint the following essays first published elsewhere, as follows:

"Rock and the facts of life," *Yearbook for Inter-American Musical Research* 7 (1971), pp. 5–15. "Changing patterns in society and music: the US since World War II," in Charles Hamm, Bruno Nettl and Ronald Byrnside, *Contemporary Music and Music Cultures* (Englewood Cliffs, 1975), pp. 35–70. "'If I Were a Voice': or, The Hutchinson Family and popular song as political and social protest," in *Yesterdays: Popular Song in America* (New York and London, 1979), pp. 147–61. "Some thoughts on the measurement of popularity in music," in David Horn and Philip Tagg, eds., *Popular Music Perspectives* [I] (Gothenburg and Exeter, 1982), pp. 3–15. "*Elvis*, a review," *Journal of the American Musicological Society* 36/2 (Summer 1983), pp. 335–40. "Home cooking and American soul in black South African popular music," *Musica/Realtá* 11 (August 1983), pp. 75–89. "Rock 'n' roll in a very strange society," *Popular Music* 5 (1985), pp. 159–74. *African-American Music, South Africa, and Apartheid* (Brooklyn, 1988). "'The constant companion of man': Separate Development, Radio Bantu, and music," *Popular Music* 10/2 (1991), pp. 147–73. "Privileging the moment of reception: music and radio in South Africa," in Steven Paul Scher, ed., *Music and Text: Critical Inquiries* (Cambridge, 1992), pp. 21–37. "Music and radio in the People's Republic of China," *Asian Music* 22/2 (Spring/Summer 1991), pp. 1–42. "Towards a new reading of Gershwin," *Musica/Realtá* 25 (April 1988), pp. 23–45. "A blues for the ages," in Richard Crawford, R. Allen Lott and Carol J. Oja, eds., *A Celebration of American Music: Words and Music in Honor of H. Wiley Hitchcock* (Ann Arbor, 1990), pp. 346–55. "*Graceland* revisited," *Popular Music* 8/3 (October 1983), pp. 299–304. "*The Role of Rock*, a review," *Notes* (June 1992), pp. 1301–2. "Genre, performance, and ideology in the early songs of Irving Berlin," *Popular Music* 13/2 (1994), pp. 143–50. "John Cage revisited," *Journal of Popular Music Studies* 5 (1993), pp. 3–7.

PREFACE

This book contains a selection of my articles and reviews on the subject of popular music, written between 1970 and the present.

When I first tried to write about this subject, in the late 1960s, the world was changing in rapid and dramatic ways, and some popular music of the day seemed to be in tune with these changes. But I found that my academic training in historical musicology, a discipline proud of its tradition of humanistic positivism, was of limited use in dealing with this music and its place in the world.

My association with John Cage proved to be more useful. Even though Cage's music and aesthetics seem remote from and even antithetical to the sounds and environments of popular music, he was saying and doing things that helped make sense of whatever new world was emerging. No one was yet using the word "postmodern," but Cage imagined a non-linear universe in which things simply existed, without the connecting tissue of cause and effect. His proto-postmodern aesthetic proposed that an uncountable number of different events take place, none of them privileged in significance or power over any others and none of them understandable from the perspective of a single dominant system of meaning. This is not rampant relativism, but rather an affirmation of the uniqueness and value of each happening. "Here we are. Let us say Yes to our presence together in Chaos" he wrote; and "now structure is not put into a work, but comes up in the person who perceives it. There is therefore no problem of understanding but the possibility of awareness."[1]

By giving such elegant intellectual support to the notion, ridiculed

[1] John Cage, *Silence* (Middletown. CT, 1961), p. 259.

xi

in academic circles of the day, that every musical event is equally worthy of attention, Cage's aesthetic helped legitimize the study of any sort of music, including popular music. Just as important, since his aesthetic insisted that each musical event is unique, it seemed to follow that the goal of popular music study shouldn't be to construct one overriding interpretative scheme, but to be receptive to any given musical event and the circumstances under which it occurred.

Most of the following essays are in the nature of case studies of a repertory, or even a single piece of music, in historical, geographical, and musical context. Focused more on methodology than theory, they share several assumptions: (1) popular music, like all music, is both an acoustical and a social phenomenon and thus must be dealt with musically, though not necessarily at a technical level, as well as culturally; (2) one cannot fully understand the nature of a given musical event unless one is present at it, or can reconstruct it from critical or historical documentation; (3) popular music has never existed in isolation from other types of music and is best considered in terms of its interaction with other genres, most certainly including the classical repertory.

Though I was trained a historical musicologist, in a sense I've been a scholar without a home discipline for the last two decades. As a result, my essays have appeared in publications in a number of fields, and the chief purpose of the present volume is to bring a number of these pieces together. Since any writing about music, like music itself, takes place in a specific context, each essay is prefaced with brief autobiographical remarks placing myself at the time of writing and mentioning then-current literature on popular music. I've resisted the temptation to revise or correct: each piece is offered here as it first appeared, except that sections have been cut here and there to avoid redundancy.

Norwich, Vermont
November 1993

I

MODERNIST NARRATIVES AND POPULAR MUSIC

Popular music, as we understand the term today, was a product of the modern era, extending from the late eighteenth century through the first two-thirds of the twentieth, or from the industrial revolution through late capitalism.[1]

The modern era brought a concentration of power in the institutions of industrialized countries and a new set of economic and social relations within the developing systems of capitalism and socialism. It was a time of the emergence of large new nation-states, swallowing up previously autonomous city-states, regions, and smaller countries; of colonialism, with a handful of European countries taking military and economic control over much of the rest of the world, and then postcolonialism, with large international conglomerates playing the same role; and of oligarchical domination within industry, finance, and both state and private institutions. In contrast, today's postmodern world is marked by fragmentation, discontinuity, ephemerality, and chaos in economics, politics, social relations, and the arts.

The intellectual and ideological climate of the modern era encouraged various writers to construct meta-narratives: broad, all-encompassing schemes purporting to yield some "special mode of representation of eternal truth."[2] Lyotard, who sees the modern–postmodern dialectic as a "crisis of narratives," defines the modernist meta-narrative (in science):

> To the extent that science does not restrict itself to stating useful regularities and seeks the truth, it is obliged to legitimate the rules

---

[1] The term "extended nineteenth century" is sometimes used as an alternative label.
[2] David Harvey, *The Condition of Postmodernity* (Cambridge, MA, and Oxford, 1990), p. 20.

1

of its own game. It then produces a discourse of legitimation with respect to its own status, a discourse called philosophy. I will use the term modern to designate any science that legitimates itself with reference to a metadiscourse of this kind making an explicit appeal to some grand narrative, such as the dialectics of Spirit, the hermeneutics of meaning, the emancipation of the rational or working subject, or the creation of wealth . . . If a metanarrative implying a philosophy of history is used to legitimate knowledge, questions are raised concerning the validity of the institutions governing the social bond: these must be legitimated as well.[3]

Historical and critical writing about popular music is itself a product of the modern era. In the spirit of its time, much of it attempts not only to "legitimate the rules of its own game" and "the validity of the institutions governing the social bond" but also attempts to "seek the truth," drawing on some "philosophy of history" to "legitimate knowledge." Some of it approaches meta-narrative; but the less pretentious term "narrative" seems more appropriate.

These narratives have common features. As befits their origin in modernist thinking, each is hierarchical and exclusionary, tending to privilege some genre or repertory of music over all others. None originated as a single essay, manifesto, or polemic; each appears in the work of various writers of common ideological bent, permeating modernist writing on music from the most utilitarian to the most arcane, as assertions and assumptions in the nature of belief systems and therefore not requiring explication or intellectual development. They often approach myth, in the general meaning of this term as "a purely fictitious narrative . . . embodying some popular idea concerning natural or historical phenomena."[4]

What follows is intended not as a comprehensive survey of writing on popular music,[5] but as an attempt to identify and describe several modernist narratives shaping this literature.

The narrative of musical autonomy

The essence and value of a piece of music resides in the text, in the music itself, not in its reception and use. Judged in this way, popular music is artistically and morally inferior to the classical repertory and is thus not deserving of serious scholarly attention. It does, however,

[3] Jean-François Lyotard, *The Postmodern Condition: A Report on Knowledge*, trans. Geoff Bennington and Brian Massumi (Minneapolis, 1984), pp. xxiii–xxiv. Originally published as *La Condition postmoderne: rapport sur le savoir* (Paris, 1979).
[4] *The Compact Edition of the Oxford English Dictionary* (Oxford, 1971), p. 1889.
[5] For a comprehensive survey and criticism of the history of popular music study, see Richard Middleton, *Studying Popular Music* (Milton Keynes and Philadelphia, 1990).

mirror the society in which it was created more directly than does
classical music.

Early in the modern era, a distinction developed in the Western
world between the music of the elite classes, comprising both
classical ("high art") music and the less technically demanding
genres of the bourgeois parlor, and that of the people, encompassing
both folk and popular music (as these two terms came to be used in
the twentieth century). Classical music, preserved in musical notation
and performed by professionals for passive audiences, was understood
to be universal and eternal, with a single repertory serving for the
entire (Western) world. The music of the people, created and passed
on chiefly in oral tradition, often in a participatory environment,
was taken to be regional and ephemeral.

By the late nineteenth century, socially based distinctions between
"highbrow" (classical) and "lowbrow" (folk and popular) music had
become even more rigid.[6] The classical repertory, symbolizing order
and permanence and thus power, continued to be associated with
and supported by the aristocracy, as before, but now more importantly
by industrialists, financiers, and the bourgeoisie. A supportive
narrative took shape, holding that the European classical repertory
was superior to all other music within and outside the Western
world. At its crudest, this narrative took the form of a set of
supposedly commonsensical assertions:

> In general terms "Classical Music," like Classical Literature, is that
> which has been recognized by the ages as of the best and highest
> class. Thus, in common acceptance, "classical" is the antithesis of
> "popular." In its stricter sense, a classical production is one that
> has stood the test of time, and has come to be acknowledged by
> scholars and teachers of the art as a model of purity of style and
> form, and most worthy of emulation . . . because of [its] purity of
> form, universality of idea and permanent value to musical art.
>
> In general terms that music is popular which makes an easy
> appeal to the masses. There can be no definition of popular music
> that will apply equally to the music of all nationalities, for the
> reason that standards of taste differ in the various countries.
>
> Less civilized peoples, even the wildest tribes of Africa or
> fiercest islanders of the South Seas, have a "music," and rude
> musical instruments which are their own. They have their battle
> songs, and their funeral dirges.
>
> Feasts, weddings, even cannibal orgies, are accompanied with
> some sort of a succession of sounds chanted with accompaniments

---

[6] See Lawrence W. Levine, *Highbrow/Lowbrow: The Emergence of Cultural Hierarchy in America* (Cambridge, MA, and London, 1988), for an account of this process in the United States.

pounded from rude instruments. The more civilized the people, the nearer to some form or rhythm and the more intelligible their music.[7]

Underlying this narrative is the assumption that music is autonomous; that is, its value resides in the musical composition itself and not in its reception and use. From this follows the notion that distinctions between "the best and highest" music and all lesser genres, as well as between "masterpieces" of the classical repertory and lesser pieces within this genre, are to be found in details of melody, harmony, form, rhythm, and instrumentation. As Dahlhaus put it, the great works of classical music came to be seen as "ideal objects with an immutable and unshifting 'real' meaning," and the function of the scholar dealing with these objects "consists in the gradual unfolding of [this] meaning,"[8] a view grounded in nineteenth-century German idealism and the concepts of genius and individual masterpieces.

> The autonomy principle was closely allied to the aesthetic of genius and the notion of originality, both survivals from the late eighteenth century. Not only was autonomous music vindicated in a formal and aesthetic sense by musical logic, it also received a philosophical legitimation – a "necessity for existing," to use Novalis's phrase – by being the product of genius . . . [though] this aesthetic was never committed to paper during the age itself.[9]

Despite the intellectual poverty of this argument, based as it is on little but assertion,[10] it came to dominate Western attitudes towards music throughout the modern era, enabling musicologists and critics to ignore all music lying outside the Western classical repertory, even to the extent of appropriating the term "music" for this repertory and this repertory alone. Consequently, virtually all the literature on popular music for the first two-thirds of the twentieth century was the work of non-academics, chiefly journalists and dilettantes, whose writings at first glance may appear to have little to do with the narrative of musical autonomy. But in fact this literature

---

[7] Nathaniel I. Rubinkam, *Masterpieces of Melody and the Musical Art* (Chicago, 1906), pp. 36–9. Rubinkam held a Ph.D. from the University of Chicago.

[8] Carl Dahlhaus, *Foundations of Music History* (Cambridge, 1983), pp. 150, 155. First published as *Grundlagen der Musikgeschichte* (Cologne, 1967). [9] Dahlhaus, *Foundations*, p. 147.

[10] Theodor W. Adorno developed a much more sophisticated set of arguments around the concept of autonomy. For a summary, see Middleton, *Studying Popular Music*, pp. 39–42. For further criticism of the modernist view of musical autonomy, see Janet Wolff, "The ideology of autonomous art," in *Music and Society: The Politics of Composition, Performance and Reception*, ed. Richard Leppert and Susan McClary (Cambridge, 1987), pp. 1–12; Rose Rosengard Subotnik, "The role of ideology in the study of Western music," *Journal of Musicology* 2/1 (Winter 1983), pp. 1–12; and Edward W. Said, *Musical Elaborations* (New York, 1991).

is so grounded in the assumption that music outside the classical repertory is not worthy of attention that it makes no attempt to deal with musical aspects of the popular repertory, in even the most general way.

Sometimes the assumed inferiority of popular music is made explicit, as in an early biography of Irving Berlin:

> [Berlin] came into the world with an unrivalled capacity for inventing themes. But to that birthright he has added little of the art, the patience, the interest in form, and the musicianly knowledge which could elaborate them. It is an injustice at once to his true achievements, to his deepest aspirations and to his honest unpretentiousness to link his name with a Wagner or Rimsky-Korsakoff. . . . In time his music will be heard from the Metropolitan's stage. There is small doubt of that. But it will be heard after other men, with less inventive genius perhaps but with far greater musicianship, have picked his tunes up from the streets and transmuted them into operas as Moussorgsky and Rimsky-Korsakoff rifled the treasure chests of Russian folk music to make their finest scores.[11]

Similarly, the author of the first book-length study of popular music, after promising to demonstrate that this genre is "a most revealing index to American life" that "sums up the ethics, the habits, the slang, the intimate character of every generation," makes it clear that he attaches no great value to the product itself:

> [Popular music] is all part of our fast-working, well-routined machine age, dealing in formulas, in slogans, in short cuts, but often side-stepping honest realities. The universe of the popular song is unique in the history of mankind. It has its own private system of absurdities and needs little more than direct quotation to receive its due of laughter in Olympus. . . . Many a fine poet or excellent composer might find it exceedingly difficult to produce anything with a wide popular appeal, simply because of his inability to make his expression convincing to the masses of listeners. To make such an appeal it is actually necessary to be one of those whose personal responses are of the naive and childlike type.
>
> In its reaction to entertainment of all kinds the human race will probably never grow up. After all, why should it?[12]

And in the first historical survey of popular music in the United States, offered as a "record of our history," this same author takes pains to explain that even though he considers popular music to be

[11] Alexander Woollcott, *The Story of Irving Berlin* (New York and London, 1925), pp. 218–20.
[12] Sigmund Spaeth, *The Facts of Life in Popular Song* (New York and London, 1934), pp. iii–iv, 148.

"historically and racially important," he is nevertheless convinced that "artistic merit has nothing to do with it":

> It would be foolish to deny the obvious fact that America's popular songwriters have written some incredibly banal, absurd, bathetic stuff, badly rhymed, often ungrammatical, with cheap, obvious, commonplace tunes. They have had this material promoted in various ways, of which the general public is quite ignorant, often involving some chicanery, even downright bribery. The personal characters of the songwriters themselves have not always been above reproach, and many of them could with difficulty command respect either as artists or as human beings.
>
> It is impossible for a history of popular music in America to be continually complimentary either to its materials or to those who produced them. But it can at least attempt to analyze the reasons for certain established successes, . . . [and] in the process of such analysis, including the mere listing of much that may be considered important only for the sake of the record, such a book may throw considerable light on what Americans were thinking and doing at certain periods, how they reacted to the common impulses of life and what emotions they inherited from their ancestors and passed on to their descendants.[13]

Most subsequent books of this sort on popular music have similarly assumed that the study of musical texts is best left to musicologists and theorists, who have the analytical tools to examine the classical repertory for evidence of order and eternal truth, while writing on popular music should concentrate on the lives of composers and performers, and on song lyrics, searching for insights into social history. One such book, for instance, is subtitled "The history of the American popular song told through the lives, careers, achievements, and personalities of its foremost composers and lyricists,"[14] while another explains that the songs of the Tin Pan Alley era were "a mirror to and a voice of America during a period of formidable growth and change. The fads and fashions, the fluctuating mores, tastes, and moral attitudes, the current events and economic crises, the passing moods and social forces – all that made up American social history – were caught, fixed, and interpreted in words and music."[15]

Even though rock 'n' roll and other popular genres of the 1950s and 60s brought a new generation of journalistic writers on popular

[13] Sigmund Spaeth, *A History of Popular Music in America* (New York, 1948), pp. 3, 584–5.

[14] David Ewen, *Great Men of American Popular Song* (Englewood Cliffs, 1970).

[15] David Ewen, *The Life and Death of Tin Pan Alley* (New York, 1964), p. xiv.

music with more enthusiasm for their subject,[16] most of them were still concerned with showing that popular music "reflected American life as it really is" by "[catching] the moods and manners of their times and express[ing] them in a way that satisfied, entertained, perhaps even thrilled the people for whom [it was] intended,"[17] and not with considering the music itself.

Even recent books of this sort, including those most dedicated to establishing the legitimacy and historical importance of popular genres, still have nothing to say about the music, and thus, even though unwittingly, continue to perpetuate the myth of its inferiority.[18]

The narrative of mass culture

Communications systems of the modern era made it possible for cultural products to be widely disseminated. Since these systems were economically driven, and since the less "cultured" classes comprise the bulk of the population, the communications industry has found it economically imperative to give priority to products geared to the inferior artistic and moral levels of the lower classes. In the process, the general cultural level sinks to the lowest common denominator, and "cultivated" artistic and moral standards are endangered.

MacDonald Smith Moore has argued that a group of American musicians and intellectuals, mostly from New England, developed the ideology of a "redemptive" culture in the decades surrounding the turn of the twentieth century.[19] Though serving most obviously to privilege the music of their choice, the classical repertory, this narrative was even more importantly a response to fears that the predominantly Anglo-American–Protestant culture of the elite classes was under siege by people of other classes and ethnicities, as first- and second-generation working-class Americans became more militant in their demands for a greater role in the country's economy and culture, at the same time that millions of immigrants from Central Europe and the Mediterranean lands were pouring into the country. Philip H. Goepp, educated at Harvard and in Germany, wrote in 1897:

[16] For a comprehensive survey of the literature on popular music, see David Horn (with Richard Jackson), *The Literature of American Music in Books and Folk Music Collections: A Fully Annotated Bibliography* (Metuchen, 1977). A supplement, with the same title, was published in 1988.   [17] Spaeth, *A History of Popular Music*, p. 6.

[18] See, for instance, Ed Ward, Geoffrey Stokes, and Ken Tucker, *Rock of Ages: The Rolling Stone History of Rock & Roll* (New York, 1986).

[19] MacDonald Smith Moore, *Yankee Blues: Musical Culture and American Identity* (Bloomington, 1985).

It is the hour for the declaration of independence, and strangely, not of the many from the leaders, but of the leaders from the many. . . . In the classical past it was our good fortune to have none but true leaders. We learned to trust them unconsciously as well as implicitly. But with later democratic stirrings there came inevitable demagoguism. Men appealed over the heads of those who had the true, the saner intuition to the ruder mob to whom clear thought was naught, sensational amusement all. Democratic as we must be in government, there is no doubt that the bursts of popular will throughout the nineteenth century have had a sinister effect upon art. The lower instincts with the lower classes have broken away from the higher. Within the right meaning, the true democrat in government not only can, he must be the true aristocrat in art.[20]

"In a symphony of Beethoven the ultimate purpose is the utterance of the high thought or feeling of a great man," Goepp insists; "where there is a beautiful expression there must be nobility of the prompting thought," elevated above the "lower instincts of the lower classes." At issue is not merely "beauty," though: the "moral quality," "high aspirations," and "honesty" of the music of a master composer "shines clear throughout his art."[21]

The elite had not been concerned with the "inferior" cultural products of the lower classes as long as they were contained within their own cultural spaces; but with the development of the new mass media – radio, phonograph, film – they moved out of this space and became available to the entire population. As a professor of music at Columbia University saw it:

The very vastness of the radio audience which [is] so exciting to the commercial mind, is seen to be, for the artistic or humane mind, a matter for apprehension rather than jubilation. To be candid, the commercial and the higher human interests seem to be here flatly opposed. For it is a fundamental axiom that majority taste is always comparatively crude and undeveloped, and that where it is allowed to dominate, art languishes and dies; on the other hand, art survives and grows only where majority taste undergoes that winnowing and progressive refining whereby minority standards emerge from it.

As an instance of this crudity of majority taste one may cite the case of jazz. The features of jazz to which it owes its popularity are precisely the ones that make it most intolerable to a sound taste: its banal melody, its commonplace and sometimes sugary and sentimental harmony, its obvious, over-accented, monotonous

---

[20] Philip H. Goepp, *Great Works of Music: Symphonies and their Meaning* (New York, 1897), pp. 15–17.   [21] *Ibid.*, pp. 19–22.

rhythm. . . . The crying trouble with our whole radio condition in America is the unenlightened commercialism of its administrators. These producers, stupid men who happen to have achieved a little financial power but have no musical feeling or experience, are complacently unaware that their own taste is far lower than that of at least the more influential minority of their public.[22]

And this from America's most celebrated composer of the early twentieth century:

Perhaps the most obvious [problem] is commercialism, with its influence tending towards mechanization and standardized processes of mind and life. Emasculating America for money! Is the Anglo-Saxon going "Pussy"? – the nice Lizzies – the cautious old girls running the broadcasting companies – those great national brain-softeners, the movies – the mind-dulling tabloids – the ladybirds – the female–male crooners – they are all getting theirs, and America is not! Is she gradually losing her manhood? . . . Music has been, to too large an extent, an emasculated art. And 98 $\frac{1}{4}$% of all radio music is worse than molly-coddle – it's the one-syllable gossip for the soft-ears-and-stomachs, easy for the bodies, and is fundamentally art prostituted for commercialism. . . . Lowest of all [are] the publishing, the broadcasting, and recording for profit. . . . helping music decline – dying – dying – dead.[23]

While the overt themes of this narrative are that "high" culture is artistically and morally superior to "low," and that new systems of mass communication are being used to disseminate intellectually and morally inferior and even dangerous cultural products, there's a critical sub-text: the assumption, usually lying just beneath the surface but occasionally made explicit, that the people creating, disseminating, and consuming these mass products are of inferior ethnic, class, or moral stock.

This narrative is not primarily critical of the economic system of capitalism that makes the production of "mass culture" possible and profitable, but is directed against producers and consumers themselves for their dissemination and consumption of artistically and morally inferior products.

---

[22] Daniel Gregory Mason, *Tune In, America* (New York, 1931), pp. 72–3, 76. Mason is using "jazz" in the context of the period, as a catch-all term for the products of the music industry, particularly Tin Pan Alley.

[23] John Kirkpatrick, ed., *Charles E. Ives: Memos* (New York, 1972), pp. 133–6. This passage was written in the early 1930s.

There are theoretical reasons why Mass Culture is not and can never be any good. I take it as axiomatic that culture can only be produced by and for human beings. But in so far as people are organized (more strictly, disorganized) as masses, they lose their human identity and quality. For the masses are in historical time what a crowd is in space: a large quantity of people unable to express themselves as human beings because they are related to one another neither as individuals nor as members of communities. . . . A mass society, like a crowd, is so undifferentiated and loosely structured that its atoms, in so far as human values go, tend to cohere only along the line of the least common denominator; its morality sinks to that of its most brutal and primitive members, its taste to that of the least sensitive and most ignorant.[24]

No one has articulated the mass culture critics' sense of superiority and loathing towards consumers of mass culture better than Allan Bloom, who reduces the object of scorn from the collective to the individual:

Picture a thirteen-year-old boy sitting in the living room of his family home doing his math assignment while wearing his Walkman headphones or watching MTV. He enjoys the liberties hard won over centuries by the alliance of philosophic genius and political heroism, consecrated by the blood of martyrs; he is provided with comfort and leisure by the most productive economy ever known to mankind; science has penetrated the secrets of nature in order to provide him with the marvelous, lifelike electronic sounds and image reproduction he is enjoying. And in what does progress culminate? A pubescent child whose body throbs with orgasmic rhythms; whose feelings are made articulate in hymns to the joys of onanism or the killing of parents; whose ambition is to win fame and wealth in imitating the drag-queen who makes the music. In short, life is made into a nonstop, commercially pre-packaged masturbational fantasy.[25]

As this passage makes achingly clear, the most important agenda of the modernist narrative of mass culture is the privileging of some repertory or genre of music over allegedly inferior cultural products, and thus the privileging of those people who understand and respond to this "superior" culture over those who produce and consume mass culture.

[24] Dwight Macdonald, "A theory of mass culture," in *Mass Culture: The Popular Arts in America*, ed. Bernard Rosenberg and David Manning White (New York, 1957), pp. 69–70.
[25] Allan Bloom, *The Closing of the American Mind* (New York, 1987), pp. 74–5.

The first narrative of authenticity

> Ethnic, racial, or national groups can develop distinctive types of
> music giving authentic expression to their culture. Such music tends
> to be compromised in the modern world through conversion into
> commercial commodities. This process can be subverted by the
> intervention of persons with the requisite knowledge and education
> to retrieve the authentic product.

The myth that commercial production separates superior from
inferior music, and that music consumed by a mass audience must,
by this fact alone, be inferior to the music of a more select group, has
taken a different turn in literature on the music of groups defined by
ethnic composition.

The historiography of ragtime is a case in point. The term itself
was first used in the last years of the nineteenth century for a
performance style originating in African-American culture, then for
newly composed pieces drawing on elements of this style. By the
mid-1910s ragtime had been superseded by a more generic syncopated
dance style, and the only literature on the genre before 1950 was the
work of early historians of jazz, who treated it as an early stage in the
evolution of that genre. The 1950s, however, brought the so-called
Ragtime Revival, sparked by the publication of the book *They All
Played Ragtime*.[26] Rather than being a holistic history of the genre,
the book dismisses most of what had been known as ragtime by
tossing out all the "well-forgotten junk" once bearing that label.

> The real story of ragtime is not that of Tin Pan Alley and its
> million-dollar hits, of hacks and copyists, of song hucksters. The
> real story of ragtime is that of a song that came from the people and
> then got lost. The commercial tunesmiths of Tin Pan Alley did
> their level best to ruin the music, to wring every last dollar from
> cheap and trumped-up imitations of a folk music, and to glut the
> market to the last extreme of surfeit. The popular nature of
> ragtime's acceptance, too, stamped it in the minds of serious
> music-lovers as mere ephemeral trash, and this a priori judgement
> still prevails.[27]

This view of ragtime was accepted by a generation of "revivalists" –
all white, incidentally – who promulgated it through their writings
and their intervention as performers and entrepreneurs. Even
Gilbert Chase's brilliant and seminal book on American music insists
that while ragtime was "deeply rooted in our folk and popular

---

[26] Rudi Blesh and Harriet Janis, *They All Played Ragtime* (New York, 1950). Revised editions
appeared in 1959, 1966, and 1971.   [27] *Ibid.*, pp. 5, 220.

traditions" and was a "movement genuinely creative at the core that produced a permanent body of music and exerted an enduring influence," the "overexploitation by commercial interests, the high-pressure promotion of pseudo ragtime, and the mechanical repetition of routine formulas soon brought about the decline of ragtime as a vital form of American music."[28]

Underlying the revivalists' writing and entrepreneurship was a stated concern with both historical authenticity (who composed, published, and performed what pieces, when and under whose influence) and stylistic authenticity (at what speed and with what touch and articulation the music was played originally, and therefore should be played now). But social authenticity was never considered: even though what was considered to be authentic ragtime had been largely the music of black Americans, the revivalists and their audiences were overwhelmingly white and highly educated, and its new social setting and cultural meaning had nothing to do with its original environment and audience.

One thread of jazz scholarship has shared a similar focus on "authenticity." Like ragtime, jazz is rooted in African-American culture and derives its most distinguishing stylistic elements from black music. Though its earliest practitioners were black, it was soon played by whites as well; and as happened with ragtime, jazz was appropriated by the music industry through the writing of songs and instrumental pieces by Tin Pan Alley composers and the production and dissemination of sheet music and phonograph records of this repertory, aimed chiefly at white consumers.

The first writings on jazz were journalistic accounts of white musicians and audiences. As noted in my essay below on George Gershwin's Concerto in F, the first purported history of the genre, Henry O. Osgood's So This Is Jazz,[29] devoted entire chapters to Irving Berlin, George Gershwin, and Paul Whiteman and dismissed black jazz musicians in a single footnote. Paul Whiteman's Jazz[30] likewise makes only passing reference to black performers, and Isaac Goldberg's George Gershwin: A Study in American Music, while admitting that jazz is "traceable in part to the Negro," argues that it

---

[28] Gilbert Chase, *America's Music: From the Pilgrims to the Present* (New York, 1955), pp. 433, 451. More recently, the revivalists' use of the term "ragtime" for only a fraction of the repertory has been challenged by Edward Berlin ("It seems that the great ragtime successes were not piano pieces at all, but songs") in *Ragtime: A Musical and Cultural History* (Berkeley, 1980), p. 70, and John Hasse ("Ragtime was piano music, surely, but it was also songs, music for banjo, band, and orchestra . . . produced by blacks and whites, but certainly most of the consumers were white") in *Ragtime: Its History, Composers, and Music* (New York, 1985), p. viii.　　[29] Boston, 1926.　　[30] New York, 1926.

was "developed, commercially and artistically, by the Jew," chiefly in New York City.[31]

But by the late 1930s some critics had begun reasserting the African-American origins of jazz and reassessing the talents of black jazz performers. The journal *Downbeat* devoted equal attention to white and black jazz musicians and bands from its inception in 1934, particularly in the writings of John Hammond. Shortly thereafter, a school of criticism began to emerge around the theme that "true" jazz, like ragtime before it, was in fact an authentic black art, threatened by, but always superior to, the products of the white-controlled music industry and media. The French jazz critic Hugues Panassié wrote in 1942:

> Since jazz is a music created by the colored people, it is very difficult and, in fact, almost impossible for a white man to get to the heart of it at first shot. . . . [At] the time my first book was finished in 1934 . . . I had had the bad luck to become acquainted with jazz first through white musicians, through the recordings of Red Nichols, Frankie Trumbauer, Bix, Ben Pollack, whose music, because it differed enormously from that of the great colored musicians, could not give an exact idea of authentic jazz. . . . I did not realize until some years after the publication of my first book that, from the point of view of jazz, most white musicians were inferior to colored musicians. . . . [T]he number of white musicians who have succeeded in assimilating the musical inspiration of the Negroes (and that is the real spirit of jazz) is far smaller than I believed a few years ago.[32]

Another French critic echoed these words:

> The day is past when [jazz] was symbolized for Europeans by the names of Paul Whiteman, George Gershwin, Ted Lewis, Jack Hylton, Jean Wiener, and Clément Doucet, and when the colored star of *The Jazz Singer* turned out to be a white man, Al Jolson, made up in blackface for local color. By now it has become evident that jazz is the Negro's art and that almost all the great jazz musicians are Negroes.[33]

The idea that jazz was an authentic black product, distinct from the bogus jazz produced for a mass audience by the music industry, was widely accepted, though not always clearly articulated, by the next

---

[31] New York, 1931.

[32] Hugues Panassié, *The Real Jazz* (New York, 1960), pp. 9–10. Revised and enlarged edition, first published in 1942.

[33] André Hodeir, *Jazz: Its Evolution and Essence*, trans. David Noakes (New York, 1956), p. 7. Originally published 1954, in French.

generation of jazz journalists, critics, and historians. Martin Williams, for instance, organized his book *The Jazz Tradition* into twenty-three essays each dealing with a single performer or group, all but one of them black.[34] Gunther Schuller, writing in 1968, found it necessary to explain why he included even brief comments about several white musicians and bands in his *Early Jazz: Its Roots and Musical Development*: "The inclusion of the Original Dixieland Jazz Band may surprise some readers," he writes; but even though he says that the group "has been exaggeratedly denigrated, and because the ODJB was a white group, many have found it difficult to accord it the recognition it deserves," his own comments are scarcely less derogatory than those of other critics:

> The ODJB reduced New Orleans Negro music to a simplified formula. It took a new idea, an innovation, and reduced it to the kind of compressed, rigid format that could appeal to a mass audience. As such it had a number of sure-fire ingredients, the foremost being a rhythmic momentum that had a physical, even visceral appeal. Moreover, this rhythmic drive was cast in the most unsubtle terms, as was the ODJB's melodic and harmonic language, with none of the flexibility and occasional subtlety shown by the best Negro bands of the period. But in its rigid substitution of sheer energy for expressive power, of rigid formula for inspiration, the ODJB had found the key to mass appeal.[35]

Elsewhere, Schuller dismisses an entire group of white jazzmen – Jimmy McPartland, Bud Freeman, Frank Teschemacher, Eddie Condon, Gene Krupa, Red Nichols, the Dorsey Brothers, Phil Napoleon, Miff Mole – with the comment that "ultimately they remain in the realm of the commercial performances geared to a thriving mass market requiring a consumer's product," and a footnote dealing with Paul Whiteman's Orchestra concludes that even though "there is in the best Whiteman performances a feeling and a personal sound as unique in its way as Ellington's or Basie's, it was just not based on a jazz conception."[36]

My point is not at all to dispute that the roots of jazz lie in African-American culture and that the best jazz musicians have been black, but to suggest that the argument that only a certain repertory played by certain black musicians is authentic, and that the genre has otherwise been subverted by media exploitation and appropriation by inferior white musicians, distorts two aspects of the history of

[34] Martin Williams, *The Jazz Tradition* (New York, 1970).
[35] Gunther Schuller, *Early Jazz: Its Roots and Musical Development* (New York, 1968), pp. 179–80.
[36] *Ibid.*, pp. 192, 194.

popular music: the critical role played by the mass media in the development of jazz and other genres by black musicians themselves; and the historical reality of repertories created by white musicians and accepted by contemporary audiences and performers as "jazz," even though these were stylistically different from the music of black performers. The attitude epitomized in the following statement functions not only to privilege one body of music above all others and thus to justify the neglect of the latter, it also serves to privilege the writer above those incapable of making the same judgements:

> Tin-Pan Alley and the production of Hit Parade tunes are a big business in which a large amount of money is invested. The investors, of course, want a good and, above all, a steady return on their investments. So they find out what will sell, reduce it to the most simple formula, and manufacture it on an assembly line like tin-cans. Expose the average person to all kinds of popular music and it is safe to say that, sooner or later, he will recognize the superior vitality and honesty of jazz.[37]

Scholars of folk and traditional musics, working within the academic disciplines of folklore, anthropology, and ethnomusicology, produced their own narrative of authenticity. As Bruno Nettl summarizes it, "this concept is rooted in the idea that each culture has a primordial musical style of its own, and that songs and traits learned at a later time in its history are not properly part of its music. An authentic song is thought to be one truly belonging to the people who sing it, one that really reflects their spirit and personality."[38]

For example, in the late nineteenth century James Francis Child designated a group of British ballads as the authentic, core repertory of that genre. He and other scholars then analyzed various versions of these ballads, seeking to discover the oldest and thus most authentic texts. Subsequently collected repertories of individual singers and of entire areas, such as the Appalachian region of the United States, were judged to be more or less authentic by the presence or absence of these canonical ballads, and more recent ballads and "corrupt" versions of older ones were judged to be inferior cultural products by scholars whose chief concern was with the so-called authentic repertory.

The notion that folk music is the authentic expression of some group of people traces back to the dawning of the modern era, in the

---

[37] Marshall Stearns, *The Story of Jazz* (New York, 1956), p. 323.
[38] Bruno Nettl, *Folk and Traditional Music of the Western Continents* (Englewood Cliffs, 1973), p. 9.

writings of Herder, among others. Cecil Sharp summed up this position in the early twentieth century:

> Folk song is essentially a communal as well as a racial product. There is no music so characteristic of the German people as German folk song, so characteristic of the Russian people as Russian folk music. . . . English folk song is distinctively national and English, and, therefore, inherently different from that of every other nation in the world.[39]

Since folk music is seen as the spontaneous expression of a culturally defined group, giving voice to its inner nature, any mediation by individuals or institutions outside this group is taken as a threat to its authenticity. Thus "folklorists tend to exclude as spurious or contaminated any supposed folklore that is transmitted largely by print, broadcasting, or other commercial and organized means";[40] authenticity and commercial production are seen as irreconcilable. And just as many scholars of ragtime and jazz have also been activists through promotion and dissemination of "authentic" products once they had been identified, so folk-music scholars bring out editions and recordings – not for dissemination among the people who created this music in the first place, but among academic and intellectual communities.

In time it became clear that the ideology of textual authenticity had been imposed on the material by scholars themselves. Most folk musicians and their audiences accept evolution and change, and the creation of new repertory, as normal and desirable; and often the various mass media not only disseminate cultural products later regarded as "authentic," they can even be instrumental in shaping such repertories.

In summary, some of the literature on ragtime and jazz puts forward a version of a modernist narrative formulated first by scholars of folk and traditional music: a stable, authentic repertory shaped in an isolated and culturally pure environment is distinct from, superior to, but unfortunately threatened by, subsequent commercial and contaminated products. Richard Middleton calls this the narrative of "romantic primitivism," whereby "one [music] is 'false', the other 'true to experience'. One is corrupt, manipulated, over-complex, mechanical, commodified or whatever; the other is more natural, spontaneous, traditional."[41] This narrative has been

---

[39] Cecil Sharp, *English Folk Song. Some Conclusions* (Belmont, CA, 1965), pp. 164–5. Fourth edition, first published in 1907.

[40] Jan Harold Brunvand, *The Study of American Folklore: An Introduction* (New York, 1968), p. 2.

[41] Middleton, *Studying Popular Music*, p. 168.

shaped not by musicians and audiences of the groups in question, but by scholars and other writers from other economic, social, and geographical backgrounds.

The narrative of classic and classical popular music

> Popular music, like classical, can produce superior individual master-pieces and even entire sub-genres. The identification and preservation of these, and the explication of the differences between them and inferior products, is the responsibility of the critic and scholar.

As noted above in the discussion of the narrative of musical autonomy, the early modern period regarded popular music as ephemeral and classical music as eternal. This perception had to do largely with different modes of dissemination between the two genres. Popular (i.e., folk or traditional) music is in fact anything but ephemeral, as the persistence of specific pieces in certain repertories over centuries will attest; but since this music exists in oral tradition, it undergoes variation, accretion, and transformation from performance to performance, and over time. Classical music, on the other hand, fixed in musical notation, retains its overall structure and its defining melodic, rhythmic, and harmonic patterns from generation to generation; only nuances of articulation, phrasing, tempo, and dynamics vary with individual performances.

As popular music itself began taking on permanent physical form in the later nineteenth and early twentieth centuries, in musical notation or on phonographic discs, some pieces showed unmistakable evidence of durability in more or less fixed form, and the eternal–ephemeral dichotomy as a distinction between classical and popular music became less tenable. As Sigmund Spaeth argued in the first history of popular music in America:

> A "classic" is after all nothing more than a work of art that has established its permanence, and in music such a masterpiece may prove to be more honestly popular than any hit song of the moment. A symphony like Beethoven's *Fifth* or Schubert's *Unfinished* has probably been played in some form more often during its lifetime than any "popular" piece. Conversely, a popular song may easily achieve the permanence that makes it in the best sense a classic, with the lyric inspirations of Stephen Foster as shining examples.[42]

The publisher John Stark and the composer Scott Joplin were

---

[42] Spaeth, *A History of Popular Music*, p. 6.

apparently the first to assign the label "classic" to items of the popular repertory, in this case some of Joplin's pieces for piano, to signal that they were of "superior artistic quality [and] worthy of serious consideration."[43] Several decades later Rudi Blesh, convinced that "Scott Joplin and his colleagues were actually 'classical' composers, the American counterparts of European art composers of the eighteenth and nineteenth centuries,"[44] set out to "separate once and for all the obviously transient music from that which may legitimately claim to have realized the ideal of permanence."[45]

The identification of "classic" pieces within the popular repertory soon spread from ragtime to jazz criticism, where it began to take on other attributes of the discourse of classical music as well. Martin Williams sees the history of jazz as a succession of great individual musicians producing a string of masterpieces. He also believes that the qualities separating these masterpieces from inferior works are internal to the music itself; in other words, he treats jazz music – and its performers – as being autonomous. Rejecting the work of unnamed "Marxist critics" who see "the complexities of man and his art as merely the transient tools of 'social forces'," Williams insists that "no music depends so much on the individual as jazz."

> No jazz player is supposed to sound like any other player. A musician's instrumental voice should be as uniquely personal as is his speaking voice, but obviously its quality must be more a matter of deliberate, conscious development than that of his speaking voice. One could probably tell the history of jazz in terms of the way in which this concept of individual sound has been developed, modified, and enlarged over the years.[46]

Singling out twenty-three men and women for inclusion in a canon of great jazz musicians, he discusses their masterpieces as isolated, autonomous works. Typical are his comments on Thelonius Monk:

> He is not an "entertainer"; he does not "show" us anything. Everything he says, he says musically, directly, unadorned; he is all music and his technique is jazz technique. His greatest importance lies in the fact that Monk is an artist with an artist's deeply felt sense of life and an artist's drive to communicate the surprising and enlightening truth of it in his own way. . . . *Jazz has had precious few of his kind.*[47]

The notion that a canon of artistically superior and hence "classic"

[43] Edward Berlin, *Ragtime*, p. 186.   [44] *Ibid.*, p. 179.
[45] Blesh and Janis, *They All Played Ragtime*, p. 6.
[46] Williams, *The Jazz Tradition*, pp. 261–3.   [47] *Ibid.*, pp. 166–7.

pieces can be identified within a given popular genre has now spread from jazz to broadway musicals, popular ballads, and even country-western music.[48]

Marshall Stearns's history of jazz not only agrees that the masterpieces of jazz must be separated from the chaff of most "commercial" music, but goes beyond that to posit a direct relationship between the musical materials of certain pieces of "classic" jazz and the classical repertory.

> In the course of assimilating more and more elements of classical music – and thereby, incidentally, gaining social status – jazz generally turns to early classical forms, especially a free kind of counterpoint. . . . Both the Dave Brubeck Quartet and the Modern Jazz Quartet were achieving this in different ways [and] . . . produced music of high quality.[49]

Following Blesh, other critics have proposed that entire sub-genres, or even the entire field of jazz, should be considered "classical" on grounds of superiority to other popular styles and genres. James Lincoln Collier distinguishes between the early and late stages of jazz and equates the latter with classical music: "jazz has travelled a long way on its journey from the disreputable subculture to social and artistic respectability. It is widely considered an art."[50] Max Harrison writes that in the course of its "evolutionary succession of styles," jazz has developed "the continuity, logic and inner necessity that characterize the real art"; he concludes by offering a quote from Schoenberg's "Theory of Form" (1924) as fitting for what he considers the best jazz: "The higher an artistic ideal stands, the greater the range of questions, complexes, associations, problems and feelings it will have to cover; and the better it succeeds in compressing this universality into a minimum space, the higher it will stand."[51]

Beginning with John Hammond, many of the critics and scholars who insisted that jazz was a "real art" were entrepreneurs as well, concert promoters or record producers, positioned to influence the

---

[48] Titles of books and recorded anthologies reflect this trend: *The Smithsonian Collection of Classic Jazz* (Washington, 1973); *Classic Cole [Porter]* (Columbia M34533, 1977); *The Smithsonian Collection of Classic Country Music* (Washington, 1981); Grover Sales, *Jazz: America's Classical Music* (Englewood Cliffs, 1984); *The Classic Hoagy Carmichael Sound Recording* (Indianapolis, 1988).

[49] Stearns, *The Story of Jazz*, pp. 323–6.

[50] James Lincoln Collier, "Jazz," *The New Grove Dictionary of American Music*, ed. H. Wiley Hitchcock and Stanley Sadie (London and New York, 1986), vol. 2, p. 559.

[51] *The New Grove Dictionary of Music and Musicians*, ed. Stanley Sadie (London, 1980), vol. 9, pp. 562, 578.

performance and marketing of jazz. Concurrently with their literary efforts to elevate jazz to the status of art, and partly as a result of their intervention, performance sites for some jazz performances shifted from interactive social settings to the concert stage, where the music inevitably took on a different meaning:

> As part of the legacy from the European art music tradition, the concert has carried with it a rich set of associations as well as considerable social prestige. The concert is a solemn rite, with music the object of reverent contemplation. Certain formalities are imposed upon the concert audience: people attend in formal dress, sit quietly and attentively with little outward bodily movement, and restrict their response to applause at appropriate moments. . . . Today the notion of a jazz concert is commonplace. We recognize jazz as a music of complexity and virtuosity, deserving the undivided attention and respect of concert performances.[52]

Leonard Feather says of Duke Ellington's Carnegie Hall concert of 23 January 1943, "at last he was to be recognized as the giant we had known him to be: not in a Harlem cabaret playing song scores, not in a Broadway theater teamed with pop singers, nor in a ballroom satisfying dancers, but on America's most renowned concert stage."[53]

I have no quarrel with the adaption of a conceptual framework based on the discourse of classical music to discussions of certain repertories of popular music. This may well be an appropriate way, and is perhaps even in keeping with the intentions of the musicians themselves, to deal with Joplin's piano rags and with much recent jazz. My purpose, rather, is to argue that the elevation of selected pieces of popular music, or of entire popular genres, to the status of "art" music has the effect of emphasizing text over context, as has happened with the classical repertory, and results in the marginalization of all pieces within that genre not singled out as "masterpieces," or, worse, of entire other genres.

Finally, as is the case with other modernist narratives, this one did not originate among musicians and audiences of the genres in question, but has been imposed from a cultural outside by critics and scholars whose musical instincts and social thinking were shaped in another environment. As Robert Walser puts it, "attempts to legitimate popular culture by applying the standards of 'high' culture . . . are rightly condemned as wrongheaded and counter-

---

[52] Scott DeVeaux, "The emergence of the jazz concert, 1935–45," *American Music* 7/1 (Spring 1989), pp. 6–7.
[53] Liner notes to *The Duke Ellington Carnegie Hall Concerts: January 1943* (Prestige P-34004). Quoted in DeVeaux, "The emergence," p. 18.

productive by those who see such friends of 'low' culture as too willing to cede the high ground. That is, the assumptions that underpin cultural value judgements are left untouched, and the dice remains loaded against popular culture."[54]

The narrative of youth culture

Post-war prosperity in the West made surplus cash and leisure time more widely accessible than ever before, particularly to young people. Industry accordingly devoted more attention to the production and promotion of commodities designed for this age group. New technology has placed recorded music well within the financial reach of teenaged and younger people; the music industry has responded with massive production of music aimed at this audience.

The study of popular music first entered academia through sociology, in the decade following the end of World War II, when the study of youth behavior was a popular theme in that discipline. In the words of sociologist Simon Frith:

Though pop interest is not exclusive to any country or class, to any particular educational or cultural background, it does seem to be connected specifically to age – there is a special relationship between pop music and youth. . . . The sociology of rock is inseparable from the sociology of youth.[55]

A first stage of this narrative, linked to the then-popular theme of juvenile delinquency, took a negative view not only of youth but also of their preferred music. A handful of sociologists joined clergy, law-enforcement officers, politicians, the mainstream press, white supremacists, classical musicians, and the music industry in positing a link between early rock 'n' roll and delinquent youth.[56] The film *Blackboard Jungle* (1955) popularized this connection by dramatically associating the criminally inclined youth in the movie's cast with rock 'n' roll, while adults and "good" youth prefered jazz, patriotic songs, and Negro spirituals.

In the late 1960s, however, a radically different representation of youth and its music emerged, not incidentally coinciding with the birth of rock music (as opposed to rock 'n' roll) and the popularity of

[54] Robert Walser, *Running with the Devil: Power, Gender, and Madness in Heavy Metal Music* (Hanover and London, 1993), pp. 58–9.
[55] Simon Frith, *Sound Effects: Youth, Leisure, and the Politics of Rock 'n' Roll* (New York, 1981), pp. 7, 9. In his later writings, Frith moved away from this rigidity, to consider a wider range of popular music.
[56] For an overview of youth, delinquency, and rock, and a useful bibliography, see Simon Frith, *The Sociology of Rock* (London, 1978), particularly pp. 19–74 and 212–15.

the Beatles.[57] There was, first of all, "rock journalism," a highly original body of writing in such new periodicals as *Crawdaddy*, *Rolling Stone*, and *Creem*. The focus, as in the sociological literature of the previous decade, was on popular music as a manifestation of the culture of young people. Now, however, in the subjective, aggressive, and highly idiosyncratic prose of Lester Bangs, Greil Marcus and their peers, youth (now taken to include college-age people and young adults as well as teenagers) was seen not as a malignancy requiring a cure but rather as a potential cure for a malignant society, with music occupying a central position in their culture. Charles Reich perhaps best summed up this new attitude:

> There is a revolution coming. It will not be like revolutions of the past. It will originate with the individual and with culture, and it will change the political structure only as its final act. . . . This is the revolution of the new generation. [It will arrive] at the moment the individual frees himself from automatic acceptance of the imperatives of society and the false consciousness which society imposes.[58]

In the "new consciousness," rock music, a "protean music capable of an almost limitless range of expression," functions as "the chief medium of expression, the chief means by which inner feelings are communicated."[59]

> The new music, most notably through the poetry of its songs, has succeeded in expressing an understanding of the world, and of people's feelings, incredibly far in advance of what other media have been able to express. Journalists, writers for opinion journals, social scientists, novelists have all tried their hand at discussing the issues of the day. But almost without exception, they have been far more superficial than writers of rock poetry. . . . [It] has become a medium that expresses the whole range of the new generation's experiences and feelings.[60]

Most American journalists and academic sociologists who addressed the theme of youth and music took youth as a monolithic cultural construct, cutting across class, and ethnic and regional boundaries. Some European scholars, mostly British, were more concerned with class, arguing that working-class youth, victims of capitalist social relations, tended to form resistant groups within the dominant

---

[57] For the distinction between rock 'n' roll and rock, see Hamm, *Yesterdays: Popular Song in America* (New York and London, 1979), pp. 435–55, and Charlie Gillett, *The Sound of the City: The Rise of Rock and Roll* (New York, 1970), pp. 3 ff.

[58] Charles A. Reich, *The Greening of America* (New York, 1970), p. 225.

[59] *Ibid.*, pp. 242–3. [60] *Ibid.*, p. 247.

society that marginalized them. The resulting school of subcultural criticism focused on the appropriation of elements of mainstream culture, particularly popular music, by such groups as the teds and skinheads, to create an oppositional "style."[61]

Youth culture was an important social factor after World War II, at least in "mainstream" Western culture, and is a valid and important subject of investigation. But the typically modernist privileging of one cultural group and its music in literature shaped by this narrative results in distortion, through omission, of the larger view of popular music. This narrative has no relevance for groups in which age distinctions are less important, such as African-Americans and other marginalized ethnic populations, nor for entire popular repertories such as country-western music which appeal to people of all ages within a given cultural field; and it's virtually useless in dealing with non-Western societies.

The second narrative of authenticity

Even though the masses of capitalist societies, the proletariat, are capable of creating cultural products giving expression to the consciousness of their class, the nature of capitalist cultural production makes it impossible for these to be conveyed authentically through commercial means. Capitalist cultural products, even when they pretend to address the concerns of the masses, in fact promote the ideology of the dominant classes and intensify the alienation of the working classes.

This narrative, developed in such an intellectually sophisticated way as to approach meta-narrative, has roots extending back through most of the modern era. In order to understand how and why it became a dominant strain of popular music study in the 1980s, one must recall certain events in the recent history of that field.

Even though a handful of sociologists, ethnomusicologists, cultural historians, and even musicologists had written articles and books on popular music in the 1960s and 70s, popular-music scholarship had established no distinctive disciplinary profile, no network or organization of its own, and no significant presence in the academic community.

1981 was a turning point, bringing the first issue of the journal *Popular Music* and the First International Conference on Popular Music Research, held in Amsterdam, at which the International

---

[61] See Middleton, *Studying Popular Music*, pp. 156 ff., for an excellent summary of this issue and the relevant literature.

Association for the Study of Popular Music (IASPM) was established. Both *Popular Music* and IASPM moved quickly and decisively towards the privileging of theoretical, critical, and ideological discourse, grounded most importantly in neo-Marxist analysis, over empirical/positivist historical narrative. This trend was already apparent at the Amsterdam conference, where the liveliest discussion was touched off by a paper dealing with the penetration of merchant capital into West Africa and its impact on popular music,[62] and the most enthusiastically received paper was "Rock music as a phenomenon of progressive mass culture" by Peter Wicke and Günter Mayer of the German Democratic Republic, which ended with the manifesto: "Here we share a common goal: aiming at the emancipation of all people and of the masses towards a social practice alternative to that of capitalism. In our century, this means socialism and its goal of communism – finding a type of society, where the free development of a universal individual will be the precondition for the free development of all."[63] The first volume of *Popular Music* included several articles likewise underlaid by neo-Marxist thought,[64] which became even more dominant in the second (1982) and third (1983) issues, entitled respectively "Theory and Method" and "Producers and Markets."

Both IASPM and *Popular Music* were based in Europe and the vast majority of organizers, participants, and contributors were European. The disposition towards theoretical argumentation couched in the language of critical discourse and indebted to Marxist dogma was an accurate reflection of the intellectual climate of the early 1980s:

> At a time when most American academics were preoccupied with either resisting or enjoying the intellectual and moral emptiness of the Reagan era, or with doomed attempts to recycle the liberal activism of the 1960s, European universities had become hotbeds of tougher and more theoretical, ideological and confrontational intellectual activity, grounded most importantly in the writings of Karl Marx and his followers, which make up one of the greatest, most powerful meta-narratives of the modern age.[65]

Prior to the 1980s, musicologists who had written about popular music had dealt chiefly with musical texts, accessed through notated

---

[62] John Collins and Paul Richards, "Popular music in West Africa: Suggestions for an interpretative framework," *Popular Music Perspectives* [1] (Gothenburg and Exeter, 1982), pp. 111–41.   [63] *Popular Music Perspectives* [1], pp. 223–31.

[64] In particular, János Maróthy, "A music of your own," pp. 15–26, and Dave Harker, "The making of the Tyneside concert hall," pp. 27–56.

[65] Charles Hamm, "Text and context," paper delivered at the Seventh International Popular Music Conference, Stockton, California, 11 July 1993.

scores or recordings, and sociologists had focused on the people who listened to this music, individually or collectively. The literature of the 1980s shifted the focus to production and mediation, stages more susceptible to economic analysis, and inevitably much of the resulting literature was as much a critique of capitalism as of popular music itself.

Underlying much of this literature is the assumption that capitalist production negates "authentic" expression by certain groups, here defined not by ethnicity but by class. Even though popular music has the potential to create or intensify class consciousness and solidarity among the working classes, this rarely happens in practice because the means of production and dissemination are in the hands of the dominant classes. Mass-produced, commercial products are not only forced on the proletariat, they can even appear to be expressions of the consciousness of this class. Richard Middleton says of the relationship between working-class young people and rock music, "demands for greater 'freedom' and 'authenticity' can often be channelled into established stereotypes of rebellion and expression, and thus articulated to the framework of the dominant musical ideology,"[66] and John Shepherd writes:

> The machinery of mass marketing takes the ideological deviance of some rock musicians and their music, and utilises it to create for the musicians a star status. The musicians are different, so the implication goes, not because of their radical life-styles and musical utterances, but because of diligent hard work which has enabled them to escape the conditions of the masses and succeed. Their essential difference, therefore, lies in the nature of their success. Many youth groups are in this way being fed the spectacle rather than the actuality of social change. Rather than acting as a catalyst for social change, much rock music thus comes to act as an agent of social control. Through rock music, youth groups are fed many of the major elements of capitalist ideology.[67]

Based broadly on Marxist dogma, this narrative derives more narrowly from the writings of Adorno, whose focus on capitalist production led him to conclude that "any sense of expressive immediacy [in popular music] is an illusion; use-value is replaced totally by value in exchange; autonomy disappears as music turns into nothing more than 'social cement'; production is reduced, in effect, to reproduction."[68] Implicit in much of the literature on

[66] Middleton, *Studying Popular Music*, p. 15.
[67] John Shepherd, "Sociomusicological analysis of popular musics," *Popular Music* 2 (1982), p. 175.   [68] As summarized by Middleton in *Studying Popular Music*, p. 36.

popular music since the early 1980s, this narrative is sometimes made absolutely explicit. Terry Bloomfield, for instance, who positions himself as being "less concerned with musicological properties than with the means of production, consumption and the associated technology and rhetoric," discusses the process of "negating the authentic" in a recent article. He sets out to dismantle what he identifies as a commonly held but erroneous "(naive-)realist (proto)theory of song production and consumption," according to which:

(1) the singer reflects on personal experience that resonates with emotion; then
(2) embodies the results of that reflection in a musico-narrative form; then
(3) delivers a performance of (2) which serves to bring out fully its (inner) meaning; then
(4) the listener reads this emotional meaning by bringing his or her personal experience to bear on the performance.

But it can't work this way in "the postmodern world of late capitalism," Bloomfield tells us, because this scenario "run[s] full tilt into the constraints of the capitalist commodity: to accept them as realisable we must first reify exchange value then imagine it as use value – a double mystification." Since "the route to the rescue of the commodity is blocked," the singer of pop songs finds it impossible to "force something human across the gulf between exchange value and use value." The only way out is for the performer to accept the impossibility of meaningful direct communication in such a system, and to create songs which don't attempt to communicate "personal experience that resonates with emotion" in the first place.[69]

Despite its intellectual sophistication and its role in legitimating the study of popular music in the wider academic world, this modernist narrative, like others, imposes severe limitations on the literature grounded in it. Based almost completely on analyses of European society by European writers of the modern era, it often makes excellent sense of European social relations in this period and of the role music has played in negotiating these. More specifically, as a result of its reliance on Marxist thought, it often helps illuminate European class structures and class struggles, both in the modern era and as they linger on into the postmodern world. It has shaped an original and compelling body of writing that deals effectively and intelligently, but nevertheless narrowly, with the social uses and

[69] Terry Bloomfield, "Resisting songs: negative dialectics in pop," *Popular Music* 12/1 (January 1993), pp. 17–19.

appropriations of various styles of African-American music – as mediated by the American and European music industries – by post-War British and other European youth.

But this is only a fragment of the popular music of the world, and attempts to use this narrative to deal with other geographical areas and other chronological periods – contemporary non-rock genres of Asia, Africa, and the Americas, for instance, and the vast and complex networks of popular music produced before the present century – have been less convincing.

The most intense and momentous conflicts of recent years have taken place between the central governments of large nation states of various political persuasions – in Africa, Asia, the United States, Central Europe, the former Soviet Union, and elsewhere – intent on maintaining control and social order, and self-defining ethnic, national, regional and other groups within these national states determined to maintain or reassert their own autonomy. These struggles, which are radically changing the political and cultural face of the globe, have little or nothing to do with class conflict and have consequently been misunderstood or ignored by writers concerned with the inability of the working classes to obtain "authentic" expression of their identity through the modern mass media.

Even more generally, Marxism itself is a modernist meta-narrative, formulated in response to conditions in the modern era, and like other modernist meta-narratives it cannot be expected to make sense of the postmodern world.

Other voices

Though the vast majority of the literature on popular music through the 1980s is grounded in one or more of these modernist narratives, a handful of writers started from a quite different assumption: that popular music has a life, a legitimacy, and an ideology of its own; and the modern mass media have played a constructive rather than a destructive role in modern culture.

Isaac Goldberg, writing in 1930, accepts the commercial nature of popular song as an inevitable but not necessarily negative starting point. Characterizing popular songwriters as "hard-boiled ladies and gentlemen" who are "not in business for their health" and suggesting that "staff notes into bank notes might be their motto, and their heraldic device a loud-speaker rampant," he proposes the term "song-factory" for Tin Pan Alley. Seemingly pursuing the "mass culture" argument, he admits that "popular music of later days is a frankly commercial pursuit. It thus tends to establish formulas, to turn out a product of robots, by robots and for robots. In a word, in its own way, it becomes aridly intellectual. . . . formulized, and only pseudo-emotional."[70]

But he goes beyond that. Even so, songwriters "weep at their ballads, and laugh to the tunes of their optimistic formulas, their smiles-through-tears," he says; and after quoting H. L. Mencken on the potential expressiveness of the vernacular American language – "In all human beings, if only understanding be brought to the business, dignity will be found, and that dignity cannot fail to reveal itself, soon or late, in the words and phrases with which they make known their high hopes and aspirations and cry out against the intolerable meaninglessness of life" – Goldberg proposes that "even the lowest type of ribald song" is capable of expressing something of "the fundamental hopes and disillusionments of this, our common living."[71] And despite his elite background (he held a Ph.D. in Romance Philology from Harvard University) Goldberg rejects the notion that classical music is inherently different from and superior to popular music.

> The distinction between so-called art music and the music of the people is one of degree, not kind. Often the two musics overlap, not only in interest but in value. To say that popular music aims only at superficial entertainment, while art music seeks to establish values inherent in esthetic relationships is to indicate a difference of critical approach, a difference in temperament on the part of the special composer and the special public. . . . Yet the aim of the composer may be one thing and his result another. Music may hardly be judged by the conscious purposes of its practitioners. And it has happened, strangely enough, that a popular composer, ignorant of his craft, has achieved a music that stands on its own as an esthetic creation.[72]

Since he is not dependent on the narratives of authenticity, Goldberg is free to discuss the impact of the mass media on popular music and its audiences without warning that these media propogate the inferior culture of the lower classes, or stifle the expression of the proletariat. He sees, for instance, that radio can preserve, not destroy, certain "traditional" repertories:

[70] Isaac Goldberg, *Tin Pan Alley: A Chronicle of the American Popular Music Racket* (New York, 1930), p. 13.   [71] *Ibid.*, pp. 1–2.   [72] *Ibid.*, pp. 13–14.

A peculiar effect of the radio has been the popularization, among the inhabitants of the hinterlands themselves, of the old hill-billy songs and of ancient Tin Pan Alley stuff in general. If, on the one hand, the radio slays new songs prematurely, it restores life to the old. There is no death . . .[73]

And he offers the first discussion of corporate mergers as they affected popular culture:

The industry of popular music . . . is fast succumbing to centralized control. . . . With the coming of the talkie [sound film] and its great dependence upon music, . . . [i]t might prove more feasible, and cheaper in the long run, if, instead of paying tribute to the publishers, the radio and the talkie would buy not the music but the firm itself. That is precisely what is happening. The combinations at present in force presage the policy of the immediate future. Gigantic mergers such as the Warner Brothers Company control every possible outlet of their products – the theaters in which their pictures are shown, the houses that publish their music. Of late, there has been a movement to acquire control of phonograph and even book publishing firms. . . . The tie-up of the various interests is even more complicated: most of the vaudeville and motion picture theaters, and even some radio chains are owned or controlled by the picture companies.[74]

Most radically, Goldberg argues that Tin Pan Alley song, the mainstream popular song of his day, is itself the authentic expression of its culture:

[The] industry [is] tainted by commercialism and insincerity. So be it. In this respect it differs not a jot or tittle from other industries the world over, and least of all from the self-styled non-commercial music publishing firms. And one thing [it] achieves that has yet to be paralleled by the humorless "art" song of the conservatories: it manages, stammeringly yet at times inimitably, to speak the yearnings, the sorrows and the joys of a new, emergent folk, different from any other people in the world; and it is most gratefully accepted by that folk in the one true way that song may be accepted: it is sung. Tin Pan Alley, in brief, has cradled a new folk song, a song of the city, synthetic in facture, as short-lived as a breath, yet not for these reasons any the less authentic. The ancient folk song, in the slow course of its evolution, was not sung by as many throats in a hundred years as is the urban folk song of to-day in a single week. Time and space, by modern invention, have been conquered, telescoped into the magic of an instant. The

---

[73] *Ibid.*, p. 316.   [74] *Ibid.*, pp. 312–14.

very concept of the folk has of necessity been altered by the whir of machinery and the accelerated tempo of contemporary life.[75]

Goldberg describes his book as "an unpretentious pioneer work," an attempt to "indicate strands of interest and to suggest the design into which – as warp and woof across the loom of our national background – they may be woven," offered in the hope that his proposed "pattern of development" might "take on something like a definitive shape" in the work of subsequent writers.[76] Unfortunately, this was not to be. Few subsequent writers were as free from stifling narratives as Goldberg, and his book gave impetus to no school of historical or critical writing on popular music.

The introduction to Charlie Gillett's *The Sound of the City: The Rise of Rock and Roll* announces the author's independence from several modernist narratives: "A number of assumptions are made here which are not always granted to popular culture, the most important one being that audiences or creators can determine the content of a popular art communicated through the mass media."[77]

Gillett, a disc jockey and record producer himself, devotes considerable space to discussions of production and promotion, without assuming that these processes are dominated by the nature of capitalist production or the inferior cultural taste of the lower classes. He is thus able to approach each production decision as a unique act, made in response to considerations of audience taste and expectations, current technology, available capital, the state of performance, even the musical preferences of the producer himself.

Since Gillett starts from the assumption that popular music is aesthetically valid *as a product*, he is free to structure his book around the music itself. From his opening sentence – "In tracing the history of rock and roll, it is useful to distinguish *rock 'n' roll* – the particular kind of music to which the term was first applied – both from *rock and roll* – the music that has been classified as such since rock 'n' roll petered out around 1958 – and from *rock*, which describes post-1964 derivations of rock 'n' roll"[78] – Gillett makes *musical* distinctions, not in the language of the academically trained music theorist but nevertheless with quite specific descriptions of critical elements of music and text. For instance:

> In the years 1954 to 1956, there were five distinctive styles, developed almost completely independently of one another, that collectively became known as rock 'n' roll: northern band rock 'n'

[75] *Ibid.*, pp. 320–1.   [76] *Ibid.*, p. 326.   [77] Gillett, *Sound of the City*, p. viii.
[78] *Ibid.*, p. 3.

roll, whose most popular exemplar was Bill Haley; the New Orleans dance blues; Memphis country rock (also known as rockabilly); Chicago rhythm and blues; and vocal rock 'n' roll. All five styles, and the variants associated with each of them, depended for their dance beat on contemporary Negro dance rhythms.[79]

A description of each of the five follows. Similarly, he later distinguishes among three blues styles within the general field of rhythm and blues: big band blues; shout, scream, and cry blues; and combo (or "jump") blues. He describes the latter:

> Of the various blues-based styles, jump blues, through its boogie rhythm – variously modified as a jump or shuffle rhythm – had the most direct impact on the first singers to become popular with rock 'n' roll. . . . Typical jump combos featured a strong rhythm section of piano, guitar, bass, and drums, and usually had a singer and a saxophonist up front, with sometimes a second sax man added. Between them, the various instrumentalists emphasized the rhythm that a boogie pianist had achieved alone with his left hand, and in the process of transcribing the effect to several instruments the difference between each beat was either emphasized more – in jump rhythms – or blurred – in shuffle rhythms.[80]

These descriptions of musical styles are put forward not to construct abstract taxonomies, but to demonstrate that the music of popular music played an active role in several contentious social issues of the 1950s and 60s: race relations ("there seemed to be increasing numbers of young white people who rejected traditional attitudes of superiority towards black people, some of them working politically with (or for) black people and others adopting black cultural styles"); and changing sexual mores ("[Rock 'n' roll] provided the context in which singers began to consider love that not only had physical aspects but also was not inevitably eternal. Absorbing this music without necessarily thinking much about it, the generations of popular music audiences since 1956 have formed quite different sensibilities from the preceding generations which were raised on sentiment and melodrama").[81] The social content of this argument is not original with Gillett, of course, but he was virtually the only writer of his day to pursue it through music.

The literature dealing with one entire genre, country-western music, was free of the constraints of modernist narratives from the beginning.

A seminal article by Archie Green, "Hillbilly music: source and

---

[79] *Ibid.*, p. 23.   [80] *Ibid.*, pp. 124, 133.   [81] *Ibid.*, pp. x, xii.

resource,"[82] sketches the stance taken by virtually all subsequent scholars: the roots of the style lie in traditional Anglo-Celtic repertories brought to the New World by peasant and working-class immigrants from the British Isles; far from remaining static, these repertories were augmented and enriched in America through the creation of new songs and dances and the incorporation of musical styles and instruments from other cultures; the earliest phonograph discs of "hillbilly" and "old time" music, recorded in the 1920s, catch this music as it existed in oral tradition at that moment, and in the next decades musicians and their audiences functioned willingly and creatively within the new mass media, particularly radio and the phonograph, as the style, repertory, and audience of this music expanded.

The theme that the genre evolved as a commercial product making constructive use of the mass media without losing its "authenticity" and its relationship with its original audience runs through almost all the literature on country-western music, distinguishing it from the negative views of mass culture, commercialism, and authenticity so characteristic of popular music study grounded in modernist narratives.

Bill Malone begins his narrative history, *Country Music, U.S.A.*, by stressing the commercial nature of the genre: "Country music is not merely a facet of southern culture, but is also southern culture's chief industry."[83] He devotes considerable attention to the role of the mass media, as for example:

> The development of southern radio broadcasting was important in the discovery, refinement, modification, and eventual standardization of southern country music. . . . The 1930s marked the heyday of live radio entertainment in the United States. The typical hillbilly musician of that decade was an itinerant entertainer, moving from station to station, seeking sponsors and working a territory until it provided no further dividends.[84]

As he sees it, "An understanding of southern rural music was hampered by the reluctance of both folk scholars and high-art exponents to see it as it really was: that is, a thoroughly hybrid form of music which shared Old World and American traits, and which revealed itself as both a commercial and a folk expression."[85]

Archie Green devotes an entire book to "recorded coal-mining

---

[82] *Journal of American Folklore* 78 (July–September 1965), pp. 257–66.
[83] Bill C. Malone, *Country Music, U.S.A.* (Austin, 1985), p. xi. Second edition, first published by the American Folklore Society in 1968.   [84] *Ibid.*, pp. 35, 95.
[85] *Ibid.*, p. 27.

songs as cultural documents and communicative devices," using a succession of commercial-recorded country-western songs as keys to "the consideration of socio-economic change introduced into folk society by industrialization, urbanization, and the technology of mass media."[86] He develops the theme that the consumption of commercial recordings can be a constructive rather than a destructive process in a so-called traditional culture:

> For a semi-literate population, or for a people still close to oral tradition, the phonograph was an instrument of compelling importance: relatively inexpensive, easy to play, natural as a source for songs, stories, and intrumental styles. It was ideal for a conservative audience which wanted familiar music, rhetoric, dialect, and values, and it was competitive with many other popular-culture forms and devices . . .
>
> In 1925 a record holding a pair of songs was something that brought 75c on a counter; it was a commodity. But this very object might also carry Celtic or African memories in its grooves. . . . When a coal miner in a company store purchased a recorded disaster ballad or blues lament, he expected a story or mood set in a familiar style. Beyond a given text and tune, he was likely to hear the pick and shovel's clatter, the hammer's roar, the drill's whine, and even the heavy underground silence when work stops. In short, miners heard the ring of truth in discs intended merely to ring coins into cash registers.
>
> Essentially, sound recordings have helped preserve coal miners' energy and emotion – their folklore. Discs holding songs are artifacts of plural function: capsules of verbal and musical data, marketable objects intended for profit, pleasure-giving devices, commentaries on the society in which records themselves are produced and purchased.[87]

Norm Cohen puts it even more directly: "the preeminent role of the record industry in the development of country music is taken for granted, and 'early years' of country music is understood to mean 'early years on phonograph records'."[88]

It's not altogether clear why the literature on country-western music could develop such a positive view of the relationship between commercially produced, media-disseminated products and their audiences. One is tempted to point out that all the seminal literature on this genre was the work of American scholars; but more

[86] Archie Green, *Only a Miner: Studies in Recorded Coal-Mining Songs* (Urbana, 1972), pp. 439, 440.
[87] *Ibid.*, pp. 58, 34, 450.
[88] "Early pioneers," in *The Stars of Country Music*, ed. Bill C. Malone and Judith McCulloh (New York, 1975), p. 3.

telling, perhaps, is the fact that these writers were themselves from the social classes producing and consuming country-western music. They were writing from within a culture, whereas most of the formative literature on ragtime, jazz, and most other popular genres was the work of persons from outside the cultures in which this music originated.

Wilfrid Mellers's writing on popular music is *sui generis*, neither dependent on modernist narratives nor fitting comfortably into any other pattern. Trained as a composer and historical musicologist, he wrote for many years about the classical European repertory, particularly the music of modernist composers. Like most musicologists, he is concerned chiefly with the musical text, the notated and/or recorded score; but he is interested more in what he takes to be the meaning of the music than in abstract technical details. That is, Mellers believes that a given piece of music has a certain impact on listeners because of details of its melodic, harmonic, rhythmic, and formal construction, and that the goal of musical analysis should be to identify and describe these details, to demonstrate why the composition "works" as the composer intended.

His history of American music,[89] undertaken after a teaching stint in the United States, was in the same mold, dealing chiefly with twentieth-century American composers of "high art" music. But he experienced an epiphany. As he puts it in the foreword to a second edition of *Music in a New Found Land*, he came to realize that the book had suffered from a major omission: it "almost totally ignored white demotic music, whether under the categories of folk, jazz, country or pop. Whatever one thinks of these musics – about some of them I had been, when working on the book, distressingly ignorant – one cannot deny that they are part of the rich, or at least multifarious, pattern of American (and everyone else's) life."[90] Accordingly, though he was well into his 60s, Mellers set out to "repair that omission" by writing books about Bob Dylan, female popular singers, and the Beatles.

Mellers wants to explain the expressive content of this music, too, through stylistic analysis set in historical context. The following is excerpted from an essay on the songs on Bob Dylan's album *Street Legal*:

> The "alienation" of the blues – the basic conflict between black and white sources – is epitomised in the phenomenon of "blue"

[89] Wilfrid Mellers, *Music in a New Found Land: Themes and Developments in the History of American Music* (New York, 1965).

[90] Mellers, *Music in a New Found Land* (New York, 1987, revised edition), p. xii.

notes: for repeatedly the "natural" flat thirds and sevenths of pentatonic and modal melodies collide with the sharpened sevenths and leading notes demanded by Western dominant–tonic harmony. . . . The phenomenon of blue notes repeats a process that had happened, in a wider and more complex context, in European history when the mystically orientated theocracy of the Middle Ages was being engulfed by the Renaissance and by the humanistically and scientifically centred modern world. The new post-Renaissance harmony called for sharpened sevenths and thirds to define cadence and mark temporal progression; while music-makers trained on folk monody and on liturgical polyphony intuitively favoured the natural, flatter intervals. Simultaneous or near-simultaneous clashes of minor and major thirds, known as false relations, occurred. Blue notes are an exactly comparable technique, likewise springing from a clash between two views of the world. They are indeed false relations which, in the context of history, may prove to be symptomatic of a change no less crucial than that between the Middle Ages and the modern world. . .

"Baby Stop Crying" is passionately heart-felt, maturely balanced between desperation and hope. It seems at first to be a straight secular love-song, the girl's sobs being broken, drooping in syncopations and appoggiaturas. Dylan's approach to her begins conversationally ("you been down to the bottom with a bad man, babe"), acquiring lyrical, almost tender, nuance as the line floats through pentatonic seconds, droops through a sixth, lifts through a sixth when he tells us that he can provide no easy answers to the pain that makes her (and us) tempestuously cry, since "I can't tell right from wrong." Yet throughout the antiphony of the chorus a private love-song grows into a public hymn; in the refrain the "crying" seems to involve us all, reflecting on the human condition; and is safe-guarded from hysteria by the fact that the music reiterates an ostinato of I III IV V I triads, purely diatonic, but not modal, and without blue notes.[91]

Modernist narratives in the postmodern era

As noted above, little of the modernist literature on popular music is devoted to the explication of narratives; rather, the latter function at a deep level as assumptions or belief systems, shaping the writing of those who depend on them without being the subject of such writing.

An Arab proverb holds that "men resemble their brothers more than they do their fathers." Though the modernist narratives noted above were shaped and used by writers of different and even

[91] Wilfrid Mellers, "God, modality and meaning in some recent songs of Bob Dylan," *Popular Music* 1 (1981), pp. 145, 148.

radically opposing ideological and political convictions, they are all products of the Western modern era and they all share features not found in, say, medieval or postmodern narratives. Each privileges one or another musical genre or style above others, on grounds of artistic superiority, or greater significance, or authenticity. As it happens, the music excluded by these narratives is invariably the most commercially successful products of the music industry, or "mainstream" popular music. As a result, popular music literature governed by modernist narratives has dealt mostly with marginal, oppositional, or so-called authentic genres or repertories, such as punk rock or Chilean "new song." Commercially viable music, if studied at all, is usually placed in an oppositional context itself, as has been done with some rock music, and reggae. One would search in vain for critical, scholarly literature on the music of Elton John, or Creedance Clearwater Revival, or Barbra Streisand, or even Stevie Wonder.

Some years ago, Philip Tagg remarked that "popular music" might be defined as all music ignored by departments of music and conservatories. In the same spirit, I would suggest that popular music is all music attacked or ignored in the literature governed by modernist narratives.

To paraphrase a famous comment by General Douglas MacArthur, modernist narratives don't die, nor do they fade away. Even as we progress deeper into the postmodern era, they persist in the work of older writers whose consciousness was shaped in the modern era and of younger scholars trained in and receptive to modernist modes of thought. The narrative of musical autonomy, for instance, is still the foundation for much, probably most, writing in musicology and music theory. Composer-theorist George Perle can still write: "I read the future of music, not in terms of politics or social questions, but only in terms of the self-contained evolution of the musical language,"[92] and musicologist Peter Burkholder can still say:

> What I want to know, ultimately, is why the creators of the music I study made the choices they did: what options they chose among, what was forbidden or did not occur to them, and what led them to select one option over others. . . . My interest in why composers make the choices they do leads to a study of musical style, the traditional core of historical musicology, for composers make choices within, among, and sometimes in defiance of the prevailing style or styles.[93]

[92] George Perle, *The Listening Composer* (Berkeley, 1990).
[93] J. Peter Burkholder, "Music theory and musicology," *Journal of Musicology* 11/1 (Winter 1993), p. 11.

The narratives of authenticity and mass culture are still with us as well. Much recent literature starts from the premise that "commercial success and artistic accomplishment are rarely joined,"[94] and we can still read, at the other end of the ideological spectrum: "In what begins to appear as a fundamental aporia of modernity, just as the (self-)denial of bourgeois expression paradoxically gave birth to an art aiming to speak to the interior subject, so giant steps towards the total commodification of music were taken under the banner of an authentic expression that was newly available for consumption."[95]

But the decade of the 1990s is also bringing the first generation of writers whose awareness and consciousness has been shaped by the fragmented, non-hierarchical postmodern world. For many of them, modernist narratives are relics of a faded intellectual climate, no more relevant to their lives and their scholarship than the modes of thought of, say, the Age of Enlightenment. Writing in 1989, Andrew Ross speaks of the divide between:

> the last generation of American intellectuals to swear unswerving allegiance to the printed word and the dictates of European taste, and the first generations to *use* their involvement with popular culture as a site of contestation in itself, rather than view it as an objective tool with which to raise or improve political consciousness; the last generation to view culture in the polarized marxist terms of a universal class struggle, and the first to accept the uneven development, across a diverse range of social groups and interests, of the contradictions of living with a capitalist culture; the last generation for whom the heroic mythologies of the unattached, dissident intellectual could still be acted out, and the first to insist that the institutionalizing or the commercializing of knowledge does not seal the fate of political criticism; the last to devolve its politics solely upon the mind, and the labor of production, the first to appeal to the liberatory body, and the creativity of consumption.[96]

Since Ross situates himself on the near side of this divide, he's in a position to point out the contradictions in modernist narratives, since they're not part of *his* world. He can write of the complex interrelations between African-American and "mainstream" popular culture:

> But I will call attention to the fragments of another, less idealized history, one that is linked to the capacity of popular music to transmit, disseminate, and render visible "black" meanings,

---

[94] Robert H. Rossberg, in a review of books about Lionel Hampton and Buddy Rich, *American Music* 11/3 (Fall 1993), p. 386.

[95] Bloomfield, "Resisting songs," pp. 17–18.

[96] Andrew Ross, *No Respect: Intellectuals & Popular Culture* (New York and London, 1989), p. 11.

precisely because of, and not in spite of, its industrial forms of production, distribution, and consumption. These commercial forms, whether on record or in performance, were, after all, the actual historical channels through which "black" meanings were made widely available, and were received and used by a popular audience, even a black audience. . .

[Baraka's] account of the perpetual cut-and-thrust between pure and impure, black and white, good and evil, always depends on his demonizing the cut-and-paste mainstream culture of musical meanings as a Gehenna of white appropriation and of black Tomming. So while [his] polemical purism ensures his sensitivity to the changes wrought within black music, it leaves him little room to consider the actual changes wrought upon mainstream popular culture by black musical influences. As a result, black meanings, in whatever form, which reach "acceptance by the general public" can only be seen as evidence of "dilution," and testimony to a "loss of contact with the most honestly *contemporary* expression of the Negro soul."[97]

Sara Cohen crisply notes and critiques the modernist narratives of musical autonomy, mass culture, authenticity, and youth culture:

Tagg and Negus have noted that musicologists studying popular music still tend to ignore social context. Hence lyrical and musical texts may be deconstructed and their "meaning" asserted, but the important question "meaning for whom?" is often neglected. . . . Rock music is frequently analysed in terms of the music industry and its networks of production, distribution and marketing, and in terms of technology, mass communication and global culture and capital. The latter are commonly depicted as acting upon individuals like "forces" or "flows." . . . There has been a focus upon global processes of homogenisation or diversification and the fears or resistance they provoke, the conditions of fragmentation, placelessness and timelessness they give rise to. . . . [Richard] Middleton refers to the privileging of the category of youth within popular music studies, and the neglect of older age groups who may use different musics and in different ways. It should also be added that it is still overwhelmingly *male* youth (particularly of the working class) which has been privileged, and that the focus on youth has often been accompanied by a concern with fast-changing commodities and trends which down plays the elements of continuity that might also be present.[98]

She then proposes an approach that, rather than setting up hierarchical, exclusionary structures, seeks to "make sense of the meaning

[97] *Ibid.*, pp. 71, 76.
[98] Sara Cohen, "Ethnography and popular music studies," *Popular Music* 12/2 (May 1993), p. 126.

derived from music . . . by specific persons, at specific times, within specific places," by

> focus[ing] upon social relationships, emphasising music as social practice and process. It should also be comparative and holistic; historical and dialogical; reflexive and policy-oriented. It should emphasise, among other things, the dynamic complexities of situations within which abstract concepts and models are embedded, and which they often simplify or obscure. The social, cultural and historical specificity of events, activities, relationships and discourses should also be highlighted.[99]

Among subjects of her case studies have been local rock bands and elderly Jewish musicians in Liverpool.

Leslie Gay proposes an "imagined local." Rejecting the modernist view of "the urban experience as ungrounded alienation," he argues that rather than being dulled or destroyed by the mass media and other conditions of postmodern life, "authentic" group identity can be aided by them.

> Besides the factors of class, gender, race, and sexuality, activities and interest groups like rock music and musicians also create their own local map defined through the interactions they share with others, through their conventions for working, patterns of communications, and the pathways, both real and symbolic, they travel. Thus, the world exists as an oddly-shaped and changing latticework of localities created by the actions of its inhabitants.[100]

Venise Berry also rejects the notion that "the 'commodification of culture' . . . into the commercial system strips [cultural products] of their original context and presses them into an image-form," and that "without a context to the interpretation of images, the products all blend into an undifferentiated, continuous flow, in which each individual image or set of images, has no particular significance."[101] Rap music, the subject of her attention, is actually a product of electronic technology and the mass media, and she insists that:

> Commodification does not negate cultural understanding and empowerment. That is obvious when I talk to black youth about their relationship with rap music. It is obvious as I talk with colleagues and we support the release of suppressed voices, and recognize the power that such voices encompass when they finally

---

[99] *Ibid.*, pp. 135, 123.

[100] Leslie Gay, "Rockin' the imagined local: New York rock in a reterritorialized world," paper read at the Seventh International Conference on Popular Music Research, Stockton, California, 11–15 July 1993.

[101] As this narrative is summarized in Ian Angus and Sut Jhally, *Cultural Politics in Contemporary America* (New York, 1989), p. 2.

emerge. It is obvious when I acknowledge my own response to the disturbing but timely messages.[102]

The music, lyrics, and style of rap musicians Public Enemy, NWA, Sister Souljah, Ice T, and Ice Cube are at the center of a new theoretical discourse in cultural politics, she argues. Since rap is "deviant and unacceptable to the mainstream" and efforts to control it have failed, efforts to destroy it have begun, centered around eliminating its dissemination through the commercial mass media.

Robert Walser, unhindered by the narrative of musical autonomy and its privileging of the classical repertory and "classic" popular pieces, is thus free to consider heavy metal music as a valid cultural product. He subjects it to close musicological analysis of the sort previously reserved for classical music, not as an abstract exercise or an attempt to show its superiority or inferiority in relation to other types of music, but to make quite specific points: "[the] appropriation and adaption of classical models sparked the development of a new kind of guitar virtuosity, changes in the harmonic and melodic language of heavy metal, and new modes of musical pedagogy and analysis."[103]

These are only samples. In the 1980s, even late in the decade, it would have taken an exhaustive search of literature on popular music to locate as many instances of writing free of modernist narratives as one can now encounter at a single conference, or in one collection of articles.

Maybe Bob Dylan was right, after all.[104]

November 1993

[102] Venise Berry, "Hardcore rap and the revolution of cultural politics," paper read at the Seventh International Conference on Popular Music Research, Stockton, California, 11–15 July 1993.

[103] Robert Walser, "Eruptions: heavy metal appropriations of classical virtuosity," *Popular Music* 11/3 (October 1992), p. 264. This article, in a slightly different form, later appeared as Chapter 3 in Walser's book *Running with the Devil*.

[104] Other authors have begun to analyze the restrictive impact of modernist thought on our understanding of music, popular or otherwise. See, for instance, Scott DeVeaux, "Constructing the jazz tradition: jazz historiography," *Black American Literature Forum* 25/3 (Fall 1991), pp. 525–60; Gary Tomlinson, "Cultural dialogics and jazz: a white historian signifies," in *Disciplining Music: Musicology and Its Canons* (Chicago and London, 1992), pp. 64–94; Philip V. Bohlman, "Musicology as a political act," *Journal of Musicology* 11/4 (Fall 1993), pp. 411–36; and Gary Tomlinson, "Musical pasts and postmodern musicologies: a response to Lawrence Kramer," *Current Musicology* 53 (1993), pp. 18–24. At the same time, other writers are attempting to disassociate some of the iconic figures of high modernism from the intellectual constraints of that era; see Martin Brody, "Music for the masses: Milton Babbitt's Cold War music theory," *The Musical Quarterly* 77/3 (Summer 1993), pp. 161–92, and J. Bradford Robinson, "The jazz essays of Theodor Adorno: some thoughts on jazz reception in Weimar Germany," *Popular Music* 13/1 (January 1994), pp. 1–25.

2

ROCK AND THE FACTS OF LIFE

When I arrived at Princeton University to begin work on a Ph.D. in musicology in 1957, with a life-long interest and involvement in various genres of American music, I discovered that:

> All books, monographs, editions, periodicals, and other materials considered necessary for successfully completing the degree had been collected in a large study-seminar room. . . . The word "canon" was never used then, but the ideology, though never articulated, could not have been clearer. The corpus of music and literature on music necessary for the pursuit of musicology was finite; it was all here in this room; and once our apprenticeship was completed and we moved out into the hard world of academia, our success would be measured by whether or not our own work would one day be brought into this room.
> The [general] stacks were situated just outside the door of our sanctuary, and occasionally, when none of my professors or fellow students was about, I would sneak a look at a score by John Cage or Charles Ives, or at a book about southern folk hymnody, or a bound collection of nineteenth-century sheet music. I felt like a teenager browsing through a collection of pornography.[1]

What Wiley Hitchcock would later label "vernacular music"[2] was no part of this canon, and my proposal to write a dissertation on nineteenth-century shape-note music was rejected out of hand. Dufay was acceptable, however, and my career as a scholar of Renaissance music was launched. But my interest in other types of music continued, and in 1970, as a member of a panel considering "Music and Higher Education in the 1970s" during a joint conference of the American

---

[1] Charles Hamm, "Expanding our musical heritage," *Harvard Library Bulletin* 2/1 (Spring 1991), p. 13.
[2] H. Wiley Hitchcock, *Music in the United States: A Historical Introduction* (Englewood Cliffs, 1969).

Musicological Society and the College Music Society in Toronto, I
suggested the following:

> The last five years have witnessed a period of intense and significant
> activity in American music almost without parallel in our history, a
> period of vitality and accomplishment in composition, performance,
> involvement of large and varied groups of people with this music, and
> above all of interaction between music – and musicians – and the
> exciting and troubling events that have made this period such a
> critical one in American history. I am speaking not only of "art"
> music, of course, but the entire range of musical activity, from John
> Cage to Jimi Hendrix, Terry Riley to Simon and Garfunkel, Cecil
> Taylor to Roger Reynolds, Gordon Mumma to The Band to Merle
> Haggard to "Hair."
> And I confess that I find it disturbing that none of this activity has
> been reflected in the publications and other official activities of the
> American Musicological Society, and very little of it in the teaching
> and other involvements of individual members of the Society.
> [I] suggest that the most sensible and profitable course for
> musicology in the coming decade would seem to be one that would
> hold fast to the methods and accomplishments that have made our
> discipline one of the fastest-growing and most respected in recent
> decades, but at the same time to enrich and revitalize the field by
> constant broadening of the types of music, stylistic and chronological,
> that our scholars and teachers are concerned with, [and] to embrace
> whatever new methodology and aesthetic is necessary to deal most
> sensibly with this larger and more varied body of material.[3]

Reaction from certain musicological quarters was immediate and
predictable. The then-director of graduate studies in musicology at
Columbia University, a noted writer on Early Music, responded in the
following issue of the same publication:

> The gist of [Hamm's] argument is that one of the best musicological
> journals in the world, familiarly and affectionately known as JAMS,
> together with those who are sufficiently misguided to receive and
> read it regularly, should be censured for failing to give publicity to
> jazz, pop, rock, folk, tape, and trick music – if indeed the Muses have
> anything at all to do with these monosyllabic forms of activity. My
> reply is that neither the Journal nor its supporters deserve censure of
> any kind or degree; and it is no more incumbent upon them to
> feature the commercial ephemerides that blight the artistic ecology
> of our sad planet than it is desirous that they should advertise cola
> drinks, greasy kid stuff, or the pill.
> We are told that "many younger people of today . . . understand
> only too well the artistic, historical, and sociological value of this
> music." Younger than whom? Perhaps this sentence should read:
> "many immature quasi-illiterates understand perfectly the atavistic,

3 Charles Hamm, "A needed change of attitude," *College Music Symposium* 11 (1971), pp. 94–5.

hysterical, and social appeal of this noise." For noise most of it is, if
you will consider the deafening volume at which most of it must be
reproduced, and the incident of permanently damaged eardrums
among its practitioners. As for hysteria, evidence is superabundant,
ranging from a kind of mass hypnosis through drug-addiction to
murder.[4]

This same gentleman had written elsewhere, in response to a suggestion
by Arthur Parris that Bach's cantatas were the "commercial" music of
their day:

> Bach wrote his cantatas as part of his duties as a director of music, and
> for the glory of Almighty God. Commercial music is written or
> improvised (the mode of transmission is of little importance) by
> decomposers as part of their duties as corrupters of public taste, and
> for the glory of the Almighty Dollar. . . . If Mr. Parris can honestly
> compare the finest of Binchois, or of any other great composer
> before or since, with the primitive vomiting noises wallowing in
> over-amplified imbecility that typifies most "commercial" non-music
> of today, he would be well advised to cure his addiction to value
> judgements.[5]

It was in this climate that I made my first attempts to write about what
I saw as America's "intense and significant" music of the 1960s and its
interaction with "the exciting and troubling events" of the day. There
was no literature in my own discipline to guide me. I knew some of the
writing on "mass culture" by Adorno and other sociologists, but I
couldn't imagine that this dour, elitist, negative approach, exhibiting
an almost total lack of familiarity with the music in question, could be
fruitful. Journalistic writing by David Ewen and his peers seemed
equally unpromising, as did the growing body of sociological "youth
and leisure" literature, since it seemed to me that popular music cut a
much wider swathe in American culture. So I struck off essentially on
my own, at first. My first attempts were shots in the dark, guided only
by the germ of a conviction that popular music should be approached
as a complex field encompassing composers, performers, audiences,
the music industry, the media, and the state.

"Rock and the facts of life" was first delivered as a lecture during the
winter of 1970–1, at Brown University and elsewhere. It seemed
pointless to offer it to a musicological journal, so I turned to my friend
and then-colleague Gilbert Chase, one of the great iconoclasts of the
day, whose seminal book *America's Music: From the Pilgrims to the
Present*[6] had rekindled and broadened my interest in American music

[4] Denis Stevens, "Lower music and higher education," *College Music Symposium* 12 (1972).
[5] Denis Stevens, *The New York Times*, 18 December 1971.
[6] New York, Toronto, and London, 1955.

of all kinds. Characteristically, Gilbert not only accepted the article for his Yearbook but defiantly placed it as the first item in the next volume.

For those who don't remember, or weren't around, Hayakawa, a college professor in California, rose to political power as a proponent of "law and order" and received wide media coverage in the late 1960s as a forceful opponent of that state's rampant student activism. Though Hayakawa doesn't acknowledge it, the title of his article invokes Sigmund Spaeth's *The Facts of Life in Popular Song*.[7]

* * *

S. I. Hayakawa, in an article called "Popular songs vs. the facts of life,"[1] explains that he is very fond of jazz and sometimes listens to popular music also, but he finds the latter disturbing. He recalls that Wendell Johnson, in *People in Quandaries*,[2] isolated a disease infecting American society that he labelled IFD: Idealization (the making of impossible and ideal demands upon life), Frustration (as a result of these demands not being met), and finally Demoralization (or Disorganization, or Despair). The products of our popular culture are some of the chief carriers of this disease. Citing lyrics of songs by George and Ira Gershwin, Rodgers and Hart, Irving Berlin and the like, Hayakawa says that popular music is concerned almost solely with idealized romantic love. He contrasts this with the lyrics of some of his favorite blues, particularly those of Bessie Smith, in which a much wider and more realistic range of what can happen between a man and a woman is portrayed – happiness, unhappiness, despair, loneliness, desertion, unfaithfulness, tenderness, and earthy passions. He concludes that blues show a willingness to acknowledge the "facts of life," suggesting, though he does not develop the point, that these "facts" include not only a wider spectrum of love but other matters as well. Citing Kenneth Burke's description of poetry as "equipment for living," he ends by saying:

> If our symbolic representations give a false or misleading impression
> of what life is likely to be, we are worse prepared for life than we
> would have been had we not been exposed to them at all. . . .
> Hence the question arises: do popular songs, listened to, often
> memorized and sung in the course of adolescent and youthful
> courtship, make the attainment of emotional maturity more

[7] New York and London, 1934.

[1] *Etc.* 12 (1955), pp. 83–95. Reprinted in *Mass Culture*, ed. Bernard Rosenberg and David Manning White (New York, 1957), pp. 393–403.   [2] New York, 1946.

difficult than it need be? . . . Cannot our poets and our songwriters try to do at least as much for our young people as Bessie Smith did for her audiences, namely provide them with symbolic experience which will help them understand, organize, and better cope with their problems?[3]

Hayakawa, writing a decade after the end of World War II, cites songs from the 1920s and 30s, the period of his youth, when he himself was in a formative and impressionable period. One wonders if the songs popular some fifteen years later, when he wrote his article, were similar. To test this, I went to *Billboard* magazine's weekly listing of the most popular songs, based on record sales and other data. Assuming that it took perhaps a year for Hayakawa's article to be written, submitted, accepted, set, proofread, and published, I went back a year from the date of publication of the article, to the chart for the week of 8 May 1954 for a sample of what was in fact popular when he was writing. The ten most popular songs were:

(1)	Wanted	Perry Como
(2)	Make Love to Me	Jo Stafford
(3)	Cross Over the Bridge	Patti Page
(4)	Oh, Baby Mine	Four Knights
(5)	Young at Heart	Frank Sinatra
(6)	Secret Love	Doris Day
(7)	Answer Me, My Love	Nat King Cole
(8)	A Girl, A Girl	Eddie Fisher
(9)	Here	Tony Martin
(10)	Man with the Banjo	Ames Brothers

This list does indeed verify Hayakawa's thesis, and makes possible some amplification of it. With one exception, these songs deal with romantic love from the point of view of the mores of American white middle- to upper-class society: one man seeking one woman, going through difficulties and perhaps even heartbreaks in his search, but eventually attaining his goal, and with it lasting happiness. If there are other aspects of the man–woman relationship, they are scarcely hinted at here. If there are any other issues in life, this body of music is silent about them.

Hayakawa was concerned only with the lyrics of these songs, not with the music. If he had been, he could have pointed out that the homogeneous nature of this repertory extends to the music itself. The songs all sound alike. Each was sung by one singer, or

---

[3] Hayakawa, "Popular songs," p. 91.

occasionally a small vocal group, to the accompaniment of an orchestra dominated by strings but making some use of winds and brass. Each uses the same melodic style (diatonic, tonal, and heavily dependent on sequential writing) supported by a common harmonic style (thick, lush chords – tonal but liberally sprinkled with post-Debussyian seventh and ninth chords). Each is written in precisely the same form, in the same meter, moving at more or less the same tempo. A person whose knowledge of music was derived from this repertory would have a remarkably limited view of the potential of the art.

Hayakawa was correct. Whether or not he was listening to these or any other popular songs in 1954, his thesis that popular music gave a narrow and distorted view of reality, that it was not facing up to the facts of life, was a sound one.

At the time that Hayakawa was writing his article, ten years after the end of World War II, Eisenhower was president, America was engaged in the Cold War, politicians and would-be politicians were making capital of Communist-hunting in and out of government, and with a few exceptions Americans felt it in their best personal interests to go along with the internal and foreign policies of the government, to fit into the life style appropriate to their social and economic class, to conduct their lives so that they were moving towards maximum material gain, and to avoid any behavior or expression of beliefs that might impede their attainment of this goal. High school and college students seemed content to play the role of careless, uninvolved, transitory people, with responsibilities, decision making and involvement in the problems of the country off somewhere in the future. Deviation in belief and behavior among them was largely confined to a rather small group, mostly male, often on the fringe of criminal activity, almost all of them the children of families low in the economic scale of the country. The image of America as a benevolent, righteous nation dispensing impartial justice at home and abroad was rarely questioned or even examined, at least by those people in the groups and classes that listened to popular music.

One of the most convincing parts of Charles Reich's *The Greening of America*[4] is his characterization of this period in American history, which he calls Consciousness II. He insists again and again that most decisions affecting the lives of Americans were made by the institutions of the country (political, religious, educational, economic,

---

[4] New York, 1970.

social), that people were under the impression that they were offered freedom of choice but this choice was from among options that were essentially the same. He illustrates this paradox of a choice that is no choice by his infamous peanut butter diatribe: American housewives going to a supermarket in search of peanut butter have a choice of different brands bearing different labels in differently shaped containers, but inside everything is essentially the same; and a person wanting something genuinely different, such as peanut butter that has not been homogenized, cannot find it, because a decision has been made that American peanut butter is homogenized.

A more telling example of this point is the situation with popular music of the time. Someone dependent on the large radio stations or certain types of record shops had a choice of what he listened to, a choice among Perry Como, Doris Day, Frank Sinatra, and Pat Boone, but in terms of musical style and content of lyrics this was a very narrow choice. Popular music was the music of middle- and upper-class white Americans, by and large, the people who held positions of power in financial, political, religious, and educational institutions; the people who listened to this music were the children of both groups, who would eventually succeed them. This music offered no view of life in America that questioned the way things were going. Of course there was jazz, blues, country music, and folk music of many sorts, and much of this music was bitterly critical of one aspect or another of American life – of the kind of life that many people were forced to live. But this was the music of minority groups, and the hard facts of life, of poverty, of repression, of apparently inescapable unhappiness, were unknown or ignored by the people who listened to Perry Como and Eddie Fisher, who heard in this music nothing that disturbed their limited and unrealistic view of what was and was not happening in the country. Bob Dylan said:

> Rudy Vallee. Now that was a lie, that was a downright lie, Rudy Vallee being popular. What kind of people could have dug him? . . . If you want to find out about those times and you listen to his music you're not going to find out anything about the times. His music was a pipedream. All escapes.[5]

That's not completely true, though, because you *can* find out something important about those times from listening to such music. You can find out that the people who produced and consumed

[5] Nora Ephron and Susan Edmiston, "Bob Dylan interview", in *The Age of Rock*, ed. Jonathan Eisen (New York, 1970), p. 70.

popular music were shielding and shielded from any contact with reality that might conflict with a certain narrow view of life in America. You can find out that the function of this music was clearly *not* to provoke or stimulate any thoughts or discussions of alternate ways of viewing American society.

Hayakawa's article was probably conceived in 1954; mine was first delivered as a lecture in May of 1970. Conditions in the United States were dramatically different then. The first general student strike in the history of American education had closed or at least impeded operation of most American colleges and universities: the strike triggered by President Nixon's decision to send troops into Cambodia and the killings of students at Kent State and Jackson State. This strike was of course no isolated, impulsive happening. It came at the end of a decade of involvement by students and other young people in protests against the Vietnam War, attempts to focus attention on and seek solutions to racial discrimination, concern with the environment, and opposition to laws and practices that seemed discriminatory. The American student with his serious involvement in such matters and his insistence on being in the middle of – and if possible shaping – political and social matters, would have been almost unrecognizable to his counterpart in 1955.

And his music would have seemed equally curious. Here is the list of the top most popular songs for the week ending 9 May 1970, the week of the strike. The list is again taken from *Billboard*.

(1)	American Woman	Guess Who
(2)	ABC	The Jackson Five
(3)	Let It Be	Beatles
(4)	Vehicle	Ides of March
(5)	Spirit in the Sky	Norman Greenbaum
(6)	Love or Let Me Be Lonely	Friends of Distinction
(7)	Everything is Beautiful	Ray Stevens
(8)	Instant Karma	John Lennon
(9)	Turn Back the Hands of Time	Tyrone Davis
(10)	Reflections of My Life	Marmalade

Comparing this list with the one from 1954, two things stand out in shocking contrast. First, the subject matter of the lyrics: only one or two deal with romantic love. The most popular song, "American Woman" by the Canadian group Guess Who, is a naive but direct criticism of some aspects of American life: "American woman, stay away from me . . . I don't need your war machines, I don't need your ghetto scenes. . . ." "Spirit in the Sky" and "Let It Be" are religious songs, and "Instant Karma" reflects the curious, highly personal religious mysticism of John Lennon. "ABC," done by a black group, deals with love – sex, rather – in a teasingly erotic fashion not unlike some blues. "Vehicle" speaks of the risks of accepting rides with strange men in large new cars. "Everything Is Beautiful" praises tolerance by offering as its main theme the notion that anything can be beautiful "in its own way." "Reflections of My Life" is quite remote from blues, musically, but offers a view of life as a difficult and troubled journey that Hayakawa would have had no difficulty in relating to the "truths" of black music: "Oh my crying, feel I'm dying, Take me back to my own life. . . . The world is a bad place, a terrible place to live, Oh but I don't want to die. . . ." If anyone was listening to the radio this week, he would have been exposed to songs that gave a wide variety of views about life and love.

From a musical point of view, each one of these songs is different from any other one in sometimes small but often great matters of style. Four are done by solo artists, six by groups of differing sizes. The instrumental backing ranges from the percussion of "Instant Karma" through the standard rock ensembles of amplified guitars and percussion of "American Woman" to the studio orchestra, with strings, of "Reflections of My Life." Harmonic style is sometimes simple, diatonic, tonal, and triadic, with reference either to rock simplicity ("American Woman") or country-music simplicity ("Spirit in the Sky"); sometimes it derives more from gospel and rhythm-and-blues style ("Everything Is Beautiful"); sometimes its reference is more to the popular music of Hayakawa's time, as in "Reflections of My Life." Melodic style is equally varied: in "American Woman" it is repetitious, fragmented, declamatory and almost non-melodic; "Everything Is Beautiful" has a simple, symmetrical, almost folk- or child-like tune; "Let It Be" has a flowing, balanced, diatonic, sequential melody; the long-spun, legato line of "Reflections of My Life" is almost operatic. There is an equally wide range of musical forms in this collection of pieces.

Thus listeners in 1970, even those who listened only to stations playing the most popular songs, were offered the sort of choice in musical style and content that had not been available in 1954. Millions of Americans, most of them young, were listening to songs concerned with a wide variety of subjects, many of them dealing with political and social issues of the day, many of them at variance with the view of American life offered by popular songs several decades earlier.

Just as the events of May 1970 were merely episodes in a chain of events stretching back at least a decade, so the songs popular that week represented no sudden new development but rather a continuation of currents that had been flowing for some time. It is not the intent of this article to discuss in any detail the history of popular music of the past decades. I will merely point out what is obvious to anyone who has been in any way involved with this music: since the mid–1950s, elements have been pouring into popular music that had not been found in it before. They have come from black music, country music, folk music of various types, art music, electronic music, and rock 'n' roll (itself indebted to black and country music). Some have come in directly, as songs in one or another of these styles that have become popular, other elements have been diluted or filtered or mixed with other styles. In sociological terms, popular music has been infiltrated by music from some of the minority cultures of our country, and this music has brought with it not just its sound, but in its lyrics the attitudes towards life prevalent in these subcultures. The main audience for popular music has been the young and the relatively affluent, the white middle- or upper-class youth. The infiltration into their popular music of music from various minority groups and subcultures, with the views of American society as seen through the eyes of these people, has exposed them to facts of life not habitually acknowledged in this layer of American society. What are these facts of life? Charles Reich says:

> The very first thing that began to happen when rock came in on a mass cultural level was it started to say "we feel lonely and alienated and frightened" and music had never said that before. Blues has always said it. . . . But white people were told how happy, how romantic, how nice, how smooth the world was. And that didn't reflect the truth.
>
> Then all of a sudden there was Elvis Presley singing about "Heartbreak Hotel" full of lonely people, and he said no matter how full it is, when you get there you're lonely, because none of these people can communicate with you and you can't communicate with them. . . . So the first truth of rock, the first big communication, was to say things aren't that good.[6]

This may not have been the first thing that rock said, but it did say, often, that the world is full of lonely, unhappy people, that lives can be or become tragic, that all people do not have an equal opportunity for happiness. Popular music of the past decade has seen a long

[6] *Rolling Stone* 75 (4 February 1971), p. 32.

parade of characters whose lives have gone in directions never hinted at in the songs done by Patti Page or Doris Day: the Beatles' "Eleanor Rigby," Simon and Garfunkel's "The Boxer," Bob Dylan's "Like a Rolling Stone," and the down-and-out aging hoofer in "Mr. Bojangles" by the Nitty Gritty Dirt Band.

Probably the first thing that rock said that "white music" had not said was that there is a physical side to love in addition to or in place of the sentimental, romanticized view of love portrayed in earlier popular music. The first wave of rock 'n' roll, in the mid-1950s, was certainly not characterized by lyrics of profound intellectual or sociological value. To the contrary, the words were unimportant. What mattered, what was different (and shocking to many people), was the feel, the beat, the excitement of the music itself, the unabashed movement and sensuality of the sound. As Dylan says:

> You gotta listen to the Staple Singers, Smokey and the Miracles, Martha and the Vandellas. That's scary to a lot of people. It's sex that's involved. It's not hidden. It's real. It's not only sex, it's a whole beautiful feeling.[7]

Elvis Presley could be added to that list, and the Rolling Stones, Sly and the Family Stone, Jim Morrison and the Doors, Ike and Tina Turner, and scores of other individuals and groups. And hundreds of songs that have been played on the Top Forty stations and risen in the charts, dealing in open and vivid fashion with the physical side of love.

Another thing that rock has been saying for some time now is that war is unhealthy for children and other living things. Bob Dylan's "Blowin' in the Wind" was written long before there was any mass opposition to the war among the young people of America. It is difficult to say if the anti-war songs of the past decade had a direct influence on swinging the sentiment of a high percentage of young Americans against the war or if this sentiment was developing anyway, but certainly the songs and also the lives of such artists as Dylan and Joan Baez have played a role in solidifying – if nothing else – the beliefs of millions of people on this matter. The earliest anti-war songs were in the stream of folk-oriented music flowing into popular music in the early 1960s, but eventually music in other styles echoed this sentiment: basic rock, which initially and for many years was politically and ideologically neutral; black music (one of the most bitter outbursts against the war was Edwin Starr's "War," in what might be called a gospel-rock style, which rose to

---

[7] Ephron and Edmiston, "Bob Dylan," p. 70.

the top of the charts in late 1970); the music of such a popular solo artist as Donovan; and, finally, even white country music. The twentieth song on the *Billboard* chart for the week of 9 May 1970 was Johnny Cash's "What Is Truth?," in style exactly what would be expected of this long-popular country singer, in content a condemnation of the hypocrisy of Americans who hide tolerance of war and repression and intolerance of people whose views and appearance differ from their own behind their own notion of what is "American."

Still another fact of life dealt with again and again in music of the last decade is that drugs have become part of American life. There is no reason to belabor this point at this date. Recognition of the fact that lyrics of hundreds of songs of the past decade make reference to drugs, their use and effects has spread even to network television newscasts – and even to the office of the Vice President of the United States. Some of the songs are sympathetic to the use of drugs, some are not, most simply accept the fact that there is a drug culture in the country.

There are songs that deal with ecology, politics, old age, historical characters, humor, religion, patriotism, family relationships, the treatment of the American Indian – indeed, with an ever-expanding range of topics.

The matter is quite simple. Hayakawa complained that popular music offered a narrow, unreal view of life, that it did nothing to prepare its consumers for what life was like outside the fantasy world of this music. He called on "poets and songwriters" to create music that would provide "symbolic experiences" to help Americans "understand, organize, and better cope with" the world they face. But he could not have guessed how quickly and effectively his call would be answered. Beginning almost exactly in the year of his essay a succession of artists – most of them drawing on the music of one or another of the minority cultures of America – began producing songs suggesting that life was difficult, unpredictable, potentially tragic and lonely, sensual, humorous, exciting, and filled with experiences that families, churches, and schools had not prepared Americans for. This music often suggested that justice was not always administered in an impartial and humane way in America, that economic and military policies were sometimes determined by factors other than moral principles. Bob Dylan, Joan Baez, Bo Diddley, Elvis Presley, Peter, Paul and Mary, the Beachboys, Little Richard, Chubby Checker, the Beatles, Simon and Garfunkel, the Jefferson Airplane, the Grateful Dead, Frank Zappa and the Mothers of Invention, the Rolling Stones, Jimi Hendrix, Joni Mitchell, Phil Spector, Jim

Morrison and the Doors, Janis Joplin, and dozens of other individuals and groups began offering "symbolic experiences" that gave young Americans a sort of preparation for life that their parents and grandparents had not had. Movies, some novels, and journalism have been saying some of the same things, but music has been the most popular and influential art in changing the consciousness of a generation of Americans.

Hayakawa went on to become a college administrator. A television newscast sequence of several years ago caught him perched atop a car, wearing a tam, facing a crowd of angry, hostile students intent on forcing changes in educational and governmental policies. These students were a new breed in America, with attitudes and opinions quite different from those held by students in Hayakawa's day. They were aware of many facts of life not known to earlier generations of students. Much of this information had come from the music that had been popular during their formative years.

A note on the title of this essay

Certainly not all the music mentioned above is rock. I have used it as a convenient term for a large, varied body of music. When popular music began to change dramatically, in the mid-1950s, the first group of songs to break in style and content with earlier popular music was rock 'n' roll, and a second major innovation came in the 1960s with West Coast and English rock, as opposed to rock 'n' roll. Other types of music also figured in the revolution of popular music. But they were all indebted to rock either stylistically or because it first opened the door for different kinds of music to enjoy the commercial popularity previously possible only for the sentimental ballads discussed at the beginning of this article. To put it another way, "rock" in my title should be understood as "rock 'n' roll, rock, and other kinds of music, mostly derived from the music of one of the minority cultures in America, that have become part of and revolutionized the popular music scene in America." But that would have been too long a title.

Epilogue

Changing attitudes of young Americans and the part that popular music has played in this have not gone unnoticed by the American government. Seventy-five radio executives were summoned to Washington in January of 1971 for an expression of concern from the Nixon administration about the airing of songs with lyrics making reference to drugs. On 5 March 1971 the Federal Communications Commission issued a "public notice" on the matter, reading in part: "Whether a particular record depicts the danger of drug abuse or, to the contrary, promotes such illegal drug usage is a question for the judgment of the licensee." It goes on to say that someone in a position of responsibility at each station should be expected to make such a judgement, and if this is not done, "it raises serious questions as to whether continued operation of the station is in the public interest. In short, we expect licensees to ascertain, before broadcast, the words of lyrics of recorded musical or spoken selections played on their stations."

Nicholas Johnson, an FCC commissioner who dissented from the notion of preparing and circulating such a notice, gave more information about its background in an interview over KSAN-FM in San Francisco:

> The thing I find most ominous is that the presentation we received was put together by the Pentagon for the President, and this Defense Department briefing on song lyrics in fact used a lot of lyrics that aren't talking about drugs at all – they're anti-war songs or songs attacking the commercial standards of society, the standards of conspicuous consumption.[8]

Reaction to the notice was varied. Some stations, particularly the FM rock stations, seemed to ignore it and continued to play the same music as before. Some of the large commercial stations were more cautious though. WLS, the most powerful Top Forty station in Chicago, immediately began playing an unprecedented number of "souvenirs," or songs popular in other years, and those selected steered clear of controversial subject matter. A study of the weekly charts in the several months after publication of the notice shows a dramatic drop in songs dealing with drugs, and a similar drop in the number of songs dealing with war or the sensitive social issues of the day. It is not clear at this moment if the action by the government will have any long-range effects; there is sentiment that the notice could not withstand a court challenge. Whatever the outcome, the government of the United States has made it perfectly clear that it is not happy with a situation whereby popular music disseminates certain opinions and facts of life.

---

[8] *Rolling Stone* 79 (1 April 1971), p. 6.

3

CHANGING PATTERNS IN SOCIETY AND MUSIC: THE US SINCE WORLD WAR II

The department of musicology at the University of Illinois at Champaign-Urbana, where I taught from 1964 to 1976, was a hotbed of radicalism in comparison with such faculties elsewhere. Under the delusion that the millenium in American education was at hand, my colleagues and I set out to dismantle barriers between historical musicology and ethnomusicology, and between all genres and styles of music. An epiphany came in the spring of 1970, when students on the campus joined others across the country in protesting the American bombing of Cambodia and the shooting of protesting students at Kent State and Jackson State. As Bruno Nettl remembers it:

> Many on campus decided that students and faculty should strike, and so on the Sunday before, the musicology faculty and graduate students met, and decided not to hold classes the next week. But of course the purpose was not to do nothing, so . . . we planned to cancel our classes and to institute instead a group of lectures and presentations which we called "liberation classes." . . . I have ever since been impressed by the ability of my colleagues to put together with hardly any notice an interesting and educational and, however one would define that, a relevant set of lectures. Charles gave a talk about music in the USSR; Alex Ringer spoke on music under the Nazis; and I pulled out my recordings of Persian popular music, . . . the most radical of musical materials generally available in Teheran, and gave a talk about the way it expressed some of the values of working-class society and expressed rebellious sentiments against the Shah. . . . There were lots of other [liberation classes], some clearly warning of the dangers of autocratic governments, others a bit outré, such as our harp instructor's talk about "The Harp and Revolution."
>
> Later we sometimes asked ourselves why, and against whom, and precisely for what purpose we had struck. But clearly it was to show

solidarity with the students' anti-war movement, to show that people who talked about music could make their area of study relevant to the political and social concerns of the day, and most of all, that whatever we thought might be the solution to the problems brought on or faced by our government, it was not a time for business as usual.[1]

The following year we offered a semester-long course on popular music, and Bruno Nettl, Ron Byrnside and I set out to write a "music appreciation" text designed to offer an alternative approach to the rote teaching of canonical masterworks of the expanded nineteenth century. Rather than being organized around historical style periods or a selection of individual "masterworks," our book dealt in concepts – the development of musical styles and the interaction of different genres and music cultures, for instance – with examples drawn from classical, popular, folk, traditional, and non-Western musics. We naively thought that with such a book on the market, music faculties across America would eagerly set aside old ways in the dawning Age of Aquarius. But we had misjudged what the 1970s would bring. To my knowledge not a single introductory music course ever used our book, which soon went out of print, and few people have ever read such pieces as Ron Byrnside's excellent musical analysis of early rock 'n' roll.

The chapter offered here addresses an issue raised in "Rock and the facts of life," the relationship between music and other simultaneously occurring events in a given culture. It became clear to me, as the essay took shape, that an analysis of this sort could not separate the products of "low" and "high" culture, nor could music be split off from the visual arts, film, and literature. A decade later this issue would be phrased differently: "Is music to be understood as an autonomous object?"

Today I would summarize the piece as follows: during the 1960s and early 70s, an era in American culture dominated by institutional control over the minds and hearts of individuals and groups was giving way to an era in which such imposed consensus was questioned and resisted. Even more simply, the modern period was giving way to a postmodern era. But the term "postmodern" was not yet in common usage, and I didn't have the imagination to invent it.

*   *   *

"The times they are a-changin'," sings Bob Dylan in one of his most popular and widely quoted songs. The times were changing in 1963,

[1] Bruno Nettl, "Persian popular music, poker games in Illinois, and the liberation classes of 1970: a memoir" (unpublished, 1992), p. 3.

when the song was written. But the times have always been changing. And so has music. Anyone can hear, listening to a piece of music from 50 or 500 years ago, that it doesn't sound like music of today. The question to be investigated here is what relationship there is between changes in the times and changes in music.

One view is that since music is an abstraction – a series of marks on paper that are transformed into patterns of sound in time when the piece is performed – there can be no connection between it and such things as political events, wars, spiritual crises, labor movements, revolutions, natural disasters, and religious upheavals. Since music is an abstraction, goes this argument, it can only be understood as an abstraction – studied, talked about, described, and analyzed as a succession of sounds obeying their own rules, related only to themselves, and following certain laws of musical structure and logic. Music is something to be understood only on its own terms. The proper study of it leads to an understanding of the rules, procedures, and laws governing the organization of the various notes making up a given composition; the best analysis shows how certain pieces of music observe these rules and procedures.

An alternate view holds that there *is* a relationship between a piece of music and what was happening in the world when it was written. While there can be no direct connection between the notes in a musical score and a political campaign, an anti-war demonstration, or a discovery in the chemical laboratory, there is a possible link between such events and music written at the time they are taking place. The link is the person who writes the music. As a human being, he may be aware of, responsive to – and in the case of an exceptional person, perhaps even partially responsible for – what is happening in the world around him. As a composer of a piece of music, he consciously chooses the notes he will write down. He may be concerned with the questions of why he is selecting certain notes, who he hopes will listen to his music when it is performed, and what effect he would like his music to have on his audience. To the extent that he is aware of, and wishes to participate in, the world in which he lives, any conscious action that he takes – including the writing of a piece of music – will be affected by this world.

This is the question to be dealt with in this chapter. The procedure will be to take a given period in history – in this case the post-World War II period in America – examine it, characterize it, summarize the most important events that took place in it, attempt to sketch a "personality" of this particular time, and then to examine some of the music written and played during this period to see if the character of the times is reflected in this music. On the basis of this investigation of a specific time in history, some generalizations will be drawn regarding relationships between music and the world surrounding the composer when he writes this music.

World War II was one of the great turning points in the history of the United States. Although the country had been steadily growing in population, wealth, and influence in the nineteenth and early twentieth centuries, and although it had made certain contributions in science and even in several of the arts, until the Second World War it was regarded as an isolated, young, and relatively unimportant country by the major European powers that had shaped the destiny of the world, or at least Western Europe, for some centuries. America's intervention in World War I was late, and from the European point of view, relatively insignificant; its refusal to participate in the League of Nations minimized its role in international politics and economic and cultural exchange; severe internal problems, centered in the Great Depression, helped to maintain a low level of participation in international affairs. Europeans tended to regard Americans as naive, crude, unsophisticated, and often vaguely comic people with little history and culture. This view was shared by many Americans, particularly musicians and other artists. Generations of American composers and performers went to Europe to study, and writers and intellectuals fled the country for such "true" centers of culture (and life) as Paris. When a truly original creative genius such as the composer Charles Ives did emerge, he was often misunderstood and ignored.

Things began changing in the late 1930s and early 40s, when American economic life was revitalized. Many world-famous scientists, scholars, and artists fled Europe for the United States, finding there the security, freedom, support, and encouragement they needed to continue their activities. Their integration into the sciences and arts of the country provided a tremendous spark to American life. World War II changed the whole image of the United States. Threatened with isolation from the rest of the world and eventual annihilation, the country mobilized its military and industrial resources to a degree unprecedented in its history. At the end of the war, American troops were in almost every part of the world, having played a major role in the eventual defeat of the Germans and Japanese, and American industry was churning out an incredible flood of weapons and supplies of every sort.

When the war ended, there was no turning back. There was no

denying the critical role American arms, men, and supplies had performed in defeating the Germans and the Japanese; neither could the dominant position the US had attained in the world be argued. American troops occupied defeated countries and supported allied ones. American money and goods continued to pour into countries all over the world. American diplomats and statesmen, even American presidents, took part in conferences and meetings to try to determine the future of the postwar world. America was a charter member of the United Nations, one of the twenty-nine nations that ratified the UN charter in October 1945; the permanent headquarters of the UN were established in New York City. Its industry undamaged by the war, its casualties small in comparison with those of most European nations, its national pride in its military victories and industrial output high, the USA was undeniably one of the two most powerful nations in the world, the other being Russia.

It was assumed by the leaders of the country, apparently without question, that this new political, military, and economic strength would be sustained at a high level. Though the majority of non-career military personnel was discharged rather quickly when the war ended, the strength of the armed services was kept at a much higher level than was ever maintained in peacetime. Occupational forces remained in defeated countries, troops and military bases were maintained in countries that had been our allies, and bargains were made to establish new bases in countries such as Spain that had remained neutral during the war. Food, money, and supplies of all sorts were sent to countries wrecked by the war; billions of dollars were made available under the Marshall Plan to various European countries, playing a critical role in their amazing recovery. It was not just allies who were helped; Japan, Germany, and Italy were given major portions of American aid for rebuilding – physically, economically, and eventually militarily.

Just as American money and goods were everywhere, so was her political influence. American isolationism was dead. The Truman Doctrine, announced in 1947, stated that "it must be the policy of the United States to support free peoples who are resisting attempted subjugation by armed minorities or by outside pressures." Under this doctrine additional billions of dollars were sent to such countries as Greece and Turkey. Direct military intervention in Korea in 1950 made clear America's determination to play an active role in Asian affairs. The Eisenhower Doctrine announced that the US would supply economic and military aid to countries in the Middle East that were determined to "stop Communist aggression."

Countless other less dramatic and less published decisions and actions reinforced the image of a new America very much concerned with political, economic, even social affairs in practically every part of the world.

American economic and military victories during World War II were possible in large part because of the unity of the country during this period. There had been widespread discontent with many internal policies of the government in the 1930s and strong support for the notion that the United States should not become involved in European affairs; but in the several years preceding America's entry into the war there was increasing sympathy for the Allies, and after the Japanese attack on Pearl Harbor there was almost unanimous support for a policy of total mobilization for victory. A smattering of pacifists and political dissenters were isolated, potentially troublesome aliens were segregated, and almost all Americans settled down to doing what they could, through military service or otherwise, to see that the country prevailed against a common foe. The hardships and dangers of military duty, separation of families, and restrictions on normal activities even in civilian life – censorship, rationing, severe shortages, overtime work, limitations on travel, priorities given to military needs – were accepted, and endured, as necessary conditions for victory. Most Americans recognized this period as a crisis in their lives, and endured conditions they might otherwise have rebelled against.

The end of the war did not bring about much change in the mood of the country. After several tentative and confusing years, Americans were once again asked to mobilize against an enemy, and conditions that most people expected to change, once the war was won, were still part of American life. This time the enemy was Communism – international Communism. The American government took the view that there was an international Communist conspiracy to overthrow or conquer the United States and the entire world, and this conspiracy had to be fought as vigorously at home and abroad as the totalitarian governments of Japan and Germany had been fought during the war.

Secretary of State James Byrnes announced a new "get tough with Russia" policy early in 1946. An advisory committee recommended to President Truman in 1947 that compulsory military training for all eighteen-year-old Americans be instituted; consequently, the Selective Service Act went into effect in 1948, requiring all males in the eighteen to twenty-five age bracket to register for a minimum of eighteen months' service. This was only the second peacetime draft in American history, the first having been that ordered by President Roosevelt shortly before America's entry into World War II.

The war against Communism was conducted as vigorously within the country as it was in the area of international politics. President Truman ordered loyalty investigations of all federal employees in March 1947, and by the following year more than two million persons had been investigated – 526 resigned and 98 others were dismissed for supporting or sympathizing with Communist causes and ideas. The search for Communist influence broadened. The House Committee on Un-American Activities began hearings in 1947 on Communist sympathizers in the motion picture industry; writers, actors, and technicians were blacklisted by the industry as a result. In 1949 the New York State legislature ordered the dismissal of public school employees who were Communists; in 1950 the Board of Regents of the University of California dismissed 157 staff members who refused to sign statements disclaiming membership in the Communist party; the Supreme Court ruled in 1952 that "subversives" could legally be barred from teaching in public schools. Millions of Americans were asked to sign "loyalty oaths" to the effect that they did not belong to or sympathize with organizations attempting to overthrow the government. General Electric announced in 1953 that all Communists on their payroll would be fired. The government pursued legal warfare: 11 top Communists were convicted late in 1949 of conspiring to overthrow the United States government, and, finally, in 1954 the Communist Party itself was outlawed in America. By this time the country was again in armed conflict. In the summer of 1950 Truman ordered American troops to Korea to help resist the invading (Communist) forces from the north; an additional ten billion dollars was immediately requested to augment the military budget; and a state of emergency was declared in the country on 16 December 1950 when it became apparent that a major effort would be needed to pursue this new war.

One must not necessarily conclude that this continuing state of confrontation, conflict, and emergency was the result of a deliberate military-political scheme to keep the country on a wartime basis. The unity and single-mindedness of purpose in the country during the war had been a very real thing, sensed, understood, and appreciated by most Americans. Pearl Harbor, D-Day, and V-Day had been profound emotional experiences. The war years had been difficult in many ways, but they were also good years. There had been a sense of common purpose, a sense of working with other people to attain a common goal, a feeling that everyone was in the same situation and, as a result, could understand and relate to everyone else. Complete strangers meeting on trains, groups of people brought together by chance, felt a comradeship and a closeness that had not been part of American life in prewar years. There was a genuine sense of national pride, a feeling that America's involvement in the war was a humane thing, that Americans were truly fighting evil. There was genuine pride in the victories of America's armed forces. The clarity of the situation during the war, when Americans identified themselves as a good and righteous people fighting to overthrow evil, appealed to and inspired many people; the role had been played with great success, and it was easy enough for America to continue the same role when the enemy was redefined as Communism.

It was not just the government that was attracted to the idea of a country united behind its policies and actions. Americans of all kinds understood how the unity of the country behind its leaders had contributed to the victories of the war years, and how the same kind of unity could help achieve economic and social victories in peacetime. Americans both in and out of military service had, during the war, sacrificed some of their traditional independence and freedoms for what was felt to be the common good. The success of this course of action persuaded many people that continued unity, even if it were brought about by outside pressures, was highly desirable. This desire for unity was buttressed by an important, Pulitzer Prize-winning book of 1948, *The Disruption of American Democracy* by Roy Franklin Nichols, who explored the causes of the American Civil War, and in doing so investigated a much more general (and quite pertinent) question: What conditions can cause a successfully functioning democratic government to become disrupted and inefficient and, perhaps, even disintegrate? The author summarized his conclusions in this way:

> Why a civil war? Most of the principal "causes" – ideological differences, institutional differences, moral differences, cultural differences, sectional differences, physiographic differences – have existed in other times and places, without necessarily causing war. Then why should they set the people of the United States to killing one another in 1861? . . .
>
> People fight under the stress of hyperemotionalism. When some compelling drive, whether it be ambition, fear, anger, or hunger, becomes supercharged, violence and bloodletting, thus far in human history, seem "inevitable." . . .
>
> So rapid and uneven a rate of social growth was bound to inflict

upon Americans this "confusion of a growing state." Characteristic of it and dominant in it were pervasive, divisive, and cohesive attitudes which, as Whitman put it, were "significant of a grand upheaval of ideas and reconstruction of many things on new bases." The social confusion in itself was the great problem confronting statesmen and politicians. . . .

This lack of understanding was accompanied by a deep-seated enjoyment of political activity by Americans which proved dangerous. They gave themselves so many opportunities to gratify their desire for this sport. There were so many elections and such constant agitation. . . .

A great disruptive fact was the baneful influence of elections almost continuously in progress, of campaigns never over, and of political uproar endlessly arousing emotions. The system of the fathers might possibly bear within itself the seeds of its own destruction.

This constant agitation certainly furnishes one of the primary clues to why the war came. It raised to an ever higher pitch the passion-rousing oratory of rivals. They egged one another on to make more and more exaggerated statements to a people pervasively romantic and protestant, isolated and confused. The men and women exhibiting these different attitudes were not isolated and separated by boundaries – they dwelt side by side, and the same person might be moved by more than one attitude at a time, or by different attitudes at different times. The emotional complex which was created by the variety of these attitudes, and the tension which their antagonisms bred, added confusion to that already provided by the chaotic electoral customs and poorly organized parties; the total precipitated a resort to arms. . . .

War broke out because no means had been devised to curb the extravagant use of the divisive forces. . . .

At certain times and in certain circumstances, cooperative behavior predominates; but competitive behavior is seldom if ever absent, and when too vigorously aroused leads to a strife which ranges from argument to war. Indeed argument is itself a form of conflict short of war, more or less, and if pressed without checks and restraints easily passes over into war.[1]

For many Americans it was scientific rather than military achievement that was most exciting and held the most promise for a better life in the future. It was America's scientists, after all, who had devised the arsenal of weapons that made her armed forces so effective – the always-improving fighter planes and bombers, radar, rockets, flame

[1] Roy Franklin Nichols, *The Disruption of American Democracy* (New York, 1948), pp. 513–17.

throwers, proximity fuses, and eventually the atomic bomb – and who had perfected methods of treatment for the wounded and sick that kept the rate of fatalities much lower than it might have been. One of the most widely read books in the years just after the war was James Phinney Baxter's *Scientists Against Time* (1946), an account of the activities of the Office of Scientific Research and Development during the war. The foreword by Vannevar Bush, director of this office, explains the subject matter:

> It begins in 1940, when this country was still asleep under the delusion of isolation – when only a few realized that a supreme test was inevitable, to determine whether the democratic form of government could survive; when none could see clearly the full revolution in the art of war that impended.
>
> It recites the extraordinarily rapid evolution of weapons, as the accumulated backlog of scientific knowledge became directly applied to radar, amphibious warfare, aerial combat, the proximity fuze, and the atomic bomb.
>
> But it tells also of something that is more fundamental even than this diversion of the progress of science into methods of destruction. It shows how men of good will, under stress, can outperform all that dictatorship can bring to bear – as they collaborate effectively, and apply those qualities of character developed only under freedom. It demonstrates that democracy is strong and virile, and that free men can defend their ideals as ably in a highly complex world as when they left the plow in the furrow to grasp the smoothbore. This is the heartening fact which should give us renewed courage and assurance, even as we face a future in which war must be abolished, and in which that end can be reached only by resolution, patience, and resourcefulness of a whole people.[2]

And at the end of his history (which brought him a Pulitzer Prize) of the stirring accomplishments of American scientists during this tense and dramatic period, Mr. Baxter expresses his view of the present and future role of America and of its scientists – a view as widely held outside the political/military leadership of the country as within it:

> Until the world creates an international organization strong enough to control the genie who escaped from his bottle at Alamogordo, we must keep our powder dry. Only a strong United States can give sufficient support to the peace structure of the United Nations during the difficult period of transition in which the statesmen of the world must build more securely the foundations

2 James Phinney Baxter III, *Scientists Against Time* (Boston, 1946), p. vii.

of international order. A generation ago some of our pacifists preached unilateral disarmament, in the belief that by setting other nations an example we should encourage them to decrease their own armaments. Such a course was dangerous then. It would be suicidal now. It would place in jeopardy both our national security and the contribution we must make to the enforcement of peace. If war comes again, it probably will come quickly, leaving us no opportunity for the lengthy preparations we made in World Wars I and II while associates and allies held the fronts.

Our preparations must, therefore, provide for great offensive and defensive power from the outset of hostilities. Much of our strength will depend on the use we make of our scientists and engineers. It is not a question of scientific preparedness versus expenditures on ships, guns, and planes. We need big battalions, fleets, and air squadrons as well as factories, pilot plants, and laboratories. . . .[3]

Scientific research had been a key to military victory, and it held promise of winning other battles, those against disease, discomfort, death, and even the poor quality of life still afflicting so many Americans. The years after the war witnessed a series of scientific discoveries and developments so astonishing and so promising of a better life that reading a newspaper or listening to a news report on the radio became an exciting event, done in anticipation of hearing yet another scientific marvel or miracle.

There were astonishing developments in transportation and communication, making the world an ever-shrinking globe. Pan American Airways began the first round-the-world passenger service in 1947. An experimental X-1 jet, piloted by Captain Yaeger, made the first supersonic flight during that same year. In 1949 an Air Force jet bomber flew across the continent in less than four hours. An Army missile reached the unheard of altitude of 259 miles the same year, arousing increased speculation that space flight might eventually be possible. Direct-dial telephone service on a nationwide basis was begun in 1951. A Bell X-1A plane reached a speed of 1600 miles per hour in 1953. A transatlantic telephone system began operation in 1956, replacing radio telephone circuits. Russia launched Sputnik 1, the first earth satellite, in 1957, and the United States took important steps towards manned space flight by launching its first satellite, Explorer 1, in 1958 and sending two monkeys on a suborbital flight (up to 350 miles) in 1959. In the same year (1959) radio beams were bounced off the moon and back to the earth, a major step towards

[3] *Ibid.*, p. 449.

direct radio and television communication over distances formerly prohibitive. It was clearly only a matter of time until man would be able to communicate instantaneously with any spot on earth, or journey to any city in the country, or even the world, in a matter of hours; it was equally certain that man would soon be exloring space.

Discoveries in medicine were just as exciting. "Miracle" drugs such as Aureomycin were being used by 1948, and cortisone was discovered the following year. Antihistamines were being widely used by 1950 to combat the symptoms of colds and other illnesses. Polio, the dread crippler of children, was conquered: Dr. Jonas E. Salk began a test program of inoculating school children in 1954 and reported the following year that the tests had been successful in the forty-four states in which they had been given; within a few years almost everyone in the country had been protected by either his method or that of Dr. Sabin. The successful use of Thorazine and Reserpine in mental illnesses was reported in 1955. Improved surgical techniques, news of progress in isolating the viruses known or suspected of causing other diseases – these and other developments gave Americans hope for longer and more healthful lives.

Science was also furnishing Americans with new uses for their leisure time. Commercial telecasts, beginning after the war, became the major amusement of millions of American families. Five million sets were owned by 1950, and in the following twenty-year period the number swelled to 93 million. The first commercial color telecast was a CBS show in June 1951.

Science programs in colleges and universities expanded enormously in size and diversity and became financial mainstays of these institutions because of the federal government's willingness to grant large sums of money for research. Students entering colleges studied the sciences in ever-increasing numbers, many of them because of the promise of high salaries in these fields, but some because of a personal conviction that the most exciting and rewarding work was being done there. Respect and admiration for science and scientists cannot be demonstrated by statistics, but these feelings were dominant in postwar American life. As one illustration, the list of men elected to the Hall of Fame for Great Americans during this period is given below. Established in 1900 on the campus of New York University, the Hall of Fame holds elections every five years. The College of Electors is made up of approximately a hundred eminent men and women from various professions. Americans with a wide range of accomplishments have been voted in: among those elected in 1900 were John Adams (statesman), John James Audubon (naturalist), Henry Ward Beecher (clergyman), Henry Clay (statesman), Peter Cooper (philanthropist), Ralph Waldo Emerson (author), Robert E. Lee (military officer), Henry W. Longfellow (poet), John Marshall (jurist), and Jefferson, Franklin, and Washington. But those elected in 1945, 1950, and 1955 were almost without exception men of science, politics, or war.

1945	Walter Reed (surgeon)
	Booker T. Washington (educator)
	Thomas Paine (author)
1950	Alexander Graham Bell (inventor)
	Josiah Willard Gibbs (physicist)
	William Crawford Gorgas (physician)
	Theodore Roosevelt (statesman)
	Woodrow Wilson (statesman)
1955	"Stonewall" Jackson (military officer)
	Wilbur Wright (inventor)

An account of historical events or a recitation of facts and statistics cannot capture the mood, the feeling, of a given period in history. It is perhaps impossible for a person who did not live then to understand the attitude in the country towards science — the excitement over scientific achievements, the anticipation of continuing ones, the admiration accorded great scientists, the faith that science was leading mankind along the road to a peaceful, healthy, happy life. Much of this is summed up in a popular movie of the time, *Breaking the Sound Barrier* (1949), starring Ralph Richardson and Ann Todd. The plot involves attempts to perfect a test plane that will fly faster than the speed of sound. There is some belief that this is impossible, that a plane will disintegrate as it reaches this speed; in earlier flights there has been excessive vibration and malfunctioning of parts of the plane's mechanism as this speed is approached. Another attempt is made at the climax of the movie. It is successful, but the plane crashes, killing the pilot. The final scene includes a brief but dramatic statement by the scientist (Ralph Richardson) in charge of the operation: the pilot just killed was his son-in-law, and he is naturally shaken; but he says that the important thing is to continue this work until it is successful. Scientific achievement is more important than a human life. Audiences left movie houses excited and thrilled by this message.

Science is necessarily linked to education. Scientists must be educated more and more as their fields become increasingly complex. This period of great scientific achievement and promise was accompanied by an unprecedented expansion of higher education in America. A combination of two factors – a growing feeling that as much education as possible was a desirable and necessary thing in the postwar world, and the possibility of obtaining a college education (because of the GI Bill for veterans, the great availability of loans for education, and the generally higher level of family income) for many people who could not have afforded it before – filled colleges and universities to capacity, and encouraged and even forced a drastic increase in the enrollment at existing schools and the opening of new schools. Here, statistics are quite eloquent. Approximately 122,500 Americans were enrolled in colleges in the academic year 1929–30, representing 18 per cent of the number of pupils in high school that year. By 1939–40 the number had risen to 186,500, but this increase reflected the population growth rather than any changing pattern; this figure was only 15 per cent of the high-school population that year. But by 1949–50 there were 432,000 college students, 36 per cent of the number of high-school students.

Musical life in America was rich and complex during this period. In some ways musical activity reached peaks rarely attained in the previous history of the country. Phonograph records sold in unprecedented numbers. Popular music on radio, television, and jukeboxes, in movies, and over public systems such as Muzak flooded the air to the extent that many people lived with music most of their waking hours. Classical music flourished likewise. The sales of phonograph records of this music soared to new highs, and occasionally a classical record rivalled the sale of a pop record. Live performance of classical music also prospered. School, community, and regional symphony orchestras were founded in unprecedented numbers, as were amateur and semiprofessional opera groups. The locus of music instruction shifted dramatically from private instruction and conservatory training to music schools and departments of music in colleges and universities. These campuses became chief centers of musical activity in the country; not only music majors, but other students (and faculty) as well, involved themselves in choral groups, school orchestras, various chamber ensembles, and opera, performing for large audiences drawn from the college community. The quality of performance in these schools steadily improved – as more and more talented young musicians chose college rather than conservatory or private training, and as professional musicians were attracted to the benefits and security of an academic position – until it sometimes equalled or even surpassed that of professional groups.

In a reversal of the situation in previous centuries, when musical life was built almost completely around contemporary music, a very large percentage of music performed during this period (excluding popular music) was from the past. Composition of new works continued to flourish, however, and it is to this body of music that we must look for parallels with what was happening in postwar American life, if indeed these exist.

It is difficult to characterize music during a period like this, when so many composers were writing music of quite different types. With popular music, it seems fair enough to select the songs that sold the most copies and that were listened to by the most people, and to say that a sampling of a certain number of these pieces gives a profile of popular music as a whole. It is not so easy with classical music, where individuality is more prized, where some composers make a deliberate effort to write music that does not sound like that of anyone else, and where measurement of popularity is not only difficult but perhaps meaningless. Music historians tend to approach this problem – that of selecting a small number of composers and compositions most representative of a given period – by resorting to the concept of "importance"; by assuming that the central figure at a given time is the man whose music and ideas seem most interesting, important, and influential to other musicians and composers, and who was most centrally involved in the important and characteristic currents flowing through the musical life of that time. Utilizing this approach to music in America during the several decades immediately after World War II, a strong case can be made for selecting Walter Piston and Milton Babbitt as two of the most important composers of the time.

Walter Piston was born in Rockland, Maine, in 1894. He was educated at Harvard and in Paris. Joining the music faculty at Harvard in 1926, he eventually became chairman of the department and held the Naumburg-endowed chair of composition until his retirement from academic life in 1960. Though he composed diligently and with considerable success before World War II, the peak of his career came in the 1940s and 50s, and his success and influence as both a composer and a teacher reached new heights during that time.

As a professor at Harvard, he helped and influenced several generations of students, including the composers Arthur Berger, Irving Fine, Ellis Kohs, Leonard Bernstein, Harold Shapero, Daniel Pinkham, Billy Jim Layton, and Gordon Binkerd. But his greatest impact on the training of musicians came after the publication of his three textbooks: *Harmony* (1941), *Counterpoint* (1947), and *Orchestration* (1955). These came out at just the right time, coinciding with the enormous increase in enrollment at colleges and universities, and the shift of musical training to these institutions. They became the most widely used music textbooks for some decades, adopted by teachers at hundreds of schools and used by tens of thousands of students. These books project Piston's basic belief about the study of music: it should be a rational thing; certain principles of music can and should be learned in a systematic, disciplined fashion; all musicians should learn these things. The introduction to his book on harmony states, with characteristic clarity and succinctness, his conviction regarding the importance and necessity of rational and systematic training in the fundamental elements of music:

> There are those who consider that studies in harmony, counterpoint, and fugue are the exclusive province of the intended composer. But if we reflect that theory must follow practice, rarely preceding it except by chance, we must realize that musical theory is not a set of directions for composing music. It is rather the collected and systematized deductions gathered by observing the practice of composers over a long time, and it attempts to set forth what is or has been their common practice. It tells not how music will be written in the future, but how music has been written in the past.
>
> The results of such a definition of the true nature of musical theory are many and important. First of all, it is clear that this knowledge is indispensable to musicians in all fields of the art, whether they be composers, performers, conductors, critics, teachers, or musicologists. Indeed, a secure grounding in theory is even more a necessity to the musical scholar than to the composer, since it forms the basis for any intelligent appraisal of individual styles of the past or present.
>
> On the other hand, the person gifted for creative musical composition is taking a serious risk in assuming that his genius is great enough to get along without a deep knowledge of the common practice of composers. Mastery of the technical or theoretical aspects of music should be carried out by him as a life's work, running parallel to his creative activity but quite separate from it. . . .[4]

The period 1945–60 was one of even greater activity, success, and acclaim for Piston the composer. He wrote merely two symphonies from the time he began composing in 1926 until the end of World

---

[4] Walter Piston, *Harmony* (New York, 1962), pp. 1–2.

War II, but after that time works began to pour from his pen. The Third Symphony was written in 1947, the Fourth in 1950, the Fifth in 1954, the Sixth the next year, and the Seventh in 1961. Other compositions were produced at a similar rate. For instance, the amount of chamber music he wrote in the fifteen years after the end of the war was greater than what he had written before that time. Whatever the conditions were in the country and whatever Piston's own situation, they were clearly favorable to his creative work.

Recognition and performance of his music matched this impressive output. Piston was awarded two Pulitzer Prizes, one in 1948 for his Third Symphony, the other in 1961 for the Seventh. His music was performed by the major orchestras in the country as frequently as any contemporary American music. For example, his Second Symphony was premièred in 1944 by the National Symphony Orchestra of Washington, DC, played the same year by the Boston Symphony Orchestra, done in New York in 1945 by the NBC Symphony, and played later the same year by the New York Philharmonic under the direction of Artur Rodzinski; it won the Music Critics' Circle Award as the best new composition of 1945. Other of his works have similar histories. Just as he was a central figure in music instruction, Piston was squarely in the center of activity in the performance of contemporary music by the major performing groups in America.

His approach to composition was as rational and as historically oriented as his teaching and writing about music theory. He was familiar with the traditions, history, and style of Western European art music, and he saw his role as composer as one which he studied, absorbed, and understood as much of this music as possible, borrowing whatever elements he chose for his own music. The formal structures, harmonies, melodies, instrumentation, and counterpoint of his compositions were his own and reflected his own musical taste and personality, but they were all firmly and obviously rooted in earlier music.

Piston had assimilated this earlier music by conscious study, intellectual examination, and a deliberate and rational dissection followed by an equally rational reassembling of their various elements. His symphonies are points in a line of symphonic history extending from Haydn to Beethoven to Schubert to Brahms to Dvořák to Sibelius to Piston to whatever composers after him who chose to continue this line. He understood his music this way; he had arrived at this point of view during his own academic work in music; other people could most readily understand his music and the assumptions behind it if they were exposed to the same sort of training. Piston was content to be a college professor. His ideas about music fit nicely into an intellectual atmosphere sympathetic to order, intellectual discipline, rational examination, and historical perspective. The composer Elliott Carter, a former student of his, says of Piston:

> The rather speculative enterprise of uniting the different styles of contemporary music into one common style and using this in an ordered and beautiful way needs the peacefulness and sense of long-term continuity nowadays more frequently found in a university than elsewhere. . . .
>
> His unique contribution is to have done this particular work with outstanding excellence in a country where few have ever made a name for themselves as thoroughly craftsman-like artists. In literature several names come to mind but in music there is hardly one to be found before our time.
>
> To have helped to establish a deep understanding of the value of craftsmanship and taste here and to have given such persuasive exemplification of these in his works is highly important for our future. For, not having as ingrained a respect and love for high artistic ideals as Europeans have had, we have often slipped into the trivial, chaotic, and transitory. Piston's work helps us to keep our mind on the durable and the most satisfying aspects of the art of music and by making them live gives us hope that the qualities of integrity and reason are still with us.[5]

In a way Piston was a "popular" composer. The area of musical activity in which he worked, contemporary art music, was not a popular one in the sense that audiences and record sales matched those of pop music; but Piston had as many pieces performed, as many recordings made, and as large an audience as any other composer of this kind of music. The same cannot be said of Milton Babbitt, however. A discussion of his role in the music scene after World War II cannot stress the number of performances and recordings of his compositions (these were scarce), or the prizes and awards he won (such things were to come to him later), but must depend on the effect that his music and his ideas had on his contemporaries. Anyone involved in any serious way with contemporary music in the 1950s knew of Babbitt, knew at least something of his ideas, discussed them, felt it necessary to either agree or disagree with them, and in general was very much aware of his presence. In other words, he was an important figure.

Born in Philadelphia in 1916, Babbitt grew up in Jackson,

---

[5] Elliott Carter, "Walter Piston," *The Musical Quarterly* 32 (1946), pp. 354, 372–3.

Mississippi, was educated in Philadelphia and at New York University, and joined the faculty of Princeton University at the age of twenty-two. He has taught at that institution ever since, eventually being appointed to an endowed chair in composition. Early in his career as a composer he combined a flair for mathematics with music. He has said:

> Some people say my music is "too cerebral." Actually, I believe in cerebral music – in the application of intellect to relevant matters. I never choose a note unless I know precisely why I want it there and can give several reasons why it and not another.[6]

He was attracted to twelve-tone (or serial) music, the system worked out by Arnold Schoenberg whereby the basis of a composition is a set series of the twelve tones of the chromatic scale. This row of notes may be used in its original form, transposed to any pitch level, inverted, or used backwards (retrograde); a single form of the row may be used, several forms may be combined, or vertical or horizontal combinations of the row – or both – may be used. Few if any listeners can follow the manipulations of the row, but it permeates the entire piece and, therefore, shapes the character of the composition regardless of whether or not it can be consciously perceived. Schoenberg's pupil Anton Webern utilized this system at another level in many of his compositions. Working in more conscious ways with symmetries, proportions, and other relationships, he fashioned a series of short but incredibly complex compositions that reveal, upon careful analysis, the amazing detail of a thoughtful, systematic, and imaginative organization.

Babbitt wrote several articles analyzing and describing Webern's methods of pitch organization; in his own compositions he went beyond Webern by organizing other elements of a composition, such as rhythm and dynamics, in a similar way. The result has been called "totally organized" music, music in which every detail can be explained by reference to certain systematic compositional procedures planned and worked out before the piece is written.

By this time Babbitt's ideas and theories were so esoteric, so remote from usual musical experiences that very few people could follow or understand them. His articles and analyses were extremely difficult to comprehend, for musicians and even for theorists and other composers. No one, with the possible exception of a handful of other composers associated with him, could hear in his compositions what he was putting into them, the incredibly involved and complex

---

[6] Milton Babbitt, *The Score* 12 (June 1955), p. 53.

relationships among notes and groups of notes that seemed so important, so basic to what he was doing. Rather than seeing this as an unfortunate situation, Babbitt regarded it as a natural and even desirable development. His article "Who cares if you listen?" published in 1958, expressed his views of the relationship between the composer and the rest of the world with admirable clarity and eloquence:

> Why refuse to recognize the possibility that contemporary music has reached a stage long since attained by other forms of activity? The time has passed when the normally well-educated man without special preparation can understand the most advanced work in, for example, mathematics, philosophy, and physics. Advanced music, to the extent that it reflects the knowledge and originality of the informed composer, scarcely can be expected to appear more intelligible than these arts and sciences to the person whose musical education usually has been even less extensive than his background in other fields. But to this, a double standard is invoked with the words "music is music," implying also that "music is *just* music." Why not, then, equate the activities of the radio repairman with those of the theoretical physicist, on the basis of the dictum that "physics is physics"? It is not difficult to find statements like the following from the New York *Times* of September 8, 1957: "The scientific level of the conference is so high . . . that there are in the world only 120 mathematicians specializing in the field who could contribute." . . .
>
> . . . I dare suggest that the composer would do himself and his music an immediate and eventual service by total, resolute, and voluntary withdrawal from this public world to one of private performance and electronic media, with its very real possibility of complete elimination of the public and social aspects of musical composition. By so doing, the separation between the domains would be defined beyond any possibility of confusion of categories, and the composer would be free to pursue a private life of professional achievement, as opposed to a public life of unprofessional compromise and exhibitionism. . . .
>
> In E. T. Bell's *Men of Mathematics*, we read: "In the eighteenth century the universities were not the principal centers of research in Europe. They might have become such sooner than they did but for the classical tradition and its understandable hostility to science. Mathematics was close enough to antiquity to be respectable, but physics, being more recent, was suspect. Further, a mathematician in a university of the time would have been expected to put much of his effort on elementary teaching; his research, if any, would have been an unprofitable luxury . . ." A simple substitution

of "musical composition" for "research," of "academic" for "classical," of "music" for "physics," and of "composer" for "mathematician," provides a strikingly accurate picture of the current situation . . .

 Granting to music the position accorded other arts and sciences promises the sole substantial means of survival for the music I have been describing . . .[7]

Pieces by Babbitt from this period are his *Composition for Four Instruments* (1948), *Composition for Viola and Piano* (1950), String Quartet No. 2 (1954), and *All Set* (1957, for jazz ensemble).

In the late 1950s he was attracted to the idea of creating electronic music. His precisely calculated rhythms and pitches were difficult for human performers to execute with absolute precision, but the most complex passages were matters of simple mathematics for an electronic instrument; and once fixed, they would stay that way forever, with not the slightest variation or imperfection in any performance. Babbitt served as a consultant in the planning of one of the largest and most complex electronic instruments in America, RCA's Mark II Electronic Music Synthesizer, and has created on it such pieces as *Composition for Synthesizer* (1960–1) and *Ensembles for Synthesizer* (1961–3). The Synthesizer is housed in the Columbia–Princeton Electronic Music Center in New York, and is available to the students and faculty members of these schools.

As different from each other as their musics may seem to be, Piston and Babbitt share many ideas and attitudes. Both believe that music is something to be approached logically, rationally, analytically, systematically, and with historical perspective. Both regard music as an abstraction; neither has professed interest in music as a sociological phenomenon, neither sees music as reflecting historical, political, or even national trends. (Piston once said, "The self-conscious striving for nationalism gets in the way of the establishment of a strong school of composition and even of significant individual expression.") Both found an academic atmosphere most congenial to their careers and creative life.

Piston and Babbitt have been singled out as representative composers of this period. Their attitudes and approaches to music were shared by a large number of other composers who enjoyed the most success at this time. Success was measured by performances of compositions, publications, prizes and awards received, and publicity, i.e., articles and criticisms in newspapers and journals. Success was rewarded by academic appointments and promotions. Other composers

[7] Milton Babbitt, "Who cares if you listen?" *High Fidelity* 8/2 (February 1958), pp. 39–40, 126–7.

who were successful by these criteria were Roger Sessions, William Schuman, Quincy Porter, Elliott Carter, Peter Mennin, David Diamond, Leon Kirchner, George Rochberg, Ross Lee Finney, Vincent Persichetti, Halsey Stevens, Arthur Berger, and Harold Shapero. These men, with Piston and Babbitt, wrote the most widely performed music, won most of the major prizes and awards, and received the most attention in articles, essays, histories, and criticisms of contemporary music. Theirs was the music most often performed, most widely discussed, most praised, and most often used as models by younger composers. Almost all of these men share with Piston and Babbitt a concern for music as a rational and intellectual thing, almost all were trained in colleges or universities, and almost all held academic positions.

A handful of composers did not fit into this pattern. Gian-Carlo Menotti wrote successful operas; Samuel Barber was able to live independently of any type of position; Roy Harris and Aaron Copland were still active, though their greatest successes had come in the period before the war, a time when composers had been more independent and more concerned with writing "American" music. Although these men enjoyed some success after World War II, they were a minority, and their music and artistic ideals were rarely taken as models by the younger generation of composers.

Other types of music changed in ways reflective of the moods and attitudes dominating American life and culture during this period. Early jazz was associated with Negro dance halls, bars, houses of prostitution, and other non-academic surroundings. Jazz musicians were largely untrained players who, usually, could not read music and had little knowledge of the Western musical tradition. Even when jazz became known to white audiences, it retained much of its original character, and for some generations most jazz musicians, black and white, continued to be individuals whose training was mostly informal and was based on the oral tradition of jazz.

The most popular, successful, and influential jazz group after World War II was the Modern Jazz Quartet. This group represented something quite different in the history of jazz: its founder and leader, pianist John Lewis, studied at the Manhattan School of Music, earning two degrees and in the process becoming familiar with a wide range of music and musical techniques; Milt Jackson, the quartet's vibraharp player, studied music at Michigan State University and was later a faculty member at the School of Jazz in Lenox, Massachusetts; bassist Percy Heath studied at the Granoff

School of Music in Philadelphia. Shortly after the group was founded in 1951, John Lewis said: "I think that the audience for jazz can be widened if we strengthen our work with structure. If there is more of a reason for what is going on, there'll be more overall sense and therefore more interest for the listener."

Their stage dress and deportment accentuated the seriousness of their approach to music. They sought to lose their individual personalities through the complete integration of their talents in their music and by dressing and acting soberly; the impression they gave on stage was compared to that of a string quartet. Their music often borrows or is based on techniques or styles of classical music. Among their most popular pieces, *Vendome* and *Concorde* are fugues, and *The Queen's Fancy* was inspired by the Elizabethan composer Giles Farnaby. Other pieces are based on more sophisticated and complex formal structures than had previously been usual in jazz. Their audiences listened quietly and seriously, rarely reacting to the rhythmic elements that appealed so much to listeners of earlier jazz, and discussions of their music were often quite intellectual. Nor was this approach to jazz unique to this group. Other important jazz musicians of this time, such as Dave Brubeck, had similar backgrounds and used similar techniques in their music.

Respect for scientific achievement, a profound belief that the best hope for the future lay with a rational and intellectual approach to the problems of man, a conviction that more and better education would bring this about, and a willingness to subjugate individual ambitions, desires, and even certain freedoms to what was felt to be the common good marked this period of American history. Music created at this time tended to be rational and logical; it would not be inappropriate to use the word "scientific" to characterize it. Musical training was undertaken primarily in academic institutions, and many musicians were convinced that more and better musical education was the key to a better musical future for America. Increasing uniformity in teaching methods and in general attitudes towards music did not seem too heavy a price to pay for this promising future.

Curious things began to happen in the early and mid-1950s. A number of seemingly isolated and unrelated events in the arts, in literature, and among scientists, had one important thing in common: they were inexplicable in terms of what had been happening in America since the end of World War II.

- In 1950–1 the artist Robert Rauschenberg did a series of all-white paintings. The viewer could see nothing but a white surface, sometimes with his shadow projected on it. Several all-black paintings followed, made of torn and crumpled newspapers covered with black enamel paint.

- John Cage's *Imaginary Landscape No. 4*, written in 1951, was performed by twenty-four players on twelve radios. One player manipulated the volume control on each radio, one the knob to change stations. The sound of the piece depended on what was being broadcast over various stations at the time of a given performance, and, thus, no two performances were alike.

- In the summer of 1952, at Black Mountain College, Cage organized a "simultaneous presentation of unrelated events." Cage read a lecture; David Tudor played the piano; Merce Cunningham danced; Robert Rauschenberg played old phonograph records on a handcranked machine; M. C. Richards read poetry while perched on a ladder; various movies were projected on the ceiling. Each individual event was timed to the second, but the combination of them was unplanned, and left to chance. In a few years, such things would be called "happenings."

- The first issue of *Mad* magazine appeared in August 1952. The early issues were devoted largely to wild parodies of popular TV shows, movies, and other comic books, but there were also satirical takeoffs on various aspects of American life and culture. From the beginning, the advertising world was attacked and ridiculed by a series of grossly parodied advertisements. Features in the first issue included "Is a Trip to the Moon Possible?" (no, because of comic inefficiency and the stupidity of scientists); a *Mad* award for outstanding commercials to Goldsmobile (showing highways impossibly cluttered with cars as a result of the effectiveness of automobile advertising); "How To Be Smart" (demonstrating how social acceptance and success of various sorts can be obtained by crude, anti-intellectual behavior); "Let's Go For A Ride" (to a picnic ground grotesquely crowded and cluttered with garbage, trash, and litter); and "Supermarkets" (inconvenient, expensive, tricking people into buying things they didn't want or need). *Mad* readers soon numbered in the millions, and subject matter expanded to parody and even ridicule of such American institutions as the government, schools, and military service.

- Jasper Johns did a painting in 1954, entitled "Flag," that was an exact reproduction of an American flag – nothing more, nothing less. He also exhibited paintings of archery targets, and his "Painted Bronze," created several years later, consisted of two Ballantine Ale cans mounted on a base.

78

- A group of scientists who had been awarded the Nobel Prize met at Lake Constance in the summer of 1955 and issued a declaration reading in part: "With pleasure we have devoted our lives to the service of science. It is, we believe, a path to a happier life for people. We see with horror that this very science is giving mankind the means to destroy itself. . . . All nations must come to the decision to renounce force as a final resort of policy. If they are not prepared to do this they will cease to exist." This statement, called the Mainau Declaration, was signed by fifty-two scientists, including Bertrand Russell, Harold Urey, Frédéric and Irène Joliot-Curie, Linus Pauling, and other scientists from Germany, Sweden, France, Switzerland, Finland, England, and Japan.

- John F. Kennedy published in 1955 a book called *Profiles in Courage*, which detailed the actions of a number of political leaders, including John Quincy Adams, Daniel Webster, Sam Houston, and Robert A. Taft, men who had followed courses of action that they believed proper even though public sentiment was against them, and whose careers were endangered or even ruined by their acts. In the first chapter of this book Kennedy says:

  > . . . our everyday life is becoming so saturated with the tremendous power of mass communications that any unpopular or unorthodox course arouses a storm of protest such as John Quincy Adams – under attack in 1807 – could never have envisioned. Our political life is becoming so expensive, so mechanized and so dominated by professional politicians and public relations men that the idealist who dreams of independent statesmanship is rudely awakened by the necessities of election and accomplishment. And our public life is becoming so increasingly centered upon that seemingly unending war to which we have given the curious epithet "cold" that we tend to encourage rigid ideological unity and orthodox patterns of thought.
  >
  > And thus, in the days ahead, only the very courageous will be able to take the hard and unpopular decisions necessary for our survival. . . .[8]

- Jack Kerouac's book *On the Road*, published in 1955, is an account of the travels and wanderings of several young people across the United States and Mexico by car and bus. They are unemployed or hold temporary, meaningless jobs, and they seem to be interested only in alcohol, jazz, sex, cars, and drugs.

- One of the most widely read and discussed books of 1956 was William H. Whyte's *The Organization Man*. Whyte examined the life-style of a group that, on the surface, appeared to have been one of the most fortunate, successful, and happy ones in postwar America – young businessmen and executives. He says of them:

---

[8] John F. Kennedy, *Profiles in Courage* (New York, 1955), p. 16.

For them society has in fact been good – very, very good – for there has been a succession of fairly beneficent environments: college, the paternalistic, if not always pleasant, military life, then, perhaps, graduate work through the G. I. Bill of Rights, a corporation apprenticeship during a period of industrial expansion and high prosperity, and, for some, the camaraderie of communities like Park Forest. The system, they instinctively conclude, is essentially benevolent.

He describes their education, professional training, jobs, family lives, homes, church activities, and relationships with other people. He concludes that in most ways they are very fortunate, that there are many good features to their lives; but he also believes that there is a latent danger in the way things are going for them. Everything about their lives is organized: most of their activities are prescribed by the way of life they have chosen, and there is little opportunity for them to make conscious choices about the way their lives will unfold. He admires the efficient organization of so many phases of life in America, but sees the dangers in this:

People do have to work with others, yes; the well-functioning team is a whole greater than the sum of its parts, yes – all this is indeed true. But is it the truth that now needs belaboring? Precisely because it *is* an age of organization, it is the other side of the coin that needs emphasis. We do need to know how to co-operate with The Organization but, more than ever, so do we need to know how to resist it. . . .

The energies Americans have devoted to the co-operative, to the social, are not to be demeaned; we would not, after all, have such a problem to discuss unless we had learned to adapt ourselves to an increasingly collective society as well as we have. . . .

But in searching for that elusive middle of the road, we have gone very far afield, and in our attention to making organization work we have come close to deifying it.

No generation has been so well equipped, psychologically as well as technically, to cope with the intricacies of vast organizations; none has been so well equipped to lead a meaningful community life; and none probably will be so adaptable to the constant shifts in environment that organization life is so increasingly demanding of them. . . . They are all, as they say, in the same boat.

But where is the boat going? No one seems to have the faintest idea; nor, for that matter, do they see much point in even raising the question. Once people liked to think, at least, that they were in control of their destinies, but few of the younger organization people cherish such notions.[9]

- A new style of popular music, rock 'n' roll, skyrocketed in popularity in 1955. From the beginning it was accepted by young people as "their" music; from the beginning it was opposed and often fought by

[9] William H. Whyte, Jr., *The Organization Man* (New York, 1956), pp. 13, 14, 438.

parents, educators, churchmen, politicians, and other members of the older generations. Derived from the music of several subcultures (black, poor, and rural white), it incorporated from the start an aura of rebellion, of rejection of the patterns and life-styles of white Middle America. Jerry Rubin wrote in *Do It!*:

> Elvis Presley ripped off Ike Eisenhower by turning our uptight young awakening bodies around. Hard animal rock energy beat/surged hot through us, the driving rhythm arousing repressed passions.
>
> Music to free the spirit.
> Music to bring us *together*.[10]

- The Supreme Court ruled in 1956 that states had no authority to punish persons advocating overthrow of the federal government. Later that year, another ruling declared that the President had violated the law by dismissing as a security risk a federal employee who held a "non-sensitive" post.

- President Eisenhower approved programs for increased exchange of information and persons between the United States and the Communist countries of Eastern Europe in the summer of 1956.

- Blacks in Montgomery, Alabama, carried out a boycott against the city's public transportation system in 1956, in protest of segregated seating; on 13 November the Supreme Court ruled that segregation on buses and street-cars was unconstitutional.

- John Hersey's short novel *A Single Pebble* (1956) told the tale of a young American engineer sent to China by a contracting firm to investigate the feasibility of proposing to the Chinese government a vast power project on the Yangtze River. He becomes convinced that dynamiting stretches of rapids and erecting a dam in one of the famous gorges would improve navigation on the river, making it faster and safer. But the Chinese cannot understand this. The river is what it is – its advantages, beauties, even its dangers, are fixed points to which humans must adapt. The river should not change; only people should change. The engineer makes his report, passionately urging that the project be undertaken. But nothing comes of it.

- Paul Goodman's *Growing Up Absurd* (1956) is a series of essays relating the "disaffection of the growing generation" to "the disgrace of the Organized System of semimonopolies, government, advertisers, etc." He believes the"organized system" to be characterized by "its role playing, its competitiveness, its canned culture, its public relations, and its avoidance of risk and self-exposure." It is

> . . . very powerful and in its full tide of success, apparently sweeping everything before it in science, education, community

---

[10] Jerry Rubin, *Do It!* (New York, 1970), p. 18.

planning, labor, the arts, not to speak of business and politics where
it is indigenous.[11]

In a series of discussions of patriotism, class structure, community,
social life, faith, marriage, and other topics he details patterns and
attitudes, prevalent in American culture, that have made some
members of his generation "sickened and enraged to see earnest and
honest effort and humane culture swamped by this muck." He says
that young people in America are faced with "the lack of bona fides
about our liberties, the dishonorable politics in the universities, the
irresponsible press, the disillusioning handling of the adventure in
space, the inferior and place-seeking high officers of the State, the
shameful neglect of our landscape and the disregard of community."
He concludes that young people are "growing up absurd" because
they "*really* need a more worthwhile world in order to grow up at all."
He is encouraged that many of them are resisting the situation they
have inherited by turning to eccentric life styles, becoming involved
in such intellectual interests as Zen Buddhism, and engaging in radical
experimentation in the arts. These "crazy young allies" give him hope
that "perhaps the future may make more sense than we dared hope."

- Allen Ginsberg wrote the poem "Howl" in San Francisco in the winter
  of 1955–6. According to the poet, it was "typed out madly in one
  afternoon, a tragic custard-pie comedy of wild phrasing, meaningless
  images for the beauty of abstract poetry." It was a wild, rambling,
  undisciplined outburst from a young poet who had been dismissed
  from college for eccentric behavior and who believed that "recent
  history is the record of a vast conspiracy to impose one level of
  mechanical consciousness on mankind." The poem begins:

  > I saw the best minds of my generation destroyed by
  >   madness, starving hysterical naked,
  > dragging themselves through the negro streets at dawn
  >   looking for an angry fix,
  > angelheaded hipsters burning for the ancient heavenly
  >   connection to the starry dynamo in the machinery
  >   of night,
  > who poverty and tatters and hollow-eyed and high sat
  >   up smoking in the supernatural darkness of cold-
  >   water flats floating across the tops of cities
  >   contemplating jazz,
  > who bared their brains to Heaven under the El and saw
  >   Mohammedan angels staggering on tenement roofs
  >   illuminated,
  > who passed through universities with radiant cool
  >   eyes hallucinating Arkansas and Blake-light
  >   tragedy among the scholars of war,
  > who were expelled from the academies for crazy &

[11] Paul Goodman, *Growing Up Absurd* (New York, 1956), p. 241.

> publishing obscene odes on the windows of the skull,
> who cowered in unshaven rooms in underwear, burning
> their money in wastebaskets and listening to the
> Terror through the wall. . . .[12]

First published in 1956, a second printing was restrained in 1957 by a government official who said that "the words and the sense of the writing is obscene. You wouldn't want your children to come across it." However, a court ruling later that year found the poem not obscene.

- Vance Packard's *The Hidden Persuaders* (1957), a widely popular book, claimed that industry's use of advertising, utilizing sophisticated and unrecognized psychological tricks, often influenced people to purchase items that they did not need or even want.

- Six Friends (members of the Quaker Church) travelled to Russia on a friendship mission in 1957. The following year five Americans entered China, the first to do so since the government banned travel to that country in 1950, and the American pianist Van Cliburn won first prize in the international Tschaikowsky piano competition in Moscow, becoming an immediate hero in both Russia and the United States.

- The Supreme Court reversed the conviction of an American labor leader, Watkins, an admitted Communist sympathizer who had refused to answer questions before the House Un-American Activities Committee. It was held that some of the questions put to him concerned matters not under the jurisdiction of the committee, and that he had not been properly informed of either the charges against him or his constitutional rights.

- The governor of Arkansas and the people of Little Rock resisted a court order for racial integration of Central High School in the fall of 1957. Black students assigned to the school were prevented from attending by public demonstrations and the intervention of armed National Guardsmen. President Eisenhower ordered US Army paratroopers there on 24 September and nine blacks entered the school the next day.

- The film *The Bridge on the River Kwai* won Academy Awards for best production, best direction, and best actor (Alec Guinness) in 1957, and was given the New York Film Critics' award as the best picture of that year. The central character, played by Guinness, is a British army officer captured, with many of his men, by the Japanese in Asia during World War II. At first, he refuses to cooperate with his captors in any way, but his pride eventually leads him to supervise the construction of a bridge over a gorge; in the process Guinness drives his own men more mercilessly than the Japanese had. The bridge is an important link in a supply route for the Japanese, and the British send an expedition through the jungle to dynamite it. At the climax of the film,

[12] Allen Ginsberg, *Howl and Other Persons* (San Francisco, 1956), p. 9.

Guinness prepares to demonstrate to his captors how well he has done his job by marching his men across, and having a Japanese train follow. The bridge is blown up just at this moment; Guinness tries to prevent it, even though the saboteurs are British (it has become *his* bridge); the bridge collapses, killing British and Japanese alike, Guinness is shot, and the commander of the British expedition mutters "Madness! Madness!" War is madness, and Guinness's blind passion to complete the job is madness. The only sanity seems to be with the natives who have guided and accompanied the expedition, who have the time and temperament to enjoy the beauties of their country and their relationships with other people.

- Scientist Ralph E. Lapp published a book in 1958 giving an account of a Japanese fishing vessel caught in nuclear fallout when it sailed into a testing area. The book, *The Voyage of the Lucky Dragon*, pointed out the dangers of nuclear testing and attacked the Atomic Energy Commission's policy of secrecy concerning its operations.

- In March 1958 four people, including three Friends, sailed from San Francisco in the ship *The Golden Rule*, heading for a nuclear weapons testing site in the Pacific. Their plan was to be in the area at the time the United States planned a test blast. They were seized and detained upon reaching Hawaii and were given sixty-day jail sentences in Honolulu.

- The artist Rockwell Kent was denied permission by the government to travel to Helsinki to attend a World Council of Peace; the government had for some time been concerned with some of his associations with "subversive" activities and persons. The Supreme Court ruled in 1958 that the State Department did not have the authority to withhold a passport from a citizen because of his "beliefs and associations."

- Scientist Linus Pauling, in public statements and in his book *No More War!* (1958), called attention to the dangers to health, life, and heredity from radioactive fallout from continued nuclear bomb testing. He claimed that there would be five million defective births and several million cases of cancer in coming generations if nuclear testing continued.

- John Kenneth Galbraith's *The Affluent Society* (1958) argued that American industry was driving itself to maximum production, even overproduction, often without concern for the market or for the genuine needs of American society. The pattern was for industry to decide what to produce, to create a market for these products by advertising, and to persuade people that they needed or wanted these things and were fortunate and affluent once they acquired them. However, millions of American families had difficulty finding enough money for such basic needs as medical and dental care, and the general affluence did not extend to such things as education.

- The Supreme Court ruled in 1958 that the State of New York could not prevent the showing of a motion picture (*Lady Chatterley's Lover*) because it advocates an idea (adultery) contrary to the moral standards or religious codes of the citizens of the state.

- Nightclub comedian Lenny Bruce began attracting widespread attention for his act, which consisted of monologues (liberally sprinkled with "obscenities") on such subjects as sexual freedom, racial and religious prejudices, the drug scene, homosexuality, and the judicial and law enforcement systems of the country. "People should be taught what is, not what should be," he said. "All my humor is based on destruction and despair. If the whole world were tranquil, without disease and violence, I'd be standing in the breadline – right back of J. Edgar Hoover." By 1959 he was commanding fees of $1,750 a week. He was arrested for possession of narcotics in Philadelphia and Los Angeles, arrested for obscenity in San Francisco, Hollywood, and Chicago, barred from entering Australia and England, and declared legally bankrupt in 1965; he died in 1966.

- Rachel Carson, author of several poetical books describing the beauties and marvels of the natural world around us (*Under the Sea-Wind*, *The Sea Around Us*, *The Edge of the Sea*), became convinced early in 1958 that man, with the aid of science, was destroying his natural environment. Her research lead to the book *Silent Spring* (1962), in which she argued that:

  > The most alarming of all man's assaults upon the environment is the contamination of air, earth, rivers, and sea with dangerous and even lethal materials. . . . Chemicals are the sinister and little-recognized partners of radiation in changing the very nature of the world – the very nature of its life. . . . Chemicals sprayed on croplands or forests or gardens lie long in the soil, entering into living organisms, passing from one to another in a chain of poisoning and death. Or they pass mysteriously by underground streams until they emerge and, through the alchemy of air and sunlight, combine into new forms that kill vegetation, sicken cattle, and work unknown harm on those who drink from once pure wells.
  >   Since the mid-1940s over 200 basic chemicals have been created for use in killing insects, weeds, rodents, and other organisms described in the modern vernacular as "pests": and they are sold under several thousand different brand names.
  >   These sprays, dusts, and aerosols are now applied almost universally to farms, gardens, forests, and homes – nonselective chemicals that have the power to kill every insect, the "good" and the "bad," to still the song of birds and the leaping of fish in the streams, to coat the leaves with a deadly film, and to linger on in soil. . . . The central problem of our age has therefore become the contamination of man's total environment with such substances of incredible potential for harm – substances that accumulate in the tissues of plants and

animals and even penetrate the germ cells to shatter or alter the very material of heredity upon which the shape of the future depends.[13]

- Criticism of the American foreign policy, of "brinkmanship," that is, keeping international tensions high by continuing to stress the opposition of the "free world" to the Communist world, reached a crescendo in 1957–9 with the publication of such widely read books as *The Causes of World War Three* (Charles Wright Mills), *The Communist World and Ours* (Walter Lippman), *What's Wrong With U.S. Foreign Policy* (C. L. Sulzberger), and *The Tragedy of American Diplomacy* (William A. Williams).

- As a continuing way of life, national mobilization – military, economic, and political – against "international Communism" was questioned, challenged, and then resisted.

- Support weakened for the idea that American political influence should affect events in nations around the world.

Though these and other events were at first seemingly isolated from one another and from anything else, they were straws in a wind that grew from random breezes in the early 1950s to a gale by the 1960s, threatening to sweep before it many of the things that had been basic to American life for decades.

National pride in American military and industrial accomplishments, so strong and universal during and after World War II, was gradually replaced by questions, doubts, and eventually hostility and opposition. Many Americans began to question the image of America as a good and righteous country unified against evil. Enforced unity at the sacrifice of certain traditional American freedoms began to appear too high a price to pay, now that there was widespread questioning of the goals that this unity was intended to achieve.

The image of science was tarnished as it continued to develop more powerful and terrible weapons for warfare, to furnish procedures and means for industry to pollute and poison air, earth, and water, and to drink up billions of dollars from the national budget for such things as the space program, an exciting adventure but of little immediate benefit to the millions of people in the country who still needed decent shelter, food, clothing, medical care, and education.

Though the number of Americans in colleges and universities continued to increase, the methods, philosophies, and goals of the educational system were questioned. American education was not training people to think and reason, claimed many critics, but,

[13] Rachel Carson, *Silent Spring* (New York, 1962), pp. 6–8.

rather, was training them to fit blindly into the economy and society of the country.

Governmental policies were openly opposed and resisted. Southern politicians fought integration; speeches led to public demonstrations, and the government eventually found it necessary to use military force against its own citizens. Blacks who felt that the equal rights movement was moving too slowly boycotted, marched, and demonstrated, and were confronted by the armed forces of local and state police and the National Guard. Black urban communities in Detroit, Washington, Watts, and other places – where miserable living conditions seemed unlikely to change, and where the affluence of many Americans was in no way evident – erupted into riots, and again there was the spectacle of American troops confronting and fighting fellow citizens. Protests against US involvement in Southeast Asia grew from small gatherings of college faculty, a few scientists, and some religious groups to mass public marches and rallies; the day came when half a million Americans gathered in the capital of their country to give public testimony of their strong disagreement with policies of their government. Students argued and then acted against certain policies and practices of their universities, in some cases physically taking over buildings and facilities and demanding immediate changes. Here too, the spectacle of law enforcement officers and troops confronting and battling their fellow citizens became common.

The 60s became the age of the underground. Underground films, using techniques and subjects that Hollywood would never have touched, were at first a curiosity and then a strong, vital artistic current. Underground political activity, scorning the two-party system in which differences between the two parties seemed to grow less and less, ranged from extreme right to extreme left and anarchy. Underground publications used language previously unheard in American journalism as a cutting edge in fiction and non-fiction that dealt in stark, direct ways with sex, radical politics, drugs, and other topics outside the mainstream of American life. This kind of journalism scandalized most people at first but eventually had an effect on American letters. Underground religious movements and underground education ("free universities") likewise explored ideas and methods that in time were more generally accepted.

The 60s was the Age of Aquarius or the age of permissiveness, according to your point of view. It was a time of the Free Speech Movement, of draft card burning, of nudity on stage and screen, of Women's Lib and Gay Lib, of Black Power, of long hair, of the miniskirt and the see-through blouse, of the virtual disappearance of censorship of movies, stage productions, books, and magazines, of topless and bottomless dancers and waitresses, of SDS and Young Americans for Freedom, of Hippies and Yippies, of marijuana and LSD, of wiretapping, mass arrests, Mace, and assassination. The breakdown of faith in American institutions and the suspicion that the state, church, schools, and family were failing to guide people to meaningful lives persuaded more and more persons – not all of them young – to, in the classic phrase of the 1960s, "do their own thing." In a curious parallel to certain earlier periods of religious upheaval, when salvation was sought inside each individual rather than in the canons and traditions of the organized church, Americans tried to find meaning in their lives by turning inwards. In every aspect of behavior – dress, speech, political and religious belief, artistic expression, personal relationships – people tried to discover and follow their own individual desires, tastes, and needs. And if what they found conflicted with traditional American behavior, customs, morals, and even laws, so much the better, because these were the things that seemed to have failed.

Musical activity, like most things at this time, continued much as it had before – on the surface. Symphony orchestras played the same kinds of programs for the same audiences, opera companies staged the same operas, the training of musicians was still done mostly in colleges and universities. Walter Piston and Milton Babbitt wrote more compositions using the techniques discussed above, and many other composers continued to write symphonies, string quartets, operas, and other compositions in the tradition of Western art music. For a composer success was still measured by performances of works by major organizations, publication of these pieces, and the winning of prizes and awards; such success was still rewarded by academic appointments or promotions, or by salary raises. The Musical Establishment remained unchanged.

Other currents were running below the surface, however. Beginning in the late 1950s, traces of new sorts of musical activity occasionally rose to the surface, activity that had no immediate effect on the course of music in America, but which grew steadily more intense and attractive to increasing numbers of younger musicians. This activity seemed purely experimental at first: new ways of shaping a musical composition; new ways of producing sounds; new ideas about structure; different ideas about what was expected of an audience and what role music should play in contemporary society.

Eventually, the entire traditional concept of what a piece of music was and what the relationships among composer, performer, and audience should and could be was challenged.

This new activity first took visible form in the way music was notated, or written down. Western music had used a standardized and effective type of notation for many centuries, a system that had remained unchanged except for certain details since the early seventeenth century. But suddenly, in the late 50s and early 60s, performing musicians found themselves asked to play music notated in ways that broke radically with the system they had learned, the system that had been used for all the other music they played. At first, each composer devised his own system, and most scores contained introductory explanations of how the performer should read it. Changes in notation had taken place before in Western music, always signalling some dramatic change in musical style; composers had found that systems devised for one type of music would no longer serve for what they wanted to do. That was the situation in the mid-twentieth century: some composers reached the point of imagining and creating music so different from that of the mainstream of classical music that they could no longer indicate to performers what they should play by using the notational system of that previous time.

Though many musicians were involved in this new activity, the composer John Cage was at the center of it. Born in Los Angeles in 1912, he spent two years at Pomona College, then dropped out of school and spent a year in Paris and other European cities writing poetry, painting, studying architecture and piano, and eventually composing music. Cage returned to California, where he studied piano and composition with Arnold Schoenberg, among others. Later, he spent several months in New York studying contemporary and oriental music at the New School for Social Research.

In 1937 he involved himself with several modern dance groups, at UCLA and then at the Cornish School in Seattle. For many years his main activity – on the West Coast, in Chicago, and in New York City (where he moved in 1942) – was to accompany, compose for, and serve as musical director of dance groups.

Cage's earliest compositions were chromatic, atonal works for traditional instruments, but by the late 1930s he was writing mostly for percussion instruments. Many pieces were written for "prepared piano"; by inserting various objects among the strings of a grand piano he transformed the usual sonorities of this instrument into a rich variety of percussive sounds. Because much of his music was written for instruments that produced sounds without specific pitch, he experimented with various ways of organizing a composition according to patterns of note durations rather than pitches. Some of his structural techniques resembled those of non-Western music.

Cage's activities were scarcely known to most other musicians; he was writing music that differed in techniques, types of instruments used, and even in intent from the music that most people were involved in. Most of his associates were people from the other arts – the dancer Merce Cunningham, the artists Robert Motherwell, Robert Rauschenberg, Allan Kaprow, and Jasper Johns, the poet Kenneth Patchen – people who knew his work. Most professional musicians and professors of music had not heard of him, or were unfamiliar with his work. He held no academic positions, won no important prizes, and his music remained unpublished.

In the late 40s Cage began a serious study of Eastern philosophies, Zen Buddhism in particular. He began to use different sources of sound in his music: *Imaginary Landscape No. 1* (1937) used two variable speed phonograph turntables; *Williams Mix* (1952) used various natural and artificial sounds on tape. The composition *4'33"* (1952) required a performer (usually a pianist) to come on stage and sit before his instrument for four minutes and thirty-three seconds without producing a sound. The composition consisted of whatever sounds occurred, within or without the auditorium, during this period of time.

His compositions of the 50s were planned to incorporate variable or chance arrangements of sounds. Each performer in the *Concert for Piano and Orchestra* (1957–8) has for a part a collection of phrases and larger units of music; each decides what he or she will play, and in what sequence. Thus, during the performance no part has a planned relationship to any other part. In other works Cage used the ancient Chinese I Ching tables to generate a random assortment of notes, or he drew a staff on paper and wrote notes on it where he found imperfections in the paper, or he gave the performer a score consisting of several transparent overlays that could be moved around to produce changeable random collections of notes. Cage believed that a person should not force preconceived notions of form and structure onto the notes of a musical composition but should, rather, be able to create his own structure from any combination of sounds. He says in his book *Silence* (1961):

> Our intention is to affirm this life, not to bring order out of a chaos
> or to suggest improvements in creation, but simply to wake up to

the very life we are living, which is so excellent once one gets one's mind and one's desires out of its way and lets it act of its own accord.[14]

This way of thinking leads to the breaking down of all barriers between life and art. Cage has said that if he were successful in getting people to hear any combination of sounds as music – because of structures and coherences imposed on them by the listeners themselves – then people would find it unnecessary to attend a concert in order to hear music; they could hear it in whatever sounds were around them at any time. Each man would be his own creator and his own critic. Standards of taste would not be imposed on an individual by others, would not be established in music schools and universities, would not be systemized and canonized. A musical experience would be a completely private, personal thing, as various as the people in the world.

The late 50s and the 60s saw Cage's position in the musical world change dramatically. At the beginning of this period he was an obscure figure working in a strange musical idiom, writing pieces that were rarely published and almost never played outside of his own circle of dancers and artists; by the end, he was considered by European critics and musicians to be the first truly original figure in American music since Charles Ives. His own countrymen held divided opinions about him. But no one could ignore his music and his ideas about music, no one could deny that what he had done and was doing was having a profound effect on the course of music in America and the world. In 1954 a concert tour, with the pianist David Tudor, through Germany, France, Belgium, Sweden, Switzerland, Italy, and England brought Cage's ideas to Europe, and led to lectures at Darmstadt and the Brussels World Fair and a four-month stay at the electronic music studio in Milan. A retrospective concert of Cage's music in New York's Town Hall in May 1958 gave many persons a first chance to hear samples of works written over a twenty-five-year period, and to more properly evaluate him as a composer; the commercial sale of the recording of this concert made Cage's music even more widely available. He was asked to teach courses in new music and mushroom identification at the New School for Social Research in 1959. Other academic appointments followed: he was appointed Fellow at the Center for Advanced Studies at Wesleyan University (Middletown, Connecticut) in 1960–1; Composer in Residence at the University of Cincinnati in 1967; an

---

[14] John Cage, *Silence* (Middletown, CT, 1961), p. 12.

Associate at the Center for Advanced Study at the University of Illinois in Urbana from 1967 to 1969; an Artist in Residence at the University of California at Davis in 1969. There was a concert tour of Japan in 1962, a world tour with the Cunningham Dance Company in 1964, and a heavy schedule of lectures and concerts at colleges and universities throughout America. He was elected a member of the National Institute of Arts and Letters in 1968. All of this recognition reflected the fact that in the 1960s John Cage was making music that large numbers of people wanted to hear, and that he was saying things about music, art, and life that were interesting, relevant, and provocative.

HPSCHD, composed in collaboration with Lejaren Hiller, is a major piece from this period, when Cage achieved his greatest success and influence. It was commissioned by Antoinette Vischer of Switzerland as a piece for harpsichord, and was performed on the evening of 16 May 1969 in Assembly Hall at the University of Illinois in Urbana.

Assembly Hall is a circular concrete building on the University of Illinois campus that seats some 14,000 persons. It was planned and constructed primarily as a sports arena. The annual state high school basketball tournament is a major event in this basketball-crazy state, and it is said that the state legislature was willing to appropriate money for such an expensive building because the prospect of a spectacular, spacious new site for this tournament was popular among most people in the state, even those who usually objected to expenditures for education. Once constructed, the hall was also used for various musical events – symphony concerts, musicals, operas – despite the fact that it is acoustically unsuited for them. The enclosed area is enormous, the distance from floor to ceiling is staggering and musical sounds, even those produced by a large orchestra, become lost in all of the space, even if they are amplified. Cage was intrigued with the challenge of filling such a huge and unsympathetic space with sound.

The piece turned out to be a vast and incredibly detailed complex of sounds and sights. Seven harpsichordists, playing amplified instruments, sat on raised platforms on the floor of the hall. Three played computer-realized versions of Mozart's "Introduction to the Composition of Waltzes by Means of Dice"; two others played collages of various piano works from the time of Mozart to the present (fragments of Beethoven's *Appassionata* Sonata, Chopin's Prelude in D Minor, Schumann's *Carnival*, Gottschalk's *The Banjo*, Ives' *Three-Page Sonata*, Schoenberg's Opus 11, No. 1, Cage's *Winter*

92

Music, and an early piano sonata by Hiller); another played a part called "Computer Print-out for Twelve-tone Gamut"; and the seventh played any pieces by Mozart he chose. Each harpsichordist was free to play his part any time he wanted to, any number of times, and he was also free to play any other player's part at any time. Fifty-one amplifiers, positioned around the circumference of the hall near its top, were used to play fifty-one different tapes of electronic music that were planned and realized on a computer. Each tape was slightly over twenty minutes long and could be played at any time, any number of times, in the course of the performance – which on this occasion lasted from 8 p.m. until midnight.

For the eye there were slides, movies, and lights. Several screens, including a mammoth continuous 340-foot one, displayed slides of abstract designs done by members of the University of Illinois art school, 5,000 slides loaned by NASA, pages of musical scores by Mozart, computer instructions, and films (most of them concerned with astronomy and space travel). Colored beams of light and spinning mirrorlike balls bathed the hall in continually changing colors.

Nothing was coordinated. Each musician and each operator of a tape recorder, slide projector, or movie camera did what he chose for whatever length of time and in whatever sequence he chose. The eye and ear could pick out any combination of sights and sounds among all there was to choose from. The audience came and went, walked around, chatted with friends and with the performers, sampled work from the perspectives of various locations. And several thousand people in the audience became part of the piece: they walked, talked, danced, sang, smoked, sat, or stretched out on the floor; some came in bizarre costumes, some painted their faces with Dayglo colors, some wore white shirts imprinted with the likenesses of Beethoven and Cage. Each person made what he wanted of the piece and, thus, it was a different event for everyone who attended; each saw and heard it from the standpoint of when he was there, where he was in the hall, how long he stayed, whom he saw and talked with while there, what mood he was in, and what attitudes he had about such events.

HPSCHD does not have to be performed in this way, or on this scale. It can be performed by from one to seven harpsichords, with any number of tapes (from one to fifty-one), in any kind of hall, for any duration of more than twenty minutes. A recorded version (Nonesuch H-71224) consists of three harpsichordists and a specially condensed version of the tapes.

The jazz world was rocked by similar unorthodoxies. Saxophonist (and occasional violinist) Ornette Coleman arrived in New York in 1959 to play at the Five Spot, after having made two albums for a small company (Contemporary) in Los Angeles. Born in Fort Worth in 1930, he was an almost completely self-taught musician. For a decade he knocked around the jazz world of the South and the West – Fort Worth, New Orleans, Baton Rouge, Natchez, Los Angeles – playing in a style all his own, a style so eccentric and so different from traditional ways of playing jazz that other musicians often refused to play with him, a style that bewildered audiences. It was not until he was in his late twenties, an advanced age for a jazz player, that Coleman found several other players sympathetic to his style who learned to play with him, and it was only then that he achieved some recognition through his two records.

Coleman was still a tremendously controversial figure when he came to New York. The Five Spot was packed for month after month; the crowd including other jazzmen who came to hear – and often to criticize and ridicule. His music was described as anarchistic and nihilistic. Critics spoke of his technical inadequacies and the "incoherence" of his saxophone playing. The famous jazz writer Leonard Feather said that "his rejection of many of the basic rules, not merely of jazz but of all music, did not entail the foundation of specific new rules." Another jazz critic wrote that "there is at least one writer on jazz who not only doesn't understand what Coleman is doing but suggests that it is not worth trying to understand. Not, that is, if you are interested in music." Many jazzmen had similar reactions. "If that's music, I've been doing something else all my life," was the comment of one. Another said, "I listened to him all kinds of ways. I listened to him high and I listened to him cold sober. I even played with him. I think he's jiving, baby. He's putting everybody on. They disregard the chords and they play odd numbers of bars. I can't follow them."

Coleman's playing seemed completely detached from the traditional harmonic foundations of jazz. His melodic lines developed with no apparent reference to the harmonic and metrical patterns that had served jazz for so many decades. He wanted the other players in his groups to do the same; the result was three or four or five independent lines unfolding simultaneously, each unrelated to any other by common beat or harmonic progression.

The album *Free Jazz* (Atlantic SD 1364) is one of the monuments of his art. Coleman collected eight jazz musicians in a New York recording studio in 1964, and grouped them in two quartets: himself, Donald Cherry (trumpet), Scott La Faro (bass), and Billy Higgins (drums) in one; Eric Dolphy (bass clarinet), Freddie Hubbard (trumpet), Charlie Haden (bass), and Ed Blackwell (drums) in the other. With no rehearsal, the eight men performed a free improvisation based on no previously known tunes, no planned chord progression, no planned structure. Sometimes one player or another improvised alone, at other times several of them improvised together. "We were expressing our minds and emotions as much as could be," said Coleman. "The most important thing was for us to play together, all at the same time, without getting in each other's way." The session lasted fifty-six minutes and twenty-three seconds, enough to fill the two sides of an LP record. In listening, one can notice that although the players listen to one another – an idea played by one may be picked up by others, who play it in their own style – each player, even the drummers and bass players, goes his own way rhythmically, harmonically, and structurally. To ears conditioned to traditional jazz, or traditional music of any kind, this music is chaos. To ears that can listen in other ways, it is a fascinating and exciting collage, rich in detail, that changes with each hearing, depending on which instrument or instruments one listens to most closely.

In summary, America went through a period during and just after World War II in which the emergency of the war, followed by pride in the country's achievement and hopes for a better future unified the country as it had rarely been before. Pride in the victories of the armed forces and American industry, faith in American leadership, a conviction that the country was morally right, the belief that science and education would lead to an even more prosperous, healthy, and happy future – these things created a climate in which Americans saw their role as one of following and trusting their leaders and trying to be good citizens by fitting as smoothly and productively as possible into the economic and social patterns of American life. The mood in the country was one of obedience, trust, conformity, cooperation, discipline, of working with others for the common good – with as little friction and disagreement as possible. Politics was left to politicians, science to scientists, war to soldiers, art to artists.

But the picture began to change. Questions began to grow in the minds of some people. Were political leaders always leading the country in safe, sane, moral directions? Was American industry really concerned about the well-being of American citizens – or were its motives purely selfish? Were the directions science was taking always desirable? Was the military really protecting citizens from some imminent threat to life and property, or was it engaged in its own games – expensive, deadly games? Were educational and religious institutions really training people to lead happy, satisfying lives? Or were they preparing them to fit quietly and unquestioningly into planned patterns in American society? Faith, obedience, and conformity gradually changed to questioning, argumentation, resistance, disobedience, and even conflict.

It is simple enough to relate the musical life of America to these changing patterns. Musical activity that is centered in traditional institutions – music schools, colleges and universities, professional performing groups – and in which new generations of musicians are trained according to methods that will insure the perpetuation of a stable and traditional musical life, is obviously well suited to a culture dominated by conformity and motivated by a belief that things become even better because of more and better education. On the other hand, musical activity based on the beliefs that every person must discover for himself what music is, that every individual must find what type of music he best responds to and most wants to create (if he is a composer), that any sounds or combinations of sounds may be music, is just as obviously appropriate in a society in which the basic precepts of government, religion, education, and social behavior are being questioned. Walter Piston, as a composer and teacher, epitomized in music the dominant trends and patterns in America from 1940 to 1955. John Cage, as a composer and philosopher, epitomized some dynamic currents in American society from about 1955 to 1970.

As the times changed, music changed.

But it is not quite that simple. Any culture, at any time, in any place, reflects a collection of individuals, each with his own personality, ideas, beliefs, and attitudes. Certain events or the force of a powerful political personality may lead numbers of people – even a majority of them – to agree on enough basic issues to give a particular culture a distinct flavor. When this stage is reached, anything else that seems to fit into the general scheme of things will appear to be part of the culture, regardless of whether there is a cause-and-effect relationship. And even when certain attitudes are predominant, there are always persons who do not share them, who are at odds with the way things are going.

John Cage was writing music from 1940 to 1955 – music that was nothing like that of Walter Piston; Piston continued to compose from 1955 to 1970, writing music that had nothing in common with that being written by Cage. There was underground, radical activity in politics and the arts from 1940 to 1955; after 1955, many individuals and organizations were determinedly committed to maintaining the status quo in America, to preserving traditional American institutions, morals, and customs. Cage's music and philosophy were representative of one thread in American society and culture during and immediately after World War II but this thread was not a dominant or even a very important one. Piston's music and his views on art were part of a continuing school of thought that was challenged and at least temporarily overshadowed in the 1960s.

Any period in history can be seen in this way. Historians can identify dominant currents in the culture, musicologists can pick out the most important composers and pieces of music; and, as a result, relationships can be drawn between what was happening in the world and in music. But it must be understood that such a process deals in generalities, that "dominant currents" flow together with less strong and less visible ones, that the "most important composers" coexist with other persons who are also writing music. A rich variety of ideas and attitudes can be found at the same time in the same culture, and events can quickly change the prevailing situation so that something obscure or seemingly unimportant can become significant or dominant.

4

"IF I WERE A VOICE": OR, THE HUTCHINSON FAMILY AND POPULAR SONG AS POLITICAL AND SOCIAL PROTEST

My book *Yesterdays* was not written as an overview of popular music but as a narrative history of the musical and social origins of a single genre, popular song, which I defined as follows:

- written for, and most often performed by, a single voice or a small group of singers, accompanied by either a single chord-playing instrument or some type of band, ensemble, or small orchestra;

- usually first performed and popularized in some form of secular stage entertainment, and afterwards consumed (performed or listened to) in the home;

- composed and marketed with the goal of financial gain;

- Designed to be performed by and listened to by persons of limited musical training and ability; and

- produced and disseminated in physical form – as sheet music in its early history, and in various forms of mechanical reproduction in the twentieth century.[1]

There was no intent of privileging this genre over others. As I pointed out myself, this definition "excludes the music of William Billings, which is for vocal ensemble; Child ballads and other traditional Anglo-American songs, which were transmitted in oral tradition; the band music of John Philip Sousa and the ragtime music of Scott Joplin and others, which is instrumental; all church music, even that for solo voice; most jazz, which is instrumental." But I emphasized that "the

[1] Charles Hamm, *Yesterdays: Popular Song in America* (New York and London, 1979), p. xvii.

98

exclusion of these and other kinds of music from this book – except as they exert direct influence on popular song – does not imply that they are less interesting or important than the music dealt with here, merely that they are something different."[2]

A first methodological problem was the selection of the repertory around which my narrative would be structured. Musicologists dealing with a genre or historical period often find it impossible to examine more than a small fraction of the repertory in question because of its sheer mass, and it goes without saying that the method of selection can have a critical effect on the resulting narrative. Among the various methodologies of selectivity have been:

- The privileging of canon. The "best" pieces of music in a given repertory are assumed to have been identified already by a process whereby a small number of masterpieces have been recognized over the years as superior products, though it is not always clear at what precise point or by whom such a canon is constructed.

- The privileging of influence. Musicologists tend to think of Western music as being in forward motion, marching inexorably onwards through a succession of musical styles and genres, each replacing earlier ones only to be replaced in turn by yet others. Accordingly, attention is paid to compositions and composers in proportion to their perceived stylistic influence on contemporaries and successors.

- The privileging of personal taste. Much writing on music, including some historical narrative, is based on those compositions, composers, and performers favored by the author.

- The privileging of ideology. Some authors begin with a political agenda, then select pieces to be dealt with on the basis of how well they support this position.

My solution in *Yesterdays* was to set up an arbitrary system of selection, adapted to the writing of historical narrative from John Cage's compositional philosophy of creating pieces free of individual taste and memory and of the literature and traditions of the art.[3] Since the topic was popular song, I chose "to let the subject define the method" by devising ways of identifying "those songs demonstrably the most popular [in the sense of being] listened to, bought, and performed by the largest number of Americans."[4] No value judgements of the music are offered or implied, nor is it suggested that this methodology is the best way to approach the subject.

A few years later William Brooks theorized a somewhat similar

[2] *Ibid.*, p. xviii.
[3] This aesthetic is defined in a number of essays in John Cage, *Silence* (Middletown, CT, 1961).
[4] This methodology is described in Hamm, *Yesterdays*, pp. xix–xxii.

position in an essay entitled "On being tasteless," arguing that we should "build our histories by selecting *systematically but arbitrarily* from the detritus left by the past." He argues that "Taste gets theorists nowhere; in fact, taste gets in the way. . . . Theory has become converted into yet another defence of taste and the need for taste – but along the way it has stopped being theory."[5]

Yesterdays was written as a textbook for undergraduate lecture courses, but in the 1980s it took on a second life as one focus of criticism of the so-called musicological approach to popular music. Richard Middleton, for instance, argues that three aspects of "the bundle of assumptions and ideologies which came to constitute mainstream musicology" are problematic in dealing with popular music: (1) terminology, "slanted by the needs and history of a particular music ('classical music')"; (2) methodology, "slanted by the characteristics of notation" into reliance on a "notional centricity" ill-suited for dealing with non-notated music; and (3) ideology, "slanted by the origins and development of musicology itself," giving it a "philosophical grounding in the aesthetic and historical theories of German idealism."[6] Curiously, I agree with much of this criticism of musicology and have made similar observations myself.[7]

I've chosen a section of *Yesterdays* dealing with the Hutchinson Family, a singing group active before, during, and after the American Civil War, self-described as more social reformers than musicians. As in the study of all popular music of the past, context must be established through documents and other evidence from the historical period in question. If I were writing this section today, I would take the further step of placing the Hutchinson's social activism in the broader context of secular humanism, a movement once praised for its criticism of the social ills of early capitalism but nowadays sometimes seen as merely calling attention to these problems without addressing their roots.

* * *

The Hutchinson boys had early contacts with alcohol and the human problems it could aggravate and initiate. John wrote:

> The drink habit was almost universal in our neighborhood and town. Old New England rum was the white-faced devil that tickled the palate of more or less of the careless individuals

---

[5] *Popular Music* 2 (1982), pp. 9–18.
[6] In *Studying Popular Music* (Milton Keynes and Philadelphia, 1990), pp. 104–7.
[7] See Charles Hamm, "Some fugitive thoughts on the historiography of Music," in *Essays in Musicology: A Tribute To Alvin Johnson*, ed. Lewis Lockwood and Edward Roesner, (Philadelphia, 1990), pp. 284–91.

comprising the population. . . . Scenes of squalor characterized the drunkard's home, as they have from time immemorial – a lack of thrift, and total neglect; rags and old hats taking the place of the panes of glass that had been rudely dashed out; together with the sad countenances of wife, mother and half-child.[1]

There were neighbors and friends who suffered as a result of their addiction: the local musician, who gave violin lessons to Judson and John, but whose "love of the art and occupation were well-nigh sacrificed and bartered away for the pleasure of the dram-shop"; and a neighboring family, with a father who "when sober . . . was considered a most capable mechanic and expert blacksmith and pleasant companion," but whose fatal weakness for alcohol turned him into a "notorious sot" and led to "the family, one by one, [being] put out to be brought up by strangers."[2]

While living in Lynn in 1841, just before the first of their concert tours, the three Hutchinson brothers – then the Aeolian Vocalists – heard Hawkins, the "reformed drunkard" who had come to the Boston area to inaugurate the Washington movement. They were so persuaded that they immediately took a temperance pledge and attended meetings for the cause, leading in the singing of such songs as "We Are All Washingtonians." Jesse was moved to fit temperance words of his own invention to the well-known tune "King Oliver," arranged as a trio for the Aeolian Vocalists; it was first sung at a great temperance rally in Salem, Massachusetts, held in the former Old Deacon Giles distillery, which had been converted into a temperance hall. The song, renamed "King Alcohol," became a great favorite on their commercial programs and was one of the four songs published by Oliver Ditson in 1843. With its lively, folkish character, and its lack of "scientific" writing – parallel octaves and fifths abound, strange doublings are the rule – its sound is close to that of the hymns and anthems written by rural musicians in New England and later the South and West for use in singing schools (see Ex. 1). Their devotion to a second great cause, the abolition of slavery, developed somewhat later. The Hutchinsons had grown up in a region remote from the institution of slavery. There they had known a freed slave – "Black as the ace of spaces, tall, well-proportioned, athletic, uneducated but witty . . ." – who was married to a white woman and had seven children, attractive and talented; but beyond remarking that the family "lived in comparative isolation," they seem to have given no thought to the matter. Their first direct

---

[1] John Wallace Hutchinson, *Story of the Hutchinsons (Tribe of Jesse)*, 2 vols. (Boston, 1896), vol. 1, p. 28.   [2] *Ibid.*, vol. I, p. 29.

Ex. 4.1 Hutchinson Family, "King Alcohol"

encounter with slavery had come in Saratoga in the summer of 1842, during their first extended concert tour.

> 'Twas now we first observed our slave-holding neighbors, clothed in their wealth, displaying the elegance of their equipages, as they rolled in extravagance and splendor on the avenues, while we remembered this show as the product of the blood and sweat of the slave, who being forced could do no less than obey his master and submit to his fate.[3]

In the meanwhile, brother Jesse had become acquainted with Frederick Douglass, who had "come panting up from the South with bloodhounds baying upon his tracks" and settled in Lynn. Jesse was soon involved in antislavery activities, and when the quartet returned from their first triumphant tour, he infected them with his ardor. There was shortly thereafter a dramatic incident: an escaped slave had found his way to Boston, pursued by his Southern owner,

[3] *Ibid.*, vol. I, p. 57.

and had been arrested by local authorities. The only alternative to returning him to slavery was for a group of citizens to put up enough money to buy his freedom. Some fifty men, including several of the Hutchinsons, marched through the streets of Boston singing "Oh, liberate the bondman" to attract more supporters, then held a rally in Marlborough Chapel. During the rally,

> . . . a man came through the aisle of the chapel, and mounting the platform, shouted out to the crowd, "He's free! He's free!" I can never forget the expression of joy on the face of every citizen present.[4]

Four hundred dollars had been paid in ransom; the slave, George Latimer, was free. He settled in Lynn and was for years a fixture at antislavery rallies.

The Hutchinsons participated in their first large antislavery meeting at a state convention held in Faneuil Hall in Boston on 25–7 January 1843. "We were inspired with the greatness of the issue, finding our hearts in sympathy with those struggling and earnest people,"[5] wrote John. "We fully resolved to buckle on the armor, feeling proud to be engaged in such a great work for humanity." Their songs opened and closed each session, others were interspersed among the speeches and exhortations of Wendell Phillips, William Lloyd Garrison, Frederick Douglass, Edmund Quincy, and the like. Some notion of the temper of the sessions is conveyed by a motion offered by Garrison the last day, and adopted with ferocious enthusiasm: "*Resolved*, That the compact which exists between the North and the South is a covenant with death and an agreement with hell – involving both parties in atrocious criminality, and should be immediately annulled." The Hutchinsons' role was eloquently described in the *Herald of Freedom*:

> The Hutchinsons were present throughout the meetings . . . and it was what they said, as well as how they said it, that sent anti-slavery like electricity to every heart. They made the vast multitudes toss and heave and *clamor* like the roaring ocean. Orpheus is said to have made the trees dance at his playing. The Hutchinsons made the thousands at Faneuil Hall spring to their feet simultaneously, "as if in a dance," and echo the anti-slavery appeal with a cheering that almost moved the old Revolutionists from their stations on the wall. On one occasion it was absolutely amazing and sublime. . . . Jesse had framed a series of stanzas on the spot, while Phillips was speaking, embodying the leading

---

[4] *Ibid.*, vol. I, p. 71.   [5] *Ibid.*, vol. I, p. 73.

arguments, and enforcing them, as mere oratory cannot, as music and poetry only can, and they poured them forth with amazing spirit, in one of the maddening Second Advent tunes. [NB: Jesse undoubtedly added stanzas to "The Old Granite State."] The vast multitude sprang to their feet, as one man, and at the close of the first strain gave vent to their enthusiasm in a thunder of unrestrained cheering. Three cheers, and three times three, and ever so many more – for they could not count – they sent out, full-hearted and full-toned, till the old roof rang again. . . . Oh, it was glorious! . . . I wish the whole city, and the entire country could have been there – even all the people. Slavery would have died of that music . . .[6]

Word of the Boston meeting spread rapidly, and in May 1843 they were invited to sing for an antislavery meeting in New York, sharing the stage with the Reverend Lyman Beecher. Immediately upon their return to New England, they sang at an antislavery rally in Concord, New Hampshire, then in similar rallies elsewhere in the area. The following summer they went to Boston again for an even larger Anti-Slavery Society meeting, at one point singing for some 20,000 persons gathered on the Boston Common for a temperance meeting.

But commitment to social and political causes in their singing was by no means total at this point. This was the period of their most successful tours of the East, and their antislavery songs were reserved for appropriate rallies; Jesse's "The Bereaved Slave Mother," for example, never appeared on their public concerts. They were quite willing, in Washington and elsewhere, to omit certain "objectionable verses and parts of songs" so as not to antagonize paying audiences.

They soon became more militant. "Get Off the Track," an adaptation of "Old Dan Tucker" with words by Jesse, was so inflammatory that no publisher would bring it out. It was finally published,[7] with a lithographed cover depicting a railway coach labelled "Immediate Emancipation" flying banners of the two leading antislavery journals – *Herald of Freedom* and *American Standard* – being pulled across the country, illustrative of the song's text:

> Ho! the car emancipation,
> Rides majestic through our nation,
> Bearing on its train the story,
> LIBERTY! a nation's glory.
> Roll it along! roll it along!

[6] *Ibid.*, vol. II, pp. 76–7.   [7] By Henry Prentiss, in Boston.

Roll it along! through the nation,
Freedom's car, Emancipation.

The effect of this song on antislavery audiences was electric. N. P. Rogers described a performance at an abolitionist rally in Boston, in the June 1844 issue of *Herald of Freedom*:

> Their outburst at the convention, in Jesse's celebrated "Get off the track," is absolutely indescribable in any words that can be penned. . . . And when they came to the chorus-cry that gives name to the song – when they cried to the heedless pro-slavery multitude that were stupidly lingering on the track, and the engine "Liberator" coming hard upon them, under full steam and all speed, the Liberty Bell loud ringing, and they standing like deaf men right in its whirlwind path – and the way they cried "Get off the track," in defiance of all time and rule, was magnificent and sublime. They forgot their harmony, and shouted one after another, or all in confused outcry, like an alarmed multitude of spectators, about to witness a terrible railroad catastrophe. . . . It was the cry of the people, into which their over-wrought and illimitable music had *degenerated* and it was glorious to witness them alighting down again from their wild flight into the current of song, like so many swans upon the river from which they had soared, a moment, wildly into the air. The multitude who have heard them will bear me witness that they transcended the very province of mere music – which is, after all, like eloquence or like poetry, but one of the subordinate departments of humanity.[8]

Warned by friends that they should avoid controversial songs on their next trip to New York, they responded that "As long as nothing was said, we could take our choice; but if we were told we must not sing a song that expressed our convictions, we then felt that, come victory or defeat, we must cry aloud and spare not";[9] accordingly, they programed "Get Off the Track" at Palmo's Opera House on 26 March 1845. They were hissed, and objects were thrown at them. Rather than having an adverse effect on their popularity, the controversy attracted even more people to their programs, and 500 were turned away from their last New York concert, at Niblo's Garden.

After their return from England, they were even less willing to continue singing one repertory for commercial concerts and another for antislavery rallies. They offered their New York audiences a new verse of "The Old Granite State" on their concerts in 1846,

[8] Hutchinson, *Story*, vol. I, pp. 117–18.   [9] *Ibid.*, vol. I, p. 138.

mentioning not only their position on slavery, but also their opposition to the war with Mexico:

> War and slavery perplex us
> And ere long will sorely vex us,
> Oh, we're paying dear for Texas,
> In the war with Mexico.

The crowd in the Broadway Tabernacle had come for pleasure, not politics, and showed their displeasure by hissing and walking out. The mood of America had changed while they were in England: there was more tension, more polarization on the issue of slavery. In Philadelphia, three concerts were given, to mixed reaction and mixed reviews. The *Courier* wrote:

> It is really time that someone should tell these people, in a spirit of friendly candor, that they are not apostles and martyrs, entrusted with a "mission" to reform the world, but only a company of common song-singers, whose performances sound very pleasantly to the great mass of the people ignorant of real music.

A fourth concert, scheduled for the Musical Fund Hall – where they had sung with such success and acclaim only three years before – was cancelled when the major insisted that "persons of color" be refused admission in order to prevent possible disorder. "Of course the Hutchinsons indignantly refused to exclude colored persons from their concerts," wrote the *Liberator*, "and consequently shook off the dust from their feet of this mobocratic city." Their way led through Manchester, Concord, Nashua, and Boston – cities where they had often sung, where they were virtually idolized – but they were hissed even here whenever they introduced "politics."

The following years saw an antislavery meeting in the Broadway Tabernacle, at which they were singing, broken up by a mob; cancellation of a scheduled concert in St. Louis, on their first trip to the West; and trouble even at the scene of their most glorious triumphs, Faneuil Hall in Boston, where a mob disrupted an antislavery meeting featuring the English abolitionist George Thompson.

There were troubles within the quartet as well. Abby married in 1849 and settled in New York with her husband, virtually giving up her singing. Judson, always moody, took to spiritualism and table rapping, and sometimes "freaked out" during concerts:

> . . . at Newburyport . . . he was impressed that it was his duty to do something for the poor of the town, [so he] proceeded to draw

from his pockets handfuls of silver half-dollars, previously secured, which he threw into the broad aisle. . . . Sometimes he would speak as if inspired . . . on the sinfulness of eating flesh, or wearing any garment that necessitated the killing of animals for its construction. Because of these theories he had discarded boots and shoes, clothing his feet in socks. His food was fruits, cereal and honey.[10]

Jesse, who had travelled with the quartet as manager and had written many of their best songs, suddenly deserted them for a rival quartet, the Alleghenians, who proceeded to sing pieces from the Hutchinsons' repertory. The Alleghenians travelled as far west as California, where Jesse became ill, dying in Cincinnatti in 1853.

Despite these tragedies and traumas, the Hutchinsons persevered in their singing, in their championing of radical causes, and in the writing and performing of songs for these causes. Asa, Judson, and John made up the group now, with John's oldest son sometimes joining them. They joined a third great crusade – universal suffrage. They were present for a Women's Rights Convention in Akron, Ohio, in 1851; back East, they sometimes shared the platforms with Lucy Stone, who dressed in bloomers and lectured on women's rights. A high point came in 1874, when John sang at the National Convention of Woman Suffrage Association, presided over by Susan B. Anthony.

Their songs were melodramatic but sympathetic to the plight of women in American society. There was Henry Russell's "The Gambler's Wife," and their own setting of Thomas Hood's "The Song of the Shirt":

> With fingers weary and worn,
>> With eye-lids heavy and red,
> A woman sat in unwomanly rags
>> Plying her needle and thread.
> Stitch, stitch, stitch,
>> In poverty, hunger and dirt,
> And still with a voice of dolorous pitch,
>> She sang the song of the shirt.
>
> Work, work, work,
>> 'Till the brain begins to swim;
> Work, work, work,
>> 'Till the eyes are heavy and dim . . .
> Oh, men with sisters dear,
>> Oh, men with mothers and wives,

[10] *Ibid.*, vol. I, pp. 281–2.

It is not linen you're wearing out,
But human creature's lives.

"Hannah's at the Window Binding Shoes" is an affecting *scena* of a woman sitting year after year at a window in a New England shoe factory, watching through a window for her husband, who will never return: "Old with watching, Hannah's at the window binding shoes. Twenty winters wear and tear the rugged shore she views; . . . Still her dim eyes silently chase the white sails o'er the sea; Hapless, faithful Hannah's at the window binding shoes."

This song, attributed to Asa B. Hutchinson, wasn't published until 1859. By this time the original Hutchinson Family quartet had disbanded and sang together again only on rare occasions. The last great tour of the three brothers (Asa, Judson, John) had taken place in 1855, characteristically in pursuit of still another cause. They set off for Kansas, after hearing a fiery speaker call for Free-Soil emigrants to Kansas to help insure that it not become a slave state. They were persuaded to give some concerts in the upper Mississippi Valley, after getting as far west as Illinois, and they fell in love with Minnesota, where they staked out a claim for land for a new town, Hutchinson. They returned to Massachusetts, rather than going further west, and for some years shuttled back and forth between New England and their new town, persuading families to settle there, trying to keep peace with the Indians.

By now each of the three brothers had his own growing family; eventually the family split into three groups. "The Tribe of Asa," made up of Asa, his wife, and their children Abby, Freddy, and "little Denett," settled in Minnesota. They were so radical as to antagonize most audiences, even those in the North; at one point they joined forces with a trio of blacks, the Luca Brothers. Judson sang programs with his daughter Kate and enjoyed some success. He had shown signs of emotional instability for many years and finally hanged himself on 11 January 1859. Soon after this, Kate joined forces with Joshua (who had not been a member of the famous quartet) and Walter Kittredge, a New Hampshire singer and composer. John, who had often sung solo programs even while the original quartet was together, now formed his own family group, with his wife Fanny and two of their children, Henry and Viola.

There were important events and interesting music in the years after the original quartet ceased to exist. Both John and Asa campaigned enthusiastically for Lincoln in 1860; John, with Horace Greeley (then editor of the *Tribune* in New York), brought out *Hutchinson's Republican*

Songster for 1860, and Asa brought out a Lincoln songster of his own. Both John and Abby went to the South after the war, heard the singing of ex-slaves in Florida and elsewhere, visited Fisk University and heard its famous choir, and were among the first singers to perform arrangements of such spirituals as "My Jesus Says There's Room Enough" on the concert stage.

Despite all this, the peak of the Hutchinson Family's popularity and influence came in the period from 1841 to 1849, when the original quartet was together and their music and the way they presented it struck audiences and critics as new and fresh and very American.

It may well be that the Hutchinsons altered the course of American history, that their music hastened the confrontations and conflicts that led inexorably to the Civil War, that their songs fanned passions and created the sense of togetherness and resolve necessary to convert ideas and ideals into action, that their singing of "John Brown's Body" converted more people to the antislavery cause than all the speeches and sermons of the time.

There is no mistaking their sincerity, their deep and genuine concern for human misery. Their memoirs and writings are filled with vignettes of human suffering which they observed and tried to alleviate:

> . . . we observed a little old house the lower storey of which had been destroyed, all except the cornerposts, by the winds and waves. I noticed smoke coming out of the chimney, although it seemed impossible such a structure could be inhabited. We went on, but not being satisfied, returned, and noticing a ladder, crawled up, and knocked on a door lying horizontally on the floor. A delicate woman, with a half-starved baby in her arms answered our summons. The woman was thinly-clad and almost frozen, for the tempest had washed nearly all her clothing away, and she was without means to get more. The next day, with Abby, we took them some clothing, and gave them money to move to a more secure dwelling.[11]

And there is no mistaking the fact that they made a deliberate choice, at a critical point in their career, to state their political and social views in public concerts, whatever the damage to their professional career.

They sang at prisons, at poorhouses, at the smallest church that asked for them. They attended temperance and abolitionist rallies,

---

[11] *Ibid.*, vol. I, pp. 132–3.

when organizers had not known of their presence, and would stand in the audience at a critical point in the rally and give out with one of their "maddening" songs. They sang for the poor, the slaves, the freedmen, the Irish, women, Republicans, sailors. They were a voice crying out for freedom, peace, equality, temperance, devotion. They said it themselves, more eloquently than anyone else, in the song "If I Were a Voice," written by Judson, sung by Abby, quoted by John at the beginning of the chapter of his memoirs entitled "American Songs and their Interpretations":

> If I were a voice, a persuasive voice,
>   That could travel the wide world through,
> I would fly on the beams of the morning light,
> And speak to men with a gentle might,
>   And tell them to be true.
> I would fly – I would fly o'er land and sea,
> Wherever a human heart might be,
> Telling a tale, or singing a song,
> In praise of the right, in blame of the wrong,
>   If I were a voice.

The Hutchinsons stressed their national origins from the beginning. A bit of doggerel verse (by Judson) was inserted on their early printed programs:

> When foreigners approach your shore,
> You welcome them with open doors,
> Now we have come, to seek our lot,
> Shall native talent be forgot?

Critics agreed that there was something very American about them, about the music they performed and the way they sang it, often equating "American" with simplicity. An early critic wrote:

> We like their music, because it is so simple and unadorned. It may not please those whose nice and critical taste love to hear music executed so that there is no music in it, but the people, the millions, appreciate their notes. . . .[12]

And a critic in New York saw them as

> . . . genuine children of the rugged New Hampshire soil on which they were born. Endowed as they were by kindly Nature with sensitive musical organizations and strong, simple characters, they brought into the atmosphere of the concert room a freshness and native sweetness of melody and motive which won a way for them, at once, to the popular heart.[13]

[12] Quoted in Philip D. Jordan, *Singin' Yankees* (Minneapolis, 1946), p. 158.
[13] Hutchinson, *Story*, vol. II, p. 303.

A more specific comment was offered by a British writer for the *Birmingham Journal* of January 1846:

> After the *staccatos* and runs of Italianized vocalism, which are all very well in their own way, it is pleasant to hear music divested of its extraneous ornament and made subservient to the holy use of promoting good-will between man and man, and clothing the deep sympathy of the poet in the appropriate and winning garb of simple and unadorned harmony. How often have we longed for the quiet strain in which the untaught minstrel sung the airs which needed no ornament. . . . We never heard these themes attempted in the concert-room without dreading the coming embellishment, which drowns all appreciation of the sentiment of the song or the music, in surprise of the artist's mechanical skill.

They were not merely Americans – they were New Englanders. They avoided European songs (they rarely performed even such favorites as "Home! Sweet Home" or any of Moore's *Irish Melodies*) and songs associated with other parts of America, such as minstrel songs or the songs of Stephen Foster. Critics often chided them for their avoidance of familiar songs that would have made for more easy listening; the *Herald of Freedom* for 9 December 1842, for instance, said in the course of a generally favorable review:

> These Canary birds have been here again, charming the ear of our Northern winter with their woodnote melody. . . . The airs were modern, most or all of them; and though very sweet, were less interesting to me than if they had been songs I knew. If they had had some of the old songs intermingled, I think it would better please everybody – some of the Burns' "Bonny Doon" or "Highland Mary," for instance. Their woodland tone, their clear enunciation and their fine appreciation of the poetry, together with their perfect freedom from all affectation and stage grimace, would enable them to do justice to the great Scottish songster; and it would do the people good to hear them sing him.

But the Hutchinsons were American, not Scottish, and they had their own ideas about what would be good for their audiences.

From the beginning of their career, their programs were made up largely of pieces by composers from New England: Lyman Heath, Bernard Covert, Henry Russell (whom they considered a New Englander at least in spirit), and themselves. Increasingly, their own arrangements and compositions made up the larger part of their programs. John described their creative process:

Ex. 4.2 Hutchinson Family, "Mrs Lofty and I"

Whenever we found in the papers or had given to us anything effective or beautiful in the way of poetry, we would pin it up on a bedpost or side of the house, and start in on a tune, each one making up his own part. Judson usually took the air, and so in a sense became the composer of the tune. We have often made our songs and sung them in public without ever having seen a note. In

With fin - gers wea-ry and worn,   With eye - lids hea-vy and red,

Ex. 4.3 Hutchinson Family, "The Song of the Shirt"

this way we composed "The Good Old Days of Yore," "The Bridge of Sighs," and other well-known songs, which were really composed by "The Hutchinsons," it being impossible to say that either [sic] of the quartet was the actual composer.[14]

The origins of their style lie in the hymns and anthems of the New England churches – the religious music designed by Lowell Mason, George Webb, Thomas Hastings, and their contemporaries to elevate the morals and musical taste of literate Americans, contained in such collections as Mason's *Boston Handel & Haydn Society Collection of Sacred Music* and *Carmina Sacra*, Hastings's *Musica Sacra*, and William R. Bradbury's *The Jubilee*. The most widely sung pieces in such collections, the music the Hutchinsons – and millions of other American families – sang at home and in church, were simple, symmetrical, diatonic tunes harmonized with the most basic chords. This was the music that established the musical vocabulary and largely defined the musical taste and tolerance of most white, Protestant Americans in the North, East, and Midwest.

Their songs make use of diatonic, repetitious, regularly phrased melodies, supported by rather rudimentary chords. "Mrs. Lofty and I," a song that enjoyed much success as an item of sheet music and was often anthologized, is a fair sample of their style (see Ex. 2).

Several of their later songs, however, exhibit more musical sophistication. "The Song of the Shirt" is a rare instance from this period of a song in a minor key, and the insistent, incessant, arpeggiated accompaniment underlining the melancholy narrative creates an effect not unlike that of Schubert's "Gretchen am

[14] *Ibid.*, vol. II, p. 301.

Oh God! that bread should be_so dear_ And hu - man flesh so cheap.

Ex. 4.4 Hutchinson Family, "The Song of the Shirt"

Spinnrad," a song the Hutchinsons most certainly did not know (see Ex. 3).

Later in the song, the rhythmic pattern of the accompaniment is broken by a series of dramatic, chromatic chords, underlining the climax of the poem (see Ex. 4) and the song modulates to a distant key (B-flat minor), where it ends. The inspiration for this more adventuresome musical language is not difficult to trace: the accompaniment and harmonic style are reminiscent of the more dramatic songs of Henry Russell.

One of the loveliest of their songs, "If I Were a Voice," combines their usual melodic clarity and simplicity with somewhat more colorful chords (see Ex. 5).

No matter how appealing their story may be, the fact remains that they outlived their songs. Not one achieved enough lasting popularity to be included in the various retrospective song anthologies of the late nineteenth and early twentieth centuries.

Their songs, stripped of the emotional climate surrounding their composition and performance, have proved to be of less musical interest than those of certain of their contemporaries less involved in the great issues of this stirring time. The Hutchinsons' great contribution to American popular music was summed up by William Lloyd Garrison in a letter to Joshua, dated 3 April 1874: "Never before has the singing of ballads been made directly and purposely subservient to the freedom, welfare, happiness, and moral elevation of the people."

Ex. 4.5 Hutchinson Family, "If I Were a Voice"

5

SOME THOUGHTS ON THE
MEASUREMENT OF POPULARITY IN
MUSIC

In the 1970s most writers on popular music, scattered through a number of different disciplines or outside academia altogether, worked in isolation from one another, in touch only through their published work. The only journal devoted to popular music was the *Journal of Research in Popular Music*, narrowly focused on sociology.

This isolation began to break down in the last years of the decade. Several panels during a conference of The International Musicological Society held in Berkeley (California) in August of 1977 brought together a handful of musicologists studying popular music. Growing British interest in the music of North America, particularly at the universities of York and Keele, prompted several conferences on popular music that led to the first International Conference on Popular Music Research in June of 1981, for which several hundred people from many (mostly European) countries gathered in Amsterdam.

My paper for this conference could have been subtitled "One week in May." The organizers had suggested that media dissemination might be taken as one defining characteristic of popular music; so it occurred to me to watch every television show aired in the United States for the week of 17–23 May 1981 that featured considerable amounts of music, and then to assemble statistics on the size of the audience for each.

The experience was critical for my subsequent work, if not for the future of popular music study in general. After determining that more than 46,000,000 Americans heard "America the Beautiful" and Stephen Foster's "Old Folks at Home" on 21 May through the medium of television, and more than 30,000,000 heard Hoagy Carmichael's "Star Dust" and a medley from *Oklahoma* on 18 May, I was less inclined than ever to think of "popular music" as being contemporary rock, to the exclusion of other styles, genres, and repertories. If popular music is taken to mean either mass-disseminated music or that music heard by the largest number of people at a given time and place, it seemed to me imperative to pay more attention to the media themselves – who controls them; what institutions and policies lie behind the selection of music for media dissemination; what audiences are exposed to this music, and how they respond to it; what part of their listening experience depends on the media.

As a result of this conference, the establishment of the International Association for the Study of Popular Music (IASPM) at its final session, and the almost simultaneous publication of the first issue of *Popular Music* by Cambridge University Press, the study of popular music established an institutional base for the first time.

Two footnotes to my paper. Perhaps in response to my opening paragraphs, the theme of a second international conference, held in Reggio Emilia in August of 1983, was "What Is Popular Music?"[1] And only several months after the Amsterdam conference and my paper, Music Television (MTV), devoted exclusively to rock music, went on the air, soon producing a flood of critical writing on the rock video. But little attention has been paid to the television production of other styles and genres of music, which still take up the vast majority of air time.

* * *

We begin this conference under a severe handicap: we're not sure what we're talking about.

This statement is not intended as a prior judgement of the individual papers to follow, which I am confident will be uniformly interesting, valuable, and informative, but as a commentary on the fact that there is no general agreement on just what is encompassed by the term "popular music."

Some take it to include a wide spectrum of music, including rock 'n' roll, Tin Pan Alley song, disco, Highlife, urban blues, country-western music, punk rock, minstrel songs of the nineteenth century, country blues, New Wave, oral-tradition Irish song, Western Swing, jazz-rock fusion, sentimental parlor songs of the previous century – and much more.

Others use it in a more restricted way.

This confusion is perhaps best epitomized by the attitude of the present conference towards jazz. Is jazz "popular music"? Is some of it "popular music" and some not? Will some of the participants

[1] Conference papers were published as *Popular Music Perspectives* 2 (Gothenburg, Exeter, Ottawa, and Reggio Emilia, 1985).

assume that jazz is "popular music" and others assume that it is not?

This is not just a question of semantics. There are practical considerations, important ones. A new yearbook to be published by Cambridge University Press, entitled *Popular Music*, will probably not have the distribution it deserves in the United States because its title does not suggest to many people just what its range of subject matter will be. I suspect that many people did not think to attend the present conference for the same reason, and I predict that some of you in attendance will be disappointed by the range of subject matter of the papers and discussions. A more specific example of the mischief resulting from disagreement on the meaning of "popular music": my recent book, *Yesterdays: Popular Song in America* (New York and London, 1979) was just reviewed in the journal of the Society for Ethnomusicology – surprising in itself, perhaps – by Charles Keil, author of an excellent book on the urban blues; unfortunately, his areas of interest and expertise intersected with the subject matter of my book in the most minimal way, and the resulting review proved to be an embarrassment to all concerned.

I will not presume to offer a definition of popular music myself, but will rather offer some comments that may help define the problem.

In America, prior to the twentieth century, there were two quite distinct bodies of music with some claim on the title of "popular":

(1) composed songs, notated and disseminated in the form of sheet music, aimed at a wide audience of amateur musicmakers (the songs of Stephen Foster, for instance);

(2) oral-tradition music stemming from various non-literate sub-cultures in the United States: Child ballads; other Anglo-American, Celtic-American and American ballads and songs; most Afro-American music; dance music of both white and black Americans; the music of other ethnic and racial minorities.

Though there was some overlap between the two, there were important differences in both musical style and function in society between the first, usually referred to as "popular song," and the second, which most scholars have thought of as "folk music."

In the first decades of the twentieth century, dissemination of the first category by means of the phonograph disc became increasingly important; in the 1920s and 30s, dissemination of this music on the radio and in sound films also became common. MacLuhan would say, I believe, that these new media became extensions of the human voice, extensions of the practice of performing this music on the stage or in the parlor. They were still composed, notated songs, still disseminated most importantly in the form of printed sheet music.

Dissemination of the second type of "popular" music via the phonograph disc and radio did not begin until the 1920s. These two media represented a logical and appropriate extension of the performance means of this music (voices and instruments), which operated within the oral tradition; for the first time, such music was able to reach a mass audience, to reach out beyond private performance for a circle of family, friends, and neighbors and public performance in medicine shows and sometimes on the minstrel stage. This first mass dissemination of oral-tradition music via the phonograph disc brought vast proliferation and rapid stylistic development to jazz, the blues, and hillbilly (later country-western) music.

In 1955, with the advent of rock 'n' roll, what had been known as "popular music" to the music industry became – for the first time – an oral music, disseminated almost exclusively in live performance and its extensions: radio, the phonograph disc, and to a more limited extent television and film. Printed sheet music, created after the fact (written down after the music had been conceived and popularized orally) played virtually no role.

At just the same time, music of the second category ("folk music") began moving slowly but inexorably in the direction of composed, notated, arranged music, a trend that would soon yield Country Pop and Black Pop.

Distinctions between the two categories eventually became matters of musical style and the socio-economic status of their performers and audiences and not – as had been the case formerly – methods of dissemination. All varieties of music in the two categories became products and users of the several mass media, and I applaud the emphasis on the term "mass media" by the organizers of the present conference as an attempt to head us all in the same general direction.

However, it must also be said that classical music is also disseminated via the mass media in the twentieth century (phonograph disc, radio, television, and film), and I sense no attempt to include the music of Beethoven, Vivaldi, Obrecht, or Stravinsky on our agenda. This is not a facetious point. Returning to my opening remarks, I fear we are not in agreement as to whether the "popular music" which is the subject of our conference is a matter of musical style – or a means of dissemination.

Certain bodies of music comprise such a limited number of compositions that a scholar may be familiar with the entire corpus: the thirteenth-century motet, for instance, or operas by Russian composers written before 1870, or string quartets by American composers of the nineteenth century. Other genres comprise so many individual pieces as to make it impossible for any single person to examine all of them: the symphony of the eighteenth century; the Romantic lied.

Whatever definition one accepts for "popular music," it clearly belongs to the second situation. In studying it, one must devise some method of restriction to limit the sample to a reasonable number of pieces.

An approach which seems logical to me is to let the term define the method: to deal with the pieces which are demonstrably the *most* popular items of "popular music," with the most widely disseminated items of music disseminated in the mass media.

Rather than developing this notion abstractly and philosophically, I'd like to offer some comments on practical means and problems that one must deal with in proceeding along this line with the mass media in America.

First, the phonograph disc, considered by most rock journalists and cultural historians to be the most important medium for the dissemination of "popular music."

Billboard,[1] published weekly, carries a number of popularity charts in each issue, the most important being:

- *Hot 100* (100 top 45 rpm singles)
- *Top LPs and Tapes* (200 top 33 ⅓ rpm albums)
- *Hot Soul Singles* (100 45 rpm singles on the black market)
- *Soul LPs* (100 top 33 ⅓ rpm albums on the black market)
- *Hot Country Singles* (100 top 45 rpm singles of country music)
- *Hot Country LPs* (100 top 33 ⅓ rpm albums of country music)

Other charts offer rankings of jazz, disco, Latin, "spiritual," "easy listening," and international discs; some of these appear weekly, others more sporadically.

These charts have a profound impact on the mass media. A syndicated weekly radio program, "American Top Forty," plays the first forty songs on *Billboard*'s "Hot 100" chart in reverse order; commercial stations all over America, hundreds of them, pick up this program. In addition, other hundreds of radio stations (mostly AM) concentrate their airplay on the "Top 40" repertory all week, again taking the *Billboard* chart as a guide to their selection of pieces. A syndicated television program, "Solid Gold," offers the "Top 10" songs from the *Billboard* chart every week. More generally, both the

---

[1] *Billboard. The International Music-Record-Tape Newsweekly* (Los Angeles).

music industry and most people who write about popular music (journalists, critics, historians) give complete credence to these charts; placing a song at or near the top of *Billboard*'s "Hot 100" list (or one of the other major charts) gives a tremendous boost to a performer, and generates additional sales of the disc in question; and many writers on popular music base their arguments and conclusions on *Billboard* rankings.

An enterprising organization in Wisconsin, Record Research Inc., has compiled and published a series of books and pamphlets in which the information from the various *Billboard* charts, over the years, has been organized and summarized.[2] Armed with these volumes, the scholar or the merely curious can quickly locate details concerning every piece that has appeared on any of the *Billboard* charts since their inception.

One can determine from a recent issue of *Billboard*, the one brought out on 23 May 1981, that "Bette Davis Eyes," as sung by Kim Carnes, was the top item on the "Hot 100" charts; "A Woman Needs Love," performed by Ray Parker Jr. & Raydio, was the no.1 item on the "Soul" charts; the album *High Infidelity* by the rock group REO Speedwagon was at the top of the album chart; and so on. And by resorting to Whitburn's several compilations, it is equally simple to find out that Little Richard's "Good Golly, Miss Molly" made its first appearance on the "Hot 100" charts on 8 February 1958, that it stayed on the charts for fifteen weeks, and its highest position was no.10; the same song first appeared on the "Rhythm & Blues" chart on 15 February of that year, persisted for only 8 weeks, and reached a top of no.6.

The easy availability of such data has vastly simplified the task of the critic or historian of popular music. But it is disconcerting to note that these charts, which have become such a powerful force in the world of music, offer no supporting statistics for their rankings. The "Hot 100" chart carries only the simple explanation (or disclaimer?) that it is "a reflection of National Sales and programing activity by selected dealers, one-stops, and radio stations as compiled by the Charts Dept. of *Billboard*," and the other charts are headed by the statement that they have been "compiled from national retail stores by the Music Popularity Chart Dept. and the Record Market Research Dept. of *Billboard*." The only hard information offered is the identification of those discs which have "gone gold" (i.e., sold a

[2] Joel Whitburn, *Top Pop Artists & Singles, 1955–1978* (Menomonee Falls, 1979). Whitburn has also compiled and published similar compilations of other popular repertories: country-western music; rhythm and blues, and soul; LP albums; "easy listening" music; etc.

million copies, for singles, or 500,000 for LPs) or "gone platinum" (sales of two million, for singles, or one million for LPs). It is impossible to avoid the impression that *Billboard's* ranking techniques are not refined enough to differentiate between sales and radio play time of, say, the song ranked no.5 for a given week and that in the tenth position – or, for that matter, that the various *Billboard* charts function to generate sales and air play as much as to measure it.

Radio is quite a different matter.

Virtually every American community of more than a few thousand inhabitants has at least one commercial radio station. Many of these are totally independent, others are affiliated with one or another of the ten national radio networks. Even the latter pick up only a small fraction of their programing from nationally syndicated sources. A typical American radio station broadcasts mostly recorded music, selected by staff members, interspersed with brief news spots and weather reports, with syndicated programs from time to time. Thus the programing for each of the thousands of stations in the United States is unique, and there is no way for anyone to determine with any accuracy how many times a given piece of music is broadcast on any given day, week, or any other period of time to the approximately 477,800,000 radio receiving sets in the country.[3]

However, approximations of what kinds of music are sent out over American airwaves are possible, and the size of the audience for each kind. Almost all American radio stations base their programing on a certain type of music – Top Forty pop songs, harder rock, music aimed at black listeners, country-western music, whatever. Listeners tend to identify with one or more stations favoring the type(s) of music they prefer, and to stay with these stations, once identified, rather than constantly redialing in search of specific songs or types of music.

Measurement of radio audiences is done by several commercial concerns, most importantly the Arbitron Company. Their technique is to distribute diaries to randomly selected households, with the request that such information as what radio stations are listened to, at what hours of the day, by which members of the family, for how long, be entered in these diaries. Arbitron concerns itself only with persons in this group; 95.2 per cent of them listen to the radio at least once a week. For purposes of testing and rating, Arbitron has divided the country into some 250 market survey areas, each

---

[3] This figure is taken from the 35th edition of *World Radio TV Handbook*, ed. J. M. Frost (London, 1981).

centered around the largest city or town in that region, the idea being that every listener in a given area has access to the same cluster of broadcasting stations. Arbitron releases statistics of audience size and composition, for each market survey area, from one to four times a year; these figures are supplied to all radio stations which subscribe to Arbitron's services, and to commercial firms which advertise over the air or may have an interest in doing so, to inform them of how many people they might expect to reach if they advertise on a given station. Since Arbitron is a service concern, and its service consists of statistics issued to its customers and subscribers, it does not make its findings public. Radio stations may release partial or full figures concerning the distribution of the listening audience once they have received these from Arbitron, if they choose; otherwise, information is available only from Arbitron, which has expressed willingness to cooperate with scholarly studies dealing with the mass media.[4]

While it is impossible to determine statistics on the nation-wide air play of individual pieces of music, it would be possible to study the dissemination of various types of music within any or all of the market survey areas established by Arbitron. This would involve establishing the musical profile of each radio station within an area (what type of music it played), obtaining audience statistics from Arbitron, converting these into numbers of listeners, and thus drawing a profile of what music goes over the air in that area, in what proportions.

For instance, the market survey area centered in Boston encompassed a population (over twelve years of age) of 2,922,100 in early 1981. There were thirty radio stations on the air in the first quarter of that year – seventeen AM, thirteen FM. The following table lists the ten stations with the largest audience, according to Arbitron's statistics for March of 1981; the percentage of the listening public which preferred each station is given, with this figure translated into numbers of listeners; each of these most successful stations is further identified as to the type of music programing it stresses.

WCOZ-FM	11.1 per cent (330,000)	hard rock–heavy metal album play
WHDH-AM	10.3 per cent (300,000)	"adult contemporary"
WBZ-AM	8.4 per cent (250,000)	Top Forty (based on *Billboard*)
WEEI-AM	6.5 per cent (200,000)	all-talk: news, weather, sports
WJIB-FM	5.3 per cent (150,000)	"easy listening"
WXKS-FM	5.0 per cent (150,000)	disco and "dance-rock"

[4] The information concerning Arbitron was kindly and generously supplied to me by Mr. Jay Billie of the Washington office of Arbitron Radio, located in Laurel, Maryland.

WBCN-FM	4.8 per cent	(140,000)	New Wave, rock
WROR-FM	4.5 per cent	(130,000)	new and old "rock standards"
WEEI-FM	3.7 per cent	(120,000)	soft rock and jazz
WVBF-FM	3.5 per cent	(105,000)	"mainstream rock"

The profile reveals a heavy emphasis on the several varieties of rock music, from old "standards" through Top Forty music all the way to New Wave and Heavy Metal bands; "easy listening" styles are a distant second; none of the ten top stations offers programing aimed at black or Hispanic listeners, nor do any of them program country-western music. This picture matches the socio-economic character of Boston, of course. The city's multitude of institutions of higher education (Harvard University, Massachusetts Institute of Technology, Boston University, Boston College, Northeastern University, Tufts University, the New England Conservatory of Music, the Berklee College of Music, and many other smaller schools) give it the highest ratio of college-age persons of any American city and account for the high proportion of youth-orientated music offered on the radio; the Boston market survey area encompasses only urban and suburban areas, with no history whatever of large-scale immigration from the South, Midwest, or Southwest, and hence virtually no market for country-western music; and though there are sizeable black and Hispanic populations, Boston remains one of the most racist spots in the United States, these minority groups play almost no role in the cultural and political life of the city, and are largely disregarded in radio programing.

The problems faced in studying the dissemination of music by radio in the United States are immense. One would have to proceed by examining each of the more than 250 market survey areas in ways suggested by the above remarks: determining the musical profile of each radio station, obtaining statistics on each area from Arbitron, understanding the ethnic and cultural mix found within each area. But such studies must be undertaken if one is to obtain a comprehensive grasp of the mass dissemination of music in America. Surely more people, many more, are exposed to music on the radio than by listening to private phonograph equipment. Surely *Billboard*'s charts give an inaccurate picture of the types of music actually heard in such areas as New York City (with its unique mix of black, Hispanic, Jewish, Irish, and professional and highly educated population), or Miami (with its curious blend of retired, elderly people, its Cuban refugees, its working class drawn partly from the rural South), or Dallas, or Los Angeles, or Chicago. It would be a difficult and complex job to consider all these factors. But it could be done.

American television is yet another different proposition.

All commercial television stations offer programing composed of three elements:

(1) Networks shows carried during prime time (several hours in the morning; early afternoon; the evening, from 7 or 8 p.m. until 11; some weekend slots), picked up from whichever of the three national commercial networks – ABC, CBS, NBC – the local station is affiliated with. Thus in television, unlike radio, audiences in all parts of the country are exposed to exactly the same material at the same time.

(2) Syndicated programs (including news shows, movies, and reruns of older television programs) picked up by local stations at their discretion, and shown in time slots chosen by each station. Much of this material is seen in various parts of the United States during a given week, but not necessarily at the same time.

(3) Local programing, consisting mostly of regional newscasts and a scattering of locally produced shows concerned with civic and community matters. These are seen only in the areas in which they are produced.

Of the several firms which make statistical measurement of the size and constitution of the audience for television programs, the oldest and most prestigious is the A.C. Nielsen Company, in operation since 1952 and so important to American television programing that the term "Nielsen rating" has crept into popular usage. Their methodology relies on:

(1) *The Sample*: statistical determination of how many American households must be tested in order to yield reliable figures for their ratings.

(2) *The Storage Instantaneous Audimeter* (SIA): an electronic meter installed in the necessary number of homes, connected to the household television set(s), which automatically registers which television programs are tuned in, for how long. All SIAs are connected by telephone line to a central computer, which may be used to retrieve information at any time.

(3) *The TV Diary*: each household fitted with an SIA is also given a diary, with the request that individuals watching any program be identified by age and sex.

The SIA and the TV diaries, taken together, yield information not only on the total television audience, but also on details of the makeup of that audience. And from calculations based on the geographical areas in which selected households are located and the socio-economic-ethnic status of participating families, the Nielsen Company can determine with some precision which age groups and which economic-cultural and ethnic groups are most responsive to various programs.

The results of all this are published every two weeks, as the *Nielsen National TV Ratings*, a detailed breakdown of the size and constitution of the audience for every network program telecast. This publication is not available to the general public; it is sent only to paid subscribers – the television networks and stations, and commercial concerns which advertise on network shows or may be considering doing so. General information is released to the press: periodic reports on the relative rankings of the three networks, information on audience size of certain programs. This publication has become the "Bible" of the commercial television industry; shows are dropped or shifted to new time slots if their Nielsen ratings are low, new shows for each television season (starting in the early fall) are planned largely on the basis of which types of programs attracted the largest audiences the previous season; directors and actors are often let go – or given more important new assignments – on the basis of the success or failure of the shows with which they have been involved.

The Nielsen Company offers other services as well, including ratings of syndicated programs, more refined breakdowns of audiences for various shows and (for a price) quicker reports on audience sizes, for television networks and advertisers who want more immediate reports on the number of people viewing specific programs.

There are an estimated 142,000,000 television sets in the United States.[5] More importantly, the Nielsen Company places "television penetration" into the country's some 75,000,000 households at 98 per cent, with little fluctuation by geographical area or economic status. Even in such regions as the rural South and the worst urban slum areas, the percentage of Americans reached by television almost never drops below 95. Putting it another way, almost 200,000,000 Americans reside in households with at least one television set. Thus far more people are reached by television than by any other mass medium; and given the saturation of every element of the population by television, surely network television programs are presently the most important common denominator of American life and culture. It is absolutely urgent that anyone wishing to understand the impact of mass disseminated music on our life pay attention to commercial television's attitudes towards music.

In order to get some idea of this factor, I watched every network television program for the week of 17–23 May 1981 made up mostly of music or including substantial amounts of music. I noted types of

---

[5] According to the *World Radio TV Handbook*.

music, and specific pieces, on each program. Mr. Bob Bregenzer of the Nielsen Company, with whom I talked about my project, kindly gave me the Nielsen ratings of each show by telephone, before they were available in print.

Now, as we used to say in American slang, let me lay some figures on you.

- On 21 May 1981, CBS aired the "Miss USA Pageant" for two hours. A considerable amount of music was interspersed between the various "competitions" involving the contestants: Donny Osmond, serving as master of ceremonies, sang several medleys, one of "country" songs (including such pieces of Country Pop as "Thank God I'm a Country Boy") and another of some of his greatest hits of recent years; and the Air Force Academy Chorus sang a group of patriotic and "traditional" American songs such as "America the Beautiful" and Stephen Foster's "Old Folks at Home." According to Nielsen, 22.9 per cent of the country's households were tuned in to this program, which translates to an approximate total of 46,332,000 individual viewers.

- On 18 May 1981, CBS offered a one-hour "Grammy Hall of Fame" honoring new inductees into the phonograph industry's honor roll. There was a medley from *Oklahoma*, sung by John Raitt and Celeste Holm; Andy Williams offered a medley of "evergreens," including Hoagy Carmichael's "Star Dust" and Vernon Duke's "April in Paris"; Ella Fitzgerald and Count Basie combined for a medley of hit songs from the Big Band era. In fact, every piece on the entire program was from the Tin Pan Alley era of the 1920s, 30s and 40s. 14.9 per cent of America's households watched – some 30,000,000 people.

- On 23 May 1981, NBC devoted a two-hour show in prime time to "50 Years of Country Music," filmed at the new Opry Land in Nashville. The panorama of performers included Glen Campbell (singing "Like a Rhinestone Cowboy"), Dolly Parton ("He'll Come Again"), Ray Charles ("Take the Chains from my Heart" by Hank Williams), Crystal Gayle ("I'll Get Over You"), Chet Atkins, Larry Gatlin, Roy Clarke, Loretta Lynn (singing a Patsy Cline medley), Mel Tillis, Johnny Cash, and a scattering of such older performers as Bill Munroe, Ernest Tubb and the Texas Playboys. All music was done in the "new" Nashville style of Country Pop, with lush orchestrations and lavish sets. 14.5 per cent of all households watched and listened – almost 30,000,000 people.

- On the same evening (23 May), 13.7 per cent of America's homes (27,000,000 people) watched the "Barbara Mandrell Show" on NBC; Barbara and her two sisters, helped out by guest star Dolly Parton, offered another helping of lush Country Pop.

- Only at this point in the list of most-watched shows for this week do we come to a program offering any variety of rock 'n' roll or rock:

127

NBCs "Saturday Night Live," airing at 11.30 p.m. on 23 May, attracted 9.0 per cent (some 18,000,000 viewers) of the potential TV audience to its comedy-variety show, featuring an appearance by the rock group Devo.

• The venerable "American Bandstand," hosted by Dick Clark, was carried by ABC at 12.30 p.m. on 23 May. Teenagers in the studio audience danced to the music of guests Rick Springfield ("Jessie's Girl") and the Bus Boys (a black "minimum-wage rock 'n' roll group" mixing comedy with middle-of-the-road funk); recorded music, making up most of the program, ranged from ABBA and the Spinners through the Whispers to Devo – touching most bases in today's Top Forty scene. Only 3.6 per cent of all households were tuned in to this program, a figure which nevertheless translates to more than 7,000,000 individuals. Detailed analyses of this program in the past have revealed that approximately 55 per cent of the audience is under seventeen years of age, and in fact the largest single age–sex group consists of girls from two to eleven (almost 20 per cent of the total audience)!

Other programs this week devoted largely or entirely to music were syndicated – not network – programs, and thus attracted smaller audiences; the tabulation of their share of the audience is much more complicated, and the results are not available until six weeks later, hence the Nielsen Company was not able to furnish me with figures in time for this presentation. These syndicated shows included NBC's "Solid Gold," hosted by Dionne Warwick and concerned mostly with heavily orchestrated versions of some portion of the current Top Forty repertory; CBS's "Hee Haw," a mixture of Country Pop and comedy; and the "Lawrence Welk Show," with its distinctive brand of middle-of-the-road classics drawn from the popular repertory of the past century or so, aimed squarely at elderly and middle-class viewers. Interestingly, in the area in which I watched TV for this week (eastern Vermont), these three shows were scheduled in direct competition with one another, at 7 p.m. on 23 May.

To put some of this in perspective: during this week, when Kim Carnes's "Bette Davis Eyes" reached the no.1 position on *Billboard*'s "Hot 100" charts and was thus regarded as the most popular song in America by journalists and critics who take the sale of phonograph discs as the most important measure of popularity, this recording had not yet sold a million copies – while some 45,000,000 Americans were exposed to a number of songs performed by Donny Osmond which were nowhere to be seen on any of the *Billboard* charts; and the REO Speedwagon LP *High Infidelity*, at the top of the album charts, had just passed the million mark in sales – but as many as 30,000,000 people heard "Oh, What a Beautiful Morning" from *Oklahoma*, a song written in 1943.

If we are to deal with the dissemination of music by the mass media, we must deal with *all* media. The above remarks have been offered as nothing more than suggestions as to how one can begin to proceed along these lines, what resources are available, what problems are encountered, and what conclusions might emerge from such a study. Needless to say, what I have done is merely suggestive, a first small step in the direction of determining what sorts of music are heard by the largest number of people in the United States. And I would be the first to point out that comparisons between the number of phonograph discs sold and the number of people hearing a given song as performed on television approach a comparison of apples and oranges; once a disc has been purchased, there is no way to determine how many times it will be played, for how many people, in a given period of time. But one must start somewhere.

My remarks have been wide ranging, as I hoped would be appropriate for an opening paper. Let me end by touching on another dimension of popular music, perhaps the most important one.

Mass-disseminated music has enormous potential for influencing the ways in which a population perceives and thinks about the world. This potential has been realized in the past for both commercial and political gain, and will be again.

If one depends on data concerning the dissemination of phonograph discs alone, one must conclude that the United States is still in the Age of Rock. The several varieties of rock music have been associated since the mid-1950s with rebellious youth and radical politics; surely this music played a critical role in helping to reverse American policy on Vietnam a decade ago, and in creating a climate which made it impossible for Richard Nixon to continue in the presidency.

If one considers the dissemination of music via other media, however, a quite different picture emerges.

One would not suspect that America is living through the rock era from sitting in front of a television set. The vast majority of music emanating from this medium is country-western music (mostly Country Pop) and music from the Tin Pan Alley era or newer music in this same style – styles associated with older and more conservative layers of American society.

There is not time here to consider whether television's neglect of rock is an honest reflection of current American taste, or whether television management has consciously and deliberately allied itself with those forces in America determined to resist and ignore the Age of Rock, the counter-culture which emerged in the 1960s, and all that these trends imply.

My point is this: if one had been truly attentive in recent years to trends in the mass dissemination of music in America via television, the medium which reaches by far the largest number of people in the country, and had refused to be blinded by the much greater attention paid to the products of a more limited medium – the phonograph – one could easily have predicted the outcome of the presidential election of 1980 and anticipated other recent events in the United States signalling a massive swing to the right, politically and socially.

The mass media can tell us a great deal about the world in which we live, and the ways in which attitudes and opinions are being formed and molded. But they can tell us such things only if we learn to look and listen in a truly objective way.

6

ELVIS, A REVIEW

Though musicology had offered little intellectual guidance in my efforts to write about popular music and was under attack in the 1980s for its dedication to empirical, positivist scholarship,[1] it nevertheless seemed that with its tradition of disciplined and responsible scholarship it should be able to deal effectively with popular music.

Albert Goldman's biography of Elvis Presley (New York, 1981), pieced together from facts, rumors, insinuations, and out-and-out fabrications, struck me as a particularly blatant instance of irresponsible and undisciplined writing about popular music. Even worse, there was no responsible or intellectually challenging biography of Presley or any other popular musician of the time against which to measure Goldman's misreadings of its protagonist and the culture from which he had come, and no satisfactory analysis or even description of the music itself against which to measure the distortions and outright absurdities of the book's frequent attempts to address musical issues.

Accordingly I wrote what was intended to be another call to action in the form of a review of Goldman's book, boldly accepted for publication in the *Journal of the American Musicological Society* by Ellen Rosand, editor-in-chief, and Edward Roesner, review editor. It was the first time that Presley, or for that matter rock 'n' roll itself, had been mentioned in that venerated journal. But the piece sparked no rush to welcome popular music into the musicological canon, and popular music study flourished elsewhere.

* * *

[1] See for instance the "Editor's introduction to Volume 2" and the essay review of *The New Grove Dictionary of Music and Musicians* in *Popular Music* 2 (1982), pp. 1–8 and 245–58, and "Popular music, class conflict and the music-historical field" by Richard Middleton in *Popular Music Perspectives* 2 (Gothenburg, Exeter, Ottawa, and Reggio Emilia, 1985), pp. 24–46.

131

Elvis is not the sort of book usually reviewed in these pages. Popular music of contemporary times has been a matter of little concern to most members of our discipline, and the present book is furthermore aimed at a non-academic readership. But in my opinion this book should engage our attention. It deals with one of the central figures in a genre of music widely regarded – elsewhere, if not yet in our discipline – as one of the most distinctive and important products of the second half of the present century; despite some negative reviews, *Elvis* has already become accepted as the standard and most complete work on its subject; and though its chief concerns are often historical and sociological, it nevertheless confronts musical matters on almost every page and passes frequent judgement both on the music of its protagonist and on the entire field of American popular music of the 1950s and 60s.

It is precisely the kind of book future generations of music scholars will turn to for contemporary information on this music, which is just as sure to be of interest to them as every scrap of music from earlier times (and every bit of contemporary writing concerned with this music) is of interest to us. In fact, they will *have* to consult books of this sort, since there is nothing else.

For the record, Albert Goldman holds advanced degrees from Chicago and Columbia; he has taught at "practically every college in New York," enjoys a second career as "cultural journalist and music critic" for various journals, and founded *Cultural Affairs*. He has no training in music; and though he once delivered a paper at a national meeting of the American Musicological Society, he reveals no knowledge of the systematic and disciplined methodology of musicology or related fields.

I submit that his book is filled with blatant misinformation about the music of Elvis Presley, and in fact the entire era. Furthermore, the mischief has been compounded by the virtual absence of a responsible critical assessment of the book, at least regarding musical matters. It could not have been otherwise, since most of Goldman's reviewers, whatever their other qualifications, have had as little experience with musical and musicological matters as the author himself.

Goldman's distortions and misconceptions are so elementary and dramatic that it will be enough to deal with only several instances of his "typical substitutions of fantasy for history that are the essence of this book," to paraphrase the author's own words (p. 60). The most destructive fantasy, one that makes it impossible for Goldman to grasp the essence of the music so central to the story he tells, is his conviction that rock 'n' roll "delved back into the past," making the 1950s a "time to reverse the course of American musical history and start driving with eyes firmly fixed on the rearview mirror":

> The motto of this music was never better articulated than in that song of the sixties that ran: "Gonna buy me a time machine and go to the turn of the century. Everything's happening at the turn of the century." Rock from the beginning was a throwback to an earlier and more naive kind of music than the commercial jazz or the Broadway show tunes that had dominated American con- sciousness during the thirties and forties (pp. 116–17).

This theme recurs constantly, in other generalizations and also in reference to more specific matters, as in the contention that Presley's style was based on "naive mimickry of the styles and sounds of the preceding generations – the introductory riffs of the swing bands, the hubba-hubba rhythm vocalizing of the twenties, the cornball glottal strokes" (p. 117). The author sometimes descends to the level of sheer absurdity, as in the suggestion that Presley's breaking of guitar strings during performance equates him with Paganini and thus "once again we see that it was Elvis Presley's function to recapture the past every time he took a step into the future" (p. 157).

The truth of the matter is that the rock 'n' roll style emerging in the 1950s was characterized by many elements strikingly different from those of Tin Pan Alley song, which had dominated American popular music for more than fifty years. Structurally, the 12-bar blues form replaced the verse-chorus patterns tracing back to the 1890s and the 32-bar, four-phase format of most songs of the last decades of Tin Pan Alley. The rock 'n' roll band was comprised of amplified and electric guitars, saxophones and occasionally other horns, and a prominent rhythm section of drums, bass, and sometimes piano – quite different in makeup and sound from the theater orchestras, the swing bands, and the string-dominated ensembles used to accompany singers in the several eras of Tin Pan Alley. A driving, percussion-punctuated, fast beat replaced the slower ballad tempo of most older songs; singing styles abandoned the lyric, legato techniques of the "Big Singers" in favor of a raucous, rasping, shouting vocal production in keeping with the instrumental sound and much higher energy level of rock 'n' roll and the sentiments of the lyrics, now concerned mostly with sex rather than idealized romantic love. These quite specific features characterize the music of all early rock 'n' roll performers, black and white – Bill Haley, Little Richard, Jerry Lee Lewis, Chuck Berry, Elvis Presley.

They made this music fresh and charged with energy for the people who liked it, and harsh and ugly for those who didn't. Both proponents and opponents correctly perceived the sound as new, though many of its components had been developing over a period of several decades in both black popular music and the more urban dialects of country-western style.

Goldman gives no evidence of understanding any of this, nor indeed the general concept of the cyclic nature of music whereby an established style eventually gives way to a newer one. His discomfort in dealing with stylistic matters is perhaps best summed up in a memorable sentence: "With the advent of Hank Ballard, Chubby Checker, the Peppermint Lounge and the Philadelphia Sound, American popular music suddenly jumped into a new groove called soul" (p. 316), in which black performers spanning several decades, and several quite different styles, are lumped together as proponents of "soul" – even though none of them fits properly into this category.

Goldman's inability to perceive the stylistic differences between early rock 'n' roll and older styles of American popular music makes it impossible for him to explain the "incongruity between [Presley's] limited talents and his limitless fame" (p. 525). Forced to concede that "nobody in the history of show business ever made it so big so fast" (p. 204), the author offers several tentative explanations for this phenomenon – Presley's effective stage presence and his innovative use of the several mass media, for instance. Goldman has even less success in dealing with less glamorous performers:

> Though today it seems hard to believe, when Bill Haley landed in England for the first time in 1956, there were riots at the docks. Riots for a moon-faced, spit-curled clod like Bill Haley! Critics and showbiz professionals of that day were driven to the limits of exasperation by the spectacle of such crude and inept performers attaining unprecedented popularity (p. 206).

The explanation is simple enough. Haley managed to become a symbol of early rock 'n' roll, and his music was the first of its sort heard by millions of Americans (and Europeans). The response was not so much to his brand of rock 'n' roll as to the impact of this new music in a general sense. As more talented and dynamic rock 'n' roll performers emerged, Haley and his group faded in public favor. To some extent Elvis Presley's early story was similar: when his first recordings for RCA Victor were released in early 1956 there was still a relatively small amount of rock 'n' roll easily available, and he soon brought this music to places where it had not been available before, such as commercial television. At least part of his early success can be explained, too, by the fact that many people were first exposed to the genre of rock 'n' roll through this music. But in addition he was a much more talented performer than Haley, and better able to adapt to a variety of song styles; thus his career endured while Haley's soon ended.

But to someone unable to distinguish one musical style from another, incapable of grasping and articulating the difference between a Tin Pan Alley ballad and an early rock 'n' roll piece, these points must of necessity remain obscure.

Elsewhere Goldman criticizes Presley on the grounds that he "short-circuited all the *customary* [italics mine] preparations for recording. Instead of spending weeks closeted with writers, arrangers and producers, selecting songs, preparing scorings and rehearsing the new material, he would walk in cold and record everything at first sight" (p. 198). There is no hint here or elsewhere that all early rock 'n' roll, not just that performed by Elvis Presley, was an oral music – like the black popular and country-western music out of which it sprang, and unlike the songs of Tin Pan Alley, which were composed, notated, disseminated as sheet music, and performed from orchestral arrangements. As a result of his failure to come to terms with the conceptual framework of an oral music,[1] Goldman entangles himself in contradictions. In one place he agrees that Presley's "first records were his best" (p. 212), elsewhere he criticizes these very discs as evidence that Presley belonged with the "musically deprived all over the world" because he had no resources beyond his "vocal chords, his rhythm guitar and his tiny two-piece band" (p. 115). Later these "primitive" early efforts are contrasted with later recordings:

> The really big breakthrough came, however, in the area of instrumental sound, which, for the first time in his entire career, was produced by a full-scale studio orchestra, [creating] a thrillingly contemporary treatment instead of the stale old sound of Sun or Nashville. Sometimes the violins fill the atmosphere with a thick blue haze. . . . Never again was Elvis to walk out onstage without thirty pieces behind him. *He had been weaned at last from the tuppenny sound of rock 'n' roll* [italics mine] (p. 427–8).

This last comment suggests a problem with the book even more

---

[1] Goldman's single mention of oral tradition comes in a brief summary of Lord Raglan's arguments (in *The Hero*) discrediting euhemerism, which he borrows to contend that "just as the hillbillies had no real awareness of the present, they had no grasp of the past" (p. 54).

profound than the author's inability to deal with musical matters: his failure to come to terms with the culture that produced his protagonist, and his music.

Virtually every page is sprinkled with terms and comments that betray an attitude of condescension and cultural superiority. Bill Monroe's "Blue Moon over Kentucky" is a "classic white-trash bluegrass song" (p. 115). Two long-time members of Presley's backing band are dismissed as "Nashville cornballs" (p. 440), and several of his associates are "country bumpkin cousins" (p. 214). Presley himself is characterized as a "pimple-faced kid" with a "mush-mouthed accent" (p. 238), who was "always professing his undying love and loyalty to Ma, Country, and Corn Pone, always an unregenerate southern redneck who stopped just short of the Klan and the John Birch Society" (p. 349). His first television performance "filled the American living room with the obscene antics and barbaric yawps of a leering, sneering juvenile delinquent" (p. 177), and one of his own concerts is compared to "one of those screeching, uninhibited party rallies which the Nazis used to hold for Hitler" (p. 266).[2] In the end the author dismisses the subject of his book as "resembling a character in a comic strip rather than a real human being" (p. 501).

It is all very well to dismiss this meanness of spirit as more a commentary on the author (and publisher) than on Elvis Presley, as some reviewers have done. But even so we are left with the dismaying suspicion that the book can offer no cultural insights of more substance than its musical judgements. I will not belabor this point either, but merely offer a single sample of Goldman's ineptness.

Early on we are told of Presley's first public performance, his singing of "Old Shep" in a children's talent competition at the annual Mississippi–Alabama Fair and Dairy Show, for which he was awarded second prize. The best Goldman can do with this incident is to suggest that the subject matter of the song – in which the singer recalls with keen nostalgia a dead pet dog – reinforces one of his own pet notions, that the death (at birth) of Presley's twin brother had a profound impact on Elvis's character. He makes nothing of the fact

[2] There is a startling similarity between Goldman's rhetoric and that used in the 1950s by the established music industry and the "responsible" press in an attempt to discredit rock 'n' roll. For comparison, Frank Sinatra was quoted in the *New York Times Magazine* (12 January 1958) as saying that rock 'n' roll "is sung, played, and written for the most part by cretinous goons" and "manages to be the martial music of every side-burned delinquent on the face of the earth." *Time* (18 June 1956) ended its first article on rock 'n' roll by suggesting that this new phenomenon "does for music what a motorcycle club at full throttle does for a quiet Sunday afternoon. The results bear passing resemblances to Hitler mass meetings."

that the winner of the competition, a certain Becky Harris, sang "Sentimental Journey," which he describes as a "sexy, Bluesy number." The song is actually a classic of latter-day Tin Pan Alley, composed by Bud Green, Ben Homer, and Les Brown and popularized in 1945 through recordings by the Big Bands of both Brown and Hal McIntyre. "Old Shep," on the other hand, was not a "very old-fashioned ballad," as Goldman would have it, but rather a recent commercial country-western song written by Clyde Julian ("Red") Foley in the latest style of such music, recorded by Foley for Decca in 1941 and disseminated by sales of this disc and through radio play to millions of Americans of all ages, few of whom had lost a twin brother.

Thus both contestants selected a currently popular, mass-disseminated song, but from different repertories: Becky's from the mainstream of urban white popular music, Elvis's from country-western music. Class distinction was at work here. Tin Pan Alley songs belonged to the culture of educated, affluent, urban Americans, in the South as elsewhere; country music was seen by these people as a culturally inferior product of the predominantly rural lower classes. Presley understood this social structure, its implications for music, and his place in the scheme of things. As he became a commercial success he had increasing dealings with persons from other strata of American society, who wanted to guide his music in directions contrary to his own cultural and musical instincts. The tensions and conflicts of these confrontations are reflected in a most direct way in the music of Presley's later years.

Goldman's perception is of an inferior musical product, "the corny old rock 'n' roll of the fifties" (p. 374), the creation of a benighted segment of American life, which can be taken seriously only to the extent that it begins to resemble the neo-Tin-Pan-Alley style of the 1950s and 60s. As noted above, he approves of Presley's instrumental backings only when they begin to resemble those used behind Frank Sinatra and Barbra Streisand. After cataloguing various vocal faults in Presley's recording of "Love Me Tender," he imagines "with what wistful beauty Bing Crosby would have voiced this pretty period piece" (p. 201). He is astonished that a song as commercially successful as "Heartbreak Hotel" could have been written by "a couple of obscure writers who had never set foot inside the Brill Building" (p. 169).

This may be Goldman's story, but it is not the story of early rock 'n' roll. The book is a disgrace. The publisher should withdraw it, and libraries should reclassify it as fiction. Neither of these is likely to happen, though; so we musicologists should take matters into our own hands by beginning to produce responsible, disciplined studies of the music of our own time, against which such a book as *Elvis* could be measured, and by subjecting the literature on popular and vernacular music to the same critical scrutiny we lavish on other books.

7

HOME COOKING AND AMERICAN SOUL IN BLACK SOUTH AFRICAN POPULAR MUSIC

In the 1960s and 70s, work on a census-catalogue of manuscripts of Renaissance polyphony took me to virtually every country in Western and Eastern Europe.[1] I listened to popular music on the radio on these trips, watched musical programs on television, attended live pop performances, and bought recordings. But it wasn't until a trip to southern Africa in the early spring of 1978 brought me into contact with a body of music so vibrant and so inseparable from the dramatic events unfolding there that I considered writing about music in a culture other than my own.

Though UN boycotts of South Africa were not yet in effect when I was invited to lecture on American music at the University of Natal in Durban, I consulted with black American friends and organizations before accepting. Their advice was to go, to experience conditions in that country at first hand.

On my arrival in February of 1978 I began to realize that my preconceptions of South Africa had not prepared me for its social and political realities, and certainly not for the richness, complexity, and vitality of its musical life. I began hearing some extraordinary music on Radio Zulu, about which I knew nothing at the time; so I visited its studios, and also obtained commercial recordings of the music I'd heard. Three things were apparent: the white population was oblivious to this music; the government was using it, cleverly and effectively, to advance its own political agenda; but despite this, black identification with this music ran deep, even in oppositional circles.

A few ethnomusicologists had written about this music in the

---

[1] *Census-Catalogue of Manuscript Sources of Polyphonic Music 1400–1550*, vol. I (Neuhausen-Stuttgart, 1979). Herbert Kellman and I co-edited this volume, then he edited subsequent volumes appearing in 1982, 1984, and 1988.

context of acculturated modern styles.[2] But it seemed to me that emphasis on its "weakened" traditional African elements missed not only the power and beauty of the music, but also the ongoing struggle over its meaning.

When I returned to South Africa in January of 1982, this time specifically to learn more about this music, I spent much of my time in Johannesburg, the center of the country's recording industry, talking with executives, producers, and musicians, sitting in on recording sessions, buying more records, and attending live performances, including an open-air rock concert in Soweto. In order to unravel the highly complex media strategy of the government, I listened to the radio constantly, taped entire programs for later analysis, and interviewed officials and program directors of the South African Broadcasting Corporation in Johannesburg, Durban, and King William's Town. I also visited the state-run radio stations of Botswana and Swaziland to get some grasp of the wider dissemination of the popular styles and genres I'd heard in South Africa. Conversations with Chris Ballantine and Muff Andersson, who were beginning to write about this music, were also useful.[3]

It was clear by now that the music itself, and the circumstances under which it was produced, mediated, disseminated, and received, were complex enough to require much more study and analysis. But at least I knew enough to begin talking about it, in private and public, and I had dozens of recordings to play for whomever I could persuade to listen.[4] Though I was not yet ready to try a scholarly article, I wrote a journalistic account of this music and the context in which it was heard for the *Village Voice*, which was just beginning to show an interest in non-Western popular music. But the piece was not in an appropriate literary style for that publication, and was never used. It first appeared

[2] David Rycroft, "Evidence of stylistic continuity in Zulu 'town' music," in *Essays for a Humanist: An Offering to Klaus Wachsman* (New York, 1977), pp. 216–60; David Rycroft, "Nguni vocal polyphony," *Journal of the International Folk Music Council* 19 (1967), pp. 88–103; David Rycroft, "The new 'town' music of Southern Africa," *Recorded Folk Music* I (September-October 1958), p. 54; David Rycroft, "African music in Johannesburg: African and non-African features," *Journal of the International Folk Music Council* 9 (1959), p. 25; Gerhard Kubik, *The Kachamba Brothers Band* (Manchester, 1974); Percival R. Kirby, "The effects of Western civilization on Bantu music," in *Western Civilization and the Natives of South Africa* (London, 1967); Hugh Tracey, "The state of folk music in Bantu Africa," *African Music* I/I (1954), pp. 8–11.
[3] Muff Andersson's *Music in the Mix: The Story of South African Popular Music* (Johannesburg, 1981) had just been published when I talked with her in Gabarone, Botswana.
[4] A preliminary version of this paper was given in 1982 at a conference of the UK branch of IASPM held in Exeter, and as part of a two-hour broadcast on KPFA, the community radio station of the California Bay Area, during which pieces by Ladysmith Black Mambazo, Steve Kekana, and the Soul Brothers were played for what was surely the first time on American radio.

as an internally distributed working paper for IASPM, then was published in an Italian translation by Umberto Fiori as "Cucina casalinga e 'soul' americano nella musica dei neri in Sud Africa."

* * *

American rock has fascinated me for twenty-five years, but I have become bored with its recent products. I suspect the problem is not with me but the music, which seems dead in its tracks.

Armed with a suspicion that the next fresh wave of popular music might come from some unexpected part of the globe, I set off in January of 1982 for southern Africa – South Africa, Swaziland, Lesotho, Botswana – where four years earlier my attention had been caught by a distinctive style of music. I found it still thriving in 1982, and I also found some surprising new developments in the musical life of the region which speak to more general social and political issues.

Contemporary black South Africa has generated a dialect of popular music quite different from the Highlife or Juju of the West Coast and the Caribbean-tinged, guitar-dominated styles of Zaire and the East Coast (Tanzania and Kenya). Sometimes called vocal jive, gumba-gumba or even jazz, it is most often labelled Mbaqanga. The literal reference is to mealie-porridge or corn mush, a staple of the black diet; the implication is that this music is a local, homely product. Home cooking. Daily bread.

A typical piece of contemporary Mbaqanga, by Moses Mchunu for instance, begins with a brief improvised passage by acoustic guitar or concertina, rhythmically ambiguous; drums and bass enter, setting the beat and establishing a four-bar sequence of chords over which the entire piece will unfold; passages for the singer, who may be backed by a small vocal group, alternate with instrumental breaks. A violin may be part of the ensemble in the most traditional groups; one or more saxophones may also be used.

Elements of African and European music are intermingled. The practice of constructing an entire song over a brief repeated pattern is purely African, as are the infectious and often complex rhythms. The tonal, triadic harmonies have their roots in Western music and the instruments come from Europe and America, though they were long ago assimilated into black African culture and are now considered "traditional." Curiously, though we tend to associate drums with the music of black Africa, the older music of the Nguni people of the region (the Zulu, Swazi, and Xhosa) makes almost no

141

use of percussion. Western music – military bands, popular music, jazz – introduced drumming to much of southern Africa, and modern drum sets, not African drums, comprise the rhythm sections of Mbaqanga.

Mchunu, a Zulu from Nkandla, has been a central figure in Mbaqanga since his first recording was brought out in the mid-1970s by Gallo, the largest commercial company in South Africa. His songs draw on remembered fragments of an older Zulu song repertory, and texts also often make reference to an older literature: praise songs of African kings and warriors, village songs of farewell, wedding songs. There are constant references to cattle, sorcery, religion, and similar topics of concern to more traditional African life. He sings in a declamatory style, with a vocal production sounding harsh and strained to Western ears; when he is backed by a vocal group (Nabafana Bengoma) there are traces of call-and-response patterns found in so much African music. Mchunu wears traditional Zulu garments and jewelry, alone or in combination with Western clothing, in live performance and in photos on album covers. His style of Mbaqanga goes back some generations, and much of his following is in the rural homelands and among township blacks born in the country.

At the other end of today's Mbaqanga spectrum are the Soul Brothers, who have sold more phonograph discs than any other black South African performers in the past five years. Their songs are underlaid by the same insistent brief harmonic patterns; but an electric organ replaces the concertina, the guitar and bass are electric, the violin has disappeared, and a synthesizer is used in recent recordings. Instrumental breaks are often taken by a horn section of three saxophones, playing riffs typical of black township jazz. And the singing, by leader David Masondo and backup vocalist American Zulu, is in smooth two-part harmony depending mostly on parallel thirds and sixths, not unlike that of Simon and Garfunkel, with no trace of call-and-response.

The Soul Brothers come from Hammarsdale, where they were factory workers, and they now live in Soweto. Recent album photos picture them in sports jackets, slacks and open-neck leisure shirts. Their most popular song to date, "Deliwe," is based on an African soap opera once carried on Radio Zulu, tracing the adventures of a young black woman just arrived in Johannesburg from a rural homeland. They offer urban Mbaqanga – home cooking adapted to life in the city.

Other Mbaqanga performers have also developed individual

styles within the framework of the genre. Amaswazi Emvelo features smooth but full-throated three-part vocal harmonies backed by a mixture of acoustic and electric instruments. The Shoe Laces, formed in 1979, make use of the latest electronic instruments and a wider range of chord progressions than is usual: "Bethela Sangoma," their hit of 1980, begins with eerie sounds on a synthesizer and is built over a short sequence of curious modal-sounding chords, all this intended to illustrate their text (a *sangoma* is a witchdoctor). Steve Kekana, the blind singer regarded by record producers as the most popular black performer in southern Africa today – CCP Records brought out four of his LPs in 1980 alone – built his reputation on Mbaqanga, developing fragments of traditional tunes over the ubiquitous four-bar chord sequences of this music but with a voice patterned after black American soul singers.

Contemporary social and political issues appear to be absent in Mbaqanga lyrics. But the conventions and traditions of black oral poetry are not the same as those of European and American song texts, and a "protest" song of the sort that was so common in the 1960s would be out of place in an African song today. Issues are addressed obliquely: Hamilton Nzimande's "Sala S'Thandwa," a farewell song addressed to a young man leaving his village based on a traditional Zulu lyric, may well be heard by blacks in the context of a familiar contemporary situation: the destruction of black family structures by the necessity for so many men to leave the impoverished homelands, where it is impossible for them to find employment, for the mines or cities.

Mbube is a special dialect of Mbaqanga, differing from the above-described styles in performance forces: five to ten male voices, singing without instrumental accompaniment. Its roots lie in traditional Nguni ceremonial music. Call-and-response patterns persist in *mbube*, with a lead singer giving out phrases and the other singers responding. Harmonies are triadic; interior sections of most songs move through persistant repetition of brief chordal sequences. Voices range from low bass to extremely high tenor and falsetto, the voices sing with a precision that would be the envy of even the best European choruses. The sound of *mbube*, with its rich sonorous chords surging with rhythmic energy, reminds an American listener of a combination of barbershop quartet singing and black gospel music.

The top *mbube* group for some years has been Ladysmith Black Mambazo, the name derived from the town in Natal (Ladysmith) where most of the members were born and the Zulu word for a kind of axe (*mambazo*). Their songs, which often make reference to an older Zulu repertory, are always credited to the leader of the group, Joseph Shabalala. First recorded in the early 1970s by Radio Zulu in Durban, they were quickly signed by Gallo; their first commercial LP, *Amabutho* ("Warriors"), has been followed by fifteen others, with total sales surpassing four million discs.

Comparisons between Mbaqanga and reggae seem obvious: both are readily accessible to Western ears, since they use familiar instruments and common-practice harmonies; these are overlaid in both cases with more exotic rhythms and conceptual references to indigenous cultures. It seems probable that Western audiences would respond to Mbaqanga if given the chance, and in fact an LP of ten-year old music of this sort released in England in 1982 enjoyed considerable commercial success (*Soweto*, Rough Trade Records, Rough 37, 1982). But the South African record industry is convinced that Mbaqanga would never sell overseas, an attitude conditioned by the undeniable fact that whites within that country will have nothing to do with it.

To understand this attitude, one must experience first hand the climate of "Separate Development," the preferred terms in South Africa for what most of the rest of the world calls apartheid.

Johannesburg today reminds an American of Atlanta, in its architecture and the mix of people on the streets and in shops. Sales personnel is mixed racially in most establishments, blacks and Asians shop side by side with whites, and increasingly one sees mixing of races in restaurants and places of entertainment. A concert by Millie Jackson in the Coliseum Theatre draws an interracial audience, with no segregated seating; the Market Theatre offers nightly performances of theatrical and musical events in its several halls, often with mixed black and white performers in front of multiracial audiences. Even outside of the larger cities one sees unexpected racial mixing, for instance in the hotels and restaurants of provincial King William's Town.

It takes some time to get the point. Blacks and whites form two streams of humanity in South Africa, often sharing the same physical space these days but moving through it separately. They patronise the same shops and restaurants and theaters, but with their own kind. The races do not greet one another in the streets, nor do they seek eye contact elsewhere. My naively American attempts to exchange comments with the blacks surrounding me at the Millie Jackson concert were met with surprise and indifference.

Henry Kolatsoeu, music programer at Radio SeSotho, cautioned me against trying to attend live performances of black popular music on the grounds that "black people just aren't used to having whites around." David Kramer, a talented folksinger with a following in university and intellectual circles, said in an interview with pop critic Muff Andersson, "I've never really considered black people as a potential audience, because to be quite honest I don't come into contact with black people that often – that's just the way things are geared." It never occurred to the music director of CCP Records, the sympathetic Howard Ipp who has since emigrated to Canada, to have me talk with his black producer, sitting in his own office just a door away. Later, when I did in fact meet black producers, they had little to say to me.

Separate Development. Each race with its own language and culture, its own role in South African society, its own living space. The white government is fond of quoting statistics to prove that its blacks have higher incomes, more education and better health care than most other African blacks. But what makes the country unique is the effectiveness with which human contact between the races has been inhibited. The vast majority of South Africans, black and white, were born after the Nationalist Party launched its policy of separate development, based firmly on foundations laid by the previous English government, soon after it came to power in 1948. They have never known anything else.

Separate radio services were established by the South African Broadcasting Corporation (SABC) in English and Afrikaans some time ago, then in 1960 the government established Radio Bantu, the collective name for various African language services of the SABC. Radio Bantu is heard today throughout South Africa, or at least wherever blacks are found: in homes and shops in Soweto and other townships, in servants' quarters, kitchens and gardens in white areas, where "domestics" and "houseboys" are at work; at sidewalk newsstands and shoeshine establishments in town; in rural areas and homelands, at bus stops and along the roads where blacks walk, endlessly, to work and to market, to fetch water and firewood, to visit friends and family, to attend church. Black identification with Radio Bantu apparently runs deep, judging from official estimates of its listenership and also from the millions of letters which pour into the offices of the various services – letters requesting favorite songs, letters containing entries in contests, letters giving the names of deceased relatives to be read on the weekly programs devoted to this ritual.

At least half of the air time on Radio Bantu is devoted to music, and the government maintains strict control over what is played. All discs, domestic or foreign, must be approved by a censorship board concerned with publications of all sorts; if officially banned, as happened to most of Bob Marley's discs and Pink Floyd's *The Wall* for instance, a record not only is barred from air play but may not even be sold or owned within the country. In addition, there are SABC review boards empowered to prevent air play of any other music judged to be objectionable or inflammatory. Government and SABC approval of their products is thus important to the recording industry, which believes that radio play is essential to sales, and they themselves shy away from songs with lyrics touching on such sensitive issues as Communism or socialism, revolution of any sort, black consciousness, and explicit reference to sex.

The popularity of American soul, disco, and gospel music among black South Africans, always great, has intensified even more in the past decade. Percy Sledge was an effective missionary for soul in the early 1970s with a series of performances in all-black theaters, so successful and so attractive to whites as well that he was declared an "honorary white." An even more important breakthrough came in the spring of 1978, with Dobie Gray's five-week tour of Johannesburg, Durban, East London, Port Elizabeth, and Cape Town which made history on both political and financial fronts. His producer (Sam Quibell) had extracted an unequivocal commitment from the government that allowed Gray to sing before multiracial audiences; and the tour grossed more than half a million dollars. The latter figure attracted a stream of other black American musicians to South Africa, among them Billy Preston, Millie Jackson, Brook Benton, Tina Turner, the Commodores, Clarence Carter, and Curtis Mayfield, even in the face of threatened boycotts from various groups. Incidentally, it seems important to differentiate between these performers who have appeared before interracial audiences in public theaters all over South Africa and such people as Frank Sinatra – who have performed only at the resort complex of Sun City before audiences comprised chiefly of well-to-do, privileged whites, for obscenely inflated fees.

These black Americans have had a great impact on the musical life of southern Africa. Sales of their discs have soared, radio play of black American music has increased, and many African performers have begun to emulate their styles. Kori Moraba, for instance, has brought out several successful LPs featuring a singing style openly imitative of Dobie Gray, and the vocal styles of many leading Mbaqanga performers have become more Americanized, soulful, and mellow.

South Africa's commercial recording companies would dearly love to "break" their products on the international market but are convinced that neither Mbaqanga nor their local white performers have a chance of global success. Their most recent attempts to solve this dilemma have consisted of bringing out recordings of black performers doing music in European or international style.

CCP tested Steve Kekana on the European market with an LP entitled *Don't Stop the Music*, featuring songs (in English) by white songwriter Malcolm Watson, in pop and soul styles, backed by a studio orchestra of strings and other non-Mbaqanga instruments played by white session musicians. The cover pictures Kekana in a three-piece European suit, sitting in a bar with an attractive woman dressed in the latest black urban fashion. The songs are mostly concerned with contemporary black city life – "Working Man," "Raising my Family," "Shine On," and "Color me Black," the latter with a text anticipating the sentiments of the Paul McCartney–Stevie Wonder "Ebony and Ivory." Several cuts were reported to have enjoyed some air play in Scandinavia; some were heard on homeland services, and on the state stations of neighboring black countries; within South Africa a few of the songs were played over Radio Bantu, and the white population ignored the music.

Minc Records has recently attempted to arouse international interest in Juluka, originally a two-man acoustic duo consisting of Johnny Clegg, a white anthropologist, and Sipho Mchunu, a Zulu gardener, which for some years performed Zulu songs on the folk and university circuit. On their first commercial release, *African Litany*, the group has grown to four persons with additional backing session musicians. Though several songs on the album are sung in Zulu, most of the pieces are new songs written and sung by Clegg, strongly reminiscent of Bob Dylan in their musical references to Anglo-American folk song, their vocal delivery by Clegg, and their poetical texts touching on issues of the day – which prevented air play on SABC.

As a result of these several recent trends, the style of most black performers in South Africa has moved even closer to that of European and particularly American music. One can take this in several ways. A folklorist or ethnomusicologist, observing from the outside, can see it as a regrettable situation, as yet another instance of a distinctive indigenous music yielding to the relentless pressure of the globally disseminated mainstream international pop and rock style. Another view, however, takes into consideration certain unique political and cultural features of contemporary South Africa.

The government has aided each tribal group to retain and treasure its own language and culture; Radio Bantu, as part of this strategy, has mounted a massive effort to collect and record the traditional and religious music of each group, and to make available on the air a great deal of recent popular music in the appropriate African languages. Large amounts of money have been spent in these efforts, and at one level it appears to be an act of great generosity and concern; one can easily think of many ethnic and minority groups in various countries scattered around the world who would like nothing more than support from their central government in preserving their cultural heritage and operating a radio service in their own language. But the South African government's support and encouragement of tribal culture and language has been interpreted, inside and outside of the country, as a clever and effective strategy to intensify tribal identity (and hence, possibly, divisiveness) and thus to facilitate black acceptance of the homelands policy, while inhibiting inter-tribal black unity.

Black leaders within the country have understood for some time that the absence of a black *lingua franca* in the region is a serious obstacle to understanding and cooperation among the numerous tribes, and that English is the most logical language to serve for inter-tribal and international communication. Thus the use of English in any context is seen as an act of progress and defiance. It is worth observing in this connection that when the Transkei opted for "independence," it immediately introduced instruction in English into its public schools, to the displeasure of the South African government. In this context, when Steve Kekana releases a disc in English rather than Zulu or Sotho, it is not necessarily a gesture to the international pop style, but can be interpreted as an attempt to communicate more easily with blacks of all language groups within his country.

In addition, for more than a century the black population of South Africa has responded to, and interacted with, the culture of black Americans. Missionaries, educators, and visiting musicians afforded a first contact with their brothers in the United States; and though American blacks continue to have legitimate complaints with certain aspects of their life within American society, from the perspective of black South Africans they have obtained a most desirable economic and political status. Music and musicians have afforded an important link: each successive phase of Afro-American music reached southern Africa and was emulated by local musicians – ragtime, syncopated dance music, early jazz, swing, and now soul, gospel, and disco.

Black American musicians and athletes have become important heroes and role models for Africans; the Reverend Xaba, vice-president of the Ciskei, momentarily forgot the inhibiting presence of several SABC officials when in an interview with me he spoke of his passion for jazz and then told me how "all the blacks" had rallied behind John Tate when he came over to fight a white South African heavyweight boxer.

The assimilation and emulation of American music by black South Africans, which is the most striking trend in their musical life in recent years, may be seen then as a positive and progressive factor, an important step towards their own future.

Selected discography

Moses Mchunu and Nabafana Bengoma, *Senzeni Madona*. Motella BL 69 (Gallo), 1976

Moses Mchunu, *Sigiya Ngengoma*. Motella BL 252 (Gallo), 1980

The Soul Brothers, *Deliwe*. Masterpiece LMS 585 (GRC), 1979

Soul Brothers, *Ke Kopa Tshwarelo*. Masterpiece LMS 585 (GRC 7421), 1981

The Shoe Laces, *Bazali Yekelani*. Black HiLights BL 262 (Gallo), 1980

Steve Kekana, *Thapelo*. EMI JPL (E) 4006, 1980

Steve Kekana, *Kodua Ea Maseru*. EMI JPL (E) 4009, 1980

Steve Kekana, *Don't Stop the Music: Ungavimbi Zomculo*. CCP (V) 1025 (EMI), 1981

8

ROCK 'N' ROLL IN A VERY STRANGE SOCIETY

On a third trip to South Africa, in the winter and spring of 1983–4, I continued to investigate the complex interrelations among popular music, the black population, the music industry, and the government's media strategies. Gaining access to several large repositories of recordings by black performers, I listened to and taped hundreds of pieces recorded from the 1930s through to the 1970s, and combed newspapers, popular journals, government publications, and the scholarly literature for contemporary accounts of musical life during these years. Travelling to every section of the country, including each of the so-called homelands, and to Namibia, I listened to and recorded samples of the various "vernacular" services of the South African Broadcasting Corporation. Other scholars had begun to address this music as well, and I benefited particularly from the work of David B. Coplan[1] and Veit Erlmann.[2]

But I still didn't have sufficient control of the complex material to consider a major publication; so I began planning another, much longer

---

[1] Coplan was awarded a Ph.D. in cultural anthropology from Indiana University in 1980 for his dissertation *The Urbanization of African Performing Arts in South Africa*, later revised and published as *In Township Tonight! South Africa's Black City Music and Theatre* (Johannesburg, 1985). Other early publications include "The urbanization of African music: some theoretical observations," *Popular Music* 2 (1982), pp. 113–30, and "The emergence of an African working-class culture," in *Industrialisation and Social Change in South Africa: African Class-Formation, Culture and Consciousness*, ed. Shula Marks and Richard Rathbone (London, 1982), pp. 358–75.

[2] Erlmann's "Black political song in South Africa: some research perspectives," a paper delivered at IASPM's Second International Conference on Popular Music Studies, was published in *Popular Music Perspectives* 2 (Gothenburg, Exeter, Ottawa, and Reggio Emilia, 1985), pp. 187–209. He also published "Apartheid, African nationalism and culture – the case of traditional African music in black education in South Africa" in *Perspectives in Education* 7/3 (1983), pp. 131–54.

research trip to the region. In the meanwhile, since no study of popular music in South Africa could ignore the impact of foreign and particularly American music and musicians, I undertook the following case study of the reception of a new musical genre in a culture other than its own.

* * *

An investigation of the reception and perception of early rock 'n' roll in various parts of the world may tell us little new about the music itself, but it can inform us on contemporary issues and attitudes in these places, and remind us of the ways in which popular music has been utilized by commercial and political forces controlling the mass media.

The present essay sketches the confrontation between rock 'n' roll and the "very strange society" (to quote Allen Drury) which South Africa had become by the 1950s.[1]

At first, the importation of this music into white South Africa followed familiar patterns, observable in other European and post-Colonial countries.

Bill Haley and Elvis Presley were early favorites, beginning in 1956, when their discs were first available in the country. 1957 brought the release of the films *Love Me Tender* and *Jailhouse Rock*, which helped spur such enthusiasm for Presley that less than two years later a poll conducted by the *Sunday Times* of Johannesburg (25 October 1959) revealed him to be the top male vocalist of all time, and "Jailhouse Rock" was voted the most popular disc in recording history. At the time of this poll, more than two million record units of Presley's music had been sold in the country. By contrast, Bing Crosby – toppled from the top position by Elvis – had sold only some one million record units during the thirty years of his popularity.

The initial issue raised by rock 'n' roll in white South Africa was the familiar confrontation between youth and adult; there was the same "War against Rock" which was erupting in so many parts of the world.[2] Journalists, who had paid scant attention to mass-disseminated music and its stars before 1956, began to echo the outrage of many "responsible" citizens, which was ostensibly directed at the music but was more importantly aimed at its young

---

[1] *A Very Strange Society* (New York, 1967).
[2] See S. Chapple and R. Garofalo, *Rock 'n' Roll is Here to Pay: The History and Politics of the Music Industry* (Chicago, 1977).

audience. The *Star*, a leading English-language newspaper, suggested that rock 'n' roll sounded like nothing more than "beating on a bucket lid" (16 December 1956) and identified its audience as those "hordes of sloppy, aggressive, be-jeaned louts and their girl friends who cause so much trouble in South Africa." When a new wave of "rock 'n' roll hysteria" swept Johannesburg in January of 1958, sparked by disc jockey David Davies (who played Presley's discs in live sessions in department stores and theaters) and by the rumor that the country was to have its first visit by an established rock 'n' roll performer, twenty citizens drafted and signed a letter to the *Star* (10 January 1958) objecting to this music on the grounds of its supposed connection with "primitive" music, the identical not-so-subtle racism which was directed at rock 'n' roll in America and Europe: "The exact same ritual and war dances may be seen at less cost, and in greater safety, at our own mine compounds."

But soon, responses which were more typically South African surfaced. Foreign-produced discs could not be sold directly in the country. It was necessary for a South African company, such as Gallo, or the South African subsidiary of an international corporation, to lease foreign recordings or release them on their own lable. Thus the choice of what records were distributed lay with the South African recording industry, not with retail outlets. Europeans (the prefered South African term for whites, no matter how far back they traced their family history in Africa) made up the largest part of the disc-buying market; they were not inclined to buy discs by non-white performers, with the exception of a handful of white jazz enthusiasts who would buy releases by some of the great American jazz performers. Therefore no discs by early black rock 'n' roll performers were available in South Africa.

The state radio service, the South African Broadcasting Corporation (SABC), was controlled by the Nationalist Party, which had been in power since 1948. Most of the political strength of the party lay with the Afrikaner population; most Afrikaans-speaking South Africans belonged to the Nederdruits Gereformeerde Kerk (NGK: Dutch Reformed Church), which impressed fundamentalist Christian behavior and thinking on its congregations and stamped its moral approval on each successive bit of legislation tightening the new government's emerging, comprehensive policy of apartheid, or "Separate Development." The SABC refused to play rock 'n' roll at first, but this music could be picked up on radio sets in most parts of South Africa by tuning to LM Radio in Laurenço Marques (now Maputo) or ZQP in Lusaka, which transmitted a strong signal over the southern third of the continent. The Government could have prevented the sale of rock 'n' roll discs within the country, through the expedient of having each individual record banned by the Publications Board; however, it chose to allow this music to be heard, while being careful to disassociate itself from any direct involvement in its dissemination.

The white population of South Africa suffers from an acute sense of geographical and cultural isolation from Europe and the United States. Popular culture is shaped, perhaps more than that of any other country, by those overseas entertainers who come to the country. These people are idolized and publicized, sometimes out of all proportion to their talents; they help shape the South African perception of contemporary style, and local performers eagerly adopt styles and mannerisms from these visitors.

In late 1957 it was announced that Tommy Steele, who had recently had a top hit on the British charts with his version of "Singing the Blues," had accepted an offer from promoter Ken Parks to undertake a fourteen-day tour of southern Africa, beginning in mid-March of 1958 in Cape Town and continuing on to Port Elizabeth, Durban, Johannesburg, Pretoria, Salisbury, and Bulawayo. This event focused even more attention on rock 'n' roll, and sharpened the reactions of the several segments of the white population to this music and its audience.

Initial response to Steele was as expected: fanatical enthusiasm from youth, disapproval from adults. The press carried sensational articles suggesting potential danger from rampaging teenagers inflamed by dangerous music. A scheduled civic reception for Steele in Cape Town, the day after his arrival, was cancelled by the mayor because of protests from well-placed people "who believe that rock 'n' roll is to blame for many of our present troubles" (*Star*, 20 March 1958). The City Council of Johannesburg informed Steele's promoter that he would be liable for all damage to the City Hall "caused by riot," and insisted that he take out insurance on the building to cover the dates of Steele's concerts there.

Despite efforts by the press to magnify the smallest incident into a civil disorder, it quickly became apparent that the capacity crowds greeting Steele wherever he went were intent only on enjoying the music, and that Steele himself, temperamentally and musically, was scarcely the sort of performer intent on whipping his audience into a frenzy. Authorities in Port Elizabeth, apprehensive because of certain sensational press items, assigned twelve extra policemen to the concert there; but the program went off "without the slightest trouble of any sort," and the police "were so bored with nothing to do that they sat down in the hall and thoroughly enjoyed the performance" (*Star*, 19 March 1958). By the time Steele reached Johannesburg for his scheduled performances on the 24th and 26th of March, the English press had resigned itself to the strong probability that nothing lurid would happen, and journalist Oliver Walker, who had prodded and provoked his readers for some time with his accounts of the horrors of rock 'n' roll, could only grumble: "Except for the noise and the people it was not so bad. But, of course, it had nothing to do with music. On the other hand, it had an awful lot to do with crowd hysteria" (*Star*, 25 March 1958).

English-speaking South Africans comprised the chief strength of the United Party, which had lost control of the government to the Nationalists in 1948; the English press was their most important public voice. When English journalists moved from prudish condemnation of rock 'n' roll to grudging acceptance of this music, during Steele's tour, this new attitude accurately mirrored a switch on the part of the English-speaking population itself towards rock 'n' roll – at least the dialect of this music represented by Tommy Steele. When the tour ended after twenty-six performances, netting him £8,666, it was clear that South Africa was a viable venue for overseas rock performers, and local promoters scrambled to line up others. In the next decade, dozens of British and American singers were persuaded to make the long journey to the tip of the African continent, among them Dickie Valentine, Cliff Richard, Connie Francis, Pat Boone, Billy Fury, Dusty Springfield, Adam Faith, Vera Lynn, and Alma Cogan. This roster both reflected and helped to shape the musical taste of white South African youth: middle-of-the-road rock; often more pop than rock; several stages removed from the rhythm and blues and country and western roots of the first wave of American rock 'n' roll of the 1950s; more often British than American. South African "rock" musicians fell into these same patterns. Adults became more and more tolerant of this music as it became evident that no real harm was being done, and that much music labelled "rock 'n' roll" was not too different from the music they had enjoyed during their youth.

The reaction of the Afrikaner press – reflecting the attitudes of the Nationalist Party, the NGK, and to some extent the entire Afrikaans-speaking population – was quite different.

Even before Steele's arrival in Cape Town, a journalistic campaign had begun. *Die Vaderland*, the leading Afrikaans newspaper published in Johannesburg, ran a front-page editorial on 25 February questioning the decision to allow "ruk-en-rol sangers" such as Steele and Terry

Dene into the country. (Dene, tentatively booked to follow Steele into South Africa, had recently been fined in England for smashing equipment during a performance and provoking the audience to riotous behavior; his tour was subsequently cancelled.) The following week, the Pretoria City Council discussed the appropriateness of allowing Steele to perform in their city, the seat of the administrative branches of the government and therefore the symbolic center of the Nationalist Party. The matter was turned over to the Finance Committee, which recommended on 16 March that "due to the fact that Mr Steele concentrates chiefly on rock 'n' roll music, the reservation should be cancelled" (Star, 17 March 1958). The decision was supported by statements issued by the NGK: the Reverend D. F. B. de Beer, Transvaal Secretary for Morals, was quoted as disagreeing with the government's decision to allow Steele into the country, and with the Board of Censors for allowing rock 'n' roll films to be shown in South Africa. De Beer took "strong exception to rock 'n' roll, dancing and music exhibition, [which exert a] demoralising influence on youth and aggravate the youth problem. We are now sowing the wind and will reap the whirlwind."

Steele was apparently bewildered by all this. "Blimey, we've got some stuffed shirts in Britain . . . but nothing like some of the chaps you seem to have here. If I'm good enough to appear before the Queen surely I'm good enough for the Pretoria City Council" (Star 20 March 1958). But the ban stood, and Minister of Justice Swart tabled a bill to "combat the delinquency problem," timed to coincide with Steele's appearances in Johannesburg, the most widely publicized of his tour. The Afrikaner press largely ignored details of Steele's presence, but ran a string of articles suggesting various evil by-products of rock 'n' roll: one spoke of interracial dancing; another contrasted Steele's financial success with the career of a young South African conductor of classical music, talented but hampered by insufficient income.

National elections were held a few weeks after Steele ended his tour of South Africa, resulting in an even more sweeping victory for the Nationalist Party. Later the political writer Robin Farquharson was quoted by the Star (19 November 1959) as suggesting that the Nationalists deliberately set out to make political capital by linking widespread concern with juvenile delinquency to rock 'n' roll, then stressing the fact that Steele and the absent Terry Dene, the most visible symbols of this music at that moment, were English. By implication the opposition party, English-speaking and mostly orientated towards British culture, was responsible for any perceived mischief resulting in South Africa from rock 'n' roll.

Throughout the 1960s, the Government continued this policy, which seemed to work well for its political purposes. Rock 'n' roll was allowed to flourish; the Afrikaans press and the NGK continued to denounce it, always ready to pounce on any excesses or scandalous incidents which could be linked to this music or its performers, at home or abroad, always ready to remind the Afrikaner population that this music was the product of an alien and dangerous culture. Dusty Springfield persisted in making adverse comments on the country's racial policies while performing in South Africa in 1964, and was asked to leave. Adam Faith was arrested while sitting on an aircraft waiting to leave the country, in January of 1965, on charges brought by his promoter, R. S. Quibell, who brought suit against him for non-appearances at scheduled concerts. The Afrikaans press duly reported and editorialized on these incidents – as did also the English press, which never seemed to grasp the political implications of the fact that these were British citizens, the cultural heroes of the white English youth of South Africa, the future strength of the United Party.

The reception of rock 'n' roll among the non-white population of South Africa was more complex. Executives of local recording companies made a decision in the mid-1950s that a potentially large audience for rock 'n' roll might exist in the non-white population, which just at this time was buying phonograph discs in unprecedented quantity. Their strategies for tapping this market included the release of a sampling of rock 'n' roll on 78 rpm discs (since most non-whites owned battery-operated playback equipment running at only this speed); distributing these discs to retail outlets catering to non-white customers; and taking out advertisements and sending review copies to the black press, which, unlike the white press, had a tradition of reviewing new recordings of popular music.

A word about the "black" press in South Africa at this time might be useful. Though a number of African-language publications had appeared in the late nineteenth and early twentieth centuries, some of them owned and edited by non-Europeans,[3] the "political and economic realities of South Africa under the Nationalist Party" had brought about a situation whereby "no African newspaper in South Africa was owned or controlled by Africans".[4] There were, however, newspapers and journals published for non-white readers during

[3] L. D. Switzer, *The Black Press in South Africa and Lesotho* (Boston, 1979).
[4] F. Barton, *The Press of Africa: Persecution and Perseverance* (New York, 1979).

the time period with which the present article is concerned. The largest circulation belonged to *Drum*, a monthly founded in 1951 by Jim Bailey, whose father had made a fortune in mining, and the daily *Post*, also owned by Bailey.

Drum employed mostly black writers and photographers, and addressed itself to matters of concern and interest to the growing non-white urban population of Johannesburg and the other larger cities and towns of South Africa; it was disseminated throughout the country, as well as in a number of neighboring nations, and eventually editions were brought out in Nairobi and other cities. The language was English, more and more widely spoken by urban blacks – forced by necessity to know a European tongue – and also increasingly useful as a common language among blacks of various tribal origins, thrown together in the townships on the fringes of every European city, where they were required by law to live. From the beginning, *Drum* devoted most of its space to issues and events of most interest to non-white South Africans: the emergence of a succession of independent black nations throughout Africa; the mushrooming enforced relocation of non-whites in both rural and urban areas; the impact of more stringent pass laws, now extending to women for the first time; instances of brutality in the enforcement of these policies, and instances of resistance and protest; urban crime; local sports, chiefly boxing and soccer; international recognition of black African statesmen and entertainers. *Drum*'s insistence on dealing with sensitive and political issues resulted in governmental banning of a number of its monthly volumes; once banned, it became a crime to sell or possess the issue in question, and even today these cannot be found in South Africa's public and copyright libraries.

Much space was given to news from the United States, particularly anything involving American blacks. Virtually every issue had an article on a famous jazz musician or some other black entertainer. The succession of black heavyweight boxing champions was given full coverage, as were the success of black American track and field athletes in the several Olympic Games of the era. Race riots were headlined; Daddy Grace and other evangelists were the subjects of articles, as were many black American political figures. *Drum* was liberally sprinkled with advertisements, for pain remedies, clothing, hats, tea, portable radios, beauty creams, food, soap, correspondence courses, deodorants. These were often American products, and often invoked American blacks in their sales pitch. Typical is a large pictorial advertisement for Vaseline products in several issues in 1958: a certain Mrs Brown stands outside her suburban New York home, tastefully dressed, posed in front of her latest-model automobile; the caption reads: "The Brown family is successful, both in business and socially. They use Vaseline to keep skin smooth and soft."

Zonk had a similar format, though it tended to avoid criticism of governmental policies, and was founded even earlier, in 1949. *Hi-Note!*, published monthly between 1954 and 1957, tended to give more coverage to matters involving the Indian and colored communities.

Each of these three monthlies devoted considerable space to popular culture, indigenous and international. In addition to frequent feature articles, there were advertisements for recently released phonograph discs, playback equipment, and radios. Each of the three ran a monthly column of reviews of selected new discs, those considered by the staff to be of greatest interest to their readers. These advertisements and reviews afford one method of tracing the specific discs bought and listened to by urban non-whites in the 1950s.

Drum's "Gramo-Go-Round" column for July 1955, written by "Hot Toddy" (Todd Matshikiza, a classically trained pianist and composer who also played and wrote jazz), reviews three discs by the Crew Cuts distributed for Mercury Records by Trutone Africa Ltd.

Mercury 305 "Crazy 'bout Ya Baby"/"Angela Mia"
Mercury 311 "Oop Shoop"/"Do Me Good Baby"
Mercury 1476 "Sh-Boom"/"Do Me Good Baby"

Matshikiza adopts what he took to be appropriate slang in writing about these American products: "Boys, it's real 'jiving' when you get to Mercury Records. American singers and bands: Just dig these numbers. The CREW CUTS – one of America's all-time high groups." He gives no indication that this is a white group, or that several of the songs are covers of releases by black performers; nor does he use the term "rock 'n' roll."

This latter term, in South Africa as elsewhere, was first used in the press in connection with the music of Bill Haley. "Rock Around the Clock" was marketed for non-whites in the spring of 1956, as Decca FM 6290 (78 rpm), with "Thirteen Women" on the flip side. All three monthlies mentioned above reviewed it prominently. Gideon Jay, in his "Pick of the Discs" column in *Zonk* (April 1956), reports that this music "comes right from the Race catalogue and has created a lot of excitement. . . . [Haley] sounds remarkably like Johnny Ray (in rock 'n' roll mood). The weak spots in the disc are the electric guitar solos and the very mundane ending." Matshikiza begins his review in *Drum* (July 1956) with: "You've probably got interested in the new

American craze the 'Rock' which pounds with rhythms even more exciting than the grooviest jive tempos." The anonymous reviewer in *Hi-Note!*, is even more enthusiastic: "Full of the four 'V's' – Vim, Vigour, Vitality and Vodecall,[5] this is one you can play around the clock. It's got all the ingredients to set the joint-a-jump, and it really does. The Rhythm is good – Rock Rhythm. The Tempo is solid – Rock solid and it's a sender."

In November of that year (1956), *Zonk* ran a cover story on rock 'n' roll, with photographs of young black South African "Rock 'n' Rolsters" in action. Subheads announce that "Rock 'n' roll has struck like the dreaded plague" and "*Zonk's* ace music critic Gideon Jay tells you about the music that is causing rioting and bloodshed." The article emphasises the most sensational press reporting of rock 'n' roll performances in America and Britain, speaks of "screaming rock 'n' roll crimes," and concludes that the problem is not so much with the music itself as with the "sexy and lush lyrics – that is where the degeneracy or delinquent trend creeps in."

There is other evidence of various sorts in the black press that rock 'n' roll was accepted by some of the non-white population. *Drum* ran an advertisement for Jive Beauty Cream throughout much of 1958, with a photograph of two black teenagers dancing, dressed in sweaters, skirts, and white bobby socks, with a caption reading "It's as new as rock 'n' roll." Casey Motsisi devoted his monthly "On the Beat" column in *Drum* for May of 1958 to an account of a midnight party in Western Native Township:

> This here midnite party is participating. There's enough booze to keep Mr Kruschev blotto for weeks on end. I go to the back of the house, where there's a tent pitched for "rockagers" who now and again want to shake a leg. . . . A busty young girl in jeans slides a disc on the battered gramophone, and some rockagers begin to dance while the Elvis of Presley accuses each and everyone of being "Nothing but a Hound Dog."

Wilfred Dhlamini wrote to *Zonk* from Durban (June 1963) to complain of the absence of recording studios in that town, adding "I have 65 copies of Elvis Presley's songs and other stars." An account of a dance for colored teenagers held in Johannesburg at Springbok Hall in *Drum* (October 1959) reports: "The music was loud, a lot of it rock 'n' roll. Some of the fellows had side-whiskers, fancy haircuts, trying to look tough, casual, just like those Beat Generation heroes over in the States."

[5] Despite repeated attempts, I was unable to find the meaning of "vodecall."

Through 1957, *Zonk*, *Drum*, and *Hi-Note!* continued to carry reviews of newly released discs advertised as rock 'n' roll music. A sampling of these: Elvis Presley, "Blue Suede Shoes"/"My Baby Left Me" (RCA 71051-2); Pat Boone, "Tutti Frutti"/"Long Tall Sally" (Dot D 163); Bill Haley, "The Saints' Rock and Roll"/"R.O.C.K." (Decca FM 6365); Jim Lowe, "The Green Door"/"The Little Man in Chinatown" (Dot D 180).

Though Todd Matshikiza reported in his review of "Rock Around the Clock" (July 1956) that "nobody has done the rock around here yet," within a matter of months various non-white South Africans were emulating this music. Many new releases by local performers were identified, in advertisements or reviews, as being examples of indigenous rock 'n' roll. For instance, the Georgetown Boys released a disc in early 1957 featuring "Masihambe," which was described by a writer in *Zonk* (September 1957) as a "rock 'n' roll Zulu number. They rock with the rhythm of this song." HMV JP 2075, recorded the same year by Elijah's Rhythm Rockers, was advertised as a "rocker." The show "Township Rock" played at Johannesburg's City Hall on 7–9 May 1958, featuring such pieces as "Woodpecker's Rock" by the Woody Woodpeckers and "P.J. Rock" by the Jazz Dazzlers. Slightly later examples of this "African rock 'n' roll" are "Rock by Boogie" (HMV JP 693) and "Red River Rock" (HMV JP 669) by the Bogard Brothers, G. Mabitsela's "Tzaneen Rock" (Drum DR 170), and Rupert Bopape's "Phatha-Phatha Rock" performed by the Killingstone Stars (EMI CEA 5451). These are all pieces in fast 12-bar blues form, or some variation on it, to guitar (often electric), percussion and sometimes horn accompaniment; texts usually consist of English phrases pieced together from rock 'n' roll classics; guitar or saxophone breaks in instrumental choruses are punctuated by ritual shouts of "Go, man, go!"

While most references to rock 'n' roll in the black press suggest an urban audience with some degree of formal education, it would be a mistake to rule out the likelihood that this music was also heard in rural areas. Battery-operated radios and phonograph playback equipment were steadily becoming less expensive in the 1950s; the system of migrant and contract labor so strongly nourished by the government resulted in a continual and large flow of population between urban and rural sectors. Hugh Tracey, in the course of making field recordings for the International Library of African Music in the 1950s, often had occasion to remark on the almost instantaneous dissemination throughout southern Africa of musical styles apparently originating in urban centers. A first nationwide survey by the SABC of "Bantu Radio Listening" patterns, in 1962, revealed that more that 50 per cent of the black population of South Africa had access to a radio; by 1974, this percentage had risen to 97.7.[6] "Tzaneen rock," mentioned above, was the work of a musician from a small town in the far northeastern corner of the Transvaal.

Despite all this, it appears that most non-whites turned away from rock 'n' roll in 1958 and afterwards, at just the time its popularity was peaking and solidifying among white South Africans.

The black press rarely reviewed rock 'n' roll discs after 1957, and then mostly to make disparaging comments. A writer in *Drum* for June 1959 remarked of a newly released disc by the Kirby Stone Four (CBS CC 290): "Big beat, nonsense lyrics and just a mixture of disorganised sounds . . . doesn't make much of anything. It's good if you don't have to listen to it. Just wiggle to it, friend, because there ain't much more you could do." Even Bill Haley fell from favor; Blake Modisane wrote in *Drum* (September 1958) of a new release by the Comets: "Come off it, Bill Haley. Nothing's as bad as rock 'n' roll when it's bad. It's nonsense; just too bad to even annoy."

Encounters with live rock 'n' roll were no more positive. Tommy Steele's manager had the idea of replacing the cancelled Pretoria date with two shows in Johannesburg for non-white audiences, on 25 March (1958), no doubt partly to spite Steele's Afrikaner detractors. These took place at the Bantu Men's Social Club, and even though it was announced that some 1800 people turned out, the "best behaved audience so far" (*Star*, 25 March 1958), later John Bolon, a board member of the Union of South African Artists, told a different story: the afternoon concert played to a virtually empty hall, the second to an audience filling no more than half the auditorium. Those attending were at best "sympathetic" and most of them found that "Mr Steele's manners, his comments . . . did not endear him to us" (*Star*, 3 May 1958).

At first glance, this disinterest in rock 'n' roll seems inexplicable. Ever since black South Africans began moving into the contemporary urban world in the late nineteenth century, they had been engaged in a struggle to forge a new collective identity which would retain important elements of their own heritage, while at the same time cutting across tribal barriers and also incorporating aspects of the contemporary European world – in the face of an unsympathetic and mostly hostile white ruling class. As Coplan explains in his discussion

[6] Market Research Africa Ltd., *A Study of Bantu Radio Listening* (Johannesburg, 1974).

of why jazz took deeper roots in South Africa than in western and central Africa, the areas which supplied the Americas with most of their black slaves, there have been deep historical parallels:

(1) Similarities in the socio-historical experience of black Americans and South Africans, including rapid urbanisation and industrialisation, and racial oppression;

(2) similarities in the kinds of musical resources available to both peoples in their urban areas, and in basic African principles of composition and performance;

(3) the value of black American models for black South African urban cultural adaptation, identity, and resistance.[7]

These factors help explain the popularity among black South Africans of an entire historical spectrum of musical styles drawing in one way or another on black American music and culture: minstrel music; ragtime; syncopated dance music of the 1910s; early jazz; Big Band jazz; and later the twist, soul, and disco. But rock 'n' roll did not join this constellation.

There seem to be three important reasons for this. First, as mentioned above, all early rock 'n' roll discs released in South Africa were by white performers, and all visiting musicians were white (and mostly British). I have found no evidence that discs by Chuck Berry, Little Richard, Fats Domino, the Platters, or any other black performers of the early rock 'n' roll era were available in South Africa in the 1950s; nor are these people mentioned in the press, white or black. With no way of knowing the role played by black musicians in the early history of rock 'n' roll, and no available samples of their music, non-white South Africans apparently took this music to be an exclusively white product – at least as a social phenomenon. By contrast, five years later when the twist came to South Africa, it was identified from the beginning with Chubby Checker and quickly became immensely popular among blacks.

Non-white journalists did make a musical connection between rock 'n' roll and jazz, however. Gideon Jay's article in *Zonk* (November 1956) claims that rock 'n' roll

is really not new at all – it is the same music, with the same beat, used as far back as the early 1930s when, carried away by enthusiasm, the atmosphere or what have you, listeners egged the musicians on "to get hot," and the boys, particularly those in the rhythm section, "gave out" with a heavy "four-in-a-bar," and an

---

[7] D. Copland, "The urbanisation of African music: some theoretical observations," *Popular Music* 2 (1982), pp. 122–3.

accented "off beat." This was the basic rhythm of what you remember as "hot music" and it's the basic rhythm of today's rock 'n' roll.

An article in *Drum* the following year (March 1957), reporting on Lionel Hampton's recent tour of England, says that "ROCK AND ROLLERS caused a near riot when they were driven into a frenzy by his pulsating music" and the remainder of the article discusses his music in the context of that of Count Basie and Duke Ellington, making no distinction between jazz and rock 'n' roll. Later Ellington himself was quoted in *Drum* (July 1968) as saying: "Rock 'n' roll is the most raucous form of jazz, beyond a doubt; it maintains a link with the folk origins, and I believe that no other form of jazz has ever been accepted so enthusiastically by so many."

Despite this accurate recognition of the musical roots of rock 'n' roll, non-whites in South Africa had no choice but to view it as a product of white society, and the controversies it generated (young versus old, Britisher versus Afrikaner) were not of primary concern to non-Europeans.

The second reason for non-white rejection of rock 'n' roll is related to the above. Enthusiasm for jazz was peaking in the 1950s and early 60s. Indigenous black jazz performance had its beginnings in the early 1930s, with the Merry Blackbirds Dance Orchestra, the Rhythm Boys, and the Jazz Maniacs. By the 1940s and 50s, large and small jazz ensembles proliferated not only in Johannesburg and other large cities, but also in towns all over South Africa. For instance Grahamstown, a provincial town in the Eastern Cape with a non-white population of perhaps 20,000, had at least three jazz groups in the 1950s, those led by Jury Mpelo, Alfred Tafeni, and Russell Planga.[8]

The success of Alfred Herbert's shows at the Windmill Theatre in Johannesburg in 1954, bringing black jazz performers to white audiences, prompted a succession of variety stage productions of "African Jazz" and then "Township Jazz," chiefly for whites but with some shows scheduled for non-white audiences. The jazz musical *King Kong*, with an all-black cast and music by Todd Matshikiza, opened in Johannesburg in 1959, toured the country, then was taken to London for a series of successful and highly publicized performances. The first large-scale jazz festival held in South Africa took place in the City Hall of Johannesburg in 1961, followed by a National Jazz Festival in Soweto's Moroka-Jabavu

---

[8] H. Tracey, *The Sounds of Africa Series* (Roodepoort, n.d.), disc 27.

Stadium in 1962 and an even larger one the following year in Orlando Stadium in Soweto, attracting an audience of some 20,000 people. Cape Town developed an active jazz scene, often involving colored musicians, sometimes with multi-racial audiences. As a result of both the intense activity in jazz within the non-white community and the increasing attention given this music in the press, a number of non-white South African jazz musicians – Dollar Brand, Hugh Masekela, Miriam Makeba, Dolly Rathebe among them – began receiving international attention, and performing abroad.

During this time, which coincided with the birth and early history of rock 'n' roll elsewhere, the black press devoted a tremendous amount of coverage to jazz. *Drum* ran a six-part feature on Louis Armstrong in 1956; Todd Matshikiza published a three-part history of "African jazz" in *Drum* in 1957: "Stars of jazz" in June, "Jazz comes to Joburg" in July, "Where's jazz going now?" in August; *Zonk* (October 1963) carried a lengthy article on "Thelonius Monk, jazz composer and pianist" by Martin Williams, reprinted from the "Saturday Review." Most of the phonograph discs reviewed were of "African Jazz" and such American performers as Art Tatum, Ella Fitzgerald, Lionel Hampton, Nat King Cole, Sonny Rollins, the Mills Brothers, John Lewis, and Harry Belafonte.

It appears that, with jazz, black South Africans already had a thriving contemporary music, ideologically proper because its origins were so clearly in black American culture and because it had taken such deep root in non-white Africa. It had been embraced by the most influential writers of the black press; Todd Matshikiza wrote in *Drum* (August 1957): "Our baby, African Jazz, will grow bigger, better, stronger and more jazzlingest than any thing under the sun." Many black intellectuals and political leaders were known to be jazz fans; many jazz musicians were outspoken critics of the policies of the Nationalist Party, and some became leaders of the resistance – Matshikiza, Miriam Makeba, Hugh Masekela, and Dollar Brand eventually became outspoken political exiles; Alcock "Sik-wenene" Gwentshe joined the African National Congress. Jazz was thus linked with rising tides of black nationalism and consciousness, while rock 'n' roll was perceived as a purely white product manipulated by white entrepreneurs for maximum profit from white consumers.

A third reason for the rejection of rock 'n' roll by most black South Africans will be mentioned only briefly here since it is the subject of an extended study which I plan to publish in the near future. At just the time rock 'n' roll was emerging in the United States and beginning to form the most important musical foundation for several decades of popular music in America and much of Europe, black musicians in southern Africa were forging an indigenous urban popular style which drew important elements from their own traditional music. This became the historical foundation for a southern African dialect of the "African pop" which is so pervasive in contemporary African society, and which is beginning to attract attention in Europe and America precisely because of the fundamental and refreshing differences between it and the mainstream pop/rock of the West. "Jive" is the most widely accepted generic term for this music, though a large and bewildering array of labels have been used for various stages of its development ("kwela," for instance) and for the several dances for which it has been used ("tsaba-tsaba," "bump jive," and a host of others). These styles show common features, over a time span extending for more than thirty years. Structures are built on repetition of a short harmonic cycle of four, eight, or twelve units – as is the case with most traditional music of the region (bow songs, choral pieces, music for mbira). Performance is by a small vocal group usually pitting a lead singer against between two and four other voices, accompanied by a small instrumental ensemble, or by instruments alone. These instruments are all of Western origin, brought to South Africa by one or another of the European groups who settled there and whose music fascinated many blacks, but a lot of them (guitar, concertina, saxophone) had been played by blacks for enough generations to be regarded as "traditional" to their culture and to develop non-European playing styles. Vocal texts are in Zulu, Sotho, Swazi, Tswana, or other African languages of the area.

Jive is dance music, the music of black bars and dance halls. It developed at grass-roots level, at first ignored and sometimes ridiculed by the black press, jazz musicians, and black educators and political leaders. As Steve Montjane wrote in *Bona* (June 1967), "our musical snobs, highbrows, would pride themselves on never playing marabi, tshaba-tshaba, gumba-gumba or mbhaqanga." Jazz festivals of the 1960s would sometimes include a special competition for "Mbaqanga" groups, but the press would not mention the performers; record companies would run advertisements for "jive" records in the black press, but these would rarely be reviewed by staff writers. Commercial discs appeared in profusion, since this music was so inexpensive to produce and enjoyed steady if not spectacular sales with little or no promotion: musicians would be brought into a recording studio for one or two takes of each piece under the nominal supervision of a black producer, paid for the session (with no royalties), and the disc would come out almost immediately. White executives and producers paid little attention to jive, at least in its first decades, and as a result interfered less with its style and substance than they did with other music recorded by blacks.

Jive was essentially apolitical. Since whites never listened to it, and were scarcely aware of its existence, it played no part in the Afrikaner–British struggle for political control of South Africa. It likewise had no appeal to the Indian and colored populations. Among blacks, it was not seen as allied to any particular type of political opinion; it enjoyed equal popularity in urban and rural areas, and audiences for specific performers were divided much more along tribal than socio-economic lines. The Nationalist Party used jive for its own purposes, however. When the SABC began large-scale development of the various "vernacular services" in the 1960s and 70s by establishing round-the-clock programming in each of the important African languages of South Africa, as part of the strategy of "Separate Development," considerable air-time was devoted to jive. It was appropriate music for this purpose: its popularity attracted listeners to Radio Bantu rather than some other program; its lyrics were in an African language, rather than English; its performers and audiences were not thought to be allied with troublesome movements; its texts were politically neutral, often dealing with traditional tribal life.

In many ways it was the South African equivalent of rock 'n' roll. By the 1960s its most common instrumentation consisted of an amplified lead guitar supported by an acoustic rhythm guitar, and a rhythm section of electric bass and a Western drum set, often augmented by one or more saxophones and a concertina. This combination, playing in a fast driving rhythm, created a sound superficially similar to that of early American rock 'n' roll. And jive occupied a social position similar to that of rock 'n' roll in its earliest stages; as Bill Haley once remarked of the latter, nobody liked it but the people.

In brief summary, rock 'n' roll was perceived in South Africa as a white music, and to some extent became part of this ideological struggle between the Nationalist Party and its English-speaking foes. Non-whites largely rejected it for this reason, and blacks in particular had little interest in it because of the contemporary popularity of jazz and jive, both of which were seen as having much more to do with black culture. Perhaps black South Africans would have responded enthusiastically to Chuck Berry and Little Richard, musically and as cultural heroes, but there was no opportunity for them to do so in that strange society.

9

AFRICAN-AMERICAN MUSIC, SOUTH AFRICA, AND APARTHEID

More precipitously than any other area of the globe, Africa was moving into the postmodern world in the 1970s and 80s. One of the cornerstones of the modern era, colonialism, had collapsed, and attempts by emergent African nation-states to emulate the modernist socio-political systems of capitalism and socialism/Communism were proving to be problematic. Everything was in flux.

It was just at this time that many popular-music scholars were embracing the Marxist-grounded, theoretical discourse that was dominating European intellectual life. Though I found this movement to be intellectually stimulating, I felt distanced from much of the resultant literature, particularly when it focused narrowly on European class struggle; it seemed to have little relevance to the battles taking place in southern Africa over the meaning of popular music.

By the time I returned to Africa in the late summer of 1984, for a stay of nine months, my work had focused on three separate but interlocking topics: social and musical relations between black Americans and the black population of South Africa; the history of "jive," a contemporary popular genre in southern Africa; and the role of music in the complex and apparently highly successful media strategy of the minority white government.

Expanding on the previous article, this monograph develops the first of these issues at length, examining the musical life of black South Africans since the middle of the nineteenth century in the context of its interaction with the culture and music of black Americans. Rather than being an ethnomusicological study of a culture from the inside, from the perspective of its own language, history, and traditions, it deals instead with foreign elements introduced into the culture and the ways in which these elements were received, altered, rejected, and assimilated.

This monograph was developed from several lectures given at Brooklyn College and the City University of New York Research and Graduate Center in the fall of 1986.

* * *

I

Paul Simon's *Graceland*, a record album released in the late summer of 1986,[1] is shot through with the rhythms and instrumental sounds of South Africa's black contemporary popular music. Simon recorded many of the preliminary tracks in Johannesburg in the summer of 1985, with local musicians, then arranged for some of them to come to the United States for the final stages of recording and mixing, and to join him in live and televised promotional performances. Even though the sound of South African jive, or Mbaqanga, was exotic for most Americans, the album quickly sold a million copies, then two million; several individual songs received a great deal of air play and placed high on *Billboard*'s "Hot 100" singles charts during the fall and winter of 1986–7; and Simon's "Graceland Tour," co-featuring some of the performers on the album as well as several expatriate South African musicians, became his most successful live appearance since his split with Art Garfunkel.

Graceland was produced at a time when the attention of the United States was very much focused on South Africa. While Simon was recording in that country, American television viewers were treated to almost nightly sequences of protests and demonstrations against the racial policies of the white minority government, brutal police and army retaliation, and intensely passionate and militant funerals for the victims. From a distance, it appeared that the country was moving towards all-out racial warfare. Demonstrations outside the South African Embassy in Washington led to daily arrests, often of public figures; students around the country attempted to persuade their schools to divest from companies doing business in South Africa; debates over the official American policy of "constructive engagement" with the South African government occupied the press and the Congress. Shortly after Simon's return to America, South Africa took even harsher steps to contain spreading unrest: a state of emergency was imposed on the most troubled areas, empowering

---

[1] Paul Simon, *Graceland* (Warner Brothers 25447; rel. 1986).

security forces to detain known or suspected political activists without charge; the press was prohibited from witnessing or reporting most aspects of the continuing turmoil; when accounts of the beating and torture of detainees became too persistent to be ignored or doubted, the government simply took steps to shield members of the security forces from prosecution for such acts. At least several thousand blacks were killed by security forces, and tens of thousands of people of all races were held in detention. By the time *Graceland* was released, the South African government had extended the state of emergency to the entire country, the US Congress was in the process of imposing economic and political sanctions, more and more educational and civil institutions were selling their stock in countries doing business in South Africa, and many American companies were closing their operations there.

Graceland was released against this backdrop, and surely the intense interest of so many Americans in anything having to do with South Africa helped its sales. The album itself created controversy. Simon was accused of violating a UNESCO boycott on performance in South Africa; the texts of his songs took no note of the struggle within the country, and Simon adamantly maintained a politically neutral stance; the South African government was delighted with Simon's "constructive engagement" with the local recording industry and apolitical elements of the black population, and songs from *Graceland* were played constantly on the state-controlled South African Broadcasting Corporation (SABC).

Simon's political insensitivity aside,[2] *Graceland* represents a historic closing of a circle. For more than a century American popular music, especially those genres derived from Afro-American styles, was imported into South Africa, influencing the music of that country. Paul Simon's successful incorporation of black South African musical styles into his own music represents one of the first important reversals of this flow.

In what follows I will address the questions of why American popular music has been so enthusiastically received in black South Africa, what cultural and political factors are involved in this history, and why the pendulum is beginning to swing in the other direction at just this moment.

For reasons to be laid out below, it seems best to deal with Afro-American/black South African relations in two stages, the first

---

[2] For the most comprehensive discussion of this issue, see Robert Christgau, "South African romance," *Village Voice*, 23 September 1986, pp. 71–3, 84.

extending from the middle of the nineteenth century to 1948, the second from 1948 to the present.

Minstrel songs and dances were the first music connected in any way with the American black to reach South Africa. Dale Cockrell has found evidence of a local minstrel troupe in Durban as early as 1858, and the American Christy Minstrels visited the city in 1865.[3] David Coplan, in his seminal study of the popular music of black South Africa, has summarized what is known about minstrelsy in that country in the middle decades of the last century:

> The publication of a number of minstrel songs, including Thomas Rice's classic, "Jim Crow," by the Cape Town weekly *Die Versammelar* helped to popularise them in the Colony. In 1848, a troupe called Joe Brown's Band of Brothers became . . . "the first band of vocalists who gave South Africa a taste for nigger part singing." In the same year, white South Africans who had recently seen performances in London of the "refined" American company, the Ethiopian Serenaders, began a local company of the same name. In 1862, the white performers of the Harvey-Christy Minstrels, who combined lively dancing and earthy humour with concert pieces and sentimental ballads, toured South Africa to such acclaim that minstrelsy became a permanent part of the country's entertainment for the rest of the century.[4]

Veit Erlmann has amplified the latter statement:

> In the next three decades [after 1862], blackface minstrel shows became the dominant form of popular white musical and theatrical entertainment in South Africa, perhaps only second in popularity to the public lecture and the circus. Amateur minstrel troupes mushroomed in the most remote provincial towns, and in the major centers of English culture like Kimberley, Durban, and Cape Town audiences were often able to choose between two minstrel entertainments on the same night. British regiments soon had their own permanent minstrel troupes that enjoyed high patronage from the colonial ruling elite.[5]

This repertory was at best one step removed from the music of black Americans (white Americans composing and performing pieces supposedly reflective of black music and culture) and at worst four steps away (white South Africans imitating white Britons imitating

---

[3] Dale Cockrell, "Of gospel hymns, minstrel shows, and jubilee singers: toward some black South African musics," *American Music* 5/4 (Winter 1987), pp. 417–32.

[4] David B. Coplan, *In Township Tonight! South Africa's Black City Music and Theatre* (Johannesburg, 1985), p. 38.

[5] Veit Erlmann, "A feeling of prejudice: Orpheus M. McAdoo and the Virginia Jubilee Singers in South Africa, 1890–1898," *Journal of South African Studies* 14/3 (1987), pp. 1–35.

the white American perception of blacks). One would not expect to learn anything about Afro-American music from studying white minstrelsy in South Africa, of course; but one can begin to see the image of black America projected through the medium of the minstrel show to white South Africans, and also to blacks, who were sometimes allowed to sit or stand in segregated areas during performances of minstrel shows for white audiences.

In the last decade of the century, South Africans had the opportunity to see and hear black American performers for the first time. Orpheus M. McAdoo, born of slave parents in Greensboro, North Carolina, landed in Cape Town in June 1890 with his Virginia Jubilee Singers and performed in various parts of the country for the next two years, for both white and black audiences, before sailing to Australia. The company returned to South Africa in 1895 for a further three years, though their performances were interrupted for some months in 1897 when McAdoo travelled to New York to recruit additional cast members.[6]

Even before the arrival of McAdoo's company, black South Africans had begun to imitate American minstrel music with as much enthusiasm as whites. Little specific information has been retrieved, since such matters were of no interest to the white population and therefore did not find their way into the press, though the *Natal Mercury* of 28 December 1880 did mention performance by the Kafir Christy Minstrels, a "troupe of eight genuine natives, bones and all, who really get through their songs very well."[7] The prolonged presence of McAdoo's troupe in the country spurred even more minstrel activity among blacks. Will P. Thompson left the Virginia Jubilee Singers to form groups of his own with African performers, including the Diamond Minstrels (in Kimberley) and the Balmoral Amateur Minstrels.[8] The "colored" population of Cape Town organized social clubs which paraded and competed against one another during Carnival season, dressed in costumes imitative of traditional minstrel garb, carrying American flags, singing pieces – to the accompaniment of banjos, among other instruments – based on various types of minstrel songs.[9] Minstrel songs were performed at school and community concerts; in the

---

[6] Erlmann's landmark article cited in note 5, gives a detailed account and analysis of this historic episode.   [7] Quoted in Erlmann, "A feeling of prejudice," p. 9.
[8] Coplan, *In Township Tonight!*, p. 41.
[9] These "Coon Carnivals" in time became great tourist attractions in Cape Town, for whites and blacks alike, and eventually toured in other parts of South Africa and even Europe. They continued until 1986, when the colored community of Cape Town decided not to stage a Carnival, as a protest against increasingly repressive actions by the government.

early twentieth century a few members of the black elite were able to purchase phonographs and thus hear recordings of minstrel music, mostly by English performers. By the first and second decades of the present century there were many black minstrel companies, often formed while their members were together in mission schools, performing in black townships throughout South Africa; among those active in Natal were the Brave Natalian Coons, the Western Minstrels (based at Adams Mission), the Highland Coons, and the Inanda Native Singers.[10] When commercial recordings by black performers began to be made in the 1920s and 30s, first by musicians taken to London and then in Johannesburg, minstrel companies supplied a substantial amount of the repertory.

The penetration of American minstrel music into black South Africa can be seen as progressing in stages:

(1) *Importation.* The music was brought into the country by foreign performers, or by local white entertainers who had heard it while abroad; later, phonograph discs were imported from abroad.

(2) *Imitation.* Black South African musicians performed minstrel songs in the style in which they were done in the United States or Britain. Sometimes pieces from the American repertory were performed in English, as when James Bland's "Oh! Dem Golden Slippers" was sung on a program in Kimberley in 1892[11] or when the Inanda Native Singers performed Stephen Foster's "Old Folks at Home" and C. A. White's "I'se Gwine Back to Dixie."[12] Sometimes American tunes were sung to African texts, or new melodies were fashioned in close imitation of American models. "Imali Yami," recorded by John Mavimbela and Company in the 1930s [Gallo Singer Bantu Records, GE 34], with a solo male voice singing to the accompaniment of a humming chorus, banjo, and harmonica, has a tune indistinguishable from nineteenth-century American popular stage melodies in melodic contour and phraseology.

(3) *Assimilation.* Stylistic features of American minstrel songs were absorbed into black South African performance traditions. Thus acculturation had taken place, a repertory had been created drawing on both indigenous and foreign elements, and new genres appeared, distinct from those found elsewhere. In order to deal with this third stage, it is necessary to have some understanding of the traditional, pre-colonization music of South Africa.

Though the region now defined by the political boundaries of the Republic of South Africa is home to a complex network of different

---

[10] See Veit Erlmann, "African popular music in Durban, 1913–1939" (unpublished), p. 8. For information on black minstrel activity of the 1920s, see Coplan, *In Township Tonight!*, pp. 123–4.

[11] Coplan, *In Township Tonight!*, p. 41.   [12] Erlmann, "African popular music," p. 9.

ethnic groups,[13] and the present white minority government has labelled and attempted to isolate a dozen or so of these for its own political purposes, all blacks in the area speak some type of Bantu language,[14] and in fact contemporary scholarship suggests a division into only two large language groups: the Nguni, subdivided into Zulu, Xhosa, and Swazi; and the Sotho, with a much larger number of sub-groups, some – such as the Venda and Tsonga – related to ethnic groups in the neighboring countries of Zimbabwe and Mozambique.[15] There is considerable traditional cultural consistency among all these peoples, who belong to pastoral and agricultural societies, with cattle at the core of their political, economic, and social structures.

Traditional music of this part of the continent differs in some ways from that of the rest of sub-Sahara Africa. The dominant performance medium is the unaccompanied chorus, usually with one or more solo voices pitted against a larger group in call-and-response patterns. This music functions in a ritual or ceremonial context, as part of communal celebration of individual rites of passage or of important points along the seasonal and agricultural cycles. But it makes little sense to impose a Western distinction between ceremonial and recreational function on these celebrations, during which dancing, singing, and beer-drinking serve as much to bring pleasure to the participants as to ritualize the occasion. At weddings, for instance, members of the two families may engage in dancing and singing competitions, in a way that strikes the Western observer as more entertainment than ritual.[16]

There is also solo song, accompanied by an ostinato-playing instrument such as the musical bow, or in the northeast some form of the *mbira*; this genre often functions to preserve the history and lineage of a clan or other social group, or as purely personal expression. There is no tradition of melodic instrumental music, with the exception of flute music played by herd boys; reed-pipe ensembles, found in some areas, assign notes of the "melody" to different instruments, as in European bell ringing. Amazingly, for Africa, there is no tradition of drumming. Choral music may be

---

[13] I will avoid use of the term "tribe," which – in addition to being virtually useless ethnographically – has too often been used in a pejorative sense.

[14] The Khoikhoi ("Hottentot") and San ("Bushmen") peoples are exceptions, with their non-Bantu "click" languages; but these languages, like the people who speak them, have virtually disappeared from modern South Africa.

[15] See Monica Wilson and Leonard Thompson, eds., *A History of South Africa to 1870* (Cape Town and Johannesburg, 1985), pp. 75–186, for a discussion of this issue.

[16] Peter Larlham, *Black Theater, Dance, and Ritual in South Africa* (Ann Arbor, 1985), particularly pp. 1–59.

accompanied by hand clapping, foot stomping, or the rattling of shells attached to the legs of the performers, but drums came to this region only with European military and dance music.

The two most important stylistic features of traditional music in South Africa might be taken as metaphors of general cultural patterns. First, both vocal and instrumental pieces unfold over brief, constantly reiterated structures: in choral music these take the form of recurring vertical combinations of notes, or "chords"; in instrumental music, and instrumental accompaniment to vocal music, one hears an insistently repeated melodic rhythmic ostinato. Life in sub-Sahara Africa is perceived as progressing cyclically – through seasons, agricultural phases, the human rites of passage. Music also moves cyclically, always turning back on itself at the most basic structural level, unlike Western music, which marches inexorably along a linear, goal-oriented path in its progress towards an inevitable denouement.

Secondly, traditional music is built horizontally of different layers of sound, each contributing to the whole while maintaining some degree of individuality. As Andrew Tracey has put it, "the independence of the various parts in a piece of [African] music, unified by the recurring cycle, can be taken as [a] metaphor for the traditional individuality of personality and behaviour allowed and even expected within the bounds of the tightly-structured social patterns of African life."[17]

The assimilation or "Africanization" of minstrel music involved the absorption of stylistic elements from the American repertory into pieces retaining the two general stylistic elements just described. Early commercial phonograph discs allow us to hear this process taking place. "Into Yami," as performed by the Willie Gumede Banjo Band (Gallotone Singer GE 948), sounds superficially like an American minstrel piece, with one banjo "picking" the tune accompanied by several strummed banjos and a bones player. Listening a bit more closely, however, one can hear that the entire piece is built over reiteration of the harmonic pattern I–IV–V–V; that the "melody" could more accurately be described as repeated and varied melodic patterning; and that the three contrapuntal threads (melody, strummed accompaniment, rhythm) persistently maintain their own individuality, with no thematic reference to the other parts. A more complex example is "Ingqaqa – Mazinyo We'Mkwenyana," recorded by Kuzwayo's Zulu Dance Band (HMV JP 19). Two lead instruments, concertina and banjo, play clearly differentiated melodic patterns,

---

[17] Personal communication, 31 May 1984.

sometimes consecutively and sometimes simultaneously; a guitar gives out a constantly repeated line which functions both as a bass part and a rhythmic accompaniment; and a drummer, playing a rudimentary trap set, completes the ensemble – all this taking place over an unchanging four-bar harmonic foundation. The piece is African, though the ancestry of some of its elements in American minstrel music is apparent enough.

Traces of the impact of minstrelsy on black South African styles persist to the present, for instance in music performed by small vocal groups of workers living in single-sex hostels, in Natal.[18] Ladysmith Black Mambazo, a contemporary *ingom 'ebusuku* group of eight to ten male singers which performed in the United States in 1986–7 following the release of Paul Simon's *Graceland*, gave American audiences a chance to see how much the stage movement of present-day groups can invoke the minstrel tradition.

The same scholarly techniques used to reconstruct the history of minstrel music in South Africa enable us to trace the same three stages of penetration of the other types of Afro-American music brought to South Africa before 1948: gospel songs, ragtime, spirituals, early syncopated dance music, early jazz, and swing. For each, documentary evidence tells us when it was imported, and under what circumstances; early recordings preserve examples of the stages of imitation and assimilation; contemporary performance practice informs us of the later stages of assimilation and the extent to which these styles persist to the present.

American vocal styles have a particularly rich history of penetration into black South Africa, which is hardly surprising in a culture so grounded in choral music itself. Cockrell has shown that an edition of Moody and Sankey's *Gospel Hymns* with texts translated into Zulu was published in Durban in 1876, that spirituals were sung in that city as early as 1889 (by a forty-voice white choir), and that McAdoo's Virginia Jubilee Singers included spirituals on their programs in 1890. He observes that gospel hymns "remain a staple of church congregations and choirs, school choirs, male quartet[s] . . . and such popular black South African recording groups as the King's Messengers Quartet" and that "by the early years of this century [the spiritual] had become a staple of the repertory of black choirs, both professional and amateur."[19] Erlmann has added more details: the title of the collection published by 1876 was *Hymns in Kafir*,

---

[18] For recorded examples of this repertory, see Veit Erlmann, ed., *Mbube Roots: Zulu Choral Music from South Africa* (Rounder Records 5025), and V. Erlmann and B. Mthethwa, eds., *Zulu Songs from South Africa* (Lyrichord LLST 7401).

[19] Cockrell, "Of gospel hymns," pp. 2–3, 21.

From Sacred Songs and Solos, By J. D. Sankey; by the early 1900s American gospel hymns were being printed in the tonic sol-fa notation used in black musical education; by 1908 the British Zonophone Company issued eight discs of Sankey and Moody hymns sung by a group of Swazi chiefs visiting England.[20] And after the first stages of penetration and imitation, indigenous choral genres combining traditional styles with American elements proliferated in the twentieth century.

Taking as another example a more recent genre, vocal swing, one sees the same processes at work. Advertisements and reviews in newspapers, information from record companies, inventories of personal and institutional collections of phonograph discs, and reminiscences by persons now in their fifties and sixties all inform us that recordings by black American vocal groups, usually trios or quartets accompanied by a rhythm section, were *imported* and widely sold in South Africa from the late 1930s into the 50s. One can even identify the Mills Brothers and the Ink Spots as the most popular of these. Documentary and recorded evidence tells us that black groups in Johannesburg and elsewhere began *imitating* this style soon after it was imported. One of the first, and surely the most successful, was the Manhattan Brothers, formed in the mid-1930s while the four of them – Ronnie Sehume, Joseph Kulwane Mogotsi, Rufus Koza, Dambuza Mdledle – were classmates at the Pimville Government School.[21] They came to widespread public attention in the 1940s through live performances on the South African Broadcasting Corporation and at the Bantu Men's Social Club in Johannesburg, and with their numerous recordings for Gallo, the largest South African recording company. Many of their early recordings are "cover" versions, sung in one of the African languages, of pieces written by white Tin Pan Alley songwriters and recorded by black American groups: "Yes-Suh" by Andy Razaf and Saxie Dowell (Gallotone Singer Bantu Records GE 937); "U Mama" ("Mamma, I Wanna Make Rhythm") by Richard Byron, M. K. Jerome, and Walter Kent (Gallotone GE 938). But *assimilation* was taking place almost from the beginning. "Umlilo" (Gallotone GE 939) is apparently as derivative of vocal swing in general style as the other early repertory of the Manhattan Brothers, but unlike the American pieces just mentioned, which all share the ubiquitous AABA pattern of late Tin Pan Alley song, this piece progresses in eight-beat phrases built over a single insistent harmonic underpinning. A somewhat later piece by the Manhattan Brothers, "Unonkisa Kae" (Gallotone GB

[20] Erlmann, "African popular music," pp. 7, 8, 27.
[21] Yvonne Huskisson, *The Bantu Composers of Southern Africa* (Johannesburg, 1969), pp. 96–7.

1819; rel. 1953), has moved even further towards "Africanization": it unfolds over a four-bar harmonic ostinato (I–IV–V–I), and there are hints of call-and-response patterns among the voices.

Vocal swing proliferated in the 1950s, and a mere listing of the names of some commercially recorded groups not only gives a sense of the popularity of this genre but underlines the indebtedness to American models: the African Ink Spots, the Boogie Five, the Boogie Brothers, the African Brothers, the Gandy Brothers, the Bogard Brothers, the Crown Brothers, the Harari Swing Brothers, the King Cole Basies, the King Cole Boogies, the King Cole Porters, the Black Broadway Boys. Nor has this genre disappeared altogether today. The Beam Brothers, whose music is still available on such LPs as *Thuli Wami* (Gallo: Motella BL 58), perform in essentially the style of the 1950s, and the Soul Brothers and other popular vocal jive or Mbaqanga groups draw on elements of vocal swing, though their rhythmic and instrumental vocabulary is more contemporary.

With time and patience, more details of the importation, imitation, and assimilation of American music before 1948 will be teased out of the materials available to scholars. This was not a process taking place in a void, however, but part of a larger complex of relations between South Africa and the United States. It is this more general picture that must be studied if one is to understand why so much American music was brought into South Africa, and what role this music played at various stages of the black African struggle for cultural and political autonomy.

Historically, American relations with South Africa have been significantly different from those with other parts of the continent. No slaves were brought directly to the New World from the geographical area now encompassed by the Republic of South Africa. First contact came with the docking of American ships at Cape Town in the eighteenth century, to establish economic and political relations with the Dutch who had settled there, and later with the British who took control; but these first American visitors had virtually no contact with the indigenous population.

The first direct American involvement with black South Africans came in the 1830s, through the church. The American Board of Commissioners for Foreign Missions, based in London, sent six missionaries to the Zulu kingdom in the 1830s, and other American missionaries found their way to the Transvaal in the same decade.[22] The American Daniel Lindley served as pastor to both Zulus and

---

[22] Wilson and Thompson, *A History of South Africa*, p. 352.

Afrikaner Voortrekkers in the 1840s, and in 1853 the American Board established a first mission school in Zululand, Adams College, which was soon followed by another at Inanda. This was consonant with Governor Sir George Gray's policy in the Cape Colony of "civilization by mingling," an attempt to lessen friction between white and black by allowing religious groups to establish schools for blacks.[23] The process of Christianization at these missions and schools included, of course, the singing of hymns from the white Protestant nineteenth-century repertory.

Two important points must be stressed before we go on. First, until the 1890s, American relations with black South Africans involved only white persons from the United States, most of them connected with the church. Second, these Americans were not cast in the role of colonizers and exploiters, as were the Dutch and British who had forcibly occupied the land and, with military and economic power, subjugated the indigenous population, depriving black people of land ownership and political autonomy. Though subsequent scholarship would assign Christianity an important role in the process of colonization, through pacification of dispossessed populations, no one at the time entertained such a notion, and white missionaries and educators were seen by blacks as doers of good deeds.

The members of Orpheus McAdoo's minstrel troupe were among the first black Americans to have direct contact with black South Africans. In 1893 several local white entrepreneurs organized an "African Native Choir" among students attending mission schools in Kimberley and Lovedale. After performing in the United Kingdom and Canada, the group came to the United States; again, music was the initiator of early relations between African and American blacks. Stranded in the Midwest when funds ran out and their white manager abandoned them, members of the group were enrolled at Wilberforce and Lincoln universities, with the aid of the black African Methodist Episcopal Church (AME). Some earned degrees, and several played important roles in the formation of a new urbanized black elite when they returned to South Africa.[24] At about the same time, two Xhosa Methodist ministers, Mangena Mokone and James Dwane, became disaffected with the policies of the English church in South Africa and announced a new affiliation with the American AME. In 1898 Bishop H. M. Turner of the AME came to South Africa to strengthen ties between the American and African branches of the church, personally ordaining sixty-five local ministers

[23] Ibid., pp. 260 ff.
[24] For a discussion and interpretation of this episode, see Coplan, In Township Tonight!, pp. 41–2.

while in the country. The result of all this was the emergence of the South African AME as a "large, well-organized all-black church with transatlantic ties, . . . the church of the educated African townspeople, whose broadened horizons led them to a strong identification with the struggles of the American Negro."[25]

The AME established Wilberforce Institute at Evaton in the Transvaal, modelled on the American Tuskeegee Institute, in 1897. John L. Dube, one of the handful of black South Africans able to pursue higher education in America, educated at Tuskeegee and elsewhere in the United States in 1887–92 and 1897–9 and a disciple of Booker T. Washington, founded Ohlange Institute in Natal in 1901. Dube also began editing *Ilanga lase Natal*, an African-language journal, in 1903.

A network for interaction between the black populations of South Africa and the United States, which was to remain in place for several decades, was thus taking shape by the beginning of the twentieth century: a handful of black Americans, probably no more than a hundred in the nineteenth century, many of them entertainers and clergymen, found their way to South Africa;[26] an even smaller number of black South Africans, mostly political and educational leaders of the tiny black elite, came to the United States. Solomon Plaatje, writer and politician and one of the founders of the African National Congress, was in America in 1920–2; Reuben Caluza, who played a central role in the creation of several genres of black South African music, studied with Nathaniel Dett at Hampton Institute early in the 1930s. But musical flow was one way, with Afro-American styles brought to Africa by occasional live performance and much more importantly by the mass media (printed music, phonograph discs, eventually films), while Americans remained ignorant of the music of South Africa.

In order to begin to understand the inordinate impact of Afro-American culture on black South Africa, out of all proportion to this amount of direct contact, one must consider the separate histories of the two black populations.

Until the end of the nineteenth century, there seemed to be little common ground between them. Africans were brought to the United States in large numbers only after the indigenous population, the American Indians, had been subdued and a plantation economy established. Black Americans were slaves in an alien country, with

---

[25] *Ibid.*, p. 43.

[26] E. de Waal, "American black residents and visitors in the South African Republic before 1899," *South African Journal* 6 (1974), pp. 52–5.

no ancestral ties to the land; their languages and social structures gradually disappeared, to be replaced by a new common language (English), a new religion (Christianity), and a new common identity (as African-Americans) pieced together over a period of time from a patchwork of pan-African cultural survivals and elements of the dominant American society in which they found themselves. They were a minority black population in a white land. Beginning in 1863 they were legally free to vote, own land, and hold public office, though these theoretical freedoms were mostly denied them by various strategies of the white population.

Most black South Africans continued to occupy their traditional lands after military subjugation, though the white population gradually took over the best land for its own use. They preserved their own languages and social structures, though the latter were gradually modified by contact with Europeans. Although a majority population, far outnumbering white colonizers, they were unable to utilize their numerical superiority for effective resistance because of superior European military and economic force, and because there was no tradition of black unity in the region. Though slavery was abolished in South Africa much earlier than in the United States – on 1 December 1834 – blacks had few legal rights in the British-controlled Natal and the Cape and virtually none in the two Afrikaner Republics, the Orange Free State and the Transvaal.

Despite these differences, by the beginning of the twentieth century the social and political condition of blacks in the two countries had come to a remarkable convergence, one of enforced racial segregation:

> Between the 1890s and the 1960s, the notorious Jim Crow laws of the southern states regulated inter-racial contacts in public places or facilities in such a way as to exclude blacks from most accommodations available to whites. The separate amenities or institutions provided for blacks were – despite the legal fiction of "separate but equal" – glaringly inferior and emblematic of a degraded social status. This pattern of mandatory social segregation was paralleled in the political sphere by the exclusion of most blacks from the electorate through a variety of voting restrictions put into effect by state legislation or constitutional provision between the 1880s and 1910 . . .
>
> In South Africa, the emergence of segregationalism as a deliberate public policy coincided quite closely with the establishment of a self-governing union [in the first decade of the twentieth century]. . . . The principal motive for prescribing separate living areas,

public facilities, and political institutions was to restrict the power and privileges of the African majority to such an extent that the preservation of white minority rule would be absolutely assured. But a more idealistic rationale was often provided for the benefit of those who doubted the justice of these policies. It was argued that Europeans and "natives" differed so greatly in cultural backgrounds and levels of civilization that it was best to allow each group to "develop along its own lines."[27]

However, both groups perceived that of the two, American blacks had attained a much more favorable position. Orpheus McAdoo, writing back to the States after his first experiences in South Africa, observed:

There is no country in the world where prejudice is so strong as here in [South] Africa. The native today is treated as badly as ever the slave was treated in Georgia. Here in Africa the native laws are most unjust; such as any Christian people would be ashamed of. Do you credit a law in a civilized country compelling every man of dark skin, even though he is a citizen of another country, to be in his house by 9 o'clock at night, or he is arrested? . . . These laws exist in the Transvaal and Orange Free State, which are governed by the Dutch, who place every living creature before the native.[28]

For their part, black Africans were impressed by the dress and demeanor of McAdoo and members of his troupe, by seeing them "[move] about with all the ease and freedom among the white people that a high state of civilization and education alone can give,"[29] and by hearing them describe the achievements of their race in America:

Hear! Today they have their own schools, primary, secondary and high schools, and also universities. They are run by them without the help of the whites. They have magistrates, judges, lawyers, bishops, ministers and evangelists, and school masters. Some have learned a craft such as building etc. etc. When will the day come when the African people will be like the Americans? When will they stop being slaves and become nations with their own government?[30]

---

[27] George M. Frederickson, *White Supremacy: A Comparative Study in American & South African History* (Oxford, 1981), pp. 239–40.

[28] Orpheus McAdoo, writing in the *Southern Workman* of November 1890, as quoted in Erlmann, "A feeling of prejudice," p. 5.

[29] From the *Southern Workman* of January 1891, as quoted in Erlmann, "A feeling of prejudice," p. 18.

[30] From *Leselinyana* for 1 October 1890, as translated by Naphtalie Morie and quoted in Erlmann, "A feeling of prejudice," p. 18.

And the few black South Africans who had found their way to America brought back similar reports.

American blacks would have been amazed by such favorable portrayals of their condition. Most of them still lived under economic and political restraints scarcely different from those of slave days. Only a few had been able to take advantage of educational opportunities and form a small black elite. The South African perception was based on limited contact with a tiny and unrepresentative group of American blacks, chiefly educators, entertainers, and religious leaders; and it was further distorted by the medium of print, largely controlled by whites in both the United States and South Africa, which persisted in offering inaccurate and even deliberately false images of black life in America.

In the capitalist society that the United States had become by the end of the nineteenth century, music was increasingly produced as a commodity to be marketed for profit, with decisions of repertory and style largely in the hands of capital and entrepreneurs. What South Africans, from a distance, took to be authentic Afro-American music was in fact selected and mediated for commercial presentation to American whites, who purchased the great majority of the printed music and phonograph discs produced in the nineteenth and early twentieth centuries. For instance:

- The music style of the minstrel show was shaped by white entertainers performing for white audiences; melodic, harmonic, and formal patterns were drawn chiefly from the traditional Anglo-American repertory and the popular stage music of the 1820s and 30s, modified in the 1850s by Stephen Foster.[31] True enough, at least two of the instruments used in early minstrel shows, the banjo and the bones, were Afro-American in origin, and the earliest banjo style (using non-harmonic ostinato patterns) appears to reflect African elements, but this type of playing had disappeared from the stage by the time the minstrel show came to South Africa. Blacks there had no opportunity to hear authentic American black dance music for banjo and fiddle, only white parodies of it.

- The gospel hymns of Sankey and Moody belong to a long tradition of religious music created by white composers for white congregations.[32] They have nothing to do with Afro-American music in melody and structure, though in time a distinctive black performance style grew

[31] Charles Hamm, *Music in the New World* (New York and London, 1983), pp. 76–82, 183–8, 236–42.
[32] Harry Eskew, "White urban hymnody," liner notes for *Brighten the Corner Where You Are: Black and White Urban Hymnody* (New World Records NW 224), pp. 4–6.

up around such music. But black South Africans had no opportunity to hear black Americans sing gospel music.

- Though spirituals drew on texts and tunes created by black slaves, they reached South Africa in triadic, tonal, homorhythmic arrangements of the sort first popularized by the Fisk Jubilee Singers in the late 1860s, then emulated by choral groups at other black schools and by professional minstrel companies. These arrangements were made first by whites (George L. White at Fisk University, Thomas Fenner at Hampton Institute), later by blacks trained in European musical styles; they were intended chiefly for white audiences.[33] South Africans knew American spirituals only in this mediated form, not as they were sung in black churches with call-and-response patterns, percussive accompaniment, and other African survivals.

- Ragtime likewise reached South Africa in a form mediated for the consumption of white Americans, as piano pieces by white composers and "coon songs" by white Tin Pan Alley songwriters. Rural ragtime and the black dance music from which it drew its characteristic rhythms were unknown in South Africa.

- No black American performers of early syncopated dance music, early jazz, or swing found their way to South Africa; so blacks there knew this music only through the media (phonograph records, films, printed music) or from an occasional white performer, usually British, who himself had only second-hand knowledge of the style. Recordings of this music available to black South Africans had gone through two levels of mediation. In America, the "jazz" offered by major record companies was played by white musicians, or by blacks playing or singing in styles thought to be appropriate for white consumption; music by black musicians intended for black audiences was marketed by small companies, and on a regional basis only, on "race records." Since blacks made up only a small percentage of the market for phonograph records in South Africa until the 1950s, the selection and marketing of American "jazz" by local record companies was based largely on its potential appeal to whites in that country, and blacks could choose only from what was made available by this process. As a result, black South Africans were able to hear "jazz" songs by Irving Berlin and instrumental "jazz" by Paul Whiteman, but no early New Orleans, Chicago, or New York jazz. They could hear Al Jolson, Bing Crosby, Lena Horne, Nat King Cole, Ella Fitzgerald, Frank Sinatra, Billie Holiday, and Johnny Mathis, but the great blues singers – from Ma Rainey, Blind Lemon Jefferson, Bessie Smith, and Papa Charlie Jackson through Leroy Carr, Sleepy John Estes, Big Bill Broonzy, and Robert Johnson – remained unknown in Africa. As noted above, the

[33] Hamm, *Music in the New World*, pp. 133–9, 375–8.

Mills Brothers and the Ink Spots became widely popular in South Africa, but blacks there never even heard of Gary Davis, the Excelsior Quartet, the Blue Jay Singers, or other black gospel groups of the era.

David Coplan has offered a brilliant and comprehensive discussion of how black South African contact with Afro-Americans in the late nineteenth and early twentieth centuries helped "foster a racial self-respect that became a basis for non-violent struggle against a society determined to crush African aspirations."[34] Elsewhere, in discussing the ways in which the music of American blacks played an important role in establishing their own self-identity, in shaping resistance to white oppression, and in furthering cultural and political aspirations, he develops the thesis that, because of "similarities in the sociohistorical experience of black Americans and South Africans, including rapid urbanisation and industrialisation, and racial oppression, [and] similarities in the kinds of musical resources available to both peoples in their urban areas, and in basic African principles of composition and performance," Afro-American music served as a model for "black South African urban cultural adaptation, identity and resistance."[35]

Coplan's work is important and convincing enough to make it unnecessary for other writers to say more on this subject. But just as African perception of the status and achievements of black Americans was shaped and distorted by the limitation of direct contact to a handful of relatively privileged individuals from each group, and by dependence on the media for information, so the African perception of black American music was limited by similar factors. It seems fair to generalize that most "Afro-American" music imported into South Africa before the middle of the twentieth century was mediated by and acceptable to white Americans. It was imprinted with white taste and white styles; and in the process of being transformed into a commodity for white consumers, it had lost much of the African identity so unmistakable in many forms of Afro-American music performed and enjoyed by blacks themselves at this time.

Black South African admiration for black American political and cultural achievement, up to the middle of the present century, was based to some degree on highly selective and often distorted information and images. The fact that this situation began to change around mid-century accounts for the gradually shifting African attitudes towards black Americans, and for the division of the present essay into two parts.

[34] Coplan, *In Township Tonight!*, p. 70 and *passim*.
[35] David Coplan, "The urbanisation of African music: some theoretical observations," *Popular Music* 2 (1982), pp. 122–3.

II

For most of the first half of the twentieth century, similarities in the social and political conditions of blacks in South Africa and the United States outweighed the many differences.

The screws of racial segregation were tightening in the United States. One state after another enacted legislation making it difficult or impossible for blacks to vote, and legalizing the segregation of public and private facilities. The Supreme Court itself upheld the segregation of public accommodations, in the *Plessy v. Ferguson* decision of 1896. Backlash against the massive new waves of immigration from the southern Mediterranean and Central Europe, stressing the threat to the culture of "native Americans" from the "impure stock" pouring into the country by the millions in the decades surrounding the turn of the century, led to much stricter immigration policies[36] and also to increasing intolerance of other ethnic minorities, blacks above all. Racist literature proliferated, and the Ku Klux Klan, revitalized, spread to all parts of the country.

In South Africa the few civil rights accorded the black population were eroded, and a steady stream of new legislation intensified racial separation. The Native Lands Act of 1913 forced blacks to live only in "reserves," and other legislation severely inhibited their migration to urban areas. The Mine and Works Act of Union Parliament (1911) established racial segregation in industry; the Colour Bar Act (1926) excluded blacks from skilled jobs on the mine fields. Only a few blacks, in Cape Province, had the franchise, and the last of these was removed from voter rolls in 1936. Both custom and law inhibited social contact, beyond employer–employee relations, between black and white.

The first organized resistance to enforced segregation, in both countries, was spearheaded by the black elite. A conference held in New York City on 30 May 1909 "for the discussion of present evils, the voicing of protests, and the renewal of the struggle for civil and political liberty" was attended largely by black educators, professional people, and religious leaders. A second conference, in May 1910, resulted in the founding of the National Association for the Advancement of Colored People (NAACP), with the educator and

---

[36] Resistance to uncontrolled immigration was first directed at Asians, with the Chinese Exclusion Act of 1882 and the subsequent Japanese and Korean Exclusion Leagues in California. A 42-volume report by a Congressional Committee on Immigration, released in 1910, assembled "scientific" evidence to demonstrate that the new immigrant stock was "racially inferior" to the older population of western and northern Europeans, and a succession of new immigration acts climaxed in 1924 with the exclusion of immigrants from many Asian and African countries and severe limitations on further influx from the Mediterranean area and Central Europe.

author W. E. B. DuBois chosen as the first executive. In South Africa, a meeting in Bloemfontein on 8 January 1912 of "several hundred of South Africa's most prominent African citizens: professional men, chieftans, ministers, teachers, clerks, interpreters, landholders, businessmen, journalists, estate agents, building contractors and labor agents"[37] led to the formation of the South African Native National Congress, renamed the African National Congress (ANC) in 1923. The first president was John Dube, founder and headmaster of the Ohlange Institute in Natal, mentioned above as having studied in the United States; Solomon Plaatje, named secretary, was later to come to America also; and the treasurer, Pixley ka Izaka Seme, had studied law in London.

But underlying these surface similarities was an overriding, fundamental difference: racial segregation was contrary to the Constitution of the United States, as amended in the middle of the nineteenth century; but racial segregation was legally enshrined in South Africa. Events of the late 1940s and early 50s were to underline this difference and result in a dramatic divergence in the civil status of the two black populations.

Soon after the end of World War II, American blacks launched an aggressive drive to achieve the equality that should have been theirs as citizens of the United States but was in practice denied them by state and municipal legislation, and by social custom. The Supreme Court decision of 1954, in *Brown v. Board of Education of Topeka*, that racial segregation in the public schools was unconstitutional, rang the death knell for the doctrine of "separate but equal" facilities. In 1956 blacks in Montgomery, Alabama, staged a boycott to protest segregated seating on city buses; on 13 November the Supreme Court ruled that such segregation on public transportation was unconstitutional. The governor of Arkansas attempted to resist court-ordered racial segregation of Little Rock High School in 1957; President Eisenhower sent members of the US armed forces to enforce the court order, and nine black students entered the school. In these and other cases, the pattern was the same: if American blacks had the determination and courage to insist on their legal rights, the federal government had no choice but to support them.

But not so in South Africa. In 1948 the National Party, after campaigning on a platform of Afrikaner nationalism and resistance to "the erosion of white power," won control of Parliament. New legislation to further strengthen and codify racial separation was put into effect almost immediately: the Prohibition of Mixed Marriages

[37] Tom Lodge, *Black Politics in South Africa Since 1945* (London and New York, 1983), p. 1.

Act (1949); the Population Registration Act (1950), requiring every South African to be classified and registered according to racial category; the Group Areas Act (1950), confining each population group to specified residential areas. In response, the ANC joined other organizations in staging the Defiance Campaign of 1952, in which thousands of blacks invaded segregated facilities, offering no resistance to arrest. A National Action Council for the Congress of the People, held near Johannesburg in 1955, adopted a "Freedom Charter" insisting that South Africa should be a non-racial society, with equal status and opportunity for all people. A three-month-long bus boycott in Alexandra township, in Johannesburg, protesting fare increases, was the most determined in a series dating back to 1940.

These strategies were similar to those pursued by American blacks, but the outcomes were strikingly different. Since national laws were being violated by the black invasion of segregated facilities, the force of the South African government was used to quell the Defiance Campaign. More than 8,000 persons were arrested,[38] many of the leaders were placed under banning orders restricting future political activity, and even more harsh racial legislation was passed. The Congress at which the Freedom Charter was adopted was "brought to an exciting close by the arrival of a large detachment of policemen bearing sten guns in the afternoon of the second day. The took over the speakers' platform, confiscated all the documents they could find, announced that they had reason to believe that treason was being contemplated, and took the names and addresses of all the delegates."[39] And the government refused to mediate in the bus boycotts, staged against a private mass transport company.

Thus the power and authority of the national government was used to maintain racial segregation and discrimination, not to lessen it as in the United States.

Rock 'n' roll, emerging in the United States as a dynamic and even revolutionary new form of popular music in the mid-1950s, played quite different roles in America and South Africa.

The first truly interracial American popular music,[40] rock 'n' roll drew elements of its style from black music, chiefly rhythm-and-blues, and also from the music of white Southerners. Its early stars were both black (Chuck Berry, Fats Domino, Little Richard) and white (Bill Haley, Elvis Presley, Jerry Lee Lewis, the Everly Brothers, Buddy Holly). The audience was likewise interracial: data in *Billboard* and

[38] For details see *ibid.*, p. 46.   [39] Lodge, *Black Politics*, p. 71.
[40] This argument is developed in Hamm, *Music in the New World*, pp. 618 ff.

other trade journals tell us that blacks and whites bought phonograph records by many of the same performers, and listened to the same music on the radio; and early live shows, such as those organized by Alan Freed or put on at military bases, played for racially mixed audiences. Whether one believes that popular music mirrors contemporary society, or agrees with Jacques Attali that music is prophetic,[41] early rock 'n' roll must be seen as a powerful statement that the United States was moving towards an interracial society in the 1950s – a view further supported by the fact that persons and institutions most resistant to racial integration were most strongly opposed to this music.[42]

Given the historic identification of black South Africans with Afro-American political struggles and music, one would have expected enthusiastic African reception of rock 'n' roll. But this is not what happened.

Rock 'n' roll arrived in South Africa in the same way it came to other European and post-Colonial countries. Phonograph records by the Crew Cuts, Bill Haley, and Elvis Presley were available soon after their release in America, and the distribution of Presley's films *Love Me Tender* and *Jailhouse Rock* in early 1957 gave such a boost to his popularity that a poll conducted by the *Sunday Times* of Johannesburg in 1959 identified him as the top male vocalist of all time – replacing Bing Crosby, incidentally – and "Jailhouse Rock" was found to be the most popular single disc in the history of the record industry in South Africa.[43]

As elsewhere, rock 'n' roll became a battleground for the generational confrontations of the 1950s. A journalist correctly linked this music to "those hordes of sloppy, aggressive, bejeaned louts and their girl friends who cause so much trouble in South Africa,"[44] and rock 'n' roll and its audiences were condemned from the pulpit and lecture podium and by the state-controlled SABC (South African Broadcasting Corporation), which refused to air rock music even into the 1960s on the grounds that "offering the young South African something more than mere beat music is in harmony with and linked to a constantly growing desire in young people nowadays for programmes of a more serious kind."[45] But South Africa was a capitalist country, and despite opposition to this music from the ruling National Party and the powerful Nederdruits Gereformeerde Kerk (NGK), recording companies continued to

---

[41] Jacques Attali, *Noise: The Political Economy of Music*, trans. Brian Massumi (Minneapolis, 1985), pp. 11–12, 57–9, and *passim*.   [42] Hamm, *Music in the New World*, pp. 623–6.
[43] *Sunday Times*, 25 October 1959.   [44] *The Star*, 16 December 1956.
[45] *Annual Report of the South African Broadcasting Corporation* (Pretoria, 1966), p. 6.

realize unprecedented profits from marketing rock 'n' roll among the white youth of the country, who were sharing the fruits of a post-war economic boom.

Some benefits of this new prosperity were filtering down to the black population as well, and in an attempt to boost record sales even more, several companies adopted strategies for marketing this music among blacks: releasing selected rock 'n' roll records on 78 rpm discs (since most blacks owned battery-operated playback equipment running only at this speed); distributing these to retail outlets catering to black customers; and sending review copies to publications aimed at black readers. Todd Matshikiza reviewed three records distributed by Trutone Africa Ltd. in the July 1955 issue of the slick monthly *Drum*: "Boys, it's real 'jiving' when you get to Mercury Records. American singers and bands: Just dig these numbers [which included "Sh-Boom"]. The CREW CUTS – one of America's all-time high groups"; and in July 1956 he began a review of Bill Haley's "Rock Around the Clock" with "You've probably got interested in the new American craze the 'Rock' which pounds with rhythms even more exciting than the grooviest jive tempos."

Reviews and feature articles dealing with rock 'n' roll give evidence that this music penetrated black South African culture to some degree between 1956 and 1958. Casey Motsisi described a party in Western Native Township, near Johannesburg, in the May 1958 issue of *Drum*:

> This here midnite party is participating. There's enough booze to keep Mr Kruschev blotto for weeks on end. I go to the back of the house, where there's a tent pitched for "rockagers" who now and again want to shake a leg. . . . A busty young girl in jeans slides a disc on the battered gramophone, and some rockagers begin to dance while the Elvis of Presley accuses each and everyone of being "Nothing but a Hound Dog."

And some black performers began imitating this new music. "Masihambe," recorded by the Georgetown Boys in early 1957, was described by the music critic of *Zonk* (September 1957) as a "rock 'n' roll Zulu number"; the stage show "Township Rock" at the Johannesburg Town Hall on 7–9 May 1958 featured "Woodpecker's Rock" by the Woody Woodpeckers and "P. J. Rock" by the Jazz Dealers; recorded examples include "Rock by Boogie" by the Bogard Brothers (HMV JP 669) and "Tzaneen Rock" by G. Mabitsela (Drum DR 170).

But within no more than two years after its introduction into black South Africa, rock 'n' roll virtually disappeared. Critics began

189

disparaging it: Blake Modisane shrugged off a new release by the Comets, writing in *Drum* of September 1958: "Come off it, Bill Haley. Nothing's as bad as rock 'n' roll when it's bad. It's nonsense, just too bad to even annoy"; and an anonymous *Drum* critic greeted another rock 'n' roll disc in June 1959 with "Big beat, nonsense lyrics and just a mixture of disorganised sounds . . . doesn't make much of anything. It's good if you don't have to listen to it. Just wiggle to it, friend, because there ain't much more you could do." Record companies, not realizing the profits they had hoped for, pulled back from distributing new rock 'n' roll discs to blacks. And black musicians stopped performing pieces with "rock" in the title. As a result, even though early rock 'n' roll progressed through the stages of importation and imitation – "rock" pieces by black performers were mostly in fast, rhythmic 12-bar blues form, often with direct melodic borrowing from Bill Haley or Elvis – it never reached the third stage, that of assimilation.

Early rock 'n' roll drew more directly on Afro-American musical styles than had any previous American music available to black South Africans. The recurring harmonic pattern of the 12-bar blues form is, after all, related to the cyclic patterns of African music. The several instruments (lead guitar, rhythm guitar, saxophone, rhythm) maintain their individuality in some sort of layering. But no elements of early rock 'n' roll penetrated popular African styles. Even the amplified guitar, which gave this music in the United States one of its most characteristic sounds, seems to have reached South Africa through jazz, not rock 'n' roll.[46]

In order to understand this rejection, one must remember that early rock 'n' roll was imported into South Africa by white-controlled record companies for sale to the white youth of the country; distribution among blacks was an afterthought. Only music by white performers was chosen, a decision made by record companies on the grounds that South African whites were unlikely to respond to music by black performers, particularly in the climate of heightened racial tension marking the 1950s. To the best of my knowledge, records by Chuck Berry and Little Richard were not distributed in South Africa at this time. When live "rock" perfomers were brought to the country, they were all white and mostly British: Tommy Steele, Cliff Richard, Dickie Valentine, Billy Fury, Connie Francis, Dusty Springfield, Pat Boone. Steele scheduled two concerts for

---

[46] Enoch Tabete, perhaps inspired by Charlie Christian, was using an amplified guitar for jazz in the late 1940s and early 50s. "Thula" (HMV JP 129) is an excellent recorded example of his playing.

black audiences in the Bantu Men's Social Club in Johannesburg during his South African tour of 1958; but the afternoon program took place in an almost empty house, the evening concert drew an audience filling no more than half the hall, and a black observer reported in *The Star* of 3 May 1958 that "Mr. Steele's manners, his comments . . . did not endear him to us."

Though a few musicians recognized rock 'n' roll's stylistic dependancy on Afro-American music, the black population as a whole saw it as music by white performers for white audiences, generating controversies among the white population of little concern to blacks. Ironically this music – recognized, praised, and condemned in America as both reflecting and furthering racial integration in the 1950s – was rejected by South African blacks because, from the information available to them, it seemed to be music having to do only with white interests and white power.[47] As before, black African perception of American music and culture had been shaped by the media.

The twist was another matter.

Hank Ballard & the Midnighters' recording of "The Twist" [King 5171], written by Ballard himself, appeared on *Billboard*'s rhythm-and-blues charts for thirteen weeks in 1960 and also on the "white" charts for sixteen weeks in the summer of that year. But it was a recording of the piece by Philadelphia-born Ernest Evans ("Chubby Checker") for Cameo-Parkway that became an international sensation. Released twice in the United States, in the summer of 1960 and the fall of 1961, it became a no.1 hit on the *Billboard* "Hot 100" charts both times and was on the rhythm-and-blues charts for the total of thirteen weeks as well. Within no more than two years of its release, the disc had sold some three million copies.

A typical rhythm-and-blues piece, in 12-bar blues form with a fast, driving beat, "The Twist" was an anomaly for 1960. By this time the music industry had succeeded in subverting the powerful response to early rock 'n' roll, retaining the term "rock 'n' roll" while substituting a musical style (invoking the aesthetic of latter-day Tin Pan Alley) and a new type of performer (Pat Boone, Paul Anka, Fabian, and a clutch of other "teen idols") more congenial to its own traditions. The success of "The Twist" suggests that the music industry had misjudged public taste by adopting this strategy. But the industry was reflecting – and perhaps helping to shape – a

---

[47] For more on this matter see Charles Hamm, "Rock 'n' roll in a very strange society," *Popular Music* 5 (1985), pp. 159–74. Reproduced as Chapter 8 in the present volume.

backlash against black gains of the mid-1950s. Southern states were devising ways to resist court-ordered school integration; social integration was proceeding slowly and bitterly; and whites outside of the South, in anticipation of action against racial segregation and discrimination in their areas, were developing their own strategies to maintain the racial status quo.

Chubby Checker's music reached South Africa by way of England, where the two releases of "The Twist" had likewise gone to the top of the charts in both 1960 and 1961. *Zonk* reported in January 1962 that "the Twist, the freshest of the new dances and a vogue in New York entertainment, is the dance that has captivated both young and old in South Africa." A 78 rpm disc pairing Chubby Checker's "The Twist" and "Twistin' USA," released in South Africa in December 1961, was reviewed in *Zonk* (April 1962) as having been "recorded by the king of them all, Chubby Checker, the teenagers' heart-throb. The Americans say nothing has risen so fast outside the Jet Age!" A cover story in the same publication for July, with photographs of twisting black teenagers in Johannesburg and Pietermaritzburg, commented that the dance was either "a depraved, wicked exhibition of sex on the dance floor or a brilliant graceful expression, depending on your point of view."

Within weeks, literally, black South African musicians were recording pieces with "twist" in the title, among them "Zulu Twist" by Victoria Mhlongo and the Durbanites (Gallo GB 303), "Hambakahle Twist" by Billy the Kid and Jesse James (Envee NV 3366), "Hambo Njalo Twist" by Sparks Nyembe (Trutone Quality TJ 695), and "New Sound Twist" by Kid Moncho's Hot Beat Kings (Gallo USA 181). Some of these were more or less literal imitations of the American twist – fast, rhythmic, cast in 12-bar blues form – but assimilation took place almost immediately. Reggie Msomi's "Get Out Baby Twist" (Gallo USA 206) is instrumental throughout, with five 12-bar saxophone choruses played by Msomi bracketed by a number of repetitions of an 8-bar phrase built over a repeated harmonic pattern. "Big Five Twist" by Spokes Mashiyane (Gallo New Sound GB 3461), recorded in 1963, is built over the four-chord harmonic cycle I–IV–I–V repeated nineteen times, and the tempo is more moderate that that of the original "The Twist."

By the end of 1963 many hundreds of such Africanized "twist" pieces had been recorded and released in South Africa, and this music and the dance associated with it persisted until 1968–9, much longer than in the United States. Two obvious factors help explain this popularity, so striking in contrast to the fate of rock 'n' roll among black South Africans. First, the twist was associated with black Americans from the beginning. Photographs and journalistic accounts identified Chubby Checker as black, and even though white Americans soon pre-empted the twist for their own amusement and profit, Africans continued to think of the twist as an Afro-American genre. Chubby Checker thus became the sort of cultural hero and role model in black South Africa that Chuck Berry and Little Richard never had the chance to be. The second factor was that the twist was a dance, with specific though flexible movements associated with the music; this had not been the case with early rock 'n' roll. In order to suggest how congenial this notion is to Africans, I can do no better than quote John Chernoff:

> If you play a recording of American music for an African friend, . . . he may say, as he sits fidgeting in his chair, "What are we supposed to do with this?" He is expressing perhaps the most fundamental aesthetic in Africa: without participation, there is no meaning. When you ask an African friend whether or not he "understands" a certain type of music, he will say "yes" if he knows the dance that goes with it.[48]

The importation, imitation, and assimilation of the twist in South Africa took place against the backdrop of an interlocking series of dramatic and traumatic events.

On 21 March 1960 a confrontation took place in Sharpeville (a black township near Vereeniging) between some 5,000 blacks gathered to protest the pass laws,[49] as part of a general campaign organized by the Pan-Africanist Congress (PAC), and 300 police sent there to control the demonstration. Early in the afternoon,

> a scuffle broke out at the gate which breached the wire fence round the police station. A police officer, accidentally or deliberately, was pushed over. The attention of the front rows was focused on the gate and they surged foward, pushed by people behind them who wanted to see what was happening. At this stage, according to police witnesses, stones were thrown at them. The more inexperienced constables began firing their guns spontaneously. The majority of those killed or wounded were shot in the back. Altogether 69 people died, including eight women and ten children. 180 people were wounded.[50]

---

[48] John Miller Chernoff, *African Rhythm and African Sensibility* (Chicago, 1979), p. 23.

[49] The Native Labour Regulation Act of 1911 had required black males to carry identity passes at all times; a revised act of 1952 made it mandatory for all blacks over the age of sixteen, male and female, to have such passes in their possession at all times. Failure to present this "dompas" on demand resulted in immediate arrest and imprisonment. An estimated half-million blacks were arrested each year for violations of the pass laws.

[50] Lodge, *Black Politics*, p. 210.

Demonstrations, protest meetings, and strikes spreading to Cape Town, Durban, and elsewhere were silenced only when the government declared a state of emergency giving the security forces extraordinary powers of detention, arrest, and civil control. The two chief black nationalist organizations, the PAC and the African National Congress (ANC), which had followed policies of non-violent protest to this point, were outlawed, and in 1964 many of their leaders, including Nelson Mandela, were sentenced to life imprisonment. Under the leadership of the prime minister, H. F. Verwoerd, the Union of South Africa was reshaped as a republic in 1961, following a referendum of the white voters on the issue of autonomy, and the new Republic of South Africa withdrew from the British Commonwealth to pursue an independent political course. International outrage at the Sharpeville massacre and subsequent events within South Africa brought condemnation and boycotts by the United Nations and many individual countries, forcing the government into the historic Afrikaner position of "laager" – embattled, surrounded by numerically superior hostile forces, determined to battle for survival at all costs. Verwoerd persuaded the vast majority of white South Africans that the country faced a Communist-inspired "total onslaught" from inside and out. His vision of "Separate Development," a much more sophisticated version of racial apartheid in which blacks would be citizens of a number of independent "homelands" or "national states" and would be allowed in "white" South Africa only under severely controlled circumstances as a temporary labor force, gradually took shape with the enactment of new legislation, beginning with the Promotion of Bantu Self-Government Act (1959).

The media were intended to play a critical role in maintaining social control over the black population, and in persuading it of the benefits and inevitability of Separate Development. A Bantu Programme Control Board of the SABC, set up in 1960, was charged with the establishment of separate radio services in each of the major African languages of the region, "bringing home to the Bantu population that separate development is, in the first place, self-development through the medium of their own language and that, by this means, there will be progress in all spheres of life."[51] The challenge for the government was to insure that blacks listened to these programs, collectively called Radio Bantu. Recognizing that "[radio] is something which you cannot force on anybody"[52] and

---

[51] *Annual Report of the South African Broadcasting Corporation* (Pretoria, 1967), p. 10.

[52] *Debates, The Senate of the Union of South Africa*, Third Session, 12th Parliament, 1960, pp. 2446–7.

that "Music constitutes, and will always constitute, the most comprehensive component of any radio service,"[53] the SABC developed and refined a strategy of using music to draw and hold black listeners to Radio Bantu so that they would also hear news and political commentary, in their own languages, written in Pretoria.

Each "vernacular" service of Radio Bantu had a committee charged with selecting appropriate music; the selection process included screening song lyrics to insure that political and moral sentiments contrary to state policy were not heard on the air. The twist was accepted by strategists and censors as appropriate music for Radio Bantu, since it seemed impossible to read revolutionary content into the song lyrics of Chubby Checker and his peers, and none of them was known to be associated with troublesome political activity. The fact that they sang in English was something of a problem, since one of the aims of Radio Bantu was to stress "tribal" identity – and thus inhibit black unity – through exclusive use of traditional languages, to counter the growing use of English as the common tongue among Africans of different linguistic groups. Since African twist music was instrumental, it was even better suited to Radio Bantu, which accordingly devoted a considerable amount of air time to it.

The government's strategy depended on having a large percentage of the black population listen to Radio Bantu, and its success in achieving this, by helping to make inexpensive transistor radios available and by offering music chosen to appeal to the largest possible audience, was remarkable. Blacks owned 103,000 radio sets in 1962; the number had reached 771,000 by 1966; and two years later (1968) there were more than two million radios in black homes.[54] Thus black radio ownership increased twenty-fold during the lifetime of the African twist; at least some of the proliferation resulted from the popularity of this music. And as elsewhere in the world, radio play stimulated record sales, and in turn recording companies produced more music of the sort already being played on the air. Though the recording industry was in private hands in capitalist South Africa, state policies governing the selection of music for radio play had a considerable impact on record-manufacturing strategy: there was little to be gained from recording music that would not be played on Radio Bantu.

In sum, the early twist was the first genre of Afro-American music to reach black South Africans in essentially the same form in which it was heard by a mass black American audience. In the United States,

[53] *Annual Report of the South African Broadcasting Corporation,* (Pretoria, 1964), p. 8.
[54] These figures are from the annual reports of the SABC for these years.

it was almost immediately co-opted by whites and played little role, symbolic or otherwise, in the continuing struggle for racial equality. In South Africa the twist was more strongly identified with black culture and aspirations, and penetrated deeply into African life. Ironically, in a time of intensified racial repression, the African twist became an effective media weapon in the hands of the racist state.

While it seems impossible to pinpoint just when "soul" was first used as a label for certain types of black American music, and difficult to define its precise musical characteristics, several things can be said with some assurance:

- The word was first widely used in 1966–7, in connection with a series of recordings by Percy Sledge ("When a Man Loves a Woman"), Aretha Franklin ("I Never Loved a Man The Way I Love You"), Wilson Pickett ("Land of 1000 Dances"), and Otis Redding ("I've Been Loving You Too Long" and "Try a Little Tenderness"), among others.

- It was adopted as a general label for all black popular music by *Billboard* magazine in 1969.

- The style itself was not new in the mid-1960s but had been evolving for many years, particularly in the music of Sam Cooke, Ray Charles, James Brown, and Bobby Bland.

- Many soul singers had begun their careers in gospel music, and the characteristically flexible, highly expressive, extravagantly embellished vocal style grew out of black church-music traditions.

- Even though white Americans began listening to soul almost immediately, there was little change in musical style as a consequence. Putting it another way, soul was the first Afro-American popular style to enjoy wide dissemination among white audiences without undergoing stylistic transformation at the hands of white arrangers, producers, and entrepreneurs. It was also the first black style resisting imitation by white performers: though some of the latter appropriated elements of soul into their singing, none dared label their music "white soul."

- More than any earlier mass-disseminated black style, soul was taken to be an expression of black ethos and black pride.

- Soul was contemporary with, and consonant with, a dramatic second push by American blacks to achieve social, educational, and economic equality.

Despite favorable court decisions and the Civil Rights Acts of 1957 and 1960, not even 2 per cent of American blacks were attending integrated schools by the early 1960s, and social integration was proceeding just as slowly. Southern blacks, led by ministers and students, mounted a massive civil disobedience campaign which reached a climax in the summer of 1963. "Blacks filled local jails from Cambridge, Maryland, to Plaquemines Parish, Louisiana, and from Greenville, Mississippi, to St. Augustine, Florida."[55] On 28 August 1963, 200,000 people marched, sang, and prayed in Washington in support of more effective civil rights legislation. Black anger directed against continuing racial inequality took more violent form outside the South, with riots in Harlem (1964), Watts (1965), Cleveland (1967), and Detroit (1968), and, following the assassination of Martin Luther King, Jr., in 125 cities all over the United States in the spring of 1968.

In order to fight effectively for equality, any oppressed group must first be convinced that it is indeed equal or superior to its oppressors. Much of the history of mass-disseminated "black" music before the 1950s, from minstrel music and "coon" songs of the nineteenth century through such later Tin Pan Alley products as "Shoeshine Boy" (recorded by Louis Armstrong in 1935) and Hoagy Carmichael's "Lazy Bones" and "Rocking Chair" (as recorded by the Mills Brothers), can be read as a continuation of the historic American strategy of depicting blacks as intellectually and morally inferior to whites.[56] Soul music, with its public representation of a positive black image (as epitomized by Aretha Franklin's "Respect" and James Brown's "Say It Loud, I'm Black and I'm Proud"), played an important role in mobilizing and vitalizing black activism in the 1960s and 70s.

Soul, both the music and the concept, reached South Africa quickly. Steve Montjane, writing in the August 1967 issue of *Bona*, reviewed two LP anthologies entitled *Solid Gold Soul* (ALA 9008 and 9018) featuring pieces by Solomon Burke, Wilson Pickett, Joe Tex, Don Covay, Ben E. King, Otis Redding, Percy Sledge, Ray Charles, and Chris Kenner, as well as two LPs by Percy Sledge (ALA 9002 and ALA 9040). In his column, titled "This Month We Look at 'Soul'," he informed his listeners about "soul jazz":

> Soul Jazz has everything: Blues, pop, rock 'n' roll, lyrics of stirring beauty, philosophy, happiness and dismal sadness, caring and not caring – the lot. Highly sophisticated American techniques, polished English lyrics, but filling us with pride, it is credited with

[55] Stephan Thernstrom, ed., *Harvard Encyclopedia of American Ethnic Groups* (Cambridge, MA, and London, 1980), p. 20.
[56] Further on this point, see Roger Hewitt, "Black through white: Hoagy Carmichael and the cultural reproduction of racism," *Popular Music* 3 (1983), pp. 33–52.

the free, uninhibited emotional content of African music. This is music of Africa which was carried to America during the slave trade and plantations, and is now emancipated to return to Africa still fresh as a breeze, with a heavy rhythm beat – but now sophisticated. Soul Jazz fans will tell you that there is no better music for combining pleasing rhythm with wise instruction and day-to-day problems. Example: Joe Tex, one of the top Soul singers in "Hold What You've Got," says: "Hold what you've got, if you feel you don't want it, throw it away, and you'll see, before you can count 1, 2, 3, somebody has taken it." . . . He gets to the crux of the problem with sweet music, as is typical of most Soul Jazz numbers.

Three more LPs of "soul jazz" were reviewed in October – *The New Boss* (Joe Tex), *Listen* (Ray Charles), and *I Never Loved a Man* (Aretha Franklin) – and 1968–9 brought the release of still more, by Sam and Dave, Otis Redding, Percy Sledge, Joe Simon, Diana Ross and the Supremes, Brook Benton, and Clarence Carter. *Drum* carried a glossy photo-story on "The King and Queen of Soul" (Percy Sledge and Aretha Franklin) in its issue of January 1969, further identifying Wilson Pickett as the "Prince" waiting on the sidelines. "Whenever there's a party these days, the records that are most likely to be in danger of wearing out first have the same sound – SOUL," the anonymous writer says, concluding that "Soul is king in South Africa. The music cries out from record players from Muizenburg to Messina!" And it was not only top American soul stars whose music was heard in South Africa: "Soul Cookin'" (1968) by Willie Bobo and other pieces virtually unknown in the United States enjoyed wide distribution in South Africa.

Despite the speed with which soul was imported into South Africa, the second and third phases of penetration were initially problematic. This music was so dependent on the sound of electric instruments (guitars, basses, organs) that imitation and assimilation could not take place without them, and few black Africans had access to the kind of money needed to buy or even rent such equipment. The earliest South African attempts to emulate soul music came from the Cape, with colored (mixed-race) groups. Cape coloreds were sometimes in better economic straits than blacks, and there was also a tradition of racially mixed audiences for musical events in this part of South Africa, making entrepreneurs more willing to subsidize talented non-white musicians. The Fantastics, four colored youths ranging in age from twelve to fourteen, were able in 1968 to obtain electric instruments costing more than 3,000 rands ($4,500). Their live performances and recordings were "full of electronic drive, short-circuiting the long road to the top in a shower of soul-searching sparks," according to *Drum* (November 1968). The Flames, from Durban, released an LP (*Burning Soul*) which "got a four star billing in America's Billboard magazine," according to *Drum* (April 1968), and the Invaders, from Uitenhagen in the Eastern Cape, "became the first Non-White group to win a golden disc" in South Africa, according to the same source.

By 1969, though, black groups playing "local soul music" had been formed in and around Johannesburg; among the first of these were the Black Hawkes and the Inne Laws. *Bona* (June 1969) carried an account of a musical entertainment for patients and staff at Baragwanath Hospital in Soweto; after an opening of "cool jazz" by the Early Mabuta Quartet,

> Out of the blue came the "Inne Laws"; music that pushed formality and chivelry [*sic*] aside and placed the hall in a frenzy mood. No part of the human joint was not shaking when these boys played "Soul Jazz music." Their music sent the audience sprawling on the ground, some sat shaking on the floor, some lay prostrate on the floor and shook violently, some stood with tears streaming down their cheeks . . . when they played their popular "Soweto Soul Music."

This "soul jazz music" of the Inne Laws, the Black Hawkes, and similar early groups – the Soul Giants, the Earthquakes, the Movers, the Teenage Lovers – represented a synthesis of American and African musical elements, rather than mere imitation of American soul. It was purely instrumental, to begin with.[57] The tempo was drastically slower than that of the African twist; the electric organ and solid-body electric guitar were introduced into South Africa with this music; and a few pieces were cast in 12-bar blues form – all reflections of African familiarity with American soul. But the majority of early African "soul" pieces unfolded over 4- or 8-bar harmonic cycles, and melodic lines were repetitious and patterned, reflecting none of the extravagantly embellished vocal lines of American soul.

Black African identification with Afro-American life and culture reached a new peak during this time. Soul reached a larger percentage of the black population than had any earlier styles based on Afro-American music. As the numbers of blacks living in urban

---

[57] One of the rare exceptions, "The Way That You Love Me," recorded by The Anchors in 1969 (City Special CYB 47), is much more in the Motown style of Diana Ross and the Supremes than an imitation of Aretha Franklin or other soul singers.

areas increased, and the government intensified its campaign to reach the entire black population by means of the mass media, the number of people with access to popular music through radio and phonograph proliferated. American styles of dress, long fashionable among the black elite, became the universal black urban attire, spurred by new strategies of mass production and marketing.

Publications targeted for black readers[58] developed an obsession with black America. *Drum*, a monthly which began publication in 1951, built its circulation on a strategy of "picture features, bright covers, jazz, girls, and crime stories."[59] At least half its stories dealt with black Americans: sports heroes, musicians, flamboyant religious leaders, politicians. American-made goods were advertised, often with pictures of attractive American blacks enjoying the "good life" with the help of these products. But as the 1960s unfolded, *Drum* and similar publications reported increasingly on less positive aspects of black life in America: race riots in urban centers; militant white opposition to the struggle for black voting rights in the South; the assassination of Martin Luther King and the resultant rioting across America; the large number of blacks fighting in Vietnam; charges of racism brought by black athletes. At the same time, in response to increasing American criticism of apartheid, the SABC and the Afrikaner press intensified their strategy of stressing racial tensions and problems in the United States as a warning against racial mixing in South Africa.[60] Though the government exerted no direct control over independent publications such as *Drum*, it reserved the right to ban publication of information and opinions contrary to its interests and strategies, and the press was wary of questioning state policy. As one of *Drum*'s editors (Tom Hopkinson) said when tendering his resignation, "it was dull work editing a magazine in which almost nothing could be said."[61] As a result of this changing media image of the condition of blacks in America, South African blacks began developing a more complex and realistic view of racial realities in the United States.

---

[58] Though there was a tradition of African-language publications edited by blacks early in the century, the policies of the National Party brought about a political and economic climate in the 1950s in which "no African newspaper in South Africa was owned or controlled by Africans." (F. Barton, *The Press of Africa: Persecution and Perseverance* [New York, 1979], p. 196.)

[59] Anthony Sampson, *DRUM: An African Adventure – and Afterwards* (London, 1983), p. 33.

[60] According to the annual report of the SABC for 1967, among the "talks" broadcast that year on the subject of racial mixing in America were "A sordid chapter in American degradation" (February), "The riot season in the United States" (June), "Flaming cities illustrate a fallacy" (July), "Negro riots open eyes" (August), and "Integration fosters hate" (November).   [61] Sampson, *DRUM*, p. 293.

Direct contact between South African and American blacks, which had declined anyway during the 1930s and 40s, was a casualty of the early years of Afrikaner rule. It became virtually impossible for an American black to obtain the necessary visa to enter South Africa, or for a black African to have a passport for travel to America. Most black South Africans in the United States were political exiles. Even though South African entrepreneurs had long suspected that a great deal of money was waiting to be made by bringing black American musicians to the country, it was only after twenty years of Afrikaner rule, in 1967, that Abe Hack of Future Promotions received permission from the government for a five-person group headed by singer Laverne Baker to give twenty performances in black townships in and around Johannesburg and Pretoria, including Sharpeville, for black audiences only. There was also a benefit show at Baragwanath Hospital in Soweto.

Even though Baker was little known in South Africa and the peak of her modest career in America had been reached a decade earlier, her shows attracted large and enthusiastic crowds, and her presence in the country piqued the interest of the white press. Judging from published interviews, the government had done an excellent screening job in choosing her as the first black American performer in the country since the Nationalists came to power: she was quoted in *The Star* for 9 June 1967 as saying, "It makes no difference to me what's going on on the political scene," and the same newspaper reported on 14 June that she had no problem with performing before blacks-only audiences, since "I do it at home, in some places where audiences are still segregated." She stayed an extra week in South Africa, expressed interest in coming back and in adopting an African child, and assured reporters that many other black American musicians would welcome the chance to come to the country.

Unlike Baker, Percy Sledge was a top international star when he came to South Africa in 1970. As noted above, he had been labelled "The King of Soul" by the South African press in 1967, and sales of his recordings there topped those of any other black American in the late 1960s and early 70s. Any remaining doubts about the commercial viability of black American performers in the country, or of the black population's ability and willingness to support them, were swept away by the wildly enthusiastic reception, at times bordering on hysteria, that greeted Sledge's extended series of concerts in black theaters and other township venues across much of South Africa. And it was not only blacks who were eager to hear him perform. The popularity of soul had spread to the white population of South Africa, just as in the United States. At a time when the likes of Patti Page, the Sandpipers, Frankie Laine, and the New Christy Minstrels made up the imported concert fare for whites-only audiences, the prospect of seeing and hearing a contemporary star of an exciting new genre of popular music excited many whites. But social custom reinforced by the Separation of Social Amenities Act, part of the government's packet of legislation intended to make a reality of Separate Development, prevented whites from attending concerts for black audiences. In a situation almost without precedent in South Africa, blacks had access to something desirable to whites, and the latter were prohibited from sharing it – inspiring many of them to try to crash Sledge's concerts disguised as blacks or Indians.

The South African government, which had been reluctant to allow black American performers in the country, could now see their presence meshing with its own strategies. Blacks performing for blacks in highly publicized events reinforced the image of racial separation; the excitement and pleasure generated among the black population helped divert energy away from more contentious matters. The 1970s brought a stream of black American musicians to South Africa, including Brook Benton, Clarence Carter, Billy Preston, the Commodores, Curtis Mayfield, Millie Jackson, Tina Turner. Entrepreneurs were careful to choose performers with no obvious history of political activity, and to instruct them to avoid controversial statements or contacts while in the country. For its part the government proclaimed these visitors Honorary Whites, allowing them the use of hotels, restaurants, and other facilities normally off-bounds to blacks, very much as Orpheus McAdoo and his troupe had been treated some seventy years before.

Direct contact intensified black South African identification with "soul." Some record producers simply used the label, even for music having nothing to do with the style of American soul. More importantly, however, elements of this music penetrated ever more deeply into indigenous popular styles, synthesizing with more traditional styles at various levels. For instance, "Sala S'thandwa," recorded in 1976 by Izintombi Zesi Manje Manje – a pioneering group in contemporary "vocal jive" – is a traditional Zulu song of farewell, but sung in this recording with harmonies and vocal style obviously indebted to Motown; the disc (GRC 486 MS71) is labelled "Zulu Vocal Soul Jive." But even here, and in the music of similar "soul" groups such as the Movers, the Young People, Cokes and the Midnight Stars, and the Vaal Express, there is little solo singing. As in all vocal jive of the 1960s and 70s, the lead singer interacts with a small vocal group, often in suggestion of traditional call-and-response patterns. It was not until a few years later, after Doby Gray and other American soul singers had performed in South Africa, that Kori Moraba and Babsy Mhlengeni began to emulate the solo vocal style of soul.[62]

In the United States, soul music asserted in practice what the Black Consciousness movement proposed in theory – that black people had a culture as good as, or better than, that of white America, and that this culture should be cultivated with pride. Black Consciousness in South Africa, linked at first with the establishment in 1969 of the all-black South African Students' Organization (SASO), had a somewhat different focus, reflecting the special imperatives of the black situation in that country.

> Its leaders . . . argued that the immediate problem in mobilising black resistance was psychological. Before one could consider the difficulties of organization and strategy the inferiority complexes engendered by oppression and paternalism had to be overcome. Jettisoning any links between black leadership and predominantly white liberal institutions was essential if all traces of a dependency mentality were to be eradicated. White liberals lacked the appropriate motivation to identify fully with black political and social aspirations. More positively, blacks had to create a social identity to replace the concepts generated by white liberal notions of integration into a western capitalist society. To this end blacks should draw on indigenous cultural traditions.[63]

Steve Biko, the most visible leader of South African Black Consciousness, envisaged "a nonracial, just and egalitarian society in which color, creed and race shall form no point of reference,"[64] but he understood that black "group power" was necessary "in the game of power politics."

> Being an historically, politically, socially and economically disinherited and dispossessed group, [blacks] have the strongest foundation from which to operate. The philosophy of Black Consciousness, therefore, expresses group pride and the determination by the Blacks to rise and attain the envisaged self.[65]

American Soul music was accepted by Biko as an expression of black pride growing out of the "indigenous cultural traditions" of black

---

[62] Examples of solo singers emulating American soul singers include *The Minerals and Kori Moraba* (RPM 7040, 1978) and *Zulu Soul Vocal* (Gallo, Mavuthela Music, Ziya Duma TL 519, 1978).　[63] Lodge, *Black Politics*, p. 323.

[64] Steve Biko and Millard Arnold, ed., *Black Consciousness in South Africa* (New York, 1979), p.v.

[65] *Ibid.*, p. xx.

America. But there was a problem with South African "soul jazz" or "soul jive." Its production and dissemination were controlled by white capital, and it was being used with telling effect by the state-run SABC, in its Radio Bantu transmissions, to propagate Separate Development. More generally, the state had pre-empted the issue of black African "indigenous culture" into its own strategies, attempting to manipulate the several different African languages and cultures to create the impression of greater differences among various "tribal" groups than in fact existed, in order to inhibit black unity. In this world turned upside down, Black Consciousness leaders were faced with a strange dilemma: if they tried to use traditional African culture as a basis for strengthening black social identity and group pride, they risked playing into the government's hands; and they had no access to the mass media to put forward an alternative view. As Muff Andersson has put it, "We can discuss whether a music that stands for the unity of the people should go through any commercial process at all: and to those who believe or not, we could argue that some powerful and politically sound music has come through these channels. Unfortunately not too much of this can reach the people it is aimed at, because of the state control of radio and because of controls on other institutions."[66] Thus black radicals of the 1970s, within the country and in exile, largely rejected contemporary commercial, mass-disseminated music in favor of older syncretic genres less contaminated by governmental appropriation – jazz, and the choral "freedom songs" so popular at rallies, funerals, and other mass gatherings.

The irony here is that the "soul jive" rejected by some black political leaders had integrated elements of Afro-American and African styles so successfully that it was instinctively heard and accepted as an expression of black consciousness by its millions of African listeners.

Disco, which dominated American popular music for several years in the mid-1970s, was in some ways more "African" than any other popular genre to date. A typical piece such as Donna Summer's "Love To Love You, Baby" of 1976 used a text of only a few lines, repeated over and over; structurally, most disco pieces were built over a brief, persistently repeating harmonic sequence, underlined by a prominent ostinato-like pattern in the electric bass. Like most African music, disco supplied a continuous, rhythmically insistent

---

[66] Muff Andersson, *Music in the Mix: The Story of South African Popular Music* (Johannesburg, 1981), p. 178.

sound pattern for dancers, extended over a long enough period of time to carry participants into a state of near-hypnosis.

The roots of disco were in Afro-American music. As far back as the late 1960s Sly Stone was playing fast pieces unfolding over an ostinato-like bass pattern, and the early 1970s brought the sub-genre of "funk" – rhythmic dance music by Edwin Starr, the Ohio Players, and George Clinton underlaid by persistent rhythms and harmonies. Then, as had happened so many times before in American popular music, white performers appropriated a style forged by blacks. K. C. & the Sunshine Band, among other groups, brought out successful pieces of funk; "The Hustle," written and recorded by Van McCoy in 1975, was the archetypical early disco piece; and America's disco culture was formalized in 1977 by the film *Saturday Night Fever* and its soundtrack album, featuring the Bee Gees.

Disco became the most truly interracial popular music since early rock 'n' roll. Performers were both black and white, as were audiences, and other minorities such as Hispanics and gays were identified with this music as well. Its reception also cut across racial, ethnic, and national boundaries; *Saturday Night Fever* not only became the top-selling LP among white Americans in 1977, it was also the first album by white performers (mostly) to reach the top position on *Billboard*'s "Soul LP" chart, while at the same time becoming a best-selling item in Canada, The Netherlands, Portugal, Finland, South Africa, Sweden, Mexico, New Zealand, and France.

For black Americans, the mid-1970s were marked both by highly visible political triumphs – the election of black mayors in several large cities, some high-level black appointments by the Carter administration – and by much slower consolidation of the social and economic gains of the 1960s. Backlash against disco at the end of the decade was an accurate barometer of an increasingly conservative mood in American life, climaxed by the election of Ronald Reagan to the presidency in 1980. Despite media attention focused on white performers, both the music of disco and its cultural milieu were quite correctly understood by most Americans as deriving from minority cultures, particularly Afro-Americans. Mass burning of disco records at baseball games, condemnation of this music by certain disc jockeys, and derogatory songs such as "Disco Sucks" were directed not so much against the music itself as the culture from which it came. For most black Americans, the 1970s reinforced the reality that racial equality was a dream not yet fully realized.

But as had always been the case, black South Africans were confronted with a far more desperate situation than were American blacks. The government's policy of Separate Development had resulted in the forced removal of millions of people to crowded, desolate, remote "homelands."[67] The separate but unequal system of Bantu Education did little more than give a useful level of literacy to the black labor force. No black could vote, at any level; even their township leadership was imposed by the government. The leaders of black unions and other organizations were jailed, banned, or harassed. Student-led protests and demonstrations in the summer of 1976, beginning in Soweto and spreading elsewhere, were met with starkly brutal force, even for South Africa, leaving 575 dead and 2,389 wounded. The Black Consciousness Movement was suppressed, its leaders detained, and Steve Biko died at the hands of security forces, bringing about even more black anger and international outrage. It did not seem a propitious time for a new, totally apolitical genre of popular dance music to flourish in the country, but old patterns persisted: South African record companies released American disco records and the SABC put them on the air; some black performers began recording music imitative of American disco; and elements of this style began penetrating indigenous popular music.

This time, however, there was even less stylistic difference to be mediated than before. Much South African soul jive of the mid-1970s already sounded very much like American disco. "Bump Jive" by the Movers (City Special CYL 1030) unfolds over a persistent harmonic ostinato in a moderate dance tempo, with a prominent electric bass; the LP has only a single piece on each side, each lasting more than fourteen minutes. Though some groups drew on the style of American disco,[68] most South African "disco" music of the late 1970s and early 80s merely appropriated the word as a label for indigenous jive, without a change of style; and the word also began to be used as a general term for dancing in bars and other township locations, to live or recorded music of any type.

Disco music in America has been taken by journalists and social commentators as signalling the beginning of the "me generation" and its narcissist fascination with self at the expense of social consciousness. Disco was in truth a more complex phenomenon than that, both musically and politically. But it was seen abroad, certainly

---

[67] See Laurine Platzky and Cherryl Walker, *The Surplus People: Forced Removals in South Africa* (Johannesburg, 1985), and Joseph Lelyveld, *Move Your Shadow: South Africa, Black and White* (New York, 1986), pp. 119–54, for accounts of the ruthless "social engineering" involved in forcing blacks to live in the so-called homelands.

[68] The Johannesburg-based black band Harari had considerable success with American-style disco music in the late 1970s and early 80s. See "Get Up and Dance" on *Flying Out* (Gallo MC 4537, 1981) and "Boogie Through the Night" on *Street Sounds* (Gallo HUC 501, 1983).

in South Africa, as mindless, apolitical entertainment, and as such it was appropriate music for the government and its agencies to encourage among blacks, in such troubled times. Black South Africans received it as pure entertainment having no connection with the continuing struggle of black Americans for personal and political power and freedom.

Thus the past hundred years has seen a shifting pattern of relations between Afro-American music and culture, and black South Africa.

Until the middle of the present century, virtually all "black" American music imported into South Africa had been doubly mediated: first by entrepreneurs and producers in the United States who shaped it for consumption by white audiences; then by South African entrepreneurs, record companies, and the government for consumption in that country by white consumers. Minstrel songs, spirituals, ragtime, syncopated dance music, and various forms of jazz also became available to South African blacks as urbanization brought more of them into contact with white life and culture, and gave them the economic means to become consumers of Western goods and entertainment. Because of the extremely limited and highly selective nature of the direct contact between American and South African blacks, the latter were in no position to understand that their images of Afro-American music were shaped largely by white media, even when the performers were black, and that they had no access to the genres of black American music now thought to be the "purest" expression of black culture – shouts and spirituals as sung in religious services rather than on the concert stage, rural dance music, field hollers, rural blues, the piano music of black dance halls, New Orleans jazz, black territorial bands of the 1920s and 30s, early urban blues, gospel music, early rhythm-and-blues. Furthermore, the handful of black South Africans who came to America found themselves unwitting prisoners of black American middle-class culture, which at this time was intent on legitimizing itself through emulation of white America.

Throughout the late nineteenth and first half of the twentieth centuries, some black Americans were able to move into more privileged positions (according to standards of American capitalism) than was possible for their brethren in South Africa, and thus Africans were justified in thinking that American blacks had achieved a degree of social and cultural identity and the beginnings of a political power base, in the face of a dominant and often hostile white population. But it is also true that this perception of black

American identity and culture was distorted by distance, by the near impossibility of direct contact, and above all by the white-controlled media. To a large extent, the image of the American black which served to focus black African aspirations in the late nineteenth and early twentieth centuries was a false one, or at best grossly incomplete.

As the twentieth century unfolded, black South African perception of Afro-American music and status slowly sharpened. By the 1930s and 40s it was possible for Africans to hear recordings of a considerable body of music performed by black Americans, as opposed to whites parodying black styles. Even though this music was still selected and mediated by whites, blacks in both America and South Africa identified with it because the performers were of their own race, even if the style was still largely white.

The 1950s and 60s brought a major turning point in black American/South African relations, as a result of three factors: a dramatic improvement in the social and political conditions of black Americans; an equally dramatic worsening of most aspects of black life in South Africa under the National Party and its policies of apartheid and Separate Development; and an ever-increasingly realistic African view of black America.

Black South Africans followed the Civil Rights movements in the United States and the rise of Black Consciousness and Black Power. They understood the role that music played in these struggles, in asserting the self-identity and aspirations of black people and in unifying them during mass actions. Soul music was accepted and imitated with even more enthusiasm than earlier genres of Afro-American music, its message of black identity and pride understood and emulated. And Africans realized that, despite some white opposition to political and social integration, the United States was a place where these things *could* happen and were happening, and that both the government and many individual white people were helping to bring them about.

But as the 1970s came and went with virtually no change in black South Africa, the long-cherished dream that the American model of revolutionary, non-violent social and political change could serve for South Africa began to fade. Black Africans tried these strategies time and again, with no results. There could be no *Brown v. Board of Education* in South Africa, because segregated education was legally institutionalized. There could be no effective Civil Rights movements, because the goals of such action were illegal, not constitutionally protected. Racial inequality was enshrined in South Africa not only in social custom but, more importantly, in law. Black Americans were still admired for their cultural products, but their political condition began to be seen as having little to do with the reality of South Africa. With the 1980s and President Reagan's policy of "constructive engagement," black attitudes towards the United States worsened. Robert Kennedy had been given a hero's welcome in Soweto in the mid-1960s, because he was seen as sympathetic to the black struggle for equality in America and thus represented hope for black South Africa as well. Twenty years later Edward Kennedy was greeted with suspicion and hostility. A frustrated black South Africa, no longer believing that the American Dream represented a solution to its problems, was turning to other models.

Individual black American musicians of the 1980s have enjoyed the same popularity in South Africa as elsewhere in the world. But Michael Jackson, Lionel Richie, and Whitney Houston are taken to be only entertainers, not political and social role models and heroes, and the same is true for local musicians who imitate them – Brenda [Fassie] and the Big Dudes, for example. Black South Africans are now able to hear that this music, heavily mediated by the white-dominated American music industry, is less dynamic and less relevant to their situation than the music of the Soul Brothers, Steve Kekana, and many other contemporary black South African musicians who have managed to create a popular style widely accepted as reflective of the spirit of a new black South Africa, even though the means of production and dissemination have remained in the hands of whites.

In the end, Paul Simon's *Graceland* is symbolic of the beginning of a new era of relations between South Africa and the United States – an era in which the music and culture of black South Africa, and their struggle for freedom, has something important to say to Americans, white and black.

10

"THE CONSTANT COMPANION OF MAN": SEPARATE DEVELOPMENT, RADIO BANTU, AND MUSIC

My study of the South African government's media strategy continued when I arrived in Grahamstown in August of 1984 to take up a post as Visiting Scholar at the Institute for Social and Economic Research at Rhodes University.

It was a time of historic confrontation in South Africa. A new black strategy of forcing political change by making the townships ungovernable brought a deadly spiral of violence. Resistance to the presence of security forces in the townships resulted in deaths of demonstrators and bystanders; funerals of these victims turned into even greater outpouring of outrage and frustration, bringing fresh clashes with security forces. Blacks collaborating with the government and its agencies were attacked and killed by fellow blacks. A state of emergency was declared throughout the country, and thousands of political and community leaders were detained without being charged or brought to trial. Resistance leaders, black and white, disappeared or died in apparent accidents, subsequently linked to security forces and paramilitary pro-apartheid groups.

Though public concerts in the black townships were impossible under such conditions, music continued to play a central role in the struggle for political power. Syncretic black "freedom songs" and hymns such as "Nkosi Sikelel' i Africa," the anthem of the African National Congress, accompanied rallies and funerals throughout the country. Though the government prohibited media dissemination of such music, television and radio coverage of the unrest carried it all over the world, and a tape released in 1985, *FOSATU Workers Choirs* (Shifty Records, L4 SHIFT 6), containing a number of these pieces sung by black choirs in Natal and the Transvaal, was somehow passed by government censors.

210

But radio, phonograph records, and cassette tapes were the chief sources of music for blacks during these times, and the government persisted in its hegemonic use of media-disseminated music. This story, narrated in the following essay, epitomizes the struggle between decaying modernity and emerging postmodernity in South Africa, with the government promoting its meta-narrative of apartheid against what it saw as the chaos of decentralization. It was a losing battle, though; developing technology made it difficult and eventually impossible to keep black audiences from alternate channels of information, and there was no way to prevent listeners from constructing their own meaning from even the music offered by the government itself. As I wrote in a review of David Coplan's *In Township Tonight!*, "media-disseminated music [in South Africa] has retained significant elements of African style and has been accepted by the mass black audience as 'their' music, even though white capital has a stranglehold on the recording industry and radio is state controlled. . . . [It] can serve to build self-identity and self-respect among an oppressed people, *even though its means of production and dissemination are firmly under the control of the oppressors.*"[1]

* * *

It is obvious that broadcasting, the constant companion of man in modern times in all his activities, moulds his intellect and his way of life. . . . Music constitutes, and will always constitute, the most comprehensive component of any radio service.[1]

It is a common argument by now that the modern mass media and the music they disseminate have been "used by economically and politically powerful interests within the state to support the capitalist relations of production and to legitimise the social, economic and political organisation of society."[2] Criticism directed more specifically at radio has focused chiefly on capitalist societies in which there are multiple channels of entertainment and information. A recent issue of *Popular Music* devoted to radio, for instance, was concerned only with the UK, Canada, and USA.[3] Little critical attention has been focused on the use of radio to "legitimise the

[1] *Popular Music* 6/3 (October 1987), p. 354.

[1] *Annual Report.* South African Broadcasting Corporation (Johannesburg, 1959), p. 4. This publication will be abbreviated as *AR* in what follows.
[2] Keyan Tomaselli, Alan Williams, Lynette Steenveld, and Ruth Tomaselli, *Myth, Race and Power: South Africans on Film and TV* (Bellville, 1986), p. 19.
[3] *Popular Music*, 9/2 (1990).

social, economic and political organisation of society" in countries in which the state assumes full control over programing and transmission.

For some years I have been analyzing the selection and dissemination of music by state-controlled radio services, particularly in relation to minority and disenfranchized national and ethnic populations within that state. The Republic of South Africa affords a particularly instructive case study. Even as this article is being written, though the white minority government has initiated talks with black political leaders and groups, there has been no crack in the formidable array of legislation which legalizes and enforces Separate Development, the more sophisticated version of apartheid put into effect in the 1960s. How has the white minority population succeeded in clinging to such a racially segregated structure, in the face of a decades-long internal black struggle for equality, supported externally by virtually every other country in the world? One factor, certainly, is that the white population of South Africa is much larger and has a much longer history than elsewhere in Africa, and has maintained and used large, efficient, and ruthless police and military forces. But I would argue, in addition, that for more than twenty years the government of the Republic of South Africa succeeded in having its entire population, black and white, listen to its own radio service, theorized and programed in accordance with state ideology, to the virtual exclusion of other radio programing; and that this radio monopoly played a major role in shaping attitudes and relations which still inhibit the formation of a multi-racial society.

In what follows, I will analyze the structural organization and program content of the South African Broadcasting System (SABC) during the three decades after the National Party came to power in 1949, to suggest how the South African state used radio and radio music as part of a highly successful strategy to entrench its policies of apartheid and then Separate Development.

Early radio in South Africa

The first public broadcast in South Africa took place on 18 December 1923, as a radio transmission by the South African Railways in connection with the British Empire Exhibition in Johannesburg. Commercial radio began in 1924, with three different independent agencies (in Johannesburg, Durban, and Cape Town) licensed to broadcast over the 100–200 mile radius of their respective transmitters. In 1927 the African Broadcasting Company (ABC), a private monopoly under the Schlesinger Organisation, took control of all three. The program language at first was English, but in 1931 the ABC began transmitting a thirty-minute program in Afrikaans as well.

The Broadcasting Act of 1936 established a single state radio service, the SABC, which absorbed much of the staff and equipment of the ABC. In the process:

> The relations of cultural production changed from being mediated through the operation of commercial capital to being mediated through the political structure of parliamentary representation . . . motivated by the ideological assumptions of liberal idealism, which placed control through government above control by capital.[4]

Administratively the SABC was placed under the Minister of Posts and Telegraphs, with a Director-General advised by a Board of Directors. Program content was modelled after that of the BBC, with emphasis on informational, educational, and cultural programing designed to reinforce the class structures of British society. Musical programing was largely confined to classical and religious items, in keeping with the BBC's conviction that the function of a state radio service was to enlighten and uplift its audience. Occasional relief was afforded by semi-classical pieces and the social dance music of the educated classes.

In 1937 a split into two separate programs was brought about; an "A" Service in English and a "B" Service in Afrikaans. Transmission was by medium-wave (AM). Because the white population of South Africa was sparsely distributed over such a large land area, and since AM transmission is subject to atmospheric and mechanical interference, SABC transmissions were received poorly or not at all in much of the country.

Radio broadcasts to "natives" were initiated by the Native Affairs Department in 1940, as an emergency war measure to dispel disruptive rumors concerning the progress of World War II and South Africa's role in the conflict. These "broadcasts" were in fact carried by telephone line to subscribing households in black "locations" near major cities. With the end of the war in 1945, the SABC proposed to initiate a new set of radio programs for black listeners, for reasons that (in contrast with what was to come soon) seem benign and paternalistic:

> It is common cause among all sections of our European community that the Bantu peoples, who constitute four-fifths of the population,

---

[4] Graham Hayman and Ruth Tomaselli, "Technology in the service of ideology: the first 50 years of broadcasting in South Africa," unpublished typescript (Grahamstown, 1986), p. 17.

are our gravest responsibility. In these critical times it is becoming more urgently necessary every day for European and non-European to understand each other and to remove the difficulties in the way of co-operation. The overwhelming majority of Africans are illiterate, and, therefore, unreachable except through the spoken word. For this purpose, the radio would be an ideal means of communication. . . . If we are agreed that radio service for the Bantu is a national necessity, then both Government and local authorities must be prepared to start this service. (*AR* 1945, pp. 10–11)

Accordingly, half-hour programs in Sotho (from Johannesburg) and Xhosa (from Cape Town) were broadcast three mornings a week as interpolations in the English and Afrikaans services, and programs in Zulu were broadcast each day from Durban. These were "compiled and presented exclusively by native announcers" (*AR* 1947, p. 33), and consisted of "talks," dramas, and, most importantly, music: some broadcast live from SABC studios and some aired from pre-recorded transcription discs. The audience was severely limited: geographically to blacks living in or near urban centers, and economically to the few who could afford to purchase radio receivers. Most of the audience came from the small black elite, comprised chiefly of two groups: the traditional petit-bourgeoisie of small-scale producers and small traders, and the new group of civil servants, non-shareholding managers, teachers, clerks, intellectuals, and journalists.[5] Music for broadcast was chosen from styles already familiar to this audience: "light" music imitative of African-American styles; secular and sacred pieces sung by black choirs; traditional African music.

The Rediffusion service

Though the national elections of 26 May 1948 brought the Afrikaner-based National Party to power with mandates for more radical racial separateness and a stronger Afrikaner identity cutting across class lines, the SABC under the leadership of Director-General Gideon Roos clung for some years to "a relatively objective style inherited from the BBC."[6] The Afrikaans Service was given "absolute

[5] Kelwyn Sole, "Class, continuity and change in black South African literature, 1948–60," in *Labour, Townships and Protest: Studies in the Social History of the Witswatersarand*, Belinda Bazzoli (Johannesburg, 1979), p. 145.
[6] Graham Hayman and Ruth Tomaselli, "Ideology and technology in the growth of South African broadcasting, 1924–1971," in *Currents of Power: State Broadcasting in South Africa* (Belville, 1989), p. 46.

equality" with the English Service (*AR* 1949, p. 7) and the SABC established its own news service, but there were still exchange programs with various European broadcasting services, daily reports from the United Nations General Assembly, and a series of international programs prepared by UNESCO.

Heightened racial tensions under the new government brought renewed attempts to use the "Bantu Services" for social control. According to the *Annual Report* for 1949, "when riots broke out in Durban, the SABC helped the police and military authorities by broadcasting accurate news and special announcements" (p. 13), and "to combat unfounded rumours among the Bantu population before the inauguration of the Voortrekker Monument [in Pretoria], the Corporation broadcast messages from the Minister of Native Affairs and the Secretary for Native Affairs" (p. 31).

The first major policy changes at the SABC under the National Party had in fact been formulated before the elections: a third service, the commercial and bilingual (English–Afrikaans) Radio Springbok, went on air on 1 May 1950; and the "programme service for the Native population" was expanded. Drawing on the wartime experience of transmission by telephone line, the SABC instituted a "rediffusion" service for the township of Orlando, near Johannesburg, on 8 August 1952. Reception was possible only by paid subscription, transmission took place between 6 a.m. and 9 p.m. on weekdays and from 9 a.m. to 9 p.m. on Sundays. In the still paternalistic language of the SABC, this service was designed "in the first place to provide the native with entertainment in his own home, and in this way to contribute towards the prevention of crime; and secondly, to contribute towards the education of the Bantu" (*AR* 1952, p. 36). Program content "consisted mainly of music," including:

> traditional Bantu music; modern light Bantu music; choral music by Bantu composers, a surprisingly large number of whom have already produced work of a high standard; and European music. The [latter] is mostly light, and consists mainly of jazz, which is very popular with listeners because of its rhythmic character. Among the more educated natives there is also a demand for light classical music, and provision has been made for this type. A special programme of light classical music, presented with a short explanatory script, was introduced on Sunday evenings, and listeners were encouraged to write in if they wanted to hear any of these pieces again. (*AR* 1952, p. 36)

The assumptions underlying this description are based on contemporaneous Euro-centric ideology: European music is "more advanced" than non-Western music; "natives" will respond more readily to rhythmic than to harmonic or melodic elements; there are four genres of music, in ascending levels of artistic and moral content (traditional, popular, light classical, and classical); the government bears the responsibility of leading at least some of its citizens up this ladder of musical taste.

Motives behind the inclusion of traditional music were positioned between South Africa's British past and Afrikaner future. Gideon Roos and other BBC-oriented personnel at the SABC were infused enough with liberal/humanist European attitudes to encourage the preservation of "folk-songs threatened with extinction," as was being done in various parts of Europe at just this time. But there was a first resonance of another attitude that was soon to be at the heart of SABC policy: to "bring the voices and music of [various] areas into the homes of the urban Bantu" (AR 1956, p. 16) in order to "heighten the listener's pride in his own culture" (AR 1953, p. 32).

The accumulation of the SABC's recorded repertory of "traditional Bantu music" was started between 1936 and 1947 by Hugh Tracey, in his capacity as Director of the Natal Studios of the SABC.[7] SABC discs of "Bantu" music were first made in the mine compounds of the Reef, "where natives from many areas are brought together and where the authorities do their best to preserve tribal bonds" (AR 1952, p. 9). With technological advances of the 1950s, the SABC "began manufacturing its own tape recorders, and the greater quality, portability and ease of editing led to their increased use, especially in the field."[8] SABC recording teams began penetrating the "native reserves of Vendaland, Thongaland, Secucunuland, Zululand and Basutoland" where "Bantu songs, which were rapidly disappearing, [could be] rescued for posterity" (AR 1957, p. 16).

The SABC's programing of "modern light Bantu music" was pragmatic. A lively black urban music culture had emerged in the 1940s and 50s, drawing partly on American jazz, swing, and popular song styles,[9] and the SABC understood that it must program some music already familiar to its intended audience, if they were to be attracted to the service.

"Choral music by Bantu composers" was seen by the SABC as a step up in musical style and social status. Black choral groups

---

[7] Hugh Tracey, "Early recordings by Hugh Tracey, 1930–1947," Sounds of Africa Series (Roodespoort, 1973), pp. 8–11.

[8] Hayman and Tomaselli, "Technology in the service," p. 21.

[9] David B. Coplan, In Township Tonight! South Africa's Black City Music and Theatre (Johannesburg, 1985), Chapters 5 and 6.

organized along European lines and trained to sing Western choral music had been established at missions and mission schools since the late nineteenth century, and by the mid-twentieth century repertories of black choral groups included such standards of the British choral tradition as Handel's "Hallelujah Chorus" and Renaissance motets.

Embedded in the colonial strategy of dealing with "native" national and ethnic populations of the old British Empire was the conviction that they could be controlled most effectively if shaped into a semblance of the British class system. A small black elite, largely mission-trained and of course Christian, was encouraged to emerge in South Africa in the late nineteenth and early twentieth centuries, with the thought that this group would have the same aspirations as the British bourgeoisie and could be dealt with in the same way. Since the British middle and upper classes aspired to an understanding and "appreciation" of classical music, the development of a similar taste was encouraged among South African's black elite. The SABC began introducing classical music on its "Bantu Services" in the 1950s, as part of a larger strategy which included:

(1) a performance of *The Mikado* at Donaldson Community Center in the township of Orlando on 29 April 1951, the "first full-scale musical presented to a non-White audience [in South Africa]" (*Zonk*, November 1951);

(2) a "gramophone record concert for Africans" featuring selections by Elgar, Handel, Irving Berlin, and Mantovani, organized by Mr W. J. P. Carr at Dube township in 1956. A receptor noted that "unfortunately there was a very small attendance" (*Zonk*, December 1956, p. 43);

(3) a performance for non-whites of *Naughty Marietta* by the Johannesburg Opera Society at Alexandra Theatre, Braamfontein, in 1961;

(4) a performance for a non-white audience by the SABC Orchestra under the direction of Igor Stravinsky, on the occasion of the latter's visit to South Africa in 1962.

In 1952, 4,300 homes subscribed to the Rediffusion Service. Since the SABC assumed that the "average Bantu family" consisted of five persons, the total listenership was calculated at 21,500. By 1956, with extension of the service to the townships of Jabavu, Dube, and Mofolo, the number of households had risen to 14,000; since the average size of each was now figured at six persons, the total had reached 84,000. But even though the Rediffusion Service was extended to Noordgesig and Zondi townships in 1957, the number of subscribers dropped. "The reason for this was that the temporary 'shelters' of Orlando were demolished and their inhabitants removed to new Native townships outside the present range of the service"

(*AR* 1957, p. 16). In other words, while the SABC was trying to expand its radio service to urban townships, the government was planning and executing policies aimed at relocating those blacks living in townships in closest proximity to white residential and business areas to new townships, such as Soweto, some distance away.

Throughout the 1950s, SABC programing for black audiences was confined to telephone-line transmission to households in black townships in the Johannesburg area, and to several daily half-hour interpolations into the English and Afrikaner Services received by an undetermined number of blacks in other areas. The targeted audience was the black urban bourgeoisie and the tiny black elite. Though transmission to mining compounds, with their dense concentrations of black workers, or to heavily populated areas of the "native reserves" would have been technically feasible, no consideration appears to have been given to doing this. The black working class was still controlled by economic and military force, not by cultural persuasion. As a consequence, virtually none of the newly emerging styles of black working class music[10] was represented on SABC programing before 1960. An expanded radio service for South Africa's black population was not seen as an item of high political priority, and in 1958 the SABC could only report:

> The Board cannot but express its deep concern about the fact that the Corporation has not been in the position to expand its services for the Bantu population of the Union. It is the Board's aim, as soon as the necessary finances have been arranged, to disseminate this service to Bantu listeners throughout the country. (*AR* 1958, p. 2)

The SABC under Separate Development

Separate Development, a vastly more sophisticated version of the racial separation of apartheid, emerged after Hendrik Verwoerd became Prime Minister in 1958. It was nothing more and nothing less than the creation of a new mythology for South Africa and the forcible construction of a new social order based on this mythology.

According to Barthes, "myth consists in overturning culture into nature or, at least, the social and cultural, the ideological, the historical into the 'natural'. Under mythical inversion, the quite contingent foundations of the utterance become Common Sense, Right Reason, the Norm, General Opinion."[11] The mythology of Separate Development, constructed by ideologues of the National

---

[10] *Ibid.*, pp. 90–112.   [11] Roland Barthes, *Mythologies* (London, 1973), p. 165.

Party, held that before the arrival of Europeans, South Africa had been populated by various "native tribes," each a homogeneous unit with a distinct language and culture, each living within clearly defined geographical boundaries. Colonizing Europeans found most of the land area of South Africa empty and claimed it for their own, occasionally skirmishing with "natives" to solidify the boundaries between "white" and "black" land. They became a "tribe" themselves, with their own land, language(s) and culture, but – because of their European and Christian heritage – a superior tribe in intelligence, industry, achievement, and morality.

Furthermore, according to this myth, both cultural separateness and the inferiority of black people were in accordance with Divine Scriptures. But geographical and cultural barriers between groups began crumbling as a result of various factors: the liberal humanism of the British, who did not understand the history, logic, and beauty of cultural separateness; urbanization, bringing migration of blacks into areas which they had not traditionally inhabited; hostile foreign interests, chiefly Communist, attempting to undermine the South African way of life; blacks misled by Communist propaganda into losing sight of their own cultural heritage and their traditional role in South African life.

Separate Development promised to restore order by a return to South Africa's mythical past. Boundaries of the traditional "homeland" of each black "tribe" were drawn clearly, once and for all. Members of any "tribe" no longer living within these boundaries were required to return there, and would eventually be given citizenship in that "homeland" or National State, as these areas were soon called. Each National State was encouraged to develop its own language and distinctive way of life, according to its "own cultural heritage," and in time each of these National States would become independent countries. The remainder of the country would be inhabited only by whites; blacks would be allowed there only on temporary labor permits, with no rights of citizenship or permanent residence. In time, then, what had once been a single state would become eleven countries, the white Republic of South Africa and ten black "tribal" National States.

This new mythology of course ignored much: that black cultural, political, and linguistic identity was infinitely more complex than a simple classification into a small number of "tribes" and "tribal languages" could suggest; that blacks had in fact formerly occupied much of the land now claimed by whites; that "tribal" boundaries had constantly shifted over the years and centuries; that cultural interaction among "tribes" had been common before and during European colonization and conquest.

An array of new legislation designed to force the country's present and future to conform to this mythology was put into place. Every South African was required to be classified according to "race." Political boundaries of the National States were drawn, and blacks by the millions were relocated from "white" areas to these "homelands," where many of them had never lived.[12] As a consequence, some 80 per cent of the population, which happened to be black, was forced to live on 17 per cent of the poorest land in South Africa. And such institutions as the educational system, the *de facto* state religion, and the state-controlled media were given the task of bringing about general acceptance of this ideologically based mythology, by persuading the entire population that this was the "way things were," according to nature, history, and common sense.

The critical Promotion of Bantu Self-Government Act, which established the legislative framework for the creation of National States, was in place by the end of 1959. A first clue to the key role planned for state radio in the implementation of Separate Development, through persuading the population of the "naturalness" and "correctness" of its mythology came with the appointment of Albert Herzog to the post of Minister of Posts and Telegraphs, and Piet Meyer to the chairmanship of the Board of Governors of the SABC. Both were prominent members of the Broederband, the secret Afrikaner political and intellectual elite,[13] and in fact Meyer was its chairperson from 1960 to 1972. The SABC's *Annual Report* for this year signalled the changing ideology of the government and the new role projected for the state radio service:

> It is obvious that broadcasting, the constant companion of man in modern times in all his activites, moulds his intellect and his way of life. [We] must, in these times, be on guard to ensure that all [we] do complies with Christian ideals. Broadcasting can render a service to the whole community by expressing the unique South African way of life, *both in its unity and great diversity. (AR* 1959, p. 4)

The year 1960 brought dramatic events. There were sixty-nine blacks killed by police at Sharpeville during a mass protest against pass laws; a large number of black leaders were banned, and 169 of them were put on trial for treason; the African National Congress and

---

[12] Laurine Platzky and Cherryl Walker, *The Surplus People: Forced Removals in South Africa* (Johannesburg, 1985).

[13] Ivor Wilkins and Hans Strydon, *The Super-Afrikaners* (Johannesburg, 1979).

the Pan-African Congress were outlawed. Strikes, boycotts, and other manifestations of the continuing and intensifying black struggle for self-determination, coupled with hostile international reaction to the South African government's policies and strategies, drove the National Party into the historic Afrikaner position of "laager," embattled by hostile and numerically superior forces and withdrawing into a defensive position to battle for survival by whatever means necessary.

Under its new Broederband leadership, the SABC shed all pretence of objectivity and autonomy and devoted itself to supporting the "rightness" of the "South African way of life." The Board of Governors "laid down the policy that the broadcasting service is not to undermine the safety and the interests of the country or promote revolutionary intentions inside or outside the country's borders" (*AR* 1961, p. 6). In defense of the decision to shape program content so as to articulate and reinforce government policy and strategy, the SABC quoted from a speech made in 1964 by Sir Hugh Greene, Director-General of the BBC:

> I believe a healthy democracy does not evade decisions about what it can never allow if it is to survive. The actions and aspirations of those who proclaim some political and social ideas are so clearly damaging to society, to peace and good order, even in their immediate effects, that, to put at their disposal the enormous power of broadcasting, would be to conspire with them against society. (*AR* 1965, p. 5)

The radio services were to air "no report contain[ing] anything which conflicts with the laws of the land and provincial ordinances of the Republic of South Africa" (*AR* 1961, p. 8). Even more specific strategies were devised for dealing with "the rapid sequence of overwhelming events [which] must be sifted and arranged so that the impact is meaningful and not confused, but placed in a perspective that promotes insight" (*AR* 1969, p. 8):

(1) events within South Africa were to be treated in a "positive" and "healthy" manner;
(2) internal problems were to be minimized, and any unrest was to be blamed on "outside agents," i.e., Communists and their sympathizers;
(3) social problems elsewhere in the world, particularly those with racial implications, were to be headlined;
(4) problems in independent (black-governed) African countries, or those moving towards independence from colonial rule, were to be given extensive coverage.

221

In addition to "sifting and arranging" news events in these ways, the SABC instituted a series of radio talks designed to "promote the survival and bounteous heritage of the White People of the Republic of South Africa" (AR 1961, p. 9) through addressing such topics as "The infiltration of Communist doctrines in Africa" and "Traces of Communism in South Africa and its subversive activities." These talks were offered daily, as "an SABC editorial in which, from a South African point of view, positive comment is made on the affairs of the day" (AR 1967, p. 52). Originally entitled "Current Affairs" and then merely "Comment," these five-minute spots were carried several times a day on all three SABC services (Afrikaans, English, Springbok), and later also on three regional services (Radio Highveld, Radio Good Hope, Radio Port Natal) when these were put into operation in the mid-1960s. A keener sense of this strategy, which remained a cornerstone of internal and external government propaganda through the late 1980s, can be gained from the titles of some of these programs, taken from the *Annual Report* for 1967:

1 January	Mineworkers alienate sympathy
25 January	Freedom of the press and assassinations
7 February	A sordid chapter in American degradation
14 February	Rhodesia, a shield for South Africa
3 March	Apartheid, a policy for balanced development
20 March	The need for a white nation in Africa
17 April	A pertinent reminder about Communism
5 May	A race problem in Britain
12 May	Racial strife in Kenya
1 June	Nigeria disintegrates
6 June	Another UN failure in the Middle East
21 June	The riot season in the United States
6 July	Unrest in Nigeria and the Congo
13 July	Indigenous people of South West reject UN
9 August	Negro riots open eyes
16 August	Flirtations with Communism in Africa
7 November	Integration fosters hate
1 December	Barry Goldwater's visit to South Africa

Since music made up the major part of the SABC's radio programing, this component needed "sifting and arranging" as well, in order for the state radio service to function effectively in its new role as "a *generator* rather than simply a *transmitter* of culture."[14] The two broad guidelines set out by the SABC in its *Annual Report* of 1959, to "express the unique South African way of life" and to "comply with

[14] Hayman and Tomaselli, "Technology in the service," p. 21.

Christian ideals," led to different programing strategies for the SABC's "white" and "black" services.

Separate Development and radio music for white audiences

Just as the government was attempting to mobilize the entire population of the country behind its policy of Separate Development, many young whites were being distracted by the first wave of rock 'n' roll. The National Party, the Afrikaans press, and the Nederdruits Gereformeerde Kerk (NGK) all took vigorous stands against the "demoralising influence on youth and the aggravation of the youth problem" brought on by rock 'n' roll, which began to filter into the country in the late 1950s,[15] and the SABC was an implacable foe of this music. The problem, of course, was that this music was (correctly) understood to be of mixed racial origin and of potential appeal to various ethnic groups.

By 1966, despite these attempts to protect the youth of South Africa from potentially corrupting music, 45 per cent of white matriculants listened chiefly to "LM," a Mozambique-based station featuring recent American and British pop and rock music, according to a survey made by the SABC. By contrast, 20 per cent preferred Radio Springbok, 19 per cent the Afrikaans Service and a mere 4 per cent the English Service.

The SABC intervened on the cultural level by refusing to play certain types of contemporary popular music, on grounds that "a high proportion of [it] is morally unacceptable" (AR 1967, p. 32), and by offering in its place "something more than mere beat music . . . in harmony with and linked to a constantly growing desire in young people nowadays for programmes of a more serious kind" (AR 1966, p. 6), always in keeping with the ideology of Separate Development. Taking as a guide its own position that "our broadcasting service for Europeans must emphasise . . . our two different cultures and languages" (AR 1959, p. 4), the SABC developed separate strategies for its "white" services:

(1) The SABC had organized a "boereorkes," in an attempt to "copy and reconstruct Afrikaans traditional music," as far back as 1938.[16] By the mid-1960s, the Afrikaans Service was financing and broadcasting the music of more than thirty such "Boereorkeste." This music, like that of the contemporaneous "Folk Revival" in the United States and

---

[15] See Charles Hamm, "Rock 'n' roll in a very strange society," *Popular Music* 5 (1985), pp. 159–74. Reproduced as Chapter 8 in the present volume.
[16] Hayman and Tomaselli, "Ideology and technology," p. 39.

some European countries, drew on traditional styles and instruments, but was mediated by professional composers, arrangers, and performers who often themselves knew little of the tradition in question. For its younger listeners, the Afrikaans Service sponsored "competition for original Afrikaans light songs as a retort to the tidal wave of foreign pops" (*AR* 1968, p. 24). Ironically, in attempting to stem the tide of Anglo-American rock and pop music and to intensify "national" consciousness, the SABC trod the same path taken by many Communist-bloc countries by depriving audiences of easy access to this music, while offering in its place a product supposedly based on its own culture.

(2) The English Service emulated the BBC by ignoring rock 'n' roll while continuing to offer "light" music of the pre-rock era, with such programs as "Journey into melody" (light music for strings), "The melody lingers on" (music and artists of the 1920s), "Dance club" (popular "Old time ballroom dances"), and swing-era dance music played by the bands of Ray Martin, Dan Hill, Nolan Ranger, and Carroll Gibbons. For younger listeners there was the "Five o'clock show," an "attempt to win the adherence of young people by contrasting three programmes a week of record requests [of modern pop music, but not rock] with two of cultural and general knowledge" (*AR* 1969, p. 19).

(3) Springbok Radio, bi-lingual and bi-cultural, programed some of the same music offered on both the Afrikaans and English services, but gave much more air time to contemporary South African and foreign pop, though not rock.

Radio Bantu

SABC strategies for black listeners were quite different.

Separate Development proposed to "serve all population groups, each according to its own cultural ideals and aspirations in such a way that the faith, hope and love of that which is one's own is strengthened and expanded" (*AR* 1963, p. 6). An insurmountable cultural gap between white and black populations was assumed. As Albert Herzog put it, testifying before the South African Senate in support of amendment of the Broadcast Act of 1936:

> The Bantu experts will tell you – and we all know it – that the taste of a White Man is not the taste of a Bantu. The taste of a Bantu is not the taste of a White Man. We live in totally different spheres; you can almost say that we live in different civilisations. I do not for a moment allow myself to be told that these programmes which

224

are broadcast for our Europeans can give great satisfaction to the Bantu because we as Europeans do not understand the desires and tastes of the Bantu.[17]

The revised Broadcast Act, passed in 1960, established a Bantu Programme Control Board, chaired by Piet Meyer, charged with expanding the existing Zulu and Xhosa services, establishing new ones in the Northern Sotho, Southern Sotho, Tswana, Venda, and Tsonga languages, and arranging for the dissemination of these services to all areas, rural and urban, where these languages were spoken. This long-delayed expansion of radio service for the black population came about just at this time for three reasons.

Politically, the Verwoerd-era strategy of Separate Development required radio transmission to the entire black population, in its own languages, with such urgency that the cost of installing and operating an enormous new broadcasting network was no object. As the *Annual Report* stated in 1966,

> it was the approval and loan facilities of the State that enabled the SABC to tackle the huge FM scheme by which good radio reception became possible for the majority of the population, and by which the technical equipment could be created to provide the Bantu population groups with radio services. (p. 3)

Economically, the National Party was determined to move the Afrikaner population beyond its traditional subservience to British and foreign capital and into more control of the country's resources. A promising strategy was to capitalize on the rapidly growing purchasing power of the black population through the establishment of new Afrikaner-based commercial enterprises, which would target black consumers and use the state-controlled media to advertise their products.

Technologically, the new capabilities of FM transmission and the development of transistor receiving sets came at a fortuitous time for the South African government. As argued by Hayman and Tomaselli:

(1) FM transmission opened up a sufficient number of broadcast frequencies to allow the SABC to continue its three "European" services while adding new services in each of the major African languages, all receivable at a much higher level of quality than had been possible with medium-wave and short-wave transmission, both subject to atmospheric and mechanical interference.

---

[17] *The Senate of the Union of South Africa: Debates.* Third Session, 112th Parliament (Cape Town, 1960), pp. 245–7.

(2) FM transmitters, with their line-of-sight propagation, have a limited range, making it possible for the SABC to target the audience for each radio service with considerable precision, and thus create separate black ethnic services keyed to the government-designated homelands, thus providing an apparent ethnic cultural basis for political and economic segregation.

(3) As a result of technological advances and government subsidy, simple transistor radios became available to blacks at quite affordable prices in the 1960s. Since these were not capable of picking up short-wave transmissions, the black population was shielded from the increasingly critical and hostile short-wave broadcasts emanating from various parts of the world in response to the government's racial policies.

(4) These transistor receivers were battery-powered, which "suited the undeveloped, non-electrified nature of the designated homelands and non-electrified urban black townships." They were also portable, which "suited the particular characteristics and needs of migrant labour, and the increasingly mobile nature of urban life."[18]

As an interim measure, while the new FM transmission network was being brought on-line, the "Bantu Services" interpolated into English and Afrikaans programing were extended to an hour and a half each day and relayed to much more of the country, as follows:

(1) Zulu. Broadcast from Durban, relayed to Pietermaritzburg and Johannesburg, and from the latter city to the East and West Rand, where the country's largest mines were located.

(2) Xhosa. Broadcast from Grahamstown, relayed to East London, Port Elizabeth, and Cape Town.

(3) Southern Sotho. Broadcast from Johannesburg, relayed to Bloemfontein and Kimberley.

(4) Northern Sotho. Broadcast from Johannesburg, relayed to Pretoria and Pietersburg.

FM transmission of Radio Bantu, as the collective services for Blacks were now called, began on 1 January 1962. Radio Zulu and Radio SeSotho were on the air sixteen and a half hours a day, Radio Lebowa (Northern Sotho) and Radio Tswana broadcast nine and a half hours a day. Radio Xhosa, expanded to a full service, continued on medium-wave bands until 1967, when FM transmission became possible; the combined Radio Venda/Radio Tsonga service began on medium-wave in 1965, then switched to FM in 1969. By the end of the 1960s, Radio Bantu was broadcasting in seven African languages, on full-day schedules.

---

[18] Hayman and Tomaselli, "Technology in the service," pp. 40–1.

Radio Bantu and racial politics

Senator Ballinger, speaking for the opposition United Party during the debate over the establishment of the Bantu Programme Control Board in 1960, anticipated government strategy:

> Is there any necessity to have this special broadcasting for the Bantu or the African people? Surely, they are quite capable of arranging for themselves what they want in the way of culture. It gives one reason to doubt what is going to happen in the future. Are we going to have special news services for Bantu people? Is the Government going to put over its own propaganda to the Bantu people? And, of course, the answer is "Yes."[19]

The SABC *Annual Report* for 1960 contains details of the organization and program content of the Bantu News Service on the new Radio Bantu. More than 2,000 "Bantu radio correspondents" had already been appointed, charged with "making Radio Bantu truly serve the purpose of interpreting Bantu thought and reflecting the daily life of the Bantu, taking into account the special language and local interests of each particular group." Since these correspondents were able to furnish "such an extensive supply of news of mainly local interest . . . [on such topics as] Decimalisation, Soil Conservation, Animal Husbandry, Health Services, Education, and Bantu Officials" there was "hardly any time left for international news" (*AR* 1960, p. 20). In 1962, with FM transmission well under way, the SABC singled out as "highlights in the broadcasts of Radio Bantu" for that year:

(1) a statement by the Prime Minister on self-government for the Transkei;
(2) coverage of the official installation of five Bantu territorial authorities for the Zulu national unit;
(3) coverage of an agricultural day for Bantu farmers at Mooifontein, Lichtenburg;
(4) ceremonies marking the opening of the Bantu secondary school at Mabieskraal, Rustenburg;
(5) coverage of the world shaft-sinking record at the Buffelsfontein mine;
(6) a live broadcast of the institution of the Lebowa territorial authority;
(7) the final round of the South African non-white tennis championships;
(8) a feature on a new translation of the Bible into Southern Sotho;
(9) a discussion program on the pros and cons of the provision of alcoholic drink (to the Bantu [*AR* 1962, pp. 32–3]).

[19] *Debates*, 1960, p. 2459.

227

In 1964, coverage of "the official opening by the State President of the First Transkeian Parliament on the 5th of May," carried live on all seven services of Radio Bantu, was singled out as the "most important broadcast" of the year.

Simply put, "Radio Bantu sets itself the task of inducing the majority of black South Africans to accept their 'homeland' status and to view it as independence and development, while at the same time socialising a smaller cadre of the urban population into a work ethic."[20]

Since the government was committed to disseminating its mythology of Separate Development to the entire black population, not just the urban and elite classes, the success of its new radio strategy could be measured by simple statistics: the size of the total audience. The Rediffusion Service had reached an estimated 84,000 persons at its peak in 1956. In 1961, with expanded daily transmissions for Blacks carried on the English and Afrikaans Services, a survey commissioned from Franklin Research (Pty) Ltd revealed that there were some 500,000 "adult Bantu listeners" to these programs. By 1963, with full-time FM transmission of Radio Bantu in its second year, the audience had doubled to more than a million, and a similar survey showed some 2,300,000 "daily listeners" by the end of the decade. In 1974, a survey commissioned by the SABC from Market Research Africa (Pty) Ltd concluded that Radio Bantu had a more or less regular audience of approximately 4,700,000 "adult Bantu" (out of an estimated 9,359,000), and that "radio penetration" of the total black population (i.e., those who had access to a radio and listened to it at least "sometimes") had reached 97.7 per cent.

Other statistics verify this dramatic increase in black listenership following the establishment of Radio Bantu. Blacks owned some 103,000 radio receivers in 1962; the number had increased to 771,000 by 1966, and only two years later there were more than 2,000,000 black-owned sets. The count of letters received by Radio Bantu studios as program requests or entries in contests, published each year in the SABC's *Annual Report*, would seem suspect as an indicator of audience size, but in fact these figures match the profile charted by other statistics:

1962   332,302
1963   699,433
1964   1,274,695

---

[20] Keyan Tomaselli and Ruth Tomaselli, "Between policy and practice in the SABC, 1970–1981," in *Currents of Power: State Broadcasting in South Africa* (Bellville, 1989), pp. 100–1.

1965   2,357,168
1966   3,412,694
1967   6,500,000 (estimated)

Radio Bantu and music

Albert Herzog, Minister of Posts and Telegraphs, said in testifying for the establishment of a Bantu Programme Control Board,

> The broadcasting service is something which you cannot force on anybody; you cannot force him to listen. What you can do, though, is to attract listeners to listen to you and it is vitally important that we should attract those Bantu to listen to those things which the Broadcasting Corporation offer for them.[21]

Since by all methods of measurement the SABC was phenomenally successful in increasing its black listenership in the 1960s and 70s, and since by the SABC's own admission "music constitutes, and will always constitute, the most comprehensive component of any radio service" (*AR* 1964, p. 8), Radio Bantu's music programing obviously played a major role in its success in building its audience.

In order to be acceptable for play on Radio Bantu, it was necessary for a piece of music to satisfy two conditions:

(1) It must be ideologically correct. Overall SABC policy, applicable to "black" services as well as "white," dictated that all material aired must "comply with Christian ideals," that it must in no way "undermine the safety and the interests of the country or promote revolutionary intentions inside or outside the country's borders," and that it should reflect a "positive and healthy view of the South African way of life" (*AR* 1961, p. 6). More specifically, in order to promote the mythology of Separate Development all music programed on Radio Bantu should relate in some way to the culture of the "tribal" group at which a given service was aimed. There should be something "Zulu" about a piece to be played on Radio Zulu, something "Xhosa" about the music broadcast on Radio Xhosa. Performers should be of the proper ethnicity, members of the proper "tribe." Beyond that, if the piece were instrumental it should draw on melodic or performance traditions of that "tribal" group, or at least have a title in its language. If vocal, the piece should have a text in the appropriate African language, to help "promote self-development through the medium of [one's] own language," and this text should preferably relate to the specific culture or history of that "tribal" group.

Each service of Radio Bantu was directed to set up a review board,

[21] *Debates*, 1960, pp. 2445–7.

and no piece of music could be aired until this board had determined that it met the above requirements. In effect, these review boards had censorship power over all music played on Radio Bantu, in addition to (and independent of) the censorship decisions of the Publications Committee in Pretoria, which was empowered to ban any publication (including a recording) throughout the entire country.

(2) It must be accessible and attractive to listeners, since the imperative of Radio Bantu was to sell ideology and commodities to the largest possible black audience, not to educate its listeners or to "elevate" their musical taste. To this end, Radio Bantu from the beginning projected an image of a positive alliance with the musical life of black South Africa, and of offering music for all tastes:

> Guiding, inspiring, encouraging the Bantu musical potential, developing all around it in South Africa, Radio Bantu has virtually become the focal point round which much of Bantu music revolves. . . . Radio Bantu continues to encourage both professional and amateur Bantu musician alike. The soloist – the choir – the group – the vocalist – the bandsmen are recorded week after week in Radio Bantu studios throughout the country.[22]

> Special attention was given to the placing of a variety of programmes ranging from traditional music to light classical presentations. Contemporary Bantu music, for example township jazz, was not ignored. Musical programmes included the following: traditional music; broadcasts by light musical groups; contemporary Bantu music; Bantu school choirs; the latest gramophone releases in the Bantu musical world; new SABC transcription recordings; regular programmes on Bantu composers; request programmes of different types; music from Africa; religious music; a musical programme for grandfathers and grandmothers; special scripted programmes on light classical music; music from the films; and music competitions. (*AR* 1962, p. 30)

In essence, all music selected for programing on Radio Bantu fell into three large genres: traditional, choral, and popular.

Traditional African music

The traditional music of black South Africans seemed ideal for the imperatives of Radio Bantu. Theoretically, no music could emphasize the separate identity of each "tribe" more emphatically than a repertory dating from a time when, according to the mythology of Separate Development, each "tribal" group formed a relatively

[22] Yvonne Huskisson, *Die Bantoe-Komponiste van Suider-Afrika* (Johannesburg, 1969), pp. xi, xxiii.

discrete cultural and political entity. Accordingly, in the first years of Radio Bantu the SABC intensified its policy of making transcription recordings of such music, "in an effort to preserve the Bantu traditional musical heritage":[23]

(1) in 1960 "a further 500 recordings of typical Bantu tribal music" were made (*AR* 1960, p. 21);
(2) nearly 1,000 recordings of "Bantu music of the various language groups" were made by SABC teams in 1961 (*AR* 1961, p. 32);
(3) during 1962, sixty-three field recording trips yielded more than 6,000 items of "traditional Bantu music" (*AR* 1962, p. 24);
(4) visits by mobile recording units to "remote parts of the Bantu homelands" added 2,000 items in 1964 (*AR* 1964, p. 32);
(5) recording expeditions were undertaken into neighboring countries, to collect music in languages spoken also in South African.

A great deal of air time was given to this music, in an attempt to attract new listeners from among those people thought to be still in contact with traditional music: blacks remaining in the rural homelands; farm workers in "white" areas; rural people migrating in such increasing numbers into the townships surrounding South Africa's cities and towns.

But in fact many of these people were in full retreat from their own cultural past, partly because they had been told so repeatedly by whites that European culture was superior to African, partly because of the strong appeal of Western (particularly American) contemporary culture. In the words of Hugh Tracey, "there is this feeling [among native peoples] that if you go back too far to being African you're going back to the bush, the unfettered, the primitive. . . . [Blacks] want to be westernised, be modern urban people."[24] A black writer agreed: "Africans almost invariably prefer Western culture – Western dress, manners, usages and speech – to their own. Western culture is associated with economic advantage as well as with status."[25] Or, as it was put even more succinctly by a patron at the Bantu Mens' Social Center in Johannesburg to Jim Bailey, editor of *Drum* magazine:

Tribal music! Tribal history! Chiefs! We don't care about chiefs! Give us jazz and film stars, man! We want Duke Ellington, Sachmo, and hot dames! Yes, brother, anything American. You can cut out this junk about kraals and folk-tales and Basutos in blankets – forget it! You're just trying to keep us backward, that's what![26]

[23] *Ibid.*, p. xxiii.
[24] As quoted in Muff Andersson, *Music in the Mix: The Story of South African Popular Music* (Johannesburg, 1981), p. 18.
[25] John Nkosi, "Africans' cultural dilemma," *African Music* 3 (1965), p. 115.

The struggle over culture thus took a curious turn in South Africa. The government itself, as part of its political agenda, focused on the perpetuation and romanticization of "native" cultures:

> From the cradle to the grave, song and dance accompany every phase of Bantu life and living. Lullabies soothe the new-born infant. The Bantu child grows up in a musical atmosphere which it cannot help but absorb. . . . The women sing as they go about their domestic rounds. . . . As the men ply their crafts, songs match the movement of their hands. Returning from the hunt, they sing of their exploits. At the Chief's place, he is praised and valorous deeds of tribal heroes related in song. Songs implore the rain to fall and are raised in joyful gratitude once it has fallen. Relaxed, round a pot of household beer, men and women sing. At a tribal celebration or social festivity, songs abound. Death itself, is mourned in song.[27]

But eventually the strategy of emphasizing and supporting "traditional" culture as a means of dividing and controlling the Black population was to become transparent to critics of the political leadership of the country.

> It is part of a reactionary policy to encourage people to look back to some mythical past. Tribal symbols are not romantic, they no longer have the same meaning, precisely because they are being used by the state to mystify the structures of oppression. . . . Against this background, tribal music sours like sorghum beer.[28]

If Radio Bantu was to attract and hold the majority of the black radio audience, it became obvious by the mid-1960s that traditional music was of limited and decreasing effectiveness.

Choral music

First introduced into mission schools in the nineteenth century, Western-style choral singing took much deeper root in black South African culture than in colonial societies elsewhere, perhaps because the traditional music of the Nguni, Sotho, and other ethnic groups of the region was itself predominantly choral. The first mission choirs sang simple four-part Christian hymns, with texts translated into the appropriate African language. As skills improved, more complex anthems and even the "Hallelujah Chorus" from Handel's *Messiah*

---

[26] Anthony Sampson, *Drum* (London, 1956), p. 20.
[27] Huskisson, *Die Bantoe-Komponiste*, p. vii.   [28] Andersson, *Music in the Mix*, p. 18.

and the occasional motet by Palestrina entered the repertories of many such groups. Graduates of mission schools in turn formed their own church and community choirs.

> It is the thousands of Bantu men and women who make up the ordinary domestic and business scene of South Africa who form the bulk membership of church and independent choirs, as an outlet for their inherent musicality. As schools and churches have come to every Bantu community, so choirs have multiplied. The standard of Bantu Choir singing in both town and country is very high.[29]

Most of this choir music seemed ideal for Radio Bantu. It was already widely popular, in the sense that so many blacks in various parts of the country, both urban and rural, already participated in choral singing. In addition, Radio Bantu in a continuing attempt to use Christianity to pacify the black population had from the beginning followed a policy of opening and closing each day's programing with prayers, and of broadcasting complete sermons and church services on Sunday. The texts of pieces sung by African choirs were mostly religious and usually sung in "tribal" languages, and were thus doubly appropriate for Radio Bantu.

Material was readily available for air play. Hundreds of commercial recordings by such groups as the Marivate's Double Quartet, the Zulu Sacred Singers, the RLD Choir, the Morija Training College Male Choir, the Xhosa Sacred Singers, Shembe's Church Choir, and the Sechuana Sacred Singers had been released by domestic and foreign record companies. Also, the SABC itself had already amassed a collection of transcription recordings of choir music, and it proceeded to augment this collection greatly in the years following the establishment of Radio Bantu. In 1963 alone, for instance, SABC mobile units visited 435 Bantu schools, recording 7,374 items.

Choral music was one of the cornerstones of Radio Bantu music programing, and Yvonne Huskisson, SABC's Organiser of Bantu Music, could write in 1969:

> The vast expansion of Radio Bantu since 1960 has seen the opening up of unprecedented scope and the providing of a stimulus for Bantu composer and choir alike. For composers to know that they are now not only keeping school and church choirs supplied with song material, but that their works are being heard on the air and so being brought to the ears of thousands of listeners, is a real

---

[29] Huskisson, *Die Bantoe-Komponiste*, pp. xx–xxi.

source of inspiration to them. There is more purpose in their music writing.[30]

Popular music

It was all very well for the English and Afrikaans Services to take a putative moral stand against certain types of popular music, under the pretense that their mission was to educate and "uplift" their audiences, but Radio Bantu had a somewhat different mission: to catch the attention of as many black people as possible and then persuade them of the "naturalness" of Separate Development. There was no question of passing moral or aesthetic judgement on music, or of attempting to "elevate" musical taste. All pieces which succeeded in "attracting listeners to listen" would do, provided they gave no evidence of attempting to subvert the goals of Separate Development, in content or association.

According to statistics compiled for the SABC,[31] only some 12 per cent of South Africa's black population had been educated to the level of Standard 6 or beyond, and at least one third had no education whatsoever. Choir music, cultivated chiefly by educated blacks, proved useful in attracting persons of this class to Radio Bantu; but if these broadcasts were to succeed in attracting black working class and unemployed populations as well, music with a much wider base would have to be programed. Consequently, by the late 1960s the bulk of music programing on Radio Bantu was given over to popular genres, on the assumption that these were best calculated to attract and hold a mass audience.

Radio Bantu went into full-scale operation at a period of transition and proliferation in black South African popular music. The 1920s and 30s had brought the development of "a single urban African musical style called *marabi*," a genre

> strongly influenced by the social and economic conditions of working-class life. Growing out of shebeen society, *marabi* was much more than just a musical style. As music it had a distinctive rhythm and blend of African polyphonic principles, restructured within the framework of the Western "three-chord" harmonic system. As a dance it placed a few limits on variation and interpretation by individuals or couples, though the emphasis was definitely on sexuality. As a social occasion it was a convivial, neighbourhood gathering for drinking, dancing, coupling, friendship and other forms of interaction.[32]

[30] *Ibid.*, p. xxi.
[31] Market Research Africa (pty) Ltd., *A Study of Bantu Radio Listening* (Johannesburg, 1974). Similar studies were made in 1975, 1976, and 1977.
[32] Coplan, *In Township Tonight!*, p. 94.

Marabi may not have been considered suitable for Radio Bantu because of its identification with illegal activities, but the point was moot, since a cluster of other popular styles had succeeded it before the birth of Radio Bantu. Among these were:

Isicathamiya, mbube. As early as the first and second decades of the twentieth century, African choral groups were developing syncretic styles combining Western harmonic progressions with the call-and-response patterns and rhythmic vitality of African styles. One of these, *isicathamiya*, was developed first in Durban around 1920 by such groups as the Crocodiles and the Dundee Evening Birds,[33] then carried to Johannesburg by Solomon Linda, whose Evening Birds became popular and influential not only with live performances but also through phonograph discs brought out in the 1930s and 40s by Gallo, the largest South African record company.[34] The title of their very first commercial release, "Mbube," soon replaced "isicathamiya" as the genre name for a range of performance styles by unaccompanied male vocal ensembles.[35]

An authentic working-class style thriving chiefly in all-night competitions among groups housed in all-male workers' hostels, *mbube* proved ideal for Radio Bantu. As a "Zulu" style, cultivated only among Zulus, sung in the Zulu language and consequently programed at first only on Radio Zulu, it served admirably to perpetuate the myth of Separate Development.

Even though some *isicathamiya* groups had performed and recorded pieces with oppositional sentiments, Radio Zulu's review board would not allow such texts to be broadcast after 1960 and commercial record companies were no longer willing to issue them, since they saw no future in recording music which could not be played on the air. The history of Ladysmith Black Mambazo, the most successful *mbube* group, illustrates the impact of Radio Bantu's policies on this genre after 1960. "Discovered" during Radio Bantu auditions in Durban, the group first made transcription discs for Radio Zulu itself, then was signed to a contract by Gallo. Within a decade they had brought out a dozen LPs, with sales of several million units. The texts of their songs avoid all controversial topics:

---

[33] Veit Erlmann, "African popular music in Durban, 1913–1939" (typescript, 1989), pp. 34–6. Parts of this study were subsequently published in *Popular Music* 8/3 (October 1989), pp. 259–74, as "Horses in the race course: the domestication of ingoma dancing in South Africa, 1929–39."

[34] Veit Erlmann, "'Singing brings joy to the distressed': the early social history of Zulu migrant workers' choral music," in *African Stars: Studies in Black South African Performance* (Chicago and London, 1991), p. 165–9.

[35] See Veit Erlmann, *Mbube Roots: Zulu Choral Music from South Africa, 1930s–1960s* (Cambridge, 1986).

"We keep the radio in mind when we compose. If something is contentious they don't play it, and then it wouldn't be known to the public anyway." [36] Their subject matter deals chiefly with either religion or Zulu customs and traditions. As a promotional brochure put it, they "emerged as messiahs restoring national pride in a shattered heritage" – this heritage being of course that of the Zulu.

Jazz. American films and phonograph records brought contemporary American popular styles to South Africa in the 1920s and 30s. Since black South African musicians had virtually no direct contact with African-Americans and their music during this time,[37] they were dependent for their models on what was made available to them through the media: commercial "jazz," usually mediated by white producers and impresarios, turned out by the American entertainment industry, as performed by Cab Calloway, the Ink Spots, Lena Horne, the Mills Brothers, Bill Robinson, Ethel Waters, and black and white swing bands. With no exposure to the black styles that many jazz scholars of today consider most "authentic," such as New Orleans jazz, the territorial bands of the Midwest, stride piano, or urban blues, the earliest black South African jazz bands and vocal groups of the 1940s – the Merry Blackbirds, the Japanese Express, the Manhattan Brothers, the Rhythm Kings, the Jazz Maniacs[38] – took commercial American jazz as their starting point.

> The Merry Blackbirds imported orchestrations. They played nothing else, and there was nobody to touch them. Don't I remember their show in Queenstown in 1940, when a capacity crowd just stood, staring, dazed, thrilled at the big band playing "In the Mood." Nobody danced. Everybody stood marvelling. Swing had arrived.[39]

Eventually these and other groups developed more characteristically African jazz styles.[40] At the same time, the term "jazz" began to be used as a generic term for a wide range of social dance music. Chiefly an urban music, appealing to both educated and working classes, African jazz was a mainstay of pre-Separate Development broadcasts for "natives." It reached its peak of popularity in the late 1950s and early 60s, when the "jazz" musical *King Kong* toured the entire

---

[36] Andersson, *Music in the Mix*, p. 870.
[37] See Charles Hamm, *African-American Music, South Africa, and Apartheid* (Brooklyn, 1988), Reproduced as Chapter 9 in the present volume.
[38] See Coplan, *In Township Tonight!*, pp. 130–80, and Chris Ballantine, "A brief history of South African popular music," *Popular Music* 8/3 (October 1989), pp. 305–10.
[39] Todd Matshikiza, *Chocolates for my Wife* (London, 1961), p. 43.
[40] Coplan, *In Township Tonight!*, pp. 130–80.

country (and eventually played in London), large jazz festivals were held in Johannesburg's City Hall (1961), Soweto's Moroka-Jabavu Stadium (1962), and Orlando Stadium (1963), and a live jazz scene flourished in Cape Town.

But true jazz became of increasingly limited usefulness to Radio Bantu after 1960, for several reasons. Its appeal never extended to the largely uneducated rural blacks who made up a majority of the population and whom the radio service was determined to reach; and some jazz musicians chose political stands and actions leading to imprisonment or exile. Jazz was gradually replaced on Radio Bantu by more broadly based, popular styles.

Kwela. In the 1940s, first in Johannesburg and then elsewhere in southern Africa, black musicians could be observed playing tin whistles on street corners and in other public places, hoping for a few pennies from passersby. Most of these street musicians were young, often in their early teens; their instrument was a small metal cylinder with six finger holes and a whistle mouthpiece, brought to South Africa by marching units attached to the British military and imitated by bands of black musicians as early as the 1910s.

This music soon caught the attention of the media. Donald Swanson used pennywhistler Willard Cele in his widely praised film of 1950, *The Magic Garden.* Gallo released a 78 rpm disc of Cele playing two pieces from the film, and other companies rushed to find other whistlers, the most successful proving to be Johannes "Spokes" Mashiyane, who by the mid-1950s had recorded more than twenty titles for Trutone and whose *Kwela Spokes* was awarded a Golden Disc (certifying sales of 50,000 copies) by the South African record industry. By now, the pennywhistle was generally accompanied by a rhythm section of acoustic guitar, bass, and a trap set, and had been discovered by the white population as well.

Some pennywhistle pieces included the word "kwela" in their titles, and Western ethnomusicologists began using this word, inaccurately, for the entire pennywhistle repertory as well as similar pieces using other instrumentation.[41] In fact, "kwela" was the correct designation only for pieces using rhythmic patterns appropriate for the kwela, a popular social dance of the time. Like African jazz, kwela was a mainstay of SABC radio programing for "natives" in the

[41] See David Rycroft, "The new 'Town Music' of southern Africa," *Recorded Folk Music* 1 (1958), pp. 54 ff.; Wolfgang Laade, *Neue Musik in Afrika, Asien und Ozeanian* (Heidelberg, 1971); Gerhard Kubik, *The Kachamba Brothers' Band* (Vienna, 1972); Gerhard Kubik, "Kwela," in *The New Grove Dictionary of Music and Musicians,* ed. Stanley Sadie (London, 1980), vol. 10, p. 330.

1950s, and the larger genre of which it was a part, jive, subsequently became the musical style most favored by Radio Bantu.

Jive. In South Africa as in the United States, the word "jive" functions both as a noun, designating a specific kind of music, and as a verb denoting what one *does* to this music:

> Beside a radiogram in the corner [of the "Back o' the Moon" in Sophiatown] sat a middle-aged African woman with glasses, in a low-cut black dress, looking through a high pile of ten-inch records. She chose a record and walked mincingly to the radiogram. The jazz noise blared against the bare walls and rattled the loudspeaker. Fatsy, without warning, jumped into a jerky jive, shaking up and down like jelly. She swayed in front of Can and me, with her podgy hands outstretched to an imaginary partner, while the floorboards creaked. Can shot up like a spring released, and jived wildly in front of her, and Fatsy shouted in delight. "Don't you jive, Mr. Tony?" shouted Fatsy. Everyone looked around at me. "Don't be shy, Mr. Tony!" sang Fatsy to the rhythm, and lunged at Can and clasped him.[42]

In the 1950s, "jive" gradually replaced "jazz" as the generic term for a large repertory of black South African social dance music descended from *marabi* and characterized by a succession of brief melodic fragments, repeated and varied but never developed in the Western sense, unfolding over a constantly reiterated harmonic cycle of four, eight, or sometimes twelve chords.

"Pennywhistle jive" was now the designation for all pennywhistle music, whether based on the kwela or some other dance rhythm, and "accordion jive" became the label for similar music featuring that instrument. When Spokes Mashiyane, Lemmy "Special" Mabaso and other whistlers switched to the soprano or alto saxophone in the late 1950s and were joined by a new generation of sax players in the early 1960s (Reggie Msomi, Albert Ralumini, Mac Tshabalala), "sax jive" became the new rage.

Also, small vocal groups accompanied by a rhythm section had moved beyond their earlier imitations of black American vocal jazz combos (the Ink Spots and Mills Brothers) to a more "African" style labelled "vocal jive," in which melodic fragments, often drawn from traditional repertories and usually in simplified call-and-response patterns, were sung over constantly repeating short harmonic cycles. As in all South African jive of this era, harmonic and rhythmic support came from guitar, bass, and drums. Early vocal

---

[42] Sampson, *Drum*, pp. 57–8.

jive groups were both male and female: a popular line-up became a female group fronted by a male singer.

In the early 1960s the electric guitar and then the electric bass were incorporated into jive, assuming roles as melodic instruments. A new style of "sax jive" resulted, in performances by Bra Sello, West Nkosi, Strike Vilakazi, Sparks Nyembe, and many others, with the saxophone alternating as lead instrument with the electric guitar, playing new melodic styles pioneered by Phuzushukela and other guitarists in response to the new capabilities of an electric instrument. With the electric bass assuming greater prominence as well, the instrumental texture became much more complex and contrapuntal. Vocal jive also began incorporating electric guitar and bass, in the music of Bkekitsche, the Mahotella Queens, Moses Mchunu, and Mahlokohloko.

As the most dynamic black popular style of the 1960s, jive was embraced by Radio Bantu with such enthusiasm and success, and came to be identified so closely with radio performance, that it was sometimes called *msakazo* ("radio music"). As a staff member of the SABC described the emergence of jive:

> The advent of RADIO BANTU in 1960s gave an additional impetus to the commercial production of LIGHT MUSIC, to serve its seven different language Programme Services. There are few original Bantu COMPOSERS in this music field. The majority of Bantu LIGHT MUSIC still consists of "hotted up" versions of the "traditional," rendered by close-harmony male/female light-vocal groups, with or without male lead, to band accompaniment, the strong rhythm of "traditional" song and dance predominating in the percussive beat, having instant "record" and "radio" appeal.[43]

Jive was the most useful music for the imperatives of Radio Bantu for several reasons. Instrumental jive, since it was textless, could not project sentiments which might "undermine the interest or the safety of the country or promote revolutionary intentions." Vocal jive, in drawing on the languages and "traditional" music of a given ethnic group, underlined the cultural uniqueness of that "tribe." The Bogard Brothers, the Gandy Brothers, the Dark City Sisters, and Gladys Setai and the Sisters performed "Sotho vocal jive," appropriate for Radio SeSotho; Izintombi Zesi Manje Manje, the Mahlokohloko Stars, and dozens of similar groups performed "Zulu vocal jive."

Even though, according to Veit Erlmann:

---

[43] Huskisson, *Die Bantoe-Komponiste*, p. ix.

In South Africa, the determination of the class basis of urban culture is rendered difficult by the fact that the rapid expansion of the capitalist mode of production was not accompanied by the formation of fully established and culturally homogeneous classes.[44]

Nevertheless some rough stratification of social structures did take place among the black population, musical preference to some extent matched social status, and radio music in pre-Separate Development days had been selected largely on the basis of its appeal to those classes of people most likely to have access to radio broadcasts. But the imperatives of Radio Bantu were different, to reach the entire black population, and the audience for jive, more than that for any earlier popular genre, cut across any class lines that might have existed. It retained African elements (fragments of older melodies, cyclic structures, call-and-response patterns), but it was also modern, in its use of contemporary instruments and triadic harmonies and its dissemination by the mass media.

Marabi, *mbube*, African jazz, and kwela had all originated in and been shaped by live performance situations and only afterwards appropriated by the media. Jive, on the other hand, was appropriated by Radio Bantu and commercial record companies almost from the beginning and adapted for live performance afterwards. It was truly "radio music."

Expansion of Radio Bantu

By the late 1970s, with seven "vernacular" services in full operation, Radio Bantu had an audience of more than five million, according to surveys commissioned by the SABC:

Radio Zulu	2,347,000
Radio SeSotho	981,000
Radio Tswana	835,000
Radio Xhosa	773,000
Radio Lebowa	488,000
Radio Tsonga	90,000
Radio Venda	85,000
	5,180,000 = total listenership for Radio Bantu

(*AR* 1980)

By the early 1980s, with the addition of Radio Swazi and Radio Ndebele to the network of Radio Bantu, each of ten "National States" was blanketed by a radio service transmitting in the "official" language, as shown in Table 10.1. In addition, one or more services

---

[44] Erlmann, "African popular music," p. 4.

Table 10.1

"National state"	Vernacular service	Broadcast language
Kwazulu	Radio Zulu	Zulu
Transkei	Radio Xhosa	Xhosa
Ciskei	Radio Xhosa	Xhosa
Bophuthatswana	Radio Tswana	SeTswana
Lebowa	Radio Lebowa	Northern Sotho
Qwaqwa	Radio SeSotho	Southern Sotho
Gazankulu	Radio Tsonga	Tsonga
Venda	Radio Venda	LuVenda
KaNgwane	Radio Swazi	SiSwati
KwaNdebele	Radio Ndebele	Ndebele

of Radio Bantu were broadcast in those urban areas with large concentrations of blacks. Radio Zulu, Radio SeSotho, and Radio Tswana could be received in the Rand, with its millions of blacks in the townships and mines surrounding Johannesburg; Radio Zulu was disseminated in Durban and other cities and towns in Natal province; Radio Xhosa was broadcast throughout the Eastern Cape.

Convinced of the importance of Namibia to its economic and political future, the South African government began applying its strategies of Separate Development to that region as well. White South Africans were enticed into the territory by the easy availability of the best farming land, while the remainder of the country was carved up in 1964 into so-called "homelands" for the several indigenous ethnic groups, with forced removals of "natives" to these areas. With the success of Radio Bantu fresh in mind, South Africa decided to commit the necessary capital to install and operate a network of state radio services for the various ethnic populations of Namibia, no matter how small their numbers. In preparation, SABC recording teams sent to Namibia had collected "987 items in thirteen dialects" by 1968 (*AR* 1968, p. 40), then concentrated on music of the Herero, Damara, and Nama peoples (*AR* 1969, p. 39). There were three services which began FM transmission on 1 December 1969: Radio Ovambo, Radio Herero, Radio Damara/Nama (*AR* 1969, p. 41). Given the extremely low population density and large land mass of Namibia, these were transmitted at first only in the Windhoek area, with its relatively large concentration of various black peoples. But in time regional transmitters extended transmission to other towns and also the newly created "homelands," and several

Table 10.2

Ethnic group	Population	Radio service
Wambo	442,939	Radio Owambo
White	110,271	Afrikaans Service
		English Service
		German Service
Damara	85,518	Radio Damara/Nama
Kavango	65,254	Radio Kavango
Herero	61,988	Radio Herero
Nama	42,865	Radio Damara/Nama
Colored	36,571	–
East-Caprivi	33,205	*
"Bushman"	29,343	–
Rehoboth Baster	22,256	–
Kaokolander	7,459	–
Tswana	4,937	*
Other	18,919	–

*Weekly programming on another service

additional services were put into operation. By the early 1980s, the structure shown in Table 10.2 was operational.

By the mid-1980s, the grand media strategy theorized in 1960 was finally in full operation. All of South Africa, and Namibia as well, was blanketed by a complex radio network ensuring that each person would have easy access to a state-controlled radio service in his/her own language, dedicated to "mould[ing] his intellect and his way of life" by stressing the distinctiveness and separateness of "his" cultural/ethnic heritage – in other words, to promoting the mythology of Separate Development. The majority of program time was given over to music, selected for its appeal to the largest possible number of listeners within that particular ethnic group, functioning to attract an audience to a radio service whose most important business was selling ideology.

Surely this media policy was an important factor in the South African government's success in carrying out its scheme of Separate Development. By the early 1980s, an entire generation of South Africans, black and white, had been subjected since birth to the relentless suggestion that each population group within their country was culturally unique, and that ethnic boundaries, not only those separating black and white but between the various African "tribes" as well, should not be breached.

Fruits of this policy, persisting to the present, include not only the inability of most white South Africans to confront the inevitability of a multi-racial government, but certainly the bitter "factional fighting" between "tribal" groups as well.

The end of radio monopoly

As detailed by Hayman and Tomaselli[45] and summarized above, the SABC made effective and often imaginative use of new communications technology in the 1960s and into the 1970s. But as Afrikaner theorists themselves recognized from the beginning, radio programing "is something which you cannot force on anybody." The success of a strategy dependent on having targeted audiences listen to given radio programs depends not only on the effectiveness with which these are made available and the attractiveness of program content, but also on the absence of alternate radio services. The SABC had achieved all this by the early 1970s, only to see its control over the latter factor begin to slip away, and with it the effectiveness of the overall strategy.

The physical vastness of the Republic of South Africa and its remoteness from most of the rest of the world initially ensured the SABC of almost total control of the airwaves. Black South Africans equipped only with inexpensive FM-AM transistor receivers could tune in neither programs from most neighboring African countries nor shortwave transmissions from Europe and North America. But despite this near-monopoly, only 70.8 per cent of the blacks interviewed in 1974 identified Radio Bantu as the service they "usually listened to," a percentage which dropped to 67.5 per cent in 1975, 64.2 per cent in 1976, and 63.9 per cent in 1977.[46]

Initially, Radio Bantu's most important competition came from "LM," a commercial radio station established in 1935 in neighboring Mozambique, which by the 1960s was transmitting a strong enough signal to be received in much of South Africa. "LM" programed the latest rock and pop hits from the USA and the UK, with David Davies and others emulating the frenetic new style of American AM disc jockeys. Audience research in the early 1970s revealed that 8.3 per cent of the black population listed "LM" as the radio service "most often listened to." This posed a problem for Radio Bantu, since by choosing a foreign radio station, South African blacks were not exposed to those "other things" which the SABC wanted them to

---

[45] Hayman and Tomaselli, "Technology in the service."
[46] A Study of Bantu Radio Listening, 1974–7.

hear. The reasons for "LM"'s popularity were surely musical, not political. Mozambique was still under Portuguese control, and no criticism of South African policy or ideology was aired from Lorenco Marques in those days; but it was the only radio station in the region devoting substantial air time to recent European and American pop music. The problem was solved in 1972 when the SABC somehow managed to take control of "LM," renaming it Radio 5 and bringing its programing more into line with SABC policy.

There was nothing to stop blacks from listening to the SABC's "European" services, and the extent to which they did so was determined largely by musical programing. Springbok Radio, devoting some 70 per cent of its air time to "light" music, was the preferred service of 7.1 per cent of the black population, while the English Service (2.2 per cent) and the Afrikaans Service (0.2 per cent), with their conservative and dour attitudes towards music, trailed far behind. By 1980, blacks made up almost half the audience for Springbok Radio and two-thirds of that for Radio 5, still largely devoted to pop music (see Table 10.3).

As Separate Development progressed to the point whereby several of the "National States" opted for nominal independence, each was allowed to establish its own radio service as one token of its supposed autonomy. Transkei (Radio Transkei, or "TKI") was first, in the mid-1960s, then Bophuthatswana (Radio Bophuthatswana, or "Radio Bop") in 1977, Venda (Radio Thohoyandou) in 1979 and Ciskei (Radio Ciskei, or "CKI") in 1981. These new services, though carefully overseen at first by the SABC, gradually developed programing patterns which ran counter to Radio Bantu's mission of stressing ethnic and linguistic separateness. English was introduced as a second program language, on all four. Considerable air time was given to European, American, and Caribbean popular songs, and to music by South African popular performers of "tribal" backgrounds other than that of the "homeland" audiences. By the 1980s, Top 10 countdowns mixing international hits with pieces by the best South African pop performers had become standard on all "homeland" services. And even though none of these stations dared broadcast pieces banned by the South African Publications Board, they sometimes played music barred by the review boards of one or another of the Radio Bantu services. Announcers began trumpeting their stations' new autonomy: "This is Radio Bop, the station with a mind of its own," and "This is Radio Transkei, the station with a difference."

Thus these new radio services, which had come into existence precisely because of Separate Development's success in creating pseudo-autonomous "National States," developed patterns of musical programing challenging the notion that each ethnic group in South Africa had a unique culture which should not be "contaminated." And the proliferation of alternative radio services did not stop with the institution of "homeland" services. As Muff Andersson put it:

> It seems as though the government's homeland policy has tripped itself up. In striving to prove that the so-called homelands of Bophuthatswana and Transkei are indeed independent countries, it has allowed those puppet governments to negotiate radio stations. The companies involved in setting up stations have made sure that the "homeland government" may in no way interfere with [policy].[47]

Capital Radio was the first independent radio service licensed to transmit from one of the "homelands," going on the air in December 1979 with transmitters located in the Transkei powerful enough to reach much of South Africa.

> The format is that of a popular music station with a core of "top 40" records which are rotated at a predetermined rate once every hour. Other musical fare is made up of rock, reggae, country music and contemporary jazz. Music is interspersed with extensive sports coverage and hourly three-minute news bulletins. The station models itself on the successful formula of the London station of the same name.[48]

Music Radio 702, broadcasting from Bophuthatswana to Johannesburg and much of the Transvaal, followed in May 1980. There were also independent Christian services, such as Southern Sounds from the Transkei.

Other services aimed at South Africa audiences began operating from neighboring countries. Swaziland Commercial Radio, which had nothing to do with Swaziland beyond the fact that most of its transmitters were located in that country, was a complex of five services: Radio 702, mentioned above, broadcasting chiefly from Bophuthatswana; Radio SR (Super Rhythm), programed for black audiences, with an emphasis on funk, soul, and disco; Radio Truro, for Indian audiences; Radio Parelelo 27, in Portuguese; and The Jewish Sound. Trans World Radio, also transmitting from Swaziland, offered religious programs in all the "native" languages spoken in South Africa. In addition, a powerful relay station for the Voice of

---

[47] Andersson, *Music in the Mix*, pp. 95–6.
[48] Tomaselli and Tomaselli, "Between policy and practice," p. 139.

America went into operation in Botswana in the mid-1980s, making it possible for South Africans to receive this service on AM frequencies for the first time.

The SABC monopoly of the airwaves had effectively ended. Listeners throughout South Africa could now choose from among a wide range of radio programs unaffiliated with the government, on easy to receive FM or AM channels. Audiences were no longer restricted to news and commentary reflecting the government's ideology and strategies, to music selected to perpetuate the mythology of Separate Development, or to religious programing designed to attract black Christians to Radio Bantu.

The carefully constructed myth of ethnic separateness perpetuated by the SABC for two decades was challenged by everyday empirical evidence, as radio audiences chose, enjoyed, and comprehended music created by persons from other ethnic backgrounds. Radio Bantu had no choice but to adapt or lose its audience to other radio services. In gradual reversals of policy, it began programing more black American and European pop music; Caribbean music, even reggae, was offered selectively, after careful screening of texts; pieces by black South African pop stars of one ethnicity were played on services of Radio Bantu aimed at other "tribal" groups. Top 20 programing, mixing recently recorded pieces by black Africans with international hits, was introduced to the various "black" services. Linguistic separateness was a casualty, as song lyrics in English and sometimes other African languages were programed on Radio Bantu's various services. In perhaps the most telling stroke of all, the inauguration of Radio Metro ("The Sound of the City"), a new "black" service, signalled the crumbling of two cornerstones of Separate Development, in accepting a permanent urban black presence and a single program language (English).

Conclusion

The above narrative suggests the following working hypotheses concerning state radio services and their use of music:

(1) Radio programing can be read as propagating, reinforcing, and sometimes predicting state ideology and strategy, which are imbedded at the first level in the structural organization of a broadcast service, and at a second level in program content.

(2) Since music usually occupies more air time than any other program component, the selection of music for air play must be coordinated with overall state ideology.

(3) The chief political and cultural impact of radio music comes not from texts of songs, but in more pervasive ways.

(4) The effectiveness of state-controlled radio in perpetuating ideology depends on the degree of "radio penetration" within a given country, and on the extent to which that population is shielded from alternative radio services.

Epilogue

The above narrative and analysis is based on research carried out in the Republic of South Africa between 1978 and 1985. I have not been in the country since then and thus my knowledge of recent events is based on second-hand information, all of which suggests that the loosening of state control of the airways has intensified, particularly since the winter of 1990. For example, one now reads:

> The South African Broadcasting Corporation [now] regularly reports on and interviews members of the ANC and other liberation groups on its nightly television news. Recent programmes on the SABC have featured a self-styled "Meet the Press" interview with Nelson Mandela and several South African reporters, and a special profile of Soweto discussing the township's people, politics and standard of living. Max Coleman, a member of the South African Human Rights Commission, told IRRC, "we're seeing things on our TV screens that we would have never seen three months ago. It's like a brain transplant."
>
> Pretoriastroika has also encouraged South Africa's semi-independent broadcasting sector to push the edge of press freedom. Radio 702 . . . now has news on township violence and political issues every hour. In the evenings the station has a call-in radio show [Talk at Ten, hosted by former rugby star John Robbie] that discusses topical local and national issues without censorship, a first for South Africa. Among its recent programmes was an interview with Joe Slovo, the Secretary General of the South African Communist Party, who answered questions from ordinary South Africans across the political spectrum. Slovo's interview is all the more striking when one considers his reputation, described by one radio announcer as "the man white South Africans most love to hate"; only six months earlier, Slovo could not be photographed, quoted or recorded.[49]

It may be too soon to judge if the SABC has indeed abandoned its decades-long campaign of entrenching racial separateness. As this article points out, "the government still retains the legislative

[49] South African Reporter 8/3 (September 1990), pp. 42–3.

powers it used to circumscribe media rights from the 1950s to the 1980s," and perhaps these recent changes "come less from a desire to expand free speech than from a need for the National Party to re-educate their own constituency after years of apartheid propaganda."

Perhaps someone within South Africa is monitoring the SABC's music programing, for clues to the government's real intentions.

Table 10.3

Radio service	Total audience	Black audience
Afrikaans	820,000	106,000
English	471,000	109,000
Springbok	1,287,000	536,000
Radio 5	774,000	479,000

11

PRIVILEGING THE MOMENT OF RECEPTION: MUSIC AND RADIO IN SOUTH AFRICA

Originating as a paper delivered at a conference organized by Steve Scher at Dartmouth College in May of 1988, this essay attempts to discover the meaning of a single piece of music in a single, specific historical setting. In a critique of the papers from this conference, Hayden White writes:

> The question of the relation of the musical work to its historical context is raised in a variety of ways in this volume, but most explicitly and most radically by Charles Hamm, John Neubauer, and Peter Rabinowitz. . . . These three critics take their point of departure from the postmodernist notions of the openness of the work of art and of the function of the performer and/or audience in the production of the work's possible meaning. . . . In his consideration of the reception in black South Africa of Lionel Richie's "All Night Long (All Night)," Hamm first stresses the difficulty of imputing any specific meaning to the work itself. . . . Specific meanings are produced, Hamm says, "only at the moment of reception" and are "shaped by the cultural capital of the listener." . . . The implications of Hamm's position could be unsettling to critics, I should think. According to Hamm, the critic's role would not consist of determining the real or true value of a given musical work, but rather – insofar as one were interested in meaning at all – in identifying the contexts in which it may have been heard and surveying the various meanings imputed to it by listeners in those contexts.[1]

The photographs accompanying the text were taken by my wife Marilyse in various black townships in 1984 and 1985. Though most townships were occupied or patrolled by security forces during this period, and whites were banned from going to them, our visits were

---

[1] Hayden White, "Commentary: form, reference, and ideology in musical discourse," in *Music and Text: Critical Inquiries*, ed. Steven Paul Scher (Cambridge, 1992), pp. 314–15.

made possible by various friends at Rhodes University and elsewhere and were sometimes facilitated by the fact that Marilyse worked in a day-care center for colored children while we were in Grahamstown.

* * *

Joseph Kerman observed in 1985 that "semiotics, hermeneutics, and phenomenology are being drawn upon only by some of the boldest of musical studies today, [and] post-structuralism, deconstruction, and serious feminism have yet to make their debuts in musicology."[1] As accurate as this statement may have been then for mainstream historical musicology in the United States, it was not applicable to the study of popular music, which was marked throughout the 1980s by attempts to apply these and other recent theories and methodologies to musical scholarship, largely through the agencies of the International Association for the Study of Popular Music (IASPM), established in 1981 during a first International Conference on Popular Music Research held in Amsterdam, and the journal *Popular Music*, published by Cambridge University Press since 1981.

Music exists as a threefold series of processes: a first stage of creation, or composition; a middle stage of mediation, involving publication, production, performance, and dissemination; and a final one of reception and perception. Historical musicologists, particularly in the United States, with their propensity for accumulating "more and more facts, [with] less and less confidence in interpreting them," as Kerman put it,[2] have tended to privilege the first of these processes to the virtual exclusion of the others, while scholars of the mass media and certain social scientists focus their attention on the second. My intent here is modest: to isolate a single moment of reception – one piece of music heard at a given time in specific place – and to test what socio-historical analysis can tell us about what is being perceived at this moment and what relationship this perception bears to what was intended by the creator of piece, and to persons or agencies involved in its mediation. I've chosen the song "All Night Long (All Night)," written by the American singer-songwriter Lionel Richie in 1983 and recorded that year for the Motown Record Corporation.

---

[1] Joseph Kerman, *Contemplating Music: Challenges to Musicology* (Cambridge, MA, 1985), p. 17. (Also published by Fontana as *Musicology* [London, 1985].)

[2] Kerman, *Contemplating Music*, p. 54.

The composition

Dave Harker's admonition that "unless we locate cultural products in history, we cannot hope to understand culture or history"[3] is a useful starting point for our analysis, though his seminal study of the early nineteenth-century English song "Bob Cranky" is of little further use to us because, like most studies of popular songs,[4] it focuses chiefly on the text. More fruitful as a model is Bill Austin's book-length analysis of three songs by Stephen Foster which explores in exhaustive detail the various socio-historical contexts in which the songs are embedded and the several resultant levels of meaning which can be teased out by close analysis.[5]

At a first contextual level, the words of our song, and in fact its very title, invoke the most venerable symbolism in rock music: music and dance as sexual imagery. Such lines as "Everybody sing, everybody dance, lose yourself in wild romance, all night long," are in a tradition extending back to Bill Haley's "Rock Around the Clock" of 1953 – "We're going to rock around the clock tonight, we're going to rock, rock, rock till broad daylight."

But while Haley's song, like so much early rock 'n' roll, draws on the black dance-hall culture of rhythm and blues of the 1940s and 50s, "All Night Long," thirty years later, is more complex and ambiguous in cultural reference. The text, on paper, often suggests contemporary, colloquial American usage: "Well my friends the time has come, to raise the roof and have some fun. . . ." But soon words and phrases from other cultures begin to appear: "parti" is a Caribbean term for a celebration involving music, dancing, eating, and drinking; "karamu" is a Swahili term for feasting and enjoyment within a community; "fiesta" is of course a Spanish word for a celebration, widely used throughout Latin America; "liming" is an English Caribbean slang expression for "hanging out," as for example at a party. The text of the second verse, beginning with "People dancing all in the street, see the rhythm all in their feet," invokes a street fest, more typical of Latin America than the United States. An apparently multi-lingual "chant" appears halfway through the song:

[3] David Harker, "The original Bob Cranky?," *Folk Music Journal* 5/1 (1985), p. 76.
[4] See, for instance, Sean Cubitt, *"Maybellene:* meaning and the listening subject," *Popular Music* 4 (1984), pp. 207–24; Umberto Fiori, "Listening to Peter Gabriel's *I Have the Touch,"* *Popular Music* 6 (1987), pp. 37–44; and Michael Roos and Don O'Meara, "Is Your Love in Vain? – dialectical dilemmas in Bob Dylan's recent love songs," *Popular Music* 7 (1988), pp. 35–50.
[5] See William Austin, *"Susanna," "Jeanie," and "The Old Folks at Home": The Songs of Stephen C. Foster from His Time to Ours* (New York and London, 1975).

> Tom bo li de say de moi ya
> Yeah, Jambo Jumbo
> Way to parti' o we goin'
> Oh, jambali
> Tom bo li de say de moi ya
> Yeah, JUMBO JUMBO!

Neither I nor my colleagues can make sense of this text beyond the fact that it is densely packed with words and phrases from various black cultures: English Caribbean, Spanish-speaking Latin American, creole, African. More specific meaning seems to depend on one's linguistic and cultural heritage. For instance, one colleague suggested that the opening phrase "Tom bo li de say" may be heard by a Trinidadian as a corruption of "Liumbo lilissay" – Liumbo being a notorious thief and folk hero in Trinidad in the second quarter of the twentieth century, "lilissay" meaning to "slide into one's premises without being caught."

Musically, Afro-Caribbean drumming patterns by percussionists Paulinho Da Costa and John Robinson, not clearly identifiable with any specific ethnic tradition, serve as an introduction and continue throughout the song. This drumming, combined with Richie's accented English and the gradual introduction of foreign words, suggests a vaguely Caribbean location, though the string and horn accompaniment (arranged by James Anthony Carmichael) is vintage 1980s Motown. The refrain, "All night long," introduces a rudimentary call-and-response pattern between Richie and his seven background vocalists, reinforced by more prominent and complex drumming, again vaguely Afro-Caribbean. The "chant," introduced by crowd sounds and blaring horns suggesting a Carnival parade, is accompanied only by percussion and shouting. Crowd noises continue intermittently as the song moves towards its close; an instrumental interlude near the end is dominated by a xylophone, invoking a steel band from Trinidad or perhaps the marimbas of Mexico and Guatemala; more blaring horns and shouts from Richie's "Hoopa Hollers" continue to suggest a street fest, up to the final fadeout.

Thus the music of "All Night Long," like the text, is shot through with references to various Afro-Caribbean and Afro-Latin cultures; there are hints of Latin street fests, of reggae, of calypso; but the song as a whole is none of these things.

Motown Records, established in the early 1960s, first produced music by black musicians in a regional black musical style, aimed at an urban black working-class audience in the industrial upper Mideast. In the mid-1960s the company targeted a national, more affluent, and mostly white audience, with outstanding commercial success. By 1983, when this record was produced, Motown had moved from Detroit to Hollywood and had entered into a long-term licensing agreement in the UK, with RCA. Thus the marketing strategies of Motown had been aimed successively at regional, national, and then international markets, and in the process the "Motown sound" had become increasingly generalized.[6] This LP was produced to be equally marketable in the USA, in Europe, in Commonwealth countries, in Latin America, and in Africa; even the iconography of the cover photo makes no visual references to a specific culture or geographic location.

Reggae music had become widely popular at this time in Latin America, Africa, and the UK,[7] particularly after Bob Marley's death in 1981. The texts of reggae songs were heard in many Third World countries as authentic expressions of the struggle of the populations of underdeveloped countries against the "new imperialism" of the late twentieth century. In the United States, reggae had remained a "cult genre . . . with limited commercial appeal. [Recording companies] had little use for these perennially stoned wild-hairs with their lackadaisical recording methods and invariably late-starting, Grateful Dead-length concerts."[8] But Americans were nevertheless exposed to the characteristic rhythms and sonorities of this music, if not its ideology, through such reggae-influenced groups as the Police ("Zenyatta Mondatta" [1980], "Ghost in the Machine" [1980], "Synchronicity" [1983]) and the Talking Heads ("Fear of Music" [1979], "Remain in Light" [1980], "Speaking Tongues" [1983]). Even such perennial stars as Stevie Wonder, Paul Simon, and Bob Dylan introduced elements of reggae into their music in the early 1980s. Thus Lionel Richie, writing a song in 1983 intended for international distribution, could have done no better than to sprinkle it with references to Caribbean music in general and reggae in particular.

We can understand "All Night Long (All Night)," then, as a deliberately generalized product, a generic pop song of the early 1980s. The text is non-narrative, repetitious, and episodic; its essence is stated in the first few lines, actually in the title itself, and there is no dramatic progression as the song unfolds. The music is

---

[6] See Charles Hamm, "The transformation of folk into popular music through mass dissemination," paper delivered at the Fourteenth Congress of the International Musicological Society, Bologna, September 1987.

[7] Roger Wallis and Krister Malm, *Big Sounds from Small Peoples: The Music Industry in Small Countries* (New York, 1984), pp. 98–9, 303.

[8] Ed Ward, Geoffrey Stokes, and Ken Tucker, *Rock of Ages: The Rolling Stone History of Rock & Roll* (New York, 1986), p. 543.

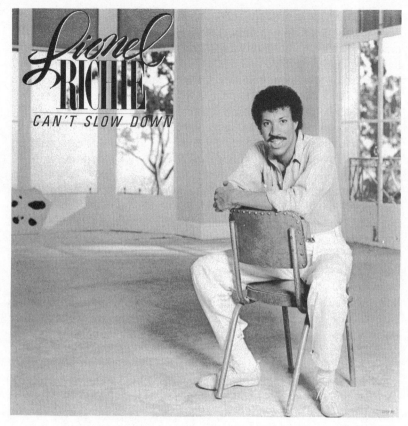

Figure 11.1 Cover for Lionel Richie's album *Can't Slow Down* (1983)

likewise episodic, additive, open-ended. Since neither text nor music is constructed in linear fashion, and neither moves to dramatic or structural climaxes, analytical systems developed to make sense of linear, goal-oriented European classical music cannot be expected to reveal structural or expressive relationships between music and text, both packed with references to specific cultures. More precise meaning comes only at the moment of reception, shaped by the cultural capital of the listener.

Reception

My analysis will be concerned with this song at the moment it was heard over the radio by two young black women in November of 1984 in a black township in the Republic of South Africa.

Figure 11.2 Two young women and radio, Fingo Village, Grahamstown, 1984

We must first note that our moment of reception takes place through the agency of one of the contemporary mass media, in this case radio.

One strand of contemporary critical thought holds that the electronic mass media have had an anti-social, dehumanizing impact on listeners, and that these media have been used to reinforce political and economic power. Attali suggests that in the present era of "repetition," "each spectator has a solitary relation with a material object: the consumption of music is individualized . . . The network is no longer a form of sociality, an opportunity for spectators to meet and communicate."[9] As a result, he says, we live in a "world now devoid of meaning," in a "present made of abstraction, nonsense, and silence," as a result of the "strategic use of music by power to *silence*, [through] mass-producing a deafening, syncretic kind of music, and censoring all other human noises."[10] Allan Bloom is even less hopeful. Taking as the symbol of our era "a thirteen-year-old boy sitting in the living room of his family home doing his math assignment while wearing his Walkman headphones or watching MTV," he laments that Western civilization now culminates in

> a pubescent child whose body throbs with orgasmic rhythms; whose feelings are made inarticulate in hymns to the joy of onanism or the killing of parents; whose ambition is to win fame and wealth in imitating the drag-queen who makes the music. In short, his life is made into a nonstop, commercially pre-packaged masturbational fantasy. . . . As long as [he] has the Walkman on, he cannot hear what the Great Tradition has to say. And, after its prolonged use, when he takes it off, he finds he is deaf.[11]

But Shuhei Hosokawa, among others, rejects the view that "with industrialisation and urbanisation, especially in recent decades, [people] lose that healthy relationship with the environment, become alienated and turn into [a] 'lonely crowd,' suffering from incommunicability."[12] Rather, he agrees with Lyotard that "the *self* [in the postmodern era] is small, but it is not isolated: it is held in a texture of relations which are more complex and more mobile than ever before."[13] For Hosokawa, the radio in general and the Walkman

---

[9] Jacques Attali, *Noise: The Political Economy of Music* (Minneapolis, 1985), p. 32. First published as *Bruits: essai sur l'economie politique de la musique* (Paris, 1977).

[10] Attali, *Noise*, pp. 3, 5, 19.

[11] Allan Bloom, *The Closing of the American Mind* (New York, 1987), pp. 74–5, 81.

[12] Shuhei Hosokawa, "The Walkman effect," *Popular Music* 4 (1984), p. 165.

[13] Jean-François Lyotard, *La Condition postmoderne: rapport sur le savoir* (Paris, 1979), p. 31.

Figure 11.3 Landscape with radio, Port Alfred township, 1984

in particular are merely the latest, and possibly the ultimate, devices allowing one to have music at home, at work, while travelling. The listener has become the *minimum, mobile, and intelligent unit* in the contemporary landscape, at the center of an "intersection of *singularities.*"[14] In other words, the person using a radio, television set, or a Walkman is not isolated and alienated from the contemporary world, but is connected to it through access to a multiplicity of simultaneously available channels of information. And far from being a solitary occupation, the consumption of music through the mass media has become a social and visible part of the contemporary landscape and soundscape, most certainly in South Africa, where the radio is omnipresent.

14 Hosokawa, "The Walkman effect," p. 165.

Figure 11.4 Landscape with radio, Northern Transvaal, 1984

Gary Burns has argued that the reception of any single piece of media-disseminated music must be examined in the context of several levels of programing. That is, a song heard on radio or television is a component of a specific program, which in turn is one part of a day's scheduling, and the radio or television service carrying this program is part of a complex of available channels.[15] An analysis of our moment of reception based on this model reveals that:

(1) "All Night Long (All Night)" at this moment of reception was heard on a request program, with listeners phoning the radio station to ask that a certain piece of music be played for specified friends or family members, and engaging the presenter in conversation and banter.

(2) The radio service in question, Radio Zulu, is devoted to omnibus, round-the-clock programing in the Zulu language; music, news,

[15] See Gary Burns, "Music video: an analysis on three levels," paper delivered at the Third International Conference on Popular Music Studies, Montreal, 10 July 1985.

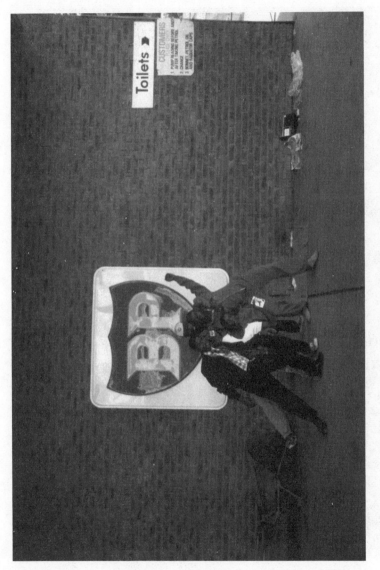

Figure 11.5 Jiving on the job, Northern Transvaal, 1984

Figure 11.6 Two children and radio, Eastern Cape, 1984

sporting events, religious messages, political commentary, announcements of deaths, children's programs, radio dramas, game shows. It is
a commercial service, with frequent advertisements of consumer
products.

(3) Radio Zulu is one of a network of nine "vernacular" services
produced by the government-controlled South African Broadcasting
Corporation (SABC), collectively called Radio Bantu.

(4) Radio Bantu is an important agent of Separate Development, a policy
formulated by theorists of the ruling National Party in 1960 as a more
sophisticated refinement of racial segregation, or apartheid. The
ultimate goal of Separate Development is for citizenship in the
Republic of South Africa to be restricted to whites, some four to five
million of them benefiting from the rich mineral and agricultural
wealth of the region. Blacks would be forced to live in, and become
citizens of, ten impoverished "homelands" (or "National States")
occupying a small fraction of the land area of South Africa, as seen in
the map on page 264. They would be allowed into "white" South
Africa only as temporary, cheap labor, and while there would be
forced to live in racially segregated townships.

Radio Bantu was designed to intensify ethnic and "national"
identity among the various black "tribes" of the region, in order to
make each of them receptive to the idea of having their own
"National State," and to inhibit Black unity. Its nine separate
services, each in the language of the ethnic group assigned to a given
"homeland," are beamed in highly selective geographical patterns,
by FM transmission, to the ten ethnically segregated "homelands"
and to the segregated townships in nearby "white" urban areas. The
network of Radio Bantu is laid out in Table 11.1.

Thus the moment of reception with which we are concerned takes
place in a context designed to elicit audience response and participation
through a phone-in format; to maximize the sales among the black
population of commodities produced by white-controlled capital;
and to intensify the ethnic identity of its Zulu-speaking audience, as
part of a larger political strategy.[16]

In this case, then, as Attali suggests, the mass medium of radio is
being used by power to promote its own objectives. The SABC
saturates its black listeners with "deafening, syncretic" music,
dulling their sensibilities, making them more receptive to its own
propaganda. "All Night Long (All Night)" was chosen for play on
Radio Bantu because its text seemed innocent of political content,
and Lionel Richie had no visible history of political activity. Its

---

[16] See Charles Hamm, *African-American Music, South Africa, and Apartheid* (Brooklyn, 1988).
Reproduced as Chapter 9 in the present volume.

Table 11.1 *Radio Bantu*

Service	Language	Dissemination
Radio Zulu	Zulu	*Kwazulu*,[1] Natal, the Rand[2]
Radio Xhosa	Xhosa	*Transkei, Ciskei*, Eastern Cape
Radio Tswana	SeTswana	*Bophutathswana*, the Rand
Radio SeSotho	Southern Sotho	*Qwaqwa*, the Ran, Free State
Radio Lebowa	Northern Sotho	*Lebowa*, Northern Transvaal
Radio Tsonga	Tsonga	*Gazankulu*, Northern Transvaal
Radio Venda	LuVenda	*Venda*, Northern Transvaal
Radio Swazi	SiSwati	*KaNgwane*, Eastern Transvaal
Radio Ndebele	Ndebele	*KwaNdebele*, Central Transvaal

Notes
[1] The "homeland" for each ethnic group is italicized
[2] "The Rand" designates the area around Johannesburg, which has a high concentration of mines and other industry and thus a heavy demand for black workers, drawn from many different ethnic groups

musical style likewise seemed devoid of political implications, and since music by black Americans is widely popular among South African blacks, it would help attract listeners to Radio Bantu.

Perception, reception

We are concerned with an individual moment of reception. If one accepts "the provocative claim made by extreme relativists that there are as many 'Eroica' Symphonies as there are listeners in our concert halls,"[17] it is impossible to move beyond this movement in our analysis. But while it is all very well for John Cage to suggest that "now structure is not put into a work, but comes up in the person who perceives it. There is therefore no problem of understanding but the possibility of awareness. . . . Here we are. Let us say Yes to our presence together in Chaos,"[18] musicologists are not at home with chaos and some of them have struggled to find a middle ground between rampant relativism and restrictive positivism. Felix Vodicka, for example, argues "that the object of reception history does not lie

[17] Carl Dahlhaus, *Foundations of Music History* (Cambridge, 1983). First published as *Grundlagen der Musikgeschichte* (Cologne, 1967).
[18] John Cage, *Silence* (Middletown, CT, 1961), pp. 259, 195.

in individual reactions but in norms and normative systems that determine how surviving texts are perceived *within groups or strata conditioned by history, society and ethnic origin.*"[19]

We must, then, locate our moment of reception in the context of such a "group or stratum conditioned by history, society and ethnic origin." To do so, I propose moving outwards in concentric circles from the individual who is the subject of our moment of reception to larger social and political structures, until we reach clear breaking points.

One can locate any number of other individual moments of reception of Lionel Richie's song which would correspond to our original.

In each case the common factors are that the subjects are black; they live in South Africa, in a black township or one of the ten so-called "National States"; each speaks an African language, and usually has some knowledge of English as a second language; each has access to a Radio Bantu service in his or her own language; each is subject to racial restrictions imposed by the Population Registration Act, the Group Areas Act, Influx Control, and the other legal bastions of Separate Development; each is denied political input into the governing of community, region, and nation. These similarities cut across so-called "tribal" distinctions in South Africa, and in any event the notion of "tribe" is now understood as being an insupportable ethnographic concept, and as having been used by the government for its own political purposes.[20]

If our subjects were to be chosen from white South Africans, however, all these conditions would change: they would be free to live wherever they choose; their first language would be European (English or Afrikaans), and they would have little or no knowledge of any African language; they do not listen to Radio Bantu; they are the beneficiaries, not the victims, of the government's racial policies and laws; they help determine the political direction of South Africa by voting for local and national representatives. Likewise if one chose subjects from beyond the political boundaries of the Republic of South Africa, from Zimbabwe or Botswana for instance, conditions would once again be different.

[19] Quoted in Dahlhaus, *Foundations*, p. 152. Vodicka's essay "Die Konkretisation des literarischen Werks. Zur Problematick der Rezeption von Nerudas Werk" was first published in *Rezeptionsässthetik*, ed. Rainer Warning (Munich, 1975), pp. 84–112.

[20] Monica Wilson and Leonard Thompson, eds., *A History of South Africa to 1870* (Cape Town and Johannesburg, 1985), pp. 75–186.

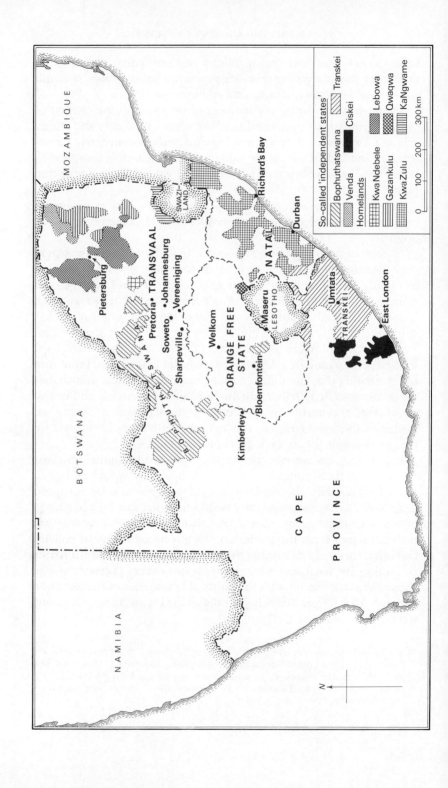

So-called 'independent states'

Homelands

Bophuthatswana   Transkei
Venda   Ciskei
KwaNdebele   Lebowa
Gazankulu   Qwaqwa
KwaZulu   KaNgwame

0 100 200 300 km

MOZAMBIQUE

SWAZI-LAND

TRANSVAAL

Pietersburg

Pretoria • Johannesburg
Soweto • Vereeniging
Sharpeville •

BOPHUTHATSWANA

Welkom

ORANGE FREE STATE

Maseru
LESOTHO

Bloemfontein

Kimberley

NATAL

Richard's Bay

Durban

Umtata

TRANSKEI

East London

CAPE PROVINCE

BOTSWANA

NAMIBIA

N

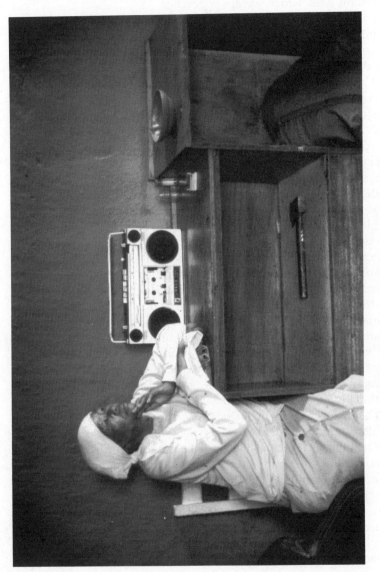

Figure 11.7 Woman and radio, Grahamstown, 1984

The question now is to define precise ways in which the "history, society and ethnic origin" of our subjects affect the moment of reception with which we are concerned.

To begin with, references to rock music's mythology and history, to Bill Haley's "Rock Around the Clock" and similar songs which equate dancing with sex, do not come into play. A historical study of the dissemination of early rock 'n' roll in South Africa reveals that few blacks had access to this music in the 1950s and 60s, that it was rejected by those who did, and that it did not exist in the consciousness of black South Africans in the 1980s.[21]

Our listener(s) can be expected to understand enough English to grasp the general thrust of Richie's song – "Everybody sing, everybody dance, come on and sing along . . . People dancing all in the street, see the rhythm all in their feet." But rather than understanding this as a metaphor for sex, our African listeners will take the text literally, as a description of communal dancing and singing – not only because the references to rock's mythology are not understood, but also because communal, celebratory singing and dancing is an important part of their traditional culture.[22]

Specific African words sprinkled through the text – "karamu," "jambo," "jambali" – are from Swahili, a language unknown this far south, and thus would not be understood literally, though they might be perceived as generically African. The "chant," however, would have a powerful resonance in South Africa. Whatever "Tom bo" means literally, it would have been perceived immediately by blacks, at this moment in South African history, as "Tambo": a reference to Oliver Tambo, the head of the outlawed African National Congress, in exile in Zambia.

The entire chorus and the extended coda of Richie's song are built on alternation between two notes (the tonic and the supertonic) and the two chords built on these pitches. As it happens, the musical bow, used to accompany much solo and choral singing in traditional South African musical cultures, is capable of playing only two notes, a major second apart. Musical patterns based on alternation of two notes and/or two chords with roots a second apart permeate other genres of traditional South African music as well, and persist in such acculturated forms of the present century as *marabi*, jive, and Mbaqanga. Though it was surely not Richie's intention, extended

---

[21] See Charles Hamm, "Rock 'n' Roll in a very strange society," *Popular Music* 5 (1985), pp. 159–74. Reproduced as Chapter 8 in the present volume.

[22] See Peter Larlham, *Black Theater, Dance, and Ritual in South Africa* (Ann Arbor, 1985).

Figure 11.8 "Beware Botha. Tambo is coming." Craddock township, 1984

sections of "All Night Long (All Night)" had a quite specific musical resonance among the black population of South Africa.

Thus, at our moment of reception, the ambiguities deliberately built into Richie's song are particularized by specific conditions of history, society, and ethnicity. The song could have been heard as a communal celebration of an exiled political leader, with several musical details appropriate to this culture. This perception could well have contributed to the enormous popularity of the song in South Africa.

More generally, individual listeners at our moment of reception, and the larger group of which they were part, knew that Richie was black, and largely through music they had a sense of belonging to a global black community encompassing Africa, the Caribbean, and black America, North and South. Even though they had not been allowed to hear reggae songs with overtly political texts, they understood the issues involved in this music, and any piece of reggae – or even a piece with clear references to Caribbean music, like Richie's – carried a clear and quite specific reference to "the wrath, aspirations and hopelessness of [black] people who feel downtrodden," whatever the literal content of the text.[23]

Thus, just as the individual moment of reception of a song can result in a perception quite different from that intended by the composer, it can also empower a piece with meaning quite different from that apparently implied by its text and musical style, and thus alter the impact of media-disseminated music intended by "power."

Most historical musicologists have assumed that the composers of the great canonical works of Western music history created "ideal objects with an immutable and unshifting 'real' meaning," and that the function of the scholar "consists in the gradual unfolding of [this] meaning."[24]

With "All Night Long (All Night)" we are dealing with a composer who deliberately created a generic piece, constructing it in such a way as to make it accessible to audiences of various cultural backgrounds, while at the same time packing it with details allowing it to be culture-specific at different moments of reception. The composer accepts and even utilizes the notion that more specific meaning will come only at reception, conditioned by factors of history, society, and ethnic origin.

---

[23] Wallis and Malm, *Big Sounds*, p. 66.   [24] Dahlhaus, *Foundations*, pp. 150, 155.

A final question, then, is whether the situation described here results from some fundamental difference between the conditions of classical and popular music, or whether the suggestions made here might also be applicable to discussions of the reception and perception of classical music.

12

MUSIC AND RADIO IN THE PEOPLE'S REPUBLIC OF CHINA

This analysis of the organization, structure, program content, and political function of the Central People's Broadcasting Station (CPBS) is based on research conducted in the People's Republic of China in September and October of 1988, when I participated in the Visiting Scholar Exchange Program administered by the Committee for Scholarly Communication. My sources are interviews with officials of the CPBS in Beijing and Shanghai; hours of listening to and taping radio programs in Beijing, Tianjin, Xian, Chengdu, Chonqin, and Shanghai, and subsequent analysis of these tapes; discussions with faculty and students at the various conservatories of music at which I lectured, and with members of the Chinese Musicians' Association in Beijing; and information and materials sent to me by Chinese colleagues after my visit.

The timing of my visit, a half-year before the saga of Tiananmen Square, was fortuitous for my work. I was able to travel freely and unaccompanied, and almost everyone I met felt free to speak openly. Many of them, including some state officials, were under the impression that the country was moving decisively towards a greater degree of democracy and free expression. But for an outsider, there was an unmistakable air of schizophrenia, with some individuals and institutions assuming that they could operate with a greater degree of autonomy from the ideology of the central state than was intended by Beijing.

As detailed in the two previous essays, the central government of South Africa became less and less successful in imposing a modernist, hierarchical ideology on its population as evolving technology opened up alternate media channels of information for virtually the entire population, and helped bring the country into the chaotic postmodern world. Though South Africa and China were bitter political enemies at this time, the hegemonic use of music in the state-controlled mass media of the two countries was strikingly familiar. What remains to be seen is whether or not the remarkable political developments in the former will be echoed in the latter.

Introduction

While lecturing in the People's Republic of China (PRC) in the fall of 1988, I undertook an analysis of the organizational structure, music programing, and political function of the Central People's Broadcasting Station (CPBS). Earlier studies of the use of music by state-controlled radio services in southern Africa and elsewhere[1] had led to the formulation of several working hypotheses:

(1) An analysis of the organizational structure of a state radio service can by itself yield information about political issues and strategies within that state.

(2) The musical content of state radio programing is not designed to reflect the musical tastes and preferences of the listening audience, but rather to enforce or reinforce political ideologies and to shape or mold certain images of the state.

(3) Most music played on state radio stations attempts to achieve its goals not through the content of song lyrics, but in other ways.

(4) The effectiveness of a given state-controlled radio service depends largely on the extent to which its programming dominates other components of the musical life of the country – live performances, listening to pre-recorded music, other radio services.

But during that trip to China, and in the course of subsequent analysis of materials collected then and afterwards, I began to understand that the situation in the PRC was much more complex than any I had dealt with before. "Schizophrenic" is the word that comes immediately to mind. One part of the state radio service did indeed function as described above, but another part seemed to operate in dramatic contrast, even opposition.

This dichotomy will shape the following analysis.

The structure of the CPBS

All radio services in the People's Republic, collectively called the Central People's Broadcasting Station, are under governmental

---

[1] Charles Hamm, "'The constant companion of man': Separate Development, Radio Bantu and music", *Popular Music* 10/2 (May 1991), pp. 147–73, and "Privileging the moment of reception: music and radio in South Africa," in *Music and text: critical inquiries*, ed. Steven Scher (Cambridge, 1991), pp. 21–37. Reproduced as Chapters 10 and 11 in the present volume.

supervision. Six services originating from the central office of the CPBS in Beijing, under the direct control of the Ministry of Radio, Film, and Television, are transmitted by satellite, this number limited by the current state of Chinese technology. Three are designated as National Programs, the official internal radio voice of the central government, broadcasting in Putonghua ("standard" Chinese, Beijing dialect) and disseminated throughout the country by a number of regional transmitters. Two programs are beamed only to Taiwan, the other is an Ethnic Nationalities Program designed for the populations of China's "autonomous regions" and for non-Han minorities elsewhere in the country, transmitted selectively to appropriate areas.

At a second level, each of China's twenty-one provinces and four Autonomous Regions has a radio service, sometimes with multiple channels, still under the direct supervision of the Ministry of Radio, Film, and Television but with administrative staff, studios, transmitters, and relay stations located in that province or region.

Three of the country's largest cities – Beijing, Tianjin, and Shanghai – are classified administratively as municipalities, falling outside the provincial structure. Each has its own radio service, under sub-government rather than Ministry supervision and thus enjoying a certain degree of autonomy. Some 200 local stations also function with varying degrees of autonomy.

The complete organizational structure of the CPBS is given in Appendix 12.1.

State ideology and music

Though to an outside observer the internal political situation of the PRC may appear to have shifted dramatically from time to time during the forty years since Liberation, in reality there has been no deviation from theories and policies outlined by Mao Zedong in the 1940s and reiterated, refined, and carried out by him and his successors ever since.

According to Mao, "the universally applicable truth" of Marxism–Leninism was first revealed to "the vanguard of the Chinese proletariat" by the events of Russia's October Revolution. The "correct thesis that the Chinese revolution is part of the world revolution," based on the writings of Stalin, was put forward as early as 1924–7 by members of the Chinese Communist Party, founded in 1921. In Mao's words:

There are two kinds of world revolutions, the first belonging to the bourgeois or capitalist category. The era of this kind of world revolution is long past, having come to an end as far back as 1914 when the first imperialist war broke out, and more particularly in 1917 when the October Revolution took place. The second kind, namely, the proletarian-socialist world revolution, therefore began. This revolution has the proletariat of the capitalist countries as its main force and the oppressed peoples of the colonies and semi-colonies as its allies.[2]

The Chinese Revolution first took the form of a struggle for national liberation from foreign forces and then from the foreign-backed Guomindang led by Chang Kaishek. With Liberation in 1949 and the establishment of the People's Republic, the revolution focused on internal class struggle.

Mao saw China's population as falling into four classes: the proletariat, the peasantry, the urban petty bourgeoisie, and the national bourgeoisie (China's own capitalists). Though the revolution had of necessity depended on "the alliance of the workers and the peasants, because these two classes comprise 80 to 90 per cent of China's population," leadership could come only from the proletariat: "the entire history of revolution proves that without the leadership of the working class revolution fails and that with the leadership of the working class revolution triumphs."[3]

Continuing class struggle within the country was taken to be inevitable. According to Mao, "the contradiction between exploiter and exploited, which exists between the bourgoisie and the working class, is an antagonistic one. But, in the concrete conditions existing in China, such an antagonistic contradiction, if properly handled, can be transformed into a non-antagonistic one and resolved in a peaceful way."[4]

> So long as [the bourgeoisie] do not rebel, sabotage or create trouble, land and work will be given to them as well, to allow them to live and remould themselves through labour into new people. . . . Propaganda and educational work will be done among them, [which cannot however] be mentioned in the same breath with the work of self-education which we carry on within the ranks of the revolutionary people.[5]

[2] Mao Zedong, "On new democracy," in *Essential Works of Chinese Communism*, ed. Winberg Chai (New York, 1969), pp. 179–80.
[3] Mao Zedong, "On people's democratic dictatorship," in *Essential Works*, ed. Chai, p. 264.
[4] Mao Zedong, "On the correct handling of contradictions among the peoples," in *Essential Works*, ed. Chai, p. 330. [5] Mao Zedong, "On people's democratic dictatorship," p. 262.

The peasantry would also have to be brought into the socialist system. "Without socialization of agriculture, there can be no complete, consolidated socialism," Mao said, and judging by the experience of the Soviet Union, this education "will require a long time and painstaking work."[6]

The Communist Party of China was to be the medium through which the proletariat would theorize and execute its leadership, by continuing education of the other classes. Since steps other than education might be necessary to bring the bourgeoisie and the peasantry into line with the "correct" policies of the proletariat, another urgent task was

> to strengthen the people's state apparatus – mainly the people's army, the people's police and the people's courts – in order to protect the people's interests. Our policy of benevolence is applied only within the ranks of the people, not beyond them to the reactionaries or to the reactionary activities of reactionary classes. . . . Democracy is practised within the ranks of the people, who enjoy the rights of freedom of speech, assembly, association and so on. The right to vote belongs only to the people, not to the reactionaries. The combination of these two aspects, democracy for the people and dictatorship over the reactionaries, is the people's democratic dictatorship.[7]

This concept of a democratic dictatorship, involving democracy for some and dictatorship over others, was later reiterated even more clearly:

> In a society where there is class struggle, when the exploiting classes are free to exploit the working people, the working people will have no freedom from being exploited; when there is democracy for the bourgeoisie there can be no democracy for the proletariat and other working people. Ours is a people's democratic dictatorship, led by the working class and based on the worker–peasant alliance. What is the dictatorship for? Its first function is to suppress the reactionary classes and elements and those exploiters in the country who range themselves against the socialist revolution, to suppress all those who try to wreck our socialist construction. Who is to exercise this dictatorship? Naturally it must be the working class and the entire people led by it.[8]

Mao insisted from the beginning that "we want to build a new China," and to transform "a China that is politically oppressed and economically exploited into a China that is politically free and

---

[6] *Ibid.*, p. 263.   [7] *Ibid.*, pp. 261. ff.
[8] Mao Zedong, "On the correct handling," pp. 330–2.

economically prosperous."[9] It was essential for the creation of this new China that the country's centuries-old isolation from the rest of the world be ended, and with it the abandonment of the cherished image of China as the "Middle Kingdom," the center of the world.

> To nourish her own culture China needs to assimilate a good deal of foreign progressive culture, not enough of which was done in the past. We should assimilate whatever is useful to us today not only from the present-day socialist and new-democratic cultures but also from the earlier cultures of other nations, for example, from the culture of the various capitalist countries in the Age of Enlightenment. However, we should not gulp down any of this foreign material uncritically, but must treat it as we do our food – first chewing it, then submitting it to the working of the stomach and intestines with their juices and secretions, and separating it into nutriment to be absorbed and waste matter to be discarded – before it can nourish us.[10]

China's new "national, scientific and mass culture" envisioned by Mao could not come about without a critical mass of highly educated people capable of dealing with the science and intellectual thought of the contemporary world, and herein lies the still-unresolved dilemma of the PRC: on the one hand, its leadership has never deviated from the early party line on class struggle, dictating that the Party (in the name of the proletariat) is responsible for the political indoctrination of the entire population in "correct" Marxist-Leninist theory and practice; on the other hand, its best-educated people either come from or tend to gravitate towards the reactionary, bourgeois classes, necessitating their periodic political education and sometimes punishment by the "democratic dictatorship" of the PRC. However, political education by the Communist Party cannot substitute for academic, scientific training in institutions of higher education at home and especially abroad; and punishment by exile, imprisonment, or death leaves skilled positions unmanned. China has not yet recovered the ground it lost during the Cultural Revolution of 1966–76, a critical decade during which Japan and other Asian countries made unprecedented advances in industrial production and international marketing strategies.

As it seemed to one visitor, "the inscrutable politics of the Chinese government continue to vacillate between anti-bourgeois left wing morality and pro-Western liberalist reforms."[11] Periods of "letting a hundred flowers bloom" have alternated with periods of suppression

---

[9] Mao Zedong, "On new democracy," p. 173.   [10] Ibid., p. 190.
[11] Johnny Rogan, Wham! The Death of a Supergroup (London, 1987), p. 100.

275

and destruction of these flowers. The pendulum has swung first one way and then the other, and sometimes it is between these two poles.

The problem now is to understand how state policies towards music, and more specifically the selection of music for broadcast by state radio, have been designed to help educate the population along Marxist–Stalinist lines.

Music programing on the National Services

In the central offices of the CPBS at 2 Fuxingmenwai Street in Beijing, Huang Bingqi, Chief of the Foreign Affairs Section, impeccably dressed in a tailored suit, sat on a couch beneath a large-character banner emblazoned with a quotation from Chairman Mao. Flanked by the Senior Editor of the Foreign Music Section and the Head of the Chinese Music Section, Huang spoke with deep conviction, in excellent, idiomatic English, of the role of the National Programs, the most official and widely disseminated radio programs in the PRC.

The CPBS itself bears the responsibility of selecting what is best for its audience, in Huang's view, and therefore there is no need for systematic market research of radio listening patterns or musical preferences.

Approximately 40 per cent of the air time of the three National Programs, totalling some 9,600 minutes each week, is devoted to music. The largest share is given over to "light" music, a genre without a precise parallel in the West. Somewhat lesser but still significant program time is allocated to Chinese opera and classical music, and to European classical music. Even less time is devoted to commercially produced Chinese and foreign pop music, and to music of China's "national minorities."

In order to understand state policies towards each of these styles and genres, they must be examined in turn, then situated in socialist-Communist theory and practice.

Light music

This genre encompasses instrumental arrangements of Chinese traditional melodies, new pieces by Chinese composers based on similar melodic material, folk songs arranged for voice(s) with instrumental accompaniment, and recent vocal compositions drawing on elements of traditional Chinese style.

Whether instrumental or vocal, light music is characterized by melodic formulas based on pentatonic scales, triadic and tonal harmonies, homophonic textures, moderate tempi and dynamic ranges, string-dominated ensembles often including both Chinese and Western instruments, and simple sectional structures. To Western ears, much of it sounds for all the world like Muzak or Easy Listening FM programing. As Bruno Nettl describes a typical piece of this genre, the "Butterfly Concerto":

> The accompanying orchestra has seventeen performers of Western instruments and nine of traditional Chinese. The overall sound, however, is that of a Western orchestra. . . . It is dominated by functional harmonies. The pentatonic themes are reminiscent of more traditional Chinese melodies, but they are also compatible with Western works that imitate (or pretend to imitate) Chinese melody. Within the context of Western composition of the mid-twentieth century, it would be extremely conservative and very likely labelled as light or semiclassical.[12]

Though the origins of this light style predate Liberation, only in the last decade or so has it become the repertory most widely disseminated and promoted by such state agencies as the CPBS, Chinese Central Television, state-organized concerts within the PRC, and foreign tours by state-sponsored musical groups. To understand this choice of music, which sometimes sounds only marginally Chinese, one must first grasp the dilemma facing the formulation of musical strategies within the PRC. Mao, convinced that "a given culture is the ideological reflection of the politics and economics of a given society,"[13] called for the creation of a new "national, scientific and mass culture," which could "be lead only by the culture and ideology of the proletariat, by the ideology of communism, and not by the culture and ideology of any other class."[14] No distinctive, nationally accepted proletarian style or genre of music had emerged among the urban working classes before Liberation, thus there was no ready-made proletarian genre to serve as a model. But even if such a style had existed, the "mass line" of the Chinese Communist Party would have dictated against its being taken over without mediation.

As early as 1934, Lu Xun had theorized a cultural policy designed to draw on both old and new styles and forms, shaped so as to be accessible to the entire population: "To work on behalf of the masses and strive to make things easy for them to understand – precisely this is the correct area of effort for the progressive artist." Teng Xiaobing elaborated:

---

[12] Bruno Nettl, *The Western Impact on World Music: Change, Adaption, and Survival* (New York and London, 1985), p. 142.   [13] Mao Zedong, "On new democracy," p. 192.
[14] *Ibid.*, p. 187.

The mass line maintains that the Party's ability to go on exercising correct leadership hinges upon its ability to adopt the method of "coming from the masses [i.e. the working classes] and going back to the masses." This means – to quote from the Central Committee's "Resolution on Methods of Leadership," drafted by Comrade Mao Zedong – "summing up (i.e., coordinating and systematizing after careful study) the views of the masses (i.e., views scattered and unsystematic), then taking the resulting ideas back to the masses, explaining and popularizing them until the masses embrace the ideas as their own."[15]

Thus the issue is not to identify a ready-made proletariat music, but rather to create a new body of music for the people, drawn from the "scattered and unsystematic" music of the masses, "coordinated and systematized after careful study" by persons qualified by political and professional training, and then given back to the masses and "explained and popularized" until they are willing to accept this new product "as their own."

Several styles and genres have been subjected to this process. In the 1920s and 30s the Communist Party of China set out to create a new body of "mass song." Some of these *geming gequ* ("revolutionary songs") drew on traditional Chinese or Russian melodies and were thus "from the people," some were newly composed in the same style by Nie Er, Xian Xinghai, and other musicians numbered among the early membership of the Party.[16] In style, these *geming gequ* belonged to the generic mass songs created at this time in Russia and other parts of the world,[17] with broad, diatonic, march-like, major-key melodies cast in simple strophic forms and designed to be sung in unison, accompanied with Western-style harmonies by whatever instruments might be available.

Nourished by the Communist Party during its struggle for control of the mainland and during the first post-Liberation decades, these mass songs fell into disfavor among much of the Chinese population after 1978, partly because of their association with attitudes prevalent during the Cultural Revolution, and also because the growing openness to foreign culture after 1978 gave the Chinese population a chance to choose from among an ever-wider range of

[15] Teng Xiaobing, "Report on the revision of the constitution of the Communist Party of China," in *Essential Works*, ed. Chai, p. 319.
[16] Isabel K. F. Wong, "Geming Gequ: songs for the education of the masses," in *Popular Chinese Literature and Performing Arts in the People's Republic of China*, ed. Bonnie S. McDougall (Berkeley, 1984).
[17] Including the USA. See Carol Oja, "Marc Blitzstein's The Cradle Will Rock and mass-song style of the 1930s," *American Music* 6/2 (1989), pp. 158–80.

musical styles. *Geming gequ* and its creators remain sacred to the leadership of the Chinese Communist Party and the country's older population, but by the early 1980s they were no longer capable of rousing and maintaining mass enthusiasm for the socialist-Communist state.

Other attempts to create a new mass repertory focused on reshaping China's store of folk and art music. It must always be kept in mind that the Chinese Communists set out to establish a revolutionary society, not merely a nationalistic one. Western music was taken to be more modern and scientific than Chinese, and since "modern" could be equated with "revolutionary," the adaption of Western models of harmony, intonation, and instrumentation seemed correct. The revolutionary composer Xian Xinghai was among those convinced that "traditional music should be improved by adding the harmony and counterpoint that he had studied in Europe."[18]

> [Xian] combined a popular style with a revolutionary content. He studied traditional Chinese music seriously, although he was not a traditionalist who clung to the past; and at the same time he also absorbed and adapted the useful elements of Western music to develop Chinese music.[19]

As Zhao Feng summed it up in 1958, "Chinese folk melodies + western professional techniques = national music culture."[20]

"Modern" also implied the use of large ensembles, in emulation of Western orchestras. Many Chinese instruments traditionally used for intimate solo or small ensemble performance weren't suitable for inclusion in such groups.

> Even though our national musical instruments are varied and colorful, from the contemporary point of view they are inadequate and archaic. Their tone quality is limited, their range is narrow, modulation is difficult (because of their system of intonation). Furthermore, many types of local ensembles are small in size, and thus not suitable to the musical needs of today's masses. The country is in the process of building a socialist society. Glorious life calls for grandiose performing ensembles.[21]

Accordingly, China's instrument makers were encouraged to devise "improved" versions of traditional instruments, and by the 1960s a

[18] Richard Curt Kraus, *Pianos and Politics in China: Middle-Class Ambitions and the Struggle over Western Music* (New York and Oxford, 1989), p. 60.
[19] Ma Ke, as quoted in Kraus, *Pianos and Politics*, p. 67.
[20] As quoted in Kraus, *Pianos and Politics*, p. 108.
[21] Yang Jingming, "The organization and improvement of the national orchestra," in *Lectures on National Instruments* (Beijing, 1957), p. 73.

more or less standardized modern Chinese orchestra had emerged, combining traditional instruments with the Western cello and double bass. Han has proposed a historical evolution of the Chinese orchestra: from ancient court groups, to the traditional Jiangnan Sizhu ensemble originating in the lower valley of the Yangtze River, to the Central Broadcasting Station Chinese Orchestra founded in 1935, to the 35-member ensemble formed at the Central People's Broadcasting Station in Beijing in 1953.[22]

The modern Chinese orchestra also drew on the Soviet model of large "folk" ensembles playing arrangements made by professional composers of traditional tunes, particularly when Chinese conservatories of music were reshaped in the 1950s according to the Russian system. Though some students were allowed to study China's ancient solo classical repertories, chief emphasis was put on the establishment of standardized ensembles of traditional instruments playing a newly created repertory by Chinese composers trained in Western music.

In accordance with the above-described policy of "coming from the masses and going back to the masses," the melodic material of this new repertory was taken from the people, who had created it as folk song or classical composition, then given back to them in a new form "coordinated and systematized after careful study," i.e., arranged and harmonized by professionally trained musicians. This new music was then "explained and popularized," through performances by state ensembles and through being publicized and praised by the state press, to "encourage the masses [to] embrace [this music] as their own." Not incidentally, in the process it was purged of ideologically incorrect associations – folk music's connection with the "superstitions" of religious or pagan ritual, and Chinese classical music's historical association with the privileged classes – and was offered in a new, ideologically correct environment: performed by state-supported people's ensembles, for people's audiences, in the setting of a "workers' stadium" or a state radio broadcast.

When an ensemble from the Central Conservatory of Music performed a program of this music in Durham (England) as part of an Oriental Music Festival in August of 1979, foreign scholarly reaction was critical on grounds that it was not "traditional" music, as claimed, since it used Western-influenced forms and harmony, tempered tuning, virtuosic effects, fixed rhythmic interpretations

[22] Han Kuo-Huang, "The modern Chinese orchestra," *Asian Music* 11/1 (1979), pp. 1–43.

and ornaments, and modern European instruments.[23] The leader of the Chinese delegation, Fang Kun, responded to this "incredible criticism and doubt" by echoing Mao:

> We really felt that they did not entirely understand the circumstances surrounding Chinese music and its development. . . . [Some of] the pieces that we played were traditional pieces of either classical or folk origin. Among the other compositions and adaptions, all were composed by a process of utilizing various minority people's songs or of drawing on the style of Peking opera or Kunqu from the stage of old. Some of them contain many newly composed elements, some a few, but all of them are linked to the same flesh and blood as Chinese traditional music. When we selected a program like this it was because we recognized that in order to understand traditional music, it is not only necessary to understand its classical and folk origins, but also to understand its modern evolution. . . . [The] approach that we suggest for traditional music [is based on] making the past serve the present, weeding out the old to bring forth the new, selecting the fine and discarding the rubbish, and eliminating the false and retaining the genuine. . . . Of course, so-called excellence must be understood as having a definite foundation among the masses.[24]

Foreign pieces which fall within the general stylistic parameters outlined above are also included on light-music programs of the CPBS. Mantovani is often heard, for instance, and is widely imitated by Chinese arrangers. The acceptable foreign light repertory ranges from songs by Stephen Foster and other nineteenth-century American and European songwriters, to popular airs from operettas and operas, to a careful selection of contemporary soft rock or pop songs. One day's listening to a light music program on the Yangtze River yielded "Danny Boy," the "Toreador Song" from *Carmen*, the theme music from "Dr. Zhivago," "Blue Eyes Crying in the Rain," Foster's "I Dream of Jeanie with the Light Brown Hair," "The Way We Were," "Yesterdays," "A Man and a Woman," and "Feelings."

The category of light music, then, is defined by general musical style and may draw from the folk, traditional, classical, and popular repertories, both Chinese and foreign. The music of choice of the CPBS in its role as the official radio voice of the socialist-Communist state, light music conforms to the mass line and is "modern" in its use of tonal and triadic harmonies, sectional forms, Western intonation, and "improved" instruments. Though other genres,

[23] Fang Kun, "A discussion of Chinese national musical traditions," *Asian Music* 12/2 (1981), p. 16.
[24] *Ibid.*, pp. 4–9.

such as certain types of pop music, were tolerated in the 1980s, official preference for light music is always evident, and new products which conform to its stylistic parameters were welcome:

> The [recent] craze for pop songs has been diverted to light music, which includes small pieces of orchestral and dance music. Among the light music, Richard Clayderman's piano pieces have been faring well. The cassette has sold over 3 million copies.[25]

I've argued elsewhere[26] that in a society with a market economy, the term "popular music" is best reserved for commodity products such as sheet music, phonograph discs, and cassettes. But in a socialist-Communist state describing itself as a democratic dictatorship and reserving to itself the right to assume the voice of the people and to maintain control over the production and dissemination of music, "popular music" in either of its two broad meanings, as music emanating from the people or as music preferred by the majority of the people, is simply what the state determines should be heard by the people. It follows, then, that light music is the contemporary popular music of the PRC.

Chinese opera and classical music

Chinese opera, a genre enjoying "prestige, popularity, and wide influence among the masses"[27] since it took definitive shape in the seventeenth century, could be considered a legitimate form of people's music. Unlike its European counterpart, its stylistic origins lie in oral tradition, not the classical music of the ruling classes, and its audiences are historically drawn from a wide range of China's population, most definitely including working people. Since Liberation, its history has closely reflected the schizophrenic nature of the struggle over culture in the PRC.

The plots and characters of many traditional Chinese operas, involving as they did the adventures of wealthy landowners, princes, generals, shopkeepers, high-born lovers, and other privileged characters from China's decadent past, seemed inappropriate to a modern revolutionary society, and many of them were revised shortly after Liberation. In addition, new operas with revolutionary plots were created. The opera-going public continued to favor

---

[25] Han Yidan, "Open policy opens ears," *China Daily*, 19 October 1988, p. 5.

[26] Charles Hamm, *Yesterdays: Popular Song in America* (New York and London, 1979).

[27] Yung Bell, "Model opera as model: from Shajiabang to Saagabong," in *Popular Chinese Literature*, ed. McDougall, pp. 144–64.

traditional, historical pieces, however, and by the early 1960s the government resorted to a more vigorous campaign to "denounce many traditional operas as feudalistic, superstitious, and vulgar, and urge the revolutionalization of the stage so that it would reflect and serve socialism."[28] The older repertory began to disappear from the stage under such pressure, and with the onset of the Cultural Revolution in 1966 the entire repertory was reduced to five newly created operas with contemporary, revolutionary plots and characters (*Shajiabang, Hong deng ji, Zhiqu Weihushan, Haigang*, and *Qixi Baihutuan*). These "model" operas were "from the people," in that they contained music adapted from traditional operas, and their characters and plots had been shaped to reflect China's new revolutionary society. They were soon adapted to various regional dialects and also began to serve as models for other new "revolutionary" operas. "Between 1966 and 1977, the model operas and their adaptions dominated the musical scene in China."[29]

Traditional operas were gradually restored to the stage after the overthrow of the Gang of Four, and audiences could once again witness the exploits of the heroic, villainous, and comic characters who traditionally inhabit the Chinese operatic stage. With this repertory now sanctioned by cultural theorists of the Communist Party, the National Programs of the CPBS and Chinese Central Television began allowing time for it.

Chinese and European classical music

Traditional Chinese classical music came under attack after Liberation on two grounds: it was not modern, and therefore not revolutionary; and it was historically associated with the decadent bourgeoisie. In the early stages of the Revolution, musicians and party theorists alike regarded "China's traditional music as old-fashioned, or even as a reactionary impediment to national progress; foreign culture was modern culture, a weapon against the oppressive feudal weight of China's own arts."[30] During the Cultural Revolution China's traditional classical music virtually disappeared, kept alive only privately among older musicians. As mentioned above, some components of it survived by being reworked into "light" style, and in fact much of what is taught and performed today as traditional classical music consists of arrangements and recompositions of the older repertory. But in the past decade there has been some

---

[28] *Ibid.*, pp. 146–7.   [29] *Ibid., passim.*   [30] Kraus, *Pianos and Politics*, pp. 100–1.

resurgence of activity in both research and performance of the unmediated classical repertory. Scholars at the Research Institute of Music and elsewhere have tested new theories of historiography on the classical genres, and younger musicians have been able to study the traditional solo repertory of various instruments, privately and even at conservatories of music.

Ironically, European classical music has often had more official support than Chinese. Even though Mao denounced foreign "imperialist" culture in his early writings, –

> There is in China an imperialist culture which is a reflection of imperialist rule or partial rule, in the political and economic fields. This culture is fostered not only by the cultural organizations run directly by the imperialists in China but by a number of Chinese who have lost all sense of shame.[31]

– by 1989 Western classical music comprised 15 to 20 per cent of all music played on the three National Programs. Most is from the nineteenth and early twentieth centuries, with emphasis on the canonical works of the Viennese school, the nationalist composers of the middle and late nineteenth century, the late Romantics, and the Impressionists. For instance, programs and individual pieces broadcast on the National Services in the fall of 1988 included the finale of Wagner's *Die Walküre*, Beethoven's *Leonora* Overtures 1, 2, and 3, Chopin's Variations on a Theme of Rossini, a harp concerto by Handel, the 43rd "Spring of Prague" International Music Festival, a piano recital by an unidentified Polish pianist, music by the Czech composer Karel Komzak, and a program of Russian compositions performed by pianist Vladimir Ashkenazy.

There are several explanations for this acceptance of Western classical music, the product of a bourgeois society, by a Marxist-Leninist government committed to the creation of a classless workers' state.

The Confucian ethic that music influences morality and social behavior continues to run deep in the Chinese character. Good music is thought to stimulate good behavior, bad music provokes bad behavior. As Kraus puts it, "one of the ironies of modern Chinese politics is that the Confucian marriage of music to statecraft has endured, with the revolutionary Communist Party as its vehicle. Revolutionary Communists and Confucians both believe that art can induce political change, a view at odds with the tradition of

---

[31] Mao Zedong, "On new democracy," p. 185.

bourgeois music in the West."[32] The strong musical and political ties with the Soviet Union just after Liberation also contributed to the acceptance of this music, since the Soviets themselves had theorized the way in which bourgeois classical music could become a "correct" component of a socialist society. More abstractly, the very nature of Western classical music, conceived and fixed in musical notation, analyzable according to "correct" rules of harmony and form, symbolizing "Harmony, Unity and Order,"[33] performed by obedient performers determined to carry out the composer's intentions as mediated by a conductor – these things are all very much in harmony with a society inclined towards order, compliance, and controlled structures by both its Confucian past and the imperatives of its Marxist-Leninist present.

Despite its transparent ethnocentricity, the argument that Western classical music is superior to all other, a theme running through the work of many Western musicologists and cultural historians, has been deeply imprinted on the consciousness of contemporary Asia. Huang Bingqi of the CPBS is convinced that young Chinese who listen to Western classical music are trying to better themselves, they will rise above their peers, and therefore the National Programs must give them substantial amounts of this music at times when they can listen to it, late in the evening for instance.

The CPBS obtains some of its Western classical music directly from overseas record companies, some from exchange agreements with National Public Radio, the BBC, and the state radio services of other socialist countries, some from the Voice of America, and some as gifts from foreign embassies and commercial companies. Symphony orchestras within the People's Republic perform and record European classical music, but their efforts are judged to be inferior to those of foreign performers. Han Yidan reported in the *China Daily* for 19 October 1988 that while "tens of thousands of the tapes of Beethoven's nine grand symphonies conducted by Herbert von Karajan" had been sold in China, "only 1,000 sets of similar music performed by the Central Philharmonic Orchestra [of Beijing] have been sold in the past five years." Chinese performances of Western classical music are infrequently heard on the National Programs, dedicated as they are to giving listeners the "best" music.

[32] Kraus, *Pianos and Politics*, p. 29.
[33] Richard Leppert, "Music, domestic life and cultural chauvinism," in *Music and Society: The Politics of Composition, Performance and Reception*, ed. Leppert and Susan McClary (Cambridge, 1987), p. 68.

Pop and pop/rock music

In the first decades of Communist rule in China, and even more so during the decade of the Cultural Revolution, contemporary foreign popular music was unavailable and unknown in the PRC, and no Chinese musicians composed or performed music in this style. But this situation changed in the late 1970s, with the gradual institution of policies of relative liberalization and openness to the outside world.

> China . . . began to produce and import cassette recorders. Popular songs from Hong Kong, Taiwan and foreign countries poured into the mainland, arousing enthusiasm among the listeners, especially the young. In recent years, pop singers on the mainland have also started to grip the hearts of millions of young people. As a result, pop songs, with soft or strong rhythmical beats and often with romantic verses, have become part of the popular culture of the country.[34]

Cassettes by Taiwanese and Hong Kong singers, beginning with Deng Lijun and Xi Xiulan and continuing through Shu Rui and Qi Qin, were imported and sold openly in the PRC. This music was in a style that might be labelled "Pacific Pop," enjoyed today by tens of millions of people in Japan, South Korea, the Phillipines, Singapore, and Indonesia, as well as Taiwan and Hong Kong. Though there are national dialects of this genre, the chief stylistic features are constant: moderate tempi, texts concerned with romantic love, string-dominated backings (now often generated by synthesizer), a singing style reminiscent of Olivia Newton-John and Barry Manilow, and the frequent use of rhythmic patterns derived from disco music of the 1970s. Except for the language of the texts and an occasional hint of pentatonic scales, there is little Asian about this music.

Chinese authorities encouraged the import of "Pacific Pop," and when private record companies, allowed to begin operation in 1978, began turning out pieces imitative of the Taiwanese and Hong Kong repertories, their efforts were supported selectively by the CPBS. Even though Huang Bingqi believes that most pop performers have little or no talent and that none of this music will stand the test of time, many pieces in this style conform so closely to the stylistic parameters of light music as to fit nicely into programs devoted to this genre. And when popular musicians began drawing on more indigenous Chinese elements in 1987, creating a style labelled Xi Bei Feng ("Northwest Wind"), Chinese radio and television embraced

[34] Han, "Open policy," p. 5.

some of this as well, again because it conformed to the mass line of drawing material from the masses and giving it back to them in mediated form.

The only contemporary American or European popular music heard on the National Services is in "pop" style, in the context of light music programing, as noted above.

In the second half of the 1980s, a few Chinese musicians began performing pieces influenced by Western rock, written by the musicians themselves rather than the classically trained composers who turn out the Chinese versions of Pacific Pop, characterized by fast tempi, prominent drumming, and electric guitar solos. The group Qiheban performed songs in a style somewhat reminiscent of late Beatles, and when they disbanded in 1986, one member, Cui Jian, composed, performed, and recorded "Rocking and Rolling on the New Long March," "I Have Nothing," "Never Cover Myself Again," and other songs which established him as China's first important rock performer. Others include the group "New Air" from Guangzhou, which incorporated elements of rap style into their pieces, and Ceng Lin, with such songs as "Xintianyou."

According to Huang Bingqi, neither this music nor any Western "hard rock" is played on the National Programs of the CPBS, and an article in the *China Daily* summarizing the impact of the "open policy" on popular music made no mention whatsoever of this style or its practitioners.[35] This music, Huang said, is strongly associated with one age group, and the CPBS as an agent of the socialist-Communist state must serve the entire population. Also, the types of contemporary Chinese pop music acceptable to the CPBS are corporately produced, usually written and arranged by conservatory trained composers, and conducted, played, and sung by other institutionally trained musicians. Pieces in rock style, on the other hand, tend to be composed and sung by a single musician who also writes the texts, often has no formal musical training, and may be backed by instruments playing in styles not taught in the country's conservatories. Rock music is associated, correctly or not, with individualism, not collectivism, and is thus inappropriate in a socialist state. Also, many listeners interpret the texts of such songs as Cui Jian's "I Have Nothing" as political statements against state policies, whether or not they were intended this way by the composer.

A program entitled "The American Music Hour" began to be broadcast twice weekly on Program Two in the late 1980s. As a result

---

[35] *Ibid.*

of being carried on one of the National Services, it was relayed to all parts of the country, and I was told repeatedly that it was the single most popular radio program in the PRC. Its American producers had been given instructions as to what types of music could be included, the lyrics of each piece had to be approved by the CPBS, and in return five minutes of each hour-long program was allotted to commercial spots. The program of 23 October 1988 was typical; an unmistakably American voice greeted listeners with:

> Nie hau. I am Dr. Don, the president of the China–America Corporation. Our company was organized to promote scientific, educational, musical, and cultural exchange between the People's Republic of China and the United States of America. We can also assist with trade between our two countries. Thank you for listening to this program, and thanks to our friends at CPBS for making this show possible.

The program began with a selection of hits by the Four Tops, moved on to a group of country-western standards, and ended with a sampling of more recent black pop. Commercials for Northwest Airlines and the Jianguo Hotel in Beijing were spotted throughout the hour.

This extraordinary deviation from CPBS policy must be understood in the context of the eagerness of the Chinese government at this moment to enter into negotiations with American business, on a limited basis and on its own terms. Chinese radio audiences were allowed to hear music not otherwise carried on the National Programs, but only in a context making it clear that the program originated in the USA, and thus did not represent the musical policies of the CPBS itself.

In summary, the decade of the 1980s brought an explosion of popular music styles to the PRC.[36] Those which seemed to fit the theoretical guidelines of being modern and collective while drawing in some way on the music of the "masses" were embraced, selectively, by state cultural agencies. Other styles less appropriate for a socialist-Communist state were largely ignored.

The music of China's "national minorities"

Approximately 93 per cent of the more than a billion people living within the present political borders of the People's Republic are

---

[36] The best accounts of this history are Ju Qihong, "Musique populaire de la Chine du XXe siècle," *Worldbeat* 1 (1991), pp. 13–21, and Zeng Suijin, "Une étude sociologique de la chanson populaire de la Chine contemporaine," *Worldbeat* 1 (1991), pp. 22–33.

considered by Chinese ethnologists to belong a single ethnic group, the Han, even though they speak a variety of dialects, not all of them mutually intelligible, and their physical features may vary considerably. The other 7 per cent, numbering perhaps 80,000,000 persons, have been classified into fifty-five "national minorities."

Some of these minority peoples live within the political boundaries of one or another of the country's twenty-one regions, usually on the geographical and social fringes of the Han population, but the majority inhabits the four desolate, sparsely peopled Autonomous Regions on the geographical periphery of the PRC, comprising almost 60 per cent of the country's land area: Guangxi Zhuang, Nei Manggu (Inner Mongolia), Xinjiang Uighur, Xizang (Tibet).

Article 3 of Chapter 1 (General Principles) of the constitution of the PRC, drawn up in September of 1954, states that:

> All the nationalities are equal. Discrimination against or oppression of any nationality, and acts which undermine the unity of the nationalities, are prohibited. All the nationalities have the freedom to use and develop their own spoken and written languages, and to preserve or reform their own customs and ways.[37]

Mao Zedong insisted that "words and actions can be judged right if they help to unite the people of our various nationalities, and do not divide them."[38] Professor Chen Yongling, Director of the Central Institute of Nationalities, has defined the government's "correct policy" towards these people even more precisely, as "assist[ing] all minority nationalities to achieve all-round development in the political, economic and cultural fields, to advance continuously along the road of socialism, and [thus] to gradually achieve *de facto* equality."[39]

> We must conscientiously sum up the profound impact exerted by the various old social and cultural patterns, and find out the negative factors in holding back their advance toward socialism so as to facilitate working out the countermeasures. These out-dated social patterns have in no way vanished completely; they are still, overtly or covertly, giving expression to their "vitality," impeding the progress of socialist construction. Old ideology as manifested in religious life is exerting adverse effects on social activities. Large amounts of manpower, materials, money and energy, for instance, are concentrated on renovating or building temples, mosques and monasteries as well as religious activities, rather than on modernization projects. Furthermore, the old funeral customs

[37] Chai, *Essential Works*, p. 273.   [38] Mao Zedong, "On the correct handling," p. 338.
[39] Chen Yongling, "New issues confronting socio-ethnic studies in contemporary China," unpublished lecture at Dartmouth College, 1988, p. 1.

and feudal superstitions are prevailing. Our main mission at the present stage is: under the principle of state assistance combined with the underdeveloped nationalities' self-reliant efforts, energetically develop their economy and culture so as to gradually narrow down the gap between them and the advanced nationalities with regard to the level of economic and cultural development.[40]

Simply put, then, the national minorities are taken to be underdeveloped peoples who need more education, political and otherwise, to bring them into the socialist mainstream.

They live mostly within specific geographical areas and can obtain permission to live in other parts of the PRC only with difficulty. Those chosen for advanced education are enrolled in college-level institutions such as the Central Institute of Nationalities in Beijing, the Southwest Institute for Nationalities in Chengdu, and the National Minorities Institute in Lanzhou, which train national minority peoples who can work as technicians, as secondary school teachers, and as administrators in the minority areas of China. They do not usually move into Han society after their college education, but are rather sent back to educate and serve their own ethnic groups. Even educated Han people regard them as outsiders: my excellent translator in Chengdu, recent recipient of a master's degree in American literature, made deprecating remarks about groups of Tibetans on the city streets, and an equally intelligent and well-educated friend in Shanghai could see a group of minority people visiting a recently opened Buddhist shrine only as "ignorant" and "superstitious."

Since the close of the Cultural Revolution, the Chinese government has developed the potential of minority cultures as tourist attractions and as public displays of tolerance towards its non-Han peoples. The Nationalities Cultural Palace in Beijing is the official state monument to these people. Chinese and foreign tourists come here to see exhibits and live entertainment, abstracted from any religious or other ritual context, and to visit the gift shop offering clothing and crafts. Gift shops selling minority items are located in other parts of the country as well, and in recent years the government has sponsored regional festivals of deritualized minority music and dance, as tourist attractions. The *China Daily* for 14 October 1988 carried a full-page photo story on the first Yunnan National Art Festival in Kunming, Dali, and Xishuangbanna, which brought together singers and dancers from twenty-four minority nationalities,

[40] *Ibid.*, pp. 3–8.

performing in regional costumes; there was also a trade fair and various exhibitions, including "seven hundred musical instruments used by ethnic minority groups."

The music of the non-Han peoples has been described as "one of the glorious contributions made by the various nationalities to the Chinese nation's house of cultural treasures."[41] Scholars from the Research Institute of Music in Beijing and the Research Division of the Central Institute of Nationalities collect this music on tape and video, in the field. The intent is not that it will be listened to in this form, however. As a promotional brochure for the Southwest Institute for Nationalities puts it, the school is "devoted to the development of the unique cultural traditions of the various minority peoples." Therefore the musical education of minority students is designed to "improve" the quality of their music. Students study European theory, repertory, and performance and the modern "traditional" music of the Han people as taught in China's conservatories, itself drawing on Western elements, then use these skills to "develop" the music of their regions when they return home after completing their education.

The most important function of the music of minority peoples is to serve as melodic material for China's conservatory trained composers, who make "light" instrumental arrangements of these tunes or weave them into more complex compositions. Fang Kun, leading an ensemble from the Central Conservatory in performances of "traditional" music abroad, defended this sort of composition, and in the process also unwittingly reflected the prevailing condescending attitude towards minority peoples:

> Concerning . . . the pipa piece *Dance Tune of the Yi People* . . . this was a pipa piece composed since Liberation which has the color of the [Yi] people and has become widely liked by the Chinese people. . . . The composition of the piece follows precisely the ABA pattern frequently used in Western pieces, but this in no way impairs the national flavor of the piece. On the contrary, it manages to depict with even greater precision the carefree enthusiasm of the Yi people. Chinese audiences like the piece, and foreign audiences also like it, so this was a successful example of the implementation of our policy of "making foreign things serve China."[42]

So-called minority music is broadcast on the Ethnic Nationalities Program originating in Beijing, on regional services directed at

---

[41] *Ibid.*, p. 11.   [42] Fang, "A discussion," p. 9.

minority peoples, and occasionally on the National Services, never in original versions as recorded on location by ethnomusicologists but in arrangement or as part of more extended pieces by trained composers. This is music drawn from the masses, then given back to them in "improved" form.

In dealing with its ethnic population, as in its relations with the other classes within the Han majority, the leadership of the Communist Party, speaking as the voice of the proletariat, intends to educate. When and if satisfactory progress is made, the national minorities will become part of the country's democracy. Until then, they are subject to the dictatorship of the proletariat, musically as well as politically.

Summary

The National Programs of the CPBS, in their role as the official radio voice of the state, broadcast music judged to be correct listening fare for the population of a socialist-Communist state in which class struggle continues to be a central issue. The vast majority of this music draws in some way or other on music of the Chinese people, whether folk, classical, or ethnic, which is then mediated by trained musicians into a more "correct" form, stylistically neutral and divorced from its original social or ritual context.

The Shanghai People's Broadcasting Station (Radio Shanghai): history and structure

Radio Shanghai was founded on 27 May 1949, the day of the city's liberation from the Japanese. It relayed central state broadcasting from Beijing, augmented by some local programing, until the onset of the Cultural Revolution in 1966, when most of its personnel was dismissed and its programs began to be controlled even more by Beijing. In 1978, with the advent of the new open policy, the station began to function as a semi-autonomous unit under members of the local Chinese Communist Party, many of whom had been banished during the Cultural Revolution. The following exerpts from an essay by one of these men, Zou Fanyang, formerly Chairman of the Shanghai Radio and Television Bureau and subsequently Chairman of the Shanghai Radio and Television Research Institute, will serve as a summary of the station's history and ideology.

After Liberation, I became a journalist, and listened to foreign radio stations, [which] required special permission. I experienced an incomparably rich world from the music programs of these foreign radio stations. Compared with [them], I found the music programs from the Chinese radio stations unsatisfactory. Why was it that so little time was spent on music? Why were the programs so limited, rigid and dull? Why were they so filled with indoctrination and pure political propaganda?

In 1960 I came to work at the radio station [in Shanghai]. At that time, music was a "danger zone." Music was called "the sacred sensor of class struggle," and was considered a sensitive area. Every time there was political turbulence, music was always the first area to be affected. The time allotted for music programs was cut time and again, many programs were banned, folk music was on the verge of being exterminated, sources of foreign music were completely cut off. After the policy that "class struggle has to be talked about every day" was re-emphasized, any mention of "peace" and "love" was prohibited. The world of music should be a vast ocean, but now there was only dead water left in the pond.

The beginning of the Cultural Revolution marked the beginning of the real disaster. All of us "old hands" were expelled from the radio station, each of us bearing some ridiculous political accusation. A music editor told me with tears in his eyes that this time would be his farewell to music, that he would never again come to the station, never listen to the radio again. His heart was broken, dripping with blood. I was deeply touched by what he said, but I was not as pessimistic. I believed that radio could not be extinguished; music, above all, could not be extinguished, [even though] in exile, on my home-made radio, all I could hear were the hoarse cries of political slogans. Was this music? Was this culture? Music had disappeared. What was left was noise. The dead water was finally drained and the pond turned into a desert, a cultural desert.

I returned to the radio station in 1979, when all the people who had been falsely accused had been rehabilitated, and was named Chairman. But the station was in ruins. Studios were destroyed, converted into offices. The past ten years had left only nothingness. Live broadcasting had been prohibited, so that announcers could not hold conversations with the audience. Only pre-recorded programs could be aired.

A technician from the Central Committee suggested that the station set aside one frequency to play music night and day, to become a music station. We decided that in order to revive interest in radio we should put emphasis on the development of FM. The problem was to find materials for stereo radio programing. At that time imported stereos and cassettes were rare. Some young people walked around the city carrying their stereo sets, to show off. One could hear recordings of popular singers from Hong Kong and Taiwan. This phenomenon was the result of the long-time policy of cultural isolation and the dullness of music radio programming. A hunger for music and culture made such people swallow anything that came along. In order to enrich our programs, we had to break the boundaries of city, province and nation, to communicate nationally and internationally. Radio is a means of communication, and music is the most suitable world of language of international communication.[43]

Li Deming, Chairman of the Entertainment Department of the Shanghai Recreational Broadcast Improvement Committee, reiterated the theme that Radio Shanghai is committed to seeking international friendship through music:

> Ancient China had a proverb: "All within the four seas are brothers." Radio Shanghai has made a constant effort to seek friendship. It is a window through which the Chinese audience understands the world.[44]

In the 1980s, Radio Shanghai grew into a complex network of eight separate services (three in stereophonic FM, five in monophonic medium-wave), organized into three units: News and Education (four programs); Arts and Literature (three); and Economic Information (one). Taken together, these eight services are on the air for 120 hours each day, reaching an audience of some 35,000,000 people throughout the Yangtze Delta. Program languages are "standard" Chinese, the Shanghai dialect, and English.[45]

To enrich its programing, Radio Shanghai established exchange programs with its twin cities: Hamhyn (North Korea), Zagreb (Yugoslavia), Yokohama (Japan), and Hamburg (Federal Republic of Germany). It also has program exchanges with the Voice of America, the BBC, the Voice of Germany (FRG), the Canadian Broadcasting Company, and Radio Luxembourg.

---

[43] Zou Fanyang, From "Radio Friends" to "Stereo Friends" (Shanghai, 1988), pp. 1–2.

[44] Li Deming, Seeking Friendship (Shanghai, 1988), p. 1.

[45] This information is taken from a promotional brochure, "Radio Shanghai: your intimate friend," published by Radio Shanghai in 1988.

Music programing on Radio Shanghai

More than sixty hours of music is aired each day. One Art and Literature channel (103.7 FM, stereo) is devoted exclusively to music. General guidelines call for three hours of Western and Japanese pop music each day, four of Western classical music, four hours of light music (which Radio Shanghai appropriately calls "background" music), and seven hours of Chinese music, including classical, operatic, popular, and traditional genres.

The program best epitomizing Radio Shanghai's cultural autonomy is "Stereo Friends." First broadcast in June of 1982, it soon "established a network connecting the hearts of thousands and millions of people. Not only does it spread music, it also disseminates friendship, beauty and love."[46]

Feng Bingyou, the founder and director of "Stereo Friends," came with a translator to my room in the guest house of the Shanghai Conservatory of Music for an interview, dressed in casual Western clothing. Relaxed and informal, he brought program schedules and informational brochures as gifts, and began by reminding me that Shanghai has had longer and closer contact with the outside world than have other cities in the PRC. The various services and programs of Radio Shanghai are designed for this cosmopolitan listenership. His program, "Stereo Friends," is designed to bring international popular music not otherwise available in the PRC to the audiences of Radio Shanghai, for their immediate listening pleasure and also to augment their personal cassette collections by taping the programs.

Each hour-long program is made up of a selection of pieces by one singer or group, put together by Feng himself from cassettes, discs, and now CDs bought from foreign countries, given by sympathetic individuals and institutions abroad, or sometimes loaned by his listeners themselves. Some European popular performers have been included, but most programs are devoted to American music. "Michael Jackson, Dolly Parton, Paul Simon, Randy Travis, and Madonna are household names in Shanghai as a result of our programs," Feng said with obvious pride. During one week of my stay in Shanghai, "Stereo Friends" aired programs no.243 (ABBA), no.244 (Michael Jackson), and no.245 (Whitney Houston).

Feng has expressed his own views on the relationship between radio programing and radio audiences.

---

[46] Zou, *From "Radio Friends,"* p. 2.

The attitude of "It's my business to broadcast, no matter what you prefer" should come to an end. I pursue the theory of equality between producer and audience, of loyally serving our audience and getting rid of bureaucratic interference. My spiritual support comes from those tens of thousands of unknown listeners who care for and support this program. I believe that the motto for "Stereo Friends" should be: popular but not vulgar; benevolent but not subversive.[47]

Even more recently, relationships with American enterprises have brought additional programs of American popular music to Radio Shanghai. While I was there, for instance, "Music World Express," produced by TelePrograms in Los Angeles and hosted by DJ Jim Hanson, treated Chinese listeners to the top five songs in America that week, interviews with several pop musicians, and an "American life style report" dealing with problems faced by unmarried couples living together – a situation quite foreign to the People's Republic.

Unlike the Central Programs, Radio Shanghai airs a full range of Chinese popular styles, including rock pieces by Cui Jian and others. It also broadcasts educational programs dealing with the history of Chinese folk, classical, and even popular music, not unlike those sometimes heard in the USA on National Public Radio. One program, for example, began with samples of a solo folk genre from the Northwest known as Xintianyou, ambulatory songs meditating on the sorrows of human life and the beauties of nature. The genre was then traced, in recorded examples, as it appeared in Chinese opera, as a Red Army song in the 1930s, as an arranged folk song in light style, and as contemporary popular song: "Xintianyou" by Ceng Lin and "I Have Nothing" by Cui Jian. The program ended with a song by Stevie Wonder, with the suggestion that it was, purely by coincidence, similar in expression and content.

Radio Shanghai has served as a window admitting Western popular music into the PRC, with consequences for Shanghai and sometimes the entire country. In August of 1988, the station conducted a mail vote of its audience to select the most popular singer, foreign or Chinese; more than 30,000 letters were received, with Michael Jackson the overwhelming winner. "We Are the World" was first heard in the PRC on "Stereo Friends" immediately after its release in 1985. It was soon recorded in Chinese by ten singers from Shanghai and published in the magazine *Light Music*, then within a few weeks pieces of this genre were being written in

---

[47] Feng Bingyou, *Thoughts on the 200th Issue of "Stereo Friends"* (Shanghai, 1988), p. 3.

China for internal mega-events, such as "Filling the World with Love," performed by 100 Chinese pop musicians in 1986 on the occasion of the International Year of Peace.

Though Radio Shanghai obviously has not felt constrained by the ideology underlying programing for the National Programs, all music is screened by a panel of editors before being broadcast to guard against air play of songs with "pornographic" content or expressing sentiments "against state policy," according to Feng Bingyou.

Summary

Attitudes and programing policies at Radio Shanghai are dramatically different from those of the National Programs of the CPBS. While Radio Shanghai does broadcast its share of the music favored by the National Programs, including light music and both Chinese and European classical repertories, it also gives considerable air time to music not programed in Beijing, most importantly a wide range of foreign and Chinese popular styles. Recurring themes both in programing and in published informational material are international understanding and the station's receptivity to the wants and needs of its audience.

Musical preference in the People's Republic

Until recently, no information on musical preference and listening habits in the People's Republic was available. But during the winter of 1988–9 Yang Xiaoxun, a graduate student at the Tianjin Conservatory of Music, undertook as his master's thesis a computer-aided survey of musical taste and patterns of consumption in the Beijing area.

Yang is particularly concerned with popular music, which he defines as "the kind of music that emerges from the cities, spreads from there to other segments of the population, and has a certain commodity value."[48] Appropriately enough for a study undertaken in a socialist-Communist state, the chief focus is on the impact of music on social behavior, and how this might be controlled:

> Listening to music is a type of social behavior. The [recent] spread
> of popular music is the result of the influence of a quite specific
> social environment and psychological demand. . . . Under the

[48] Yang Xiaoxun, *The Theory and Practice of Predicting the Propagation of Chinese Popular Music* (Tianjin, 1989), p. 7.

influence of specific historical backgrounds and social conditions, various psychological demands will manifest differences in human behavior. By studying and predicting these behavioral tendencies, we will be able to control artificially the impact of the dissemination of music and make it possible to accurately intensify or suppress such impact.[49]

Yang posits a four-part control system, designed to enable "the controlled object to act according to the predetermined goal of the controlling object."[50] The controlling object (1) is music itself, the controlled object (2) is the audience for this music. Controlling information (3) about the controlling object (i.e., the music) comes from newspapers, radio, television, and film. The effectiveness of the controlling object on the controlled object can then be measured by feedback information (4) which can take two forms: non-predictive feedback, such as statistics of the size of the audience for radio and television programs or letters and phone calls from this audience, giving information only about the controlled object; and predictive feedback, audience surveys of the sort undertaken in Yang's thesis or analyses of non-predictive feedback, which can "find inner patterns and thus predict future behavior of the controlled object" as a result of dealing with the controlled object (the audience). Yang suggests that predictive feedback is becoming increasingly important in the contemporary world, because it can "directly influence and propel forward the development of the audio and video industry, control of music and art, music education, and musical propaganda."[51]

Of the 1,150 questionnaires distributed by Yang, 952 were completed, anonymously. Institutions chosen for participation included two middle schools, four universities, two large department stores, five factories, seven sub-departments of the Central Organizational Department, one medical institution, one social science institution, two hospitals, two departments of the National Physical Training Committee, four professional music and dance companies, and two conservatories of music. 52.9 per cent of the respondents were female, 47.1 per cent male; ages ranged from fourteen to over fifty, with an average age of twenty-six.

This survey makes it possible to test the correspondence between the music offered on the National Programs of the CPBS and actual musical taste in the PRC. Two factors must be kept in mind, however. First, Yang chose his sample from people with a relatively

---

[49] *Ibid.*, p. 3.   [50] *Ibid.*   [51] *Ibid.*, pp. 3–4.

high level of education. A mere 3.1 per cent of his respondents had only a primary school education, 7.5 per cent had done postgraduate work. Thus the results reflect the cultural tastes of a segment of the Chinese people historically inclined towards "reactionary, bourgeois" attitudes. Secondly, the survey was taken in Beijing, where musical activity (including radio programing) most directly reflects the cultural strategies of the state. The results might well have been different had the survey been taken in Shanghai, with its much wider range of music available on Radio Shanghai and elsewhere.

Informants were asked to indicate their first, second, and third choices from a list of eight types of music, with the following results:

type of music	1	2	3	total
(1) pop	370	218	150	738
(2) dance music (disco, etc.)	65	169	258	492
(3) classical (Western style)	146	141	131	418
(4) foreign instrumental (jazz, etc.)	108	146	117	371
(5) traditional or folk	137	130	80	347
(6) traditional opera	59	45	45	149
(7) Chinese instrumental	28	38	67	133
(8) chorus (mass songs)	2	24	42	68

Interpreting these findings in relation to what I've written in the first part of this study is problematic, since the categories chosen by Yang don't coincide precisely with mine. However, one sees immediately that popular vocal and instrumental genres (including jazz) given little air time on the CPBS are far and away the favored music, occupying three of the top four spots. There is agreement on Western classical music, favored with a great deal of air time on the National Services and third on the list of preferences. Light music, most favored by the CPBS, is not one of the categories listed by Yang, but his categories of "traditional and folk" and "Chinese instrumental music," fifth and seventh choices of his informants, encompass light music as I've defined it. A complicating factor, as pointed out above, is that certain types of Chinese and foreign pop songs are stylistically indistinguishable from light music and are in fact often included on light music programs.

Despite these problems of interpretation, the survey seems to indicate substantial disagreement between the types of music given most air time on the National Services and the actual music preferences of the respondents to this poll.

Dissemination of music in the PRC

Yang's survey also makes it possible to measure, albeit on a limited scale, the extent to which the Chinese people depend on radio, as opposed to other means of dissemination, for their music. A brief summary of the several ways in which music is disseminated in contemporary China is necessary first.

According to Huang Bingqi of the CPBS, there are approximately 400,000,000 radio receivers in the People's Republic, and "most people have access to a radio." The number of different radio services available varies widely, depending on location within the country. In the largest cities one can receive two or three of the National Programs, several different regional services, and in Beijing, Tianjin, or Shanghai a number of municipal services as well. When I was in Shanghai, for instance, twenty-four different radio programs could be heard at certain times of the day. In more rural areas the choice may be limited to one or two National Programs and perhaps a regional or local broadcast.

Radios are not a part of the urban or rural landscape and soundscape in the People's Republic as elsewhere, in southern Africa and the urban USA for instance. Radio sets are listened to in the home, almost never on public streets and certainly not in the workplace. On the other hand, involuntary public listening to radio broadcasts or tapes takes place in certain environments: in the lobbies and restaurants of hotels and other public places, and, when one is travelling, through the loudspeakers with which most passenger trains and boats are equipped.

According to statistics released by the Audio and Visual Department of the Ministry of Broadcasting, Film, and Television, 102,000,000 cassette tapes were produced for sale in the PRC in 1987. These are sold in small, privately operated stalls or "record bars" throughout the PRC, whose stock is legally limited to tapes produced by the some 200 record companies operating within the country and a small number of officially approved imported items. However, many shops also offer pirated foreign and domestic tapes, and one can find entire enterprises (often mobile) offering a wide selection of nothing but pirated items. Incidentally, the only music heard in the streets of the cities I visited came not from radios, but from these record bars, loudly advertising their products to passers-by.

Home taping, of commercial tapes or from the radio, is epidemic. In Yang's survey, 78.7 per cent of the respondents indicated that they owned cassette tapes of music. Of this number, 45.4 per cent said that their collections were made up chiefly of copied tapes, 23.5 per cent reported owning a mixture of original and duplicated tapes, and 31.1 per cent indicated that their collection consisted chiefly of commercially purchased tapes.[52] A very rough estimate of the total number of cassette tapes made in a year, including commercial, pirated, and home-taped items, might be 350,000,000.

Phonographs are so expensive as to be owned only by the most privileged individuals and by instititions, and compact discs are as yet virtually unknown in the PRC.

Until the advent of cassette tapes, "film enjoy[ed] perhaps the largest popular audience of all the cultural media of contemporary China. More people, and a wider range of people, watch movies than read novels, see television, or attend stage performances."[53] Music has two functions in Chinese films: to serve as dramatic accompaniment to the images on the screen; and as interpolated songs in light or pop style. By the late 1980s, composers of the Chinese Musicians Association had succeeded in combining the potential of the country's two most popular mass media by writing songs to be introduced in films and then marketed on cassette tapes.

Chinese Central Television (CCTV) reported that some 10,000,000 television sets were owned in the country at the beginning of 1988. Program 1, on the air thirteen hours each day is relayed to all parts of the country. In addition, there are some forty-six provincial and municipal services, many of them largely devoted to educational programing. The National Program of CCTV carries the same range of music as the CPBS: light vocal and instrumental music, Chinese opera, and European and Chinese classical music. Additionally, dramatic shows and series written and produced for television often contain interpolated songs in pop style, which are then brought out on cassette. In fact, many of the most successful pop songs of the late 1980s were introduced either in film or on television.

For a visitor from the West, live musical performance seems remarkably limited in the PRC. Pop or light music concerts are sometimes scheduled in large public arenas. Folk music ensembles, offering mostly light arrangements of traditional tunes, perform at conservatories of music and in public halls large enough to accommodate groups of tourists. Small clubs, clustered usually around universities, are the usual venues for rock music, though there are sometimes arena performances by Cui Lian and other stars of this genre. Chinese opera is performed in theaters, or on open-air

[52] *Ibid.*, p. 31.
[53] Paul Clark, "The film industry in the 1970s," in *Popular Chinese Literature*, ed. McDougall, p. 31.

stages. Street musicians are rare, and inappropriate in a socialist-Communist society.[54] Disco clubs, with dancing to recorded music, have proliferated in recent years. There are also bars and restaurants where patrons, for a fee, can sing to the backing of taped instrumental accompaniment. According to *The China News* for 1 February 1990, the repertory at one of these establishments, the Yanhai Restaurant in Beijing, consists of popular songs from Hong Kong and Taiwan as well as 364 American titles, including "Rock Around the Clock," "Tennessee Waltz," "Moon River," and more recent hits by Madonna and Janet Jackson.

In a survey related to his thesis, Yang Xiaoxun asked respondents to indicate what means of dissemination they depended on most for their music, with the following results:[55]

tape or phonograph	59.8 per cent
television or film	15.7 per cent
radio	11.5 per cent
live performance	10.0 per cent
participation, or listening to friends	3.0 per cent

At least within the limited sample of this survey, the CPBS appears to play a minor role in shaping the musical taste of the Chinese people through "explaining and popularizing" the kinds of music deemed best for them, simply because such a small percentage of them depend on the radio as a major source for their music.

Final summary

The Communist Party of the People's Republic of China, exercising the leadership demanded in a "democratic dictatorship," has formulated a policy governing the choice of music to be broadcast by the state-controlled radio network and performed by state ensembles. Faithful to the writings of Mao Zedong and his successors, this policy is based on the "mass line" theory; on the notion that culture in contemporary China should be "modern"; and on the conviction that music can affect social behavior and morality. It is not so much concerned with disseminating political texts through vocal music as with offering music intended to speak to the largest possible audience, and to encourage socially correct behavior among the Chinese population.

[54] My translator in Xian, a bassoon instructor at the Conservatory, was amused at my interest in a blind singer from the countryside crouched on a street corner, accompanying himself with an er-hu. "You've come all the way from America to hear *that*?"

[55] Yang, *Theory and Practice*, 6.

The three National Programs, disseminated throughout the PRC from Beijing and understood to be the official radio voice of the central government, base their music programing on these "correct" principles, as do also the provincial services. However, municipal and local radio services are now under decentralized, sub-government control, and since 1979 many of them, including Radio Shanghai, have pursued increasingly independent policies of music programing.

In the three decades after Liberation, and particularly during the Cultural Revolution, the central government was able to impose the music of its choice on virtually the entire population of the PRC, through monopoly control of cultural production and radio programing. In the 1980s, however, the situation changed dramatically. The decision to decentralize major components of the state radio network had the effect of decentralizing music programing in large areas of the country. Even more important has been the impact of cassette technology. With tape playback and recording equipment now affordable for a major part of the population, the state has simply lost control over the listening habits of its people. In an era in which as much as two thirds of the population depends on cassettes for the major share of its music, and at least two thirds of the tapes owned are pirated or copied at home, the music over which the state can exercise direct control (through radio programs under its direct supervision, or live public performance, or officially approved imported cassette tapes) makes up a small percentage of the music listened to within the country.

Postscript

The situation described above existed in the PRC in late 1988, when I visited the country. Foreign television coverage of the democracy movement in the spring of 1989, particularly from Tiananmen Square, often focused on music: Beethoven's Ninth Symphony blaring from cassette players and loudspeakers, young people clustered around pop musicians, the pop star Hou Dejien leading a hunger strike and then negotiating with the army to allow protestors to leave the square peacefully.

Only scattered information has been available to me to suggest the extent to which the Chinese government linked music in general, and popular music in particular, to the democracy movement, and what steps have been taken in reprisal. Minister of Culture Wang Meng, who expressed enthusiasm for both American and Chinese popular music when he met with me, was the highest ranking official deposed in the aftermath of the demonstrations, though his musical taste may not have been an important factor in his fall from grace. Public rock/pop concerts were discontinued after May. Hou Dejien took refuge in the Australian embassy for several months, reappeared in public only when the government promised not to arrest him, but has not been able to resume his career. Chinese scholars scheduled to read papers at the Fifth International Popular Music Conference of IASPM, held in Paris in July of 1989, had their visas withdrawn. One informant recently reported that even less pop/rock music is played on the state radio services now, and that the style of Chinese pop has been appropriated for new songs praising the army and the members of the proletariat who resisted the democracy movement. There have been changes in music programing at Radio Shanghai.

On the other hand, Cui Jian was allowed to perform in February 1990, in the Beijing Workers' Gymnasium. As the *China Post* for 5 February 1990 reported the event:

> A roar went up as mainland China's No. 1 and only rock 'n' roll singer, Cui Jian, bounded on stage Sunday night. The band surged into heavy-metal high gear. Colored strobes blinked zanily. Fans waved their arms for Cui's first concert in nearly a year, and the first rock event since last June. It was about as crazy as a crowd in socialist China can get, and hundreds of police were there to make sure it didn't get any crazier. Uniformed police occupied the entire front row, sitting stolidly while the audience behind them erupted with cheers. But that didn't stop the nearly 10,000 fans, most in their teens and 20s, from jumping up and down in place and waving posters. A plainclothes member of the People's Armed Police stood by scowling. "I don't like his music," he said. "I don't like the way he sings it. I like someone like Fei Xiang" – a Taiwanese-American pop singer who recently toured mainland China.

It isn't clear the extent to which the Communist Party of China has taken steps to enforce its policies on music more forcefully since June of 1989, and the situation has been too sensitive to find out much from musicians within the country. Two things are clear, however: music is an important site of political struggle within the PRC; and the Chinese government will find it more difficult now than in the past to control musical taste, if it attempts to do so.

Appendix 1

Directly under the Ministry of Radio, Film, and Television

Radio Beijing (external shortwave service, forty-three languages)

Central People's Broadcasting Station (Beijing)
National Program 1 (Putonghua)
National Program 2 (Putonghua)
National Program 3 (Putonghua, stereo, FM)
Taiwan, Program 1 (Putonghua)
Taiwan, Program 2 (Amoy, Hakka)
Ethnic Nationalities Program (in Putonghua and various national languages)

Provincial Services (in Putonghua and various regional dialects)

Anhui	Heilingjiang	Jiangsu	Shaanxi
Fujian	Henan	Jiangxi	Shandong
Gansu	Hubei	Liaoning	Shanxi
Guangdong	Hunan	Qunghai	Yunnan
Guizhou	Jilin	Sichuan	Zhejiang
Hebei			

Fujian Front Station (to Taiwan)
Program 1 (Putonghua)
Program 2 (Putonghua, Amoy)

Voice of Jinling (to Taiwan)

Under sub-government supervision

Municipal Services (in Putonghua and local dialects)
Beijing   Tianjin   Shanghai [Radio Shanghai]

Services for Autonomous Regions (in Putonghua and various national languages)

Guangxi Zhuang	Niangxia Hui	Xizang (Tibet)
Nei Menggu [Inner Mongolia]	Xinjiang Uighur	

Local Services (in Putonghua, and various dialects and national languages)
179 (171 FM, 8 shortwave)

13

TOWARDS A NEW READING OF GERSHWIN

Six months after returning from my last trip to southern Africa, an invitation from Brooklyn College to lead a seminar on the music of George Gershwin shifted my attention back to the musical life of the United States.

As far back as 1945 my first professor of musicology, Steve Tuttle – gentle, Harvard-educated, passionately devoted to the great master-pieces of the classical repertory and with no apparent interest in popular music – had confessed to me that the music of Gershwin troubled him. Inclined by his education and musical tastes to dismiss it out of hand, he somehow kept coming back to it, attracted and repelled at the same time. I'd had somewhat of the same problem. Though I was fond of many of the songs and had found *Porgy and Bess* to be an outstanding piece of musical theater, Gershwin's orchestral compositions had always struck me as being unsatisfactory compromises between irreconcilable musical styles, or genres, or concepts.

This article, growing out of my first lecture for the seminar, sets out to identify and analyze the several strands of modernist thought that had shaped attitudes, mine included, towards Gershwin and his music. Though I wouldn't go so far as to suggest that Gershwin was a proto-postmodernist, some of the conceptual confusion surrounding him was clearly a reaction to his attempts to free music from the rigidity of modernist form and function.

Some years after I wrote this essay, a book by Joan Peyser set out to demolish the family-controlled image of Gershwin's character, without, however, offering any new insights on the obstacles to understanding his music.[1]

* * *

[1] Joan Peyser, *The Memory of All That: The Life of George Gershwin* (New York, 1993).

The United States has not produced a more famous composer than George Gershwin, who died half a century ago, on 11 July 1937. Many of his popular songs became standards or "evergreens" throughout the Western world from the 1920s through the 1950s, and some even survived the evolution of popular music style from Tin Pan Alley to rock. Jazz musicians have always found his songs particularly suitable for improvisation, and much of the bebop repertory is built over the chord changes of several of them. His concert pieces, particularly *Rhapsody in Blue*, *An American in Paris*, the *Concerto in F* for piano and orchestra, and the preludes for piano, are among the most widely performed "classical" works of the twentieth century, and his *Porgy and Bess* has become the most popular opera of the century. He is said to have written popular classical music, and classic popular pieces. A large literature has grown up around his music and his life, much of it dealing with the latter point.

Given all this, it might seem strange to suggest that Gershwin is in any sense an unknown composer; it seems likely that more people know *something* about Gershwin than about any other composer of recent times. In point of fact, however, there has been a remarkable absence of disciplined theoretical, analytical, or historical discourse on Gershwin and his music. Much of what we think we "know" about him and his music is based on popular, journalistic literature, much of it highly problematic in theory and method. As a result, in a very real sense certain aspects of Gershwin have indeed remained unexplored, obscure, even unknown.

My intent in what follows is to identify and confront several factors which have contributed to this situation, and to suggest possible ways to correct the problem.

Donald Grout states at the beginning of the Preface to his *A History of Western Music*[1] that "the history of music is primarily the history of musical style," then offers a reading of music history as a succession of chronological "style periods," each defined by melodic, formal, rhythmic, tonal, contrapuntal, and timbral elements unique to compositions of that particular era. One style "progresses" to another, and evaluation of composers and individual pieces is based largely on their contribution to this inexorable forward march of musical progress. Of course Grout was not the first scholar to construct a history of music around an examination of stylistic

---

[1] New York, 1960, p. xiii.

elements of selected compositions and to suggest a linear progression of style periods: the notion was developed in the nineteenth century, and has dominated the thinking of mainstream musicology, at least in the United States, ever since. I mention Grout's book only because, as the most widely used text for academic courses in music history in the English-speaking world, it both reflects and reproduces this ideology. One encounters a similar view of music history wherever one looks in the standard literature, particularly in the United States. Selecting at random, Rey M. Longyear's *Nineteenth-Century Romanticism in Music*, one of six books in a series "present[ing] a panoramic view of the history of music of Western civilization, divided among the major historical periods – Medieval, Renaissance, Baroque, Classical, Romantic, and Twentieth-Century," deals with "Romantic" music by stylistic analysis of selected compositions making up the "panorama of mountains, some in shadow, separated by mist-shrouded valleys," as he sees the landscape of nineteenth-century music.[2]

Acceptance of the concept of historical style periods as the proper framework for the study of Western music has the immediate effect of defining the arena in which discussion and analysis of this music will take place. That is, the study of individual composers and pieces of music will tend to focus on the ways in which they do (or do not) conform to the stylistic parameters of the style period within which they fall, and value judgements will be based on such analyses.

Thus: an examination of certain pieces by Beethoven has suggested that they contain stylistic details not found in the music of earlier composers; a similar examination of compositions by certain composers younger than Beethoven has suggested that they drew on elements of his style; as a result, Beethoven is seen as an "important" composer, whose music is then worthy of even more intensive study. But Louis Spohr, highly esteemed by his contemporaries and as prolific and widely performed as Beethoven, has been relegated to near oblivion by musicologists, since "despite a capacity for free expression, he adhered to the discipline of Classical form and only occasionally exceeded its limits in experimentation"[3] and "[he] rejected most of Beethoven's music from the Fifth Symphony onwards."[4]

Charles Ives, whose music was virtually unknown during his lifetime, is now thought to be "the first great American composer of concert music, and unarguably the most original and significant one

---

[2] Englewood Cliffs, 1988, p. vii.
[3] *New Grove Dictionary of Music and Musicians*, ed. Stanley Sadie (London, 1980), vol. 18, p. 11.
[4] Longyear, *Nineteenth-Century Romanticism*, p. 63.

of the late 19th and early 20th centuries,"[5] largely on the basis of his experimentation with polytonality, multi-rhythms and free atonality at a time when these devices were not in the vocabulary of most composers. But the music of Sergei Rachmaninoff, "the last great representative of Russian late Romanticism" whose creative life overlapped that of Ives, has been of little interest to musicologists since "it has not had any important lasting effect on the development of Russian music."[6]

Music history is taken to be linear and "progressive," and in line with the importance assigned to individualism in bourgeois culture, each composer has been judged on his ability to create pieces different from, and more "advanced" than, those of earlier composers.

Judged in this way, Gershwin's compositions have proved to be highly problematic and, at best, marginal. At a time when Schoenberg, Stravinsky, Bartók, and others were seen to be creating a radically new twentieth-century harmonic, formal, tonal, and instrumental language, Gershwin was writing tonal, triadic music, and shaping his pieces according to nineteenth-century formal structures. Accordingly, his *Concerto in F* (1925) was judged to be "conventional and dull" by such critics as Lawrence Gilman, and even sympathetic reviewers pointed out that since the piece was a "classic piano concerto in three movements," it should be discussed according to critical standards already established for such pieces. Likewise with his songs: Alec Wilder expressed surprise that "a man so concerned with the wide scope of larger forms of music" would not "have experimented more with the popular song form," finding that "the bulk of his songs are in the conventional A–A–B–A pattern."[7]

Thus Gershwin's compositions fit uneasily into the conceptual framework adopted by so many Western music historians and critics. Since all empirical evidence suggests that his music has been more central to the cultural life of the twentieth century than is revealed by this sort of analysis, one is forced to question this way of thinking about music history, in connection with Gershwin and also in general.

Until quite recently, the vast majority of descriptive and critical writing on Gershwin centered around his putative relationship to jazz. In order to deal with this issue, one must first understand that three quite different bodies of music were labelled "jazz" in the 1920s:

[5] *The New Grove Dictionary of American Music*, ed. H. Wiley Hitchcock and Stanley Sadie (London and New York, 1986), vol. 2, p. 503.   [6] *New Grove*, vol. 15, p. 550.
[7] Alec Wilder, *American Popular Song: The Great Innovators, 1900–1950* (New York, 1972), p. 122.

(1) Jazz (and blues) performed by black musicians for black audiences within the social context of black American culture. Phonograph discs of this music were marketed as "race records" by small independent record companies, or by subsidiaries of major companies. This music was rarely heard on commercial radio, and then only locally. Given the social structures of American life at this time, few whites (including Europeans) heard this music, which is now regarded by jazz historians as the most authentic and important type of jazz.

(2) Jazz (and blues) performed by black musicians for white audiences within the social context of white American culture. By the late 1920s, and throughout the 1930s, major record companies were distributing such music nationally, and some of it could be heard on network radio. Decisions of repertory and even musical style were usually made by white entrepreneurs and producers.

(3) So-called jazz performed by white musicians for white audiences within the social context of white American culture. This repertory made up the major share of all commercially recorded popular music in the 1920s, and was widely broadcast both locally and nationally.

Virtually all writing on "jazz" during Gershwin's lifetime was concerned with category (3). Henry O. Osgood's *So This Is Jazz*,[8] the first book on this topic, devotes entire chapters to Irving Berlin, Paul Whiteman, and Gershwin, and only a single footnote to jazz by black musicians. Paul Whiteman's *Jazz*[9] also concentrates on white musicians. Isaac Goldberg's biography of Gershwin mentions "jazz" repeatedly in connection with his music, and concludes with essays on "Jazz-analysis" and "Jazz and the machine age"; he insists that even though "[jazz] is traceable in part, to the Negro, it is developed, commercially and artistically, by the Jew," and he traces its history through successive stages of "Tin Pan Alley . . . The Musical Show Racket . . . Operetta . . . Lady Jazz in the Concert Hall . . . The Wedding of Jazz to Symphonic Art."[10]

The decade of the 1920s has been labelled "The Jazz Age" by cultural historians: its central characters are taken to be such men as F. Scott Fitzgerald, Babe Ruth, Gershwin, Al Capone – not black jazz musicians in the South, Chicago, and the Midwest. Irving Berlin's songs of the early 1920s were labelled "jazz songs," and his first biographer insisted that "[Berlin] must be regarded as a pioneer in jazz."[11] Al Jolson was known as a "jazz singer," performing such songs as Berlin's "Blue Skies" in the landmark film *The Jazz Singer* of

[8] Boston, 1926.   [9] New York, 1926.
[10] Isaac Goldberg, *George Gershwin: A Study in American Music* (New York, 1931), pp. 278, 292.
[11] Alexander Woolcott, *The Story of Irving Berlin* (New York and London, 1925), p. 212.

1927. Paul Whiteman, the "King of Jazz," was one of hundreds of white musicians leading white "jazz" bands; among others were Roger Wolfe Kahn, Ben Selvin, Ben Pollack, Ted Lewis, Sam Lanin, Vincent Lopez, even Jimmy Durante.

This conceptual confusion between "jazzed" popular songs in Tin Pan Alley style and authentic black jazz was widespread in both America and Europe in the 1920s. Even the French, with their great enthusiasm for jazz, had virtually no contact with "authentic" black jazz at this time, and were exposed instead to performers like Josephine Baker, whose music was mediated for consumption by white European audiences.

Here again a questionable theoretical assumption – that "jazz" was a product of white American culture in the 1920s, and that it grew out the New York based Tin Pan Alley style of songwriting – has shaped and informed discourse on Gershwin. But it should be noted that none of Gershwin's compositions uses the word "jazz" in its title or subtitle. *Rhapsody in Blue* was written for "Jazz Band and Piano," true enough, but merely because Paul Whiteman, who commissioned the piece, called his orchestra a "jazz band." And even though Gershwin did write a brief article entitled "Jazz is the Voice of the American Soul"[12] during the height of the initial excitement over his *Rhapsody*, he otherwise avoided the word in connection with his own music. "Jazz is a word which has been used for at least five or six different types of music," he wrote near the end of his life. "It is really a conglomeration of many things (ragtime, the blues, classicism and spirituals). . . . An entire composition written in jazz could not live."[13]

It should also be noted that Gershwin, more than any other composer (or critic, or historian) of his time, constantly sought out black musicians and listened to the widest possible range of black music. He knew Will Vodery, Lucky Roberts, Duke Ellington; he heard New York "stride" pianists play downtown, and often visited the Cotton Club and other spots in Harlem to hear the bands of Ellington and Cab Calloway; through his friendship with Carl Van Vechten, he heard Bessie Smith and other black singers perform at social gatherings; and while in South Carolina to work on *Porgy and Bess*, he heard and even participated in rural black church singing.

---

[12] *Theatre Magazine* (June 1926).

[13] George Gershwin, "The composer in the machine age," in *Revolt in the Arts*, ed. Oliver M. Sayler (New York, 1930), p. 142. Duke Ellington, in his book *Music is My Mistress* (Garden City, 1973), p. 471, insisted that "Jazz is only a word and really has no meaning. We stopped using it."

Gershwin's reluctance to use the term "jazz" in connection with his own music was a result of his knowing enough about black music to understand, more clearly than his critics, that jazz was essentially a form of Afro-American music, not a product of New York's Tin Pan Alley.

Why, then, have so many writers concentrated on the "jazz connection" in Gershwin's music? For the same reason they have discussed his compositions in the context of historical style periods: it is easier to measure any music against pre-existent theory than to search for a new context. Also, discussions of "jazz" elements and influences in Gershwin's concert pieces were useful to critics in explaining the favorable reception of this music in the 1920s and 30s. Classical music was not supposed to be taken seriously unless it was "progressive" in some way. It was difficult for critics to discover anything "new" in Gershwin's harmonic, melodic, or structural techniques. But by calling attention to his use of "jazz" rhythms, tricks of instrumentation, and "blue" notes, these writers were able to suggest that his music was "progressive" in the sense that it introduced such elements to classical music, and thus reconcile popular reception of his music with their own critical ideology.

A clearer understanding of Gershwin's music has also been hindered by family intervention, following his death.

When Gershwin died in 1938, at the age of thirty-nine, he was survived by his brother Ira, who had written lyrics for most of his songs; Ira's wife Leonore; his sister Frances; and her husband, Leopold Godowsky II, son of the well-known pianist and composer. This group, headed by Ira, inherited Gershwin's physical possessions, including his musical manuscripts and personal papers, and also took control of copyrights, permissions, and performance rights to his music. Over the years most (but not all) of Gershwin's manuscripts, and a selection of his correspondence, have been given to the Library of Congress in Washington, where they can be studied, but other materials remain unavailable, in the private Gershwin Archives.

With a single exception, biographers of Gershwin have had close ties to one or another member of the family. Isaac Goldberg's early biography, mentioned above, appeared while Gershwin was still alive and was based on information and material supplied by Gershwin himself. The most recent biography is by Edward Jablonski,[14] who was for many years a friend and confidant of Ira

---

[14] Edward Jablonski, *Gershwin: A Biography* (New York, 1987).

Gershwin; he had access to Ira's diaries, and quotes selectively from them, but no other scholar has been able to see this material. As a result of this situation, most writing about Gershwin has reflected the attitudes and wishes of his immediate family.

Family control over personal information about famous people after their death is common, of course. The Gershwin family was close knit and proud of George's fame, and it is understandable that they would want a favorable and positive image projected to the world. As Jablonski sketches this image, "the young composer typified eternal youth in a vibrant, strident America wakening to its potential and power in the arts, business, industry, finance, sports, in a world only recently shocked into the twentieth century. . . . Besides his musical gifts, [he had] other attractive attributes: youth, fame, success in an era that venerated success."[15] He made a great deal of money, he became a media "personality," he consorted with a succession of attractive and talented women. He appeared to epitomize the "American Dream," and his success was cherished and cultivated by a family headed by a father who had been a worker in a shoe factory in Russia before emigrating to New York.

It is not of much importance to scholars that this mediated image of Gershwin ignores or marginalizes some details of his personal life. Even if it were true that he frequented brothels, or fathered an illegitimate child, or was a "sleazy opportunist," as the one dissident biography insinuates,[16] these things would have little effect on our understanding of his music and its relations to his contemporary world. What might help, however, would be a clearer understanding of what sort of person he was, intellectually. The family-approved image is of a cheerful, apolitical, non-intellectual extrovert, too absorbed in his music and his career to give much thought to such issues as the place of music in America's evolving democratic, capitalistic society. If one searches, though, there are many hints that Gershwin was a more complex and thoughtful person than this.

As a member of the artistic and intellectual Jewish community of New York, he must have known of the involvement of members of his community in radical politics in the early 1930s. There was, for instance, the Composers Collective of New York, affiliated with the Workers' Music League (an arm of the American Communist Party), which "sought to make an American contribution to the international working-class music movement then flourishing in Europe under writers such as Bertolt Brecht and composers such as Hanns

[15] *Ibid.*, pp. ix–x.
[16] Charles Schwartz, *Gershwin, His Life and Music* (Indianapolis, 1973).

Eisler."[17] Members of this group wrote most of the pieces in the *Workers' Songbook* published by the WML in 1934–5.

While there is no evidence whatsoever that Gershwin was connected with this group, whose membership included Marc Blitzstein, Aaron Copland, and Elie Siegmeister, one can see a clear change in Gershwin's own rhetoric at this time, in his interviews with the press and in the few surviving bits of his writing. For instance, the concept of "folk music" seems not to have interested him before, but this term begins to creep into his vocabulary in the early 1930s, sometimes in connection with his own music, at just the time folk music was becoming an issue in American radical circles. In the above-mentioned "The composer in the machine age" (1930), he wrote that "the only kinds of music which endure are those which possess form in the universal sense and folk music. All else dies. Folk songs are being written and have been written which contain enduring elements of jazz." He insisted that *Porgy and Bess* (1935) was a "folk opera," because the story was a "folk tale" and "its people would naturally sing folk music." Gershwin was both praised and criticized for the opera's portrayal of blacks; but he insisted in a press interview that such criticism was beside the point, since he intended *Porgy and Bess* to be understood in a more general context, as "exemplifying the typical American proletariat point of view in its fundamentals, regardless of race or color."[18] There is none of this sort of rhetoric from him in the 1920s, and it should also be noted that his works for the musical stage progress (though not always in a straight line) from early topical, entertaining shows such as *Lady Be Good!* (1924), *Oh, Kay!* (1926), and *Girl Crazy* (1930) through the political satire of *Strike Up the Band* (1927, 1930), *Of Thee I Sing* (1931), and *Let 'Em Eat Cake* (1933), to the celebration of the "typical American proletariat" in *Porgy and Bess* in 1935.

According to Gershwin's aesthetic, as well as it can be pieced together from scattered sources, he believed that popular songs "die at an early age and are soon completely forgotten," as a result of being "sung and played too much when they are alive, especially since the invention of the phonograph and more so since the widespread conquest of the radio." Because of their nature, they "cannot stand the strain of their very popularity."[19] Music can endure over a period of time only if it possesses "form in the universal sense," or is written "in serious form. When I wrote the

[17] *The New Grove Dictionary of American Music*, vol. 1, p. 479.
[18] *The New York Times*, 20 October 1935.
[19] George Gershwin, *George Gershwin's Song-Book* (New York, 1932), p. ix.

Rhapsody in Blue I took 'blues' and put them in a larger and more serious form. That was twelve years ago and the *Rhapsody in Blue* is still very much alive, whereas if I had taken the same themes and put them in songs they would have been gone years ago."[20]

Piecing these two attitudes together, one can see that Gershwin's ideological position and strategies resemble those of many politically aware European and American musicians of the 1930s. If Gershwin did indeed set out to "exemplify the American proletariat" in *Porgy and Bess,* he did so by using his skill and training as a composer to create a stage work representing their relations to the power stucture of contemporary American society, not by drawing on proletariat music itself; but at the same time this music was written in a style accessible to the proletariat as well as to theater audiences. He pointedly refused to use "authentic" musical materials in *Porgy and Bess*; but he insisted that the composed spirituals and songs were indeed "folk" music, since they were part of a "folk opera." And though there was some black criticism of the opera, J. Rosamund Johnson called Gershwin "a musical Abe Lincoln," Warren Coleman (who created the role of Crown) felt that the composer had a "serious and dignified" approach to his black characters, and Todd Duncan, the first Porgy, remembered that Gershwin "loved what the unspoiled South Carolina Negro stood for" and told the cast: "They're beautiful. They're not educated, but they have such virtues."[21] It should be noted in this connection that one of the earliest performances of *Porgy and Bess* was an amateur production by the "maids and porters" – all black, of course – at Bryn Mawr College in Pennsylvania.

Nothing more than these tantalizing scraps of information are available to help us reconstruct Gershwin's ideology, and if more documentation exists, in the form of letters or diaries, it remains under family control. There may not be enough to build a case that Gershwin underwent political transformation in the last years of his life, but enough to suggest that he was more intellectually and politically alert than the family-approved portrait would have us believe.

Family intervention of another sort is easier to document. Gershwin died at the height of his career, at a time when some of his compositions had been assimilated into the standard performance repertory but others were still rarely performed. He had performed much of his concert music himself, as pianist or conductor, and also

---

[20] *The New York Times*, 20 October 1935.   [21] *Opera News* (16 March 1985), p. 35.

insisted on certain controls over other performers who wanted to play his music. After his death, his family tended to authorize performances which gave the most promise of financial return or favorable publicity, with less regard for quality or integrity. Some pieces not available in commercial editions before his death – *Concerto in F, An American in Paris, Variations on "I Got Rhythm"*, and *Second Rhapsody* – were published in editions, prepared from Gershwin's manuscripts, which often violated the composer's intentions in small and even large details. The original version of *Rhapsody in Blue*, as orchestrated for Paul Whiteman's "Jazz Band" by Ferde Grofe, was never published; instead, the piece was available only as scored for full symphony orchestra by Grofe in 1926. Gershwin's songs became known to later generations through such commercially successful but artistically questionable recordings as *Ella Fitzgerald Sings the George and Ira Gershwin Song Books* (Verve, V-29-5), in which Nelson Riddle's arrangements and conducting style impose a neo-Romantic, 1950s ethic on the music, robbing it of all vitality and rhythmic life.

Most revealing has been the fate of *Porgy and Bess*. Gershwin was intimately involved in the first production of his opera, by the Theatre Guild, which opened at the Alvin Theatre in New York on 10 October 1935. In the course of rehearsals and a try-out performance in Boston, Gershwin (working closely with the stage director, Rouben Mamoulian, and the musical director, Alexander Smallens) made extensive revisions in his score: tightening dramatic action, shortening or eliminating musical numbers that proved to be less effective on stage than he had hoped, interpolating new material. *Porgy and Bess* as it took the stage in New York in 1935 was some forty-five minutes shorter, and in the opinion of Gershwin and Mamoulian a tighter and more effective show than when it first went into rehearsal. But Gershwin had died before Cheryl Crawford mounted her radically revised production in 1941, with most of the recitative eliminated and the cast and orchestra reduced by half; one cannot imagine that the composer would have allowed such violations of his score, had he been alive. And even though the Everyman Opera production of 1952–8, directed by Blevins Davis and Robert Breen, taking Gershwin's opera all over the United States and also to Eastern and Western Europe, North Africa, and Latin America, was more faithful to Gershwin's intentions, it too had its idiosyncrasies and distortions.

Equally problematic have been recent performances of *Porgy and Bess* by the Cleveland Orchestra, the Houston Grand Opera Company, and the Metropolitan Opera. These purport to be musicologically correct, "complete" performances, the opera "as Gershwin intended it to be played," based on the published piano-vocal score. But this score was completed and in the hands of the publisher some six months before the first performance, in order for it to be commercially available when the opera was premièred, and has never been revised. Thus the extensive revisions made and approved by Gershwin himself have never been incorporated into the score, and these recent pseudo-musicological "complete" performances are in fact serious misrepresentations of *Porgy and Bess*.[22]

My argument here, simply, is that Gershwin's premature death shifted artistic control of his music from himself to his family, with the unfortunate result that his pieces are now known through performances violating both the letter and the spirit of the music. Journalistic and scholarly discourse has been based to a large extent on these faulty scores and performances of Gershwin's music.

For more than a century, historical musicology has been concerned with the recovery of musical compositions from the past and the preparation of scholarly editions of these pieces, to make it possible for this music to be heard as the composer intended. An important secondary and complementary concern has been the study of performance practice in earlier times: since "the history of music . . . cannot be grasped except by first-hand knowledge of the music itself,"[23] it is not enough to hear the correct notes, but they must also be performed with proper phrasing, tempi, dynamics, articulation, instrumentation. According to the historical musicologist, we must have any piece of music in "accurate" form before we can move on to theoretical and contextual studies of it; thus the ideology of studying a piece of music as an autonomous object.

As suggested above, there are problems with Gershwin's music at this level. We "know" his music mostly from corrupt texts, and from performances having little to do with the easily documented performance style of the 1920s. Gershwin's own recordings as pianist, accompanist, and conductor inform us of the intensely rhythmic, brisk, brittle nature of the sound and style he favored. But if one depends on more recent interpretations, by Leonard Bernstein or Michael Tilson Thomas for instance, one hears Gershwin's music as lush, rhythmically insipid and erratic, neo-Romantic.

---

[22] These matters are discussed in more detail in Charles Hamm, "The Theatre Guild production of *Porgy and Bess*," *Journal of the American Musicological Society* 40/3 (Fall 1987), pp. 495–532.   [23] Grout, *A History of Western Music*, p. xiii.

Thus we should be able to "know" Gershwin's music better if musicologists were to recover the authentic texts of his compositions, as they have for Haydn, Handel, and Palestrina, and if musicians were to study performance style of the 1920s, rather than playing and singing music as though it were from another era. It would also help if critics were to inform themselves on these issues, in order to comment with more perception on performances of Gershwin's music.

But even if historical musicologists were to furnish us with accurate texts of Gershwin's compositions, and his music were to be performed in a more accurate and responsible manner, larger conceptual problems would remain. How are we to understand Gershwin's music, if we are not to measure it against a sliding scale of historical style periods, or mindlessly chatter about its relationship to jazz?

The more general question, of course, is how *any* work of art can best be understood. Literary criticism is an instructive battleground to examine, in connection with this issue. In reaction to the nineteenth century's fascination with empiricism (the collection and organization of historical "fact" with no apparent theoretical basis) on the one hand, and the twin spectres of Marxist scholarship and the social sciences on the other, academically based literary scholars developed what was called the New Criticism, and then Structuralism, "formal, structural and text-centered literary studies" taking as a point of departure the conviction that whatever was important in literature could be found in the "texts" themselves, which were to be studied as "self-enclosed verbal constructs, or looped intertextual fields of autonomous signifiers and signifieds." The Deconstructionist school, led by Jacques Derrida, represented a first influential rejection of the theoretical assumptions underlying the New Criticism, and in the 1980s various scholars have "[shared] a commitment to explore the social and historical dimensions of literary works [and to] reconstruct sociohistorical methods and interests as the heart of literary studies."[24]

One can see, from this brief summary, obvious parallels between the recent histories of literary criticism and historical musicology. Both embraced the notion of "autonomous art" for a good part of the twentieth century; and just as recent literary criticism has forcefully challenged the New Criticism and its assumptions, some music historians are now beginning to question the long-held tenets of

[24] Jerome J. McGann, "A point of reference," in *Historical Studies and Literary Criticism* (Madison, 1985), pp. 3, 21.

318

their discipline, proposing a shift to socio-historical methodologies. The recent literature suggesting that music is best understood as a product of social and economic forces, not as an autonomous object, is too numerous to be listed here. I will merely state the obvious: most of this writing derives from Marxist and neo-Marxist theory, often by way of the Frankfurt School; and American musicologists have lagged far behind Europeans in exploring alternative ways of understanding the history of music. Janet Wolff, in a recent essay challenging the notion that "Art . . . transcends the social, the political and the everday," gives a useful summary:

> The social and economic factors relevant to the understanding of an art include: contemporary forms of patronage; dominant institutions of cultural production and distribution (workshops, academies, art schools, publishers, galleries, concerts, music publishers, broadcasting companies, and so on – each of which has its own social history and specific social relations); the relationship of the State to cultural production (censorship, control of certain institutions, funding); the sociology of cultural producers (background, class, gender); and the nature and constitution of consumers. The history of any art is a history of the interplay of these many factors.[25]

Despite the variety of approaches suggested by different writers, there is virtual consensus on two points: socio-historical analysis must replace historical positivism; and works of art are "modelling rather than mirroring forms."[26] That is, works of literature (or music) do not "point to a prior, authorizing reality, they themselves *constitute* – in both the active and passive senses – what must be taken as reality."[27] Or, as Jacques Attali puts it in a slightly different way, music is a "prophetic" art, on the cutting edge of the onward march of human affairs and relations.[28]

The task, then, if we are to apply any of this to the understanding of Gershwin's music, is to identify critical socio-historical issues in which American music of the 1920s and 30s was embedded, and to measure Gershwin's role in "modelling" these. I'll suggest three large areas which might reward closer attention:

(1) Some scholars are now suggesting alternative periodizations of the history of music, based on economic and social relations rather

[25] Janet Wolff, "The ideology of autonomous art," in *Music and Society: The Politics of Composition, Performance and Reception*, ed. Richard Leppert and Susan McClary (Cambridge, 1987), p. 5. See also Rose Subotnik, "The role of ideology in the study of Western Music," *Journal of Musicology* 2/1 (1983), pp. 1–12.   [26] McGann, "A point of reference," p. 4.
[27] *Ibid.*   [28] Jacques Attali, *Bruits: essai sur l'economie politique de la musique* (Paris, 1977).

than musical style. For instance, a team of European musicologists,[29] in preparation for the writing of Volume VII of *Music in the Life of Man: A World History*, a multi-volume global history sponsored by UNESCO, has proposed the following overview of Western music history:

(a) From Prehistory to the Birth of Europe (until *c*. 500)
(b) Church (from *c*. 500 to *c*. 1520)
(c) Court and Town (from *c*. 1520 to *c*. 1740)
(d) Concert Life (from *c*. 1740 to World War I)
(e) Mass Media (from World War I to the present)

And Jacques Attali has suggested a more abstract four-fold periodization of music (sacrificial ritual, representation, repetition, and composition), agreeing in broad outline with the above.[30]

Gershwin's music comes into different focus when measured against these new frameworks. His first compositions appear at the very beginning of an era of "Mass media" or "repetition," rather than several decades into a "Modern" or "twentieth-century" style period. The critical issues of his time become the impact of the electronic mass media on the invention, production, and consumption of music – not experiments in abstract manipulation of tones. The following should be noted about Gershwin:

- He enthusiastically embraced the mechanical player piano, producing more than 100 commercial piano rolls, beginning in 1916.

- He was the first American composer whose early career was built largely on the success of sales of phonograph records of his songs. For instance, his first hugely popular song, "Swanee," as recorded by Al Jolson (Columbia 2884), was the best-selling record in America for nine weeks in 1920.[31]

- "It should be kept in mind [in connection with his extraordinary popularity] that the advent of radio occurred just as his career was getting under way. The enormous exposure provided by this medium had much to do with the public's enthusiasm for his songs."[32]

- Gershwin's only extended essay, "The composer in the machine age," develops the argument that "the composer, in my estimation, has been helped a great deal by the mechanical reproduction of music."[33]

- Gershwin not only wrote songs for a number of films, beginning with *Delicious* in 1931, but his *Second Rhapsody* (for piano and orchestra)

[29] Janos Karpati, Budapest; Jens Brincker, Finn Gravesen, Carsten E. Hatting, and Niels Krabbe, Copenhagen.   [30] Attali, *Bruits*.
[31] Joel Whitburn, *Pop Memories, 1890–1954* (Menomonee Falls, 1986), p. 233.
[32] Wilder, *American Popular Song*, pp. 122–3.
[33] Gershwin, "The composer in the machine age."

was written for that film as well, for a ballet sequence, though only a section of the concerto was used in the film.

- In 1934, Gershwin began hosting a twice-weekly radio show for CBS, "Music by Gershwin," on which he chatted about his music, talked with guests, played the piano, and introduced pieces by himself and other composers, later played by a studio orchestra. The program was carried by stations all across the country, making Gershwin and his music accessible to millions of people who had never been able to hear live performances of his music.

- The first production of *Porgy and Bess*, by the Theatre Guild in 1935, had only a moderate run, but a later production by Cheryl Crawford ran for almost four years, in New York and on the road. Many observers, including the librettist DuBose Heyward, insisted that the second production was much more successful than the first because so many people had become familiar with "Summertime," "I Got Plenty o' Nuttin'" and "It Ain't Necessarily So" in the meanwhile, from hearing this music on the radio and phonograph.

From these and other facts of his career, it emerges that Gershwin was not a mere passive observer of the technology of his age, but to the contrary he enthusiastically explored and exploited ways of utilizing the new electronic mass media for the production and dissemination of his music. By contrast, Charles Ives despised and shunned all mass communications: radio, phonograph, telephone. Thus by a shift of conceptual framework, away from privileging the moment of creation of a piece of music (and thus forcing one to study it as an autonomous object) towards considering the issues of production and reception, Gershwin can be seen as progressive and Ives as reactionary – a reversal of the judgement handed down by mainstream historical musicology.

(2) During Gershwin's own lifetime, the United States was struggling to absorb many millions of new immigrants. The older "mainstream" American population was mostly Protestant, tracing back to the British Isles, Western Europe, and Scandinavia; the new immigrants were overwhelmingly Catholic (Roman or Orthodox) or Jewish, from the Mediterranean, or Central and Eastern Europe. Relations between the two groups became highly problematic in the first decades of the twentieth century. "Older" Americans, fearing the possible economic consequences of the presence of millions of new workers in the country (many of them highly skilled and most of them willing to work for low wages in order to establish themselves in an alien land), resorted to attacks on the new population on ethnic grounds. A Congressional Committee issued a

"scientific" report in 1911 detailing the problems stemming from the presence of so much "inferior ethnic stock." New laws were passed putting an end to further immigration from Mediterranean, Eastern European, and Third World countries. The revived Ku Klux Klan spread from the South to all regions of the United States, and social and economic discrimination became even more entrenched at various levels of American life.

Faced with such a hostile climate, many minority ethnic groups, including America's Jews, adopted a twofold strategy: (a) trying to become "invisible," by modifying all obvious signs of ethnic origin (dress, language, sometimes their names and even physical appearance) in an attempt to be indistinguishable from "mainstream" Americans; and (b) trying to make positive and visible contributions to American life and culture.[34] In no area were they more successful than in entertainment. The contributions of American Jews to music (as Tin Pan Alley songwriters and singers), stage, comedy, and film in the 1910s, 20s, and 30s put them in the absolute center of American popular culture,[35] and played a major role both in improving their social relations with other Americans and in setting the stage for the next generation's contributions to education, law, and other fields which they could now enter.

In this context, Gershwin was clearly a "modeller." The popular success of his songs, musical comedies, concert pieces, and films represented an important contribution to American culture by a Jew; and his public image as a "celebrity" and a member of the social, artistic, and intellectual "scene" of New York and Hollywood helped establish those positive social relations between Jews and non-Jews that were becoming such a positive factor in American society.

Here too Ives pursued a conservative course, retreating from New York City and its burgeoning new popular arts to the cultural isolation of a small New England town. He quoted, with approval, Daniel Gregory Mason's sour dismissal of the contemporary world:

> If indeed the land of Lincoln and Emerson has degenerated until nothing remains of it but a "jerk and a rattle," then we at least are free to repudiate the false patriotism of "My country, right or wrong," to insist that better than bad music is no music, and to let our beloved art subside finally under the clangor of the subway gongs and the automobile horns, dead but not dishonored.

[34] For an excellent discussion of these issues see Irving Howe, *World of Our Fathers* (New York and London, 1976).

[35] Charles Hamm, *Yesterdays: Popular Song in America* (New York and London, 1979), pp. 326–57.

Ives then added, "And so may we ask: Is it better to sing inadequately of the 'leaf on Walden floating,' and die 'dead but not dishonored,' or to sing adequately of the 'cherry on the cocktail,' and live forever?"[36]

(3) In America, as elsewhere, classical music had first been associated with the most privileged layers of society. As a distinctively American form of democracy emerged in the nineteenth century, populist criticism of classical music mounted, and by the end of the century it appeared that classical music would become even more marginal to American life, and might disappear altogether.

Of course this did not happen. By the late twentieth century, the number of symphony orchestras, opera companies, choral groups, community concert series, schools of music, new compositions, attendance at concerts and recitals, sales of phonograph discs, and radio programs of classical music have all proliferated far beyond what the nineteenth century could have imagined. All this has come about as a result of a sweeping democratization of every aspect of classical music in the first half of the century: repertory (programing based largely on a "standard" repertory); the education of musicians and composers; social relations, with the gradual shift of patronage from the most privileged classes to public, municipal, and state support corresponding to a similar change in the constitution of the audience itself; the education of potential listeners.

If the issue is defined as the gradual demystification of classical music and the severing of its exclusive ties to the moneyed classes, there can be no mistaking Gershwin's role in this revolution. Simply put, he was the first American composer to write concert pieces accessible to those people who already enjoyed the now-standard classical repertory, and also many people whose listening tastes had not included classical music. Contrary to common belief, the proliferation in classical music in the critical era of the 1920s, 30s, and 40s in the United States was accompanied by, and to some extent the result of, the growth of a popular repertory by contemporary American composers. Gershwin played and conducted his own compositions for large crowds in Lewisohn Stadium and elsewhere; orchestras could be sure of attracting good audiences if they programed his music. Soon other composers as well – Ferde Grofe, Morton Gould, Aaron Copland, Virgil Thompson, Roy Harris, and then Leonard Bernstein – began to write concert works similar to those of Gershwin, in making use of the basic harmonic, tonal, and

[36] Charles Ives, *Essays Before a Sonata, and Other Writings* (New York, 1962), pp. 94–5.

structural vocabulary of the standard symphonic repertory, with references to contemporary popular and ethnic styles.

Charles Ives, on the other hand, had become the epitome of the Romantic, misunderstood genius, the artist as neglected visionary. After failing to find an audience for his early composition, he withdrew into a contemptuous isolation, scornful of performers and audiences who seemed unable to comprehend his music.

Tin Pan Alley, as a musical style and as an industry for producing and disseminating popular music, was well established when Gershwin began writing his songs and musical comedies. He worked within already established boundaries, both musically and socially, and even though many of his songs have become "classics" of the Tin Pan Alley repertory in the sense of being "of the first or highest class or rank," he was in no sense an innovator, and his popular songs are no more "classical," in the sense of using techniques of classical music, than those of his peers.

But his "classical" pieces did become widely popular. There were no important precedents for them, and socio-historical analysis enables us to see them as important "modelling" and "prophetic" works, much more so than his popular songs.

This merely confirms Gershwin's own judgement on these matters.

14

A BLUES FOR THE AGES

Gershwin lived at the height of the modern era, and though his instincts led him to violate some of the tenets of modernism, nevertheless his thinking was shaped by the age in which he lived and he accepted the modernist narrative claiming that popular music is more transitory and of less value than classical. As this essay demonstrates, in the second movement of his *Concerto in F* Gershwin set out to transform a popular genre of the day, the band blues, into a "larger and more serious" piece with a better chance of enduring than the popular genre on which it was based.

* * *

All books on George Gershwin have stressed the ease with which he moved between the composition of popular and classical music,[1] and Richard Crawford begins his recent essay on Gershwin by pointing out that "by the time he was 20 he had established himself as a composer of Broadway shows, and by the age of 30 he was America's most famous and widely accepted composer of concert music."[2] Recent scholarly attention to popular music has made it possible for some music historians to accept the possibility that some of it constitutes a product of equal, if different, value to classical music. But this idea would have been strange to Gershwin himself, who

---

[1] Isaac Goldberg, *George Gershwin: A Study in American Music* (New York, 1931); David Ewen, *A Journey to Greatness: The Life and Music of George Gershwin* (New York, 1956); Merle Armitage, *George Gershwin: Man and Legend* (New York, 1958); Edward Jablonski and Lawrence D. Stewart, *The Gershwin Years* (New York, 1958); Charles Schwartz, *Gershwin: His Life and Music* (New York and Indianapolis, 1973); Edward Jablonski, *Gershwin: A Biography* (New York, 1987).

[2] Richard Crawford, "George Gershwin," in *The New Grove Dictionary of American Music*, ed. H. Wiley Hitchcock and Stanley Sadie (London, 1986), vol. 2, pp. 199–211.

made it clear on various occasions that he recognized a hierarchical ranking of classical and popular music. His thinking on this matter affords us a valuable clue as to why he turned increasingly to the composition of more "serious" music in the second half of his career.

In Gershwin's opinion even the best popular music was of slight and transitory musical content, unable to endure repeated hearings or changes in musical fashion. In an attempt to give some of his songs a better chance of survival, he published eighteen of them in complex pianistic arrangements as *George Gershwin's Song-Book*, in the apparent hope that adding one level of sophistication – technical dexterity – would elevate these pieces above the usual sheet-music arrangements of songs, "arranged with an eye to simplicity . . . since the majority of the purchasers of popular music are little girls with little hands, who have not progressed very far in their study of the piano."

> Unfortunately, most songs die at an early age and are soon completely forgotten by the selfsame public that once sang them with such gusto. The reason for this is that they are sung and played too much when they are alive, and cannot stand the strain of their very popularity. This is especially true since the invention of the phonograph and more so since the widespread conquest of the radio.[3]

He elaborated on this attitude in an interview just after the New York première of *Porgy and Bess*. Writing in the *New York Times* of 20 October 1935, he explained why he had composed his own "spirituals and folksongs" rather than taking over traditional material:

> I believe that music lives only when it is in serious form. When I wrote the "Rhapsody in Blue" I took "blues" and put them in a larger and more serious form. That was twelve years ago and the "Rhapsody in Blue" is still very much alive, whereas if I had taken the same themes and put them in songs they would have been gone years ago.

Gershwin's *Concerto in F* was his first extended "serious" composition. *Rhapsody in Blue* was written in 1924 for a program entitled "An Experiment in Modern Music" by Paul Whiteman and his Palais Royal Orchestra. *Lullaby* for string quartet (*c.* 1919) and *Novelettes* for violin and piano (1925) were brief sketches. *Blue Monday*, his "Opera Ala Afro-American" of 1922, was part of *George White's Scandals of 1933*, withdrawn after opening night. But Gershwin's concerto, a full-blown "piece of absolute music"[4] in three movements

---

[3] George Gershwin, *George Gershwin's Song-Book* (New York, 1932), p. ix.   [4] *Ibid.*

scored for large orchestra, had been commissioned by Walter
Damrosch for performance by the New York Symphony Society and
was premièred at Carnegie Hall on 3 December 1925 before an
audience and music critics assembled to hear classical music.

Gershwin originally thought to call his piece the *New York
Concerto* and the second movement was first entitled "Song (Blues)."
The composer wrote in the *New York Tribune* of 29 November 1925
that this movement "has a poetic nocturnal atmosphere which has
come to be referred to as the American blues, but in a purer form
than that in which they are usually treated." In other words,
Gershwin took a popular form, the blues, and cast it in a more
"serious" form, in an attempt to create a piece that – according to his
thinking – had a better chance of "living" than in its original form. It
is my intention to examine this movement in some detail, in an
attempt to better understand Gershwin's aesthetic of popular/classical.

A starting point must be to understand what Gershwin, and the
musical world he inhabited, understood by "blues" in 1925.

Then, as now, blues were understood to belong to the larger
family of jazz. And for the New York musical world, "jazz" meant
something quite different from what jazz historians now take it to be.
Henry O. Osgood devoted entire chapters of his early book on jazz to
Irving Berlin, Gershwin, and Paul Whiteman; black jazz is mentioned
only in a single footnote, reading in part:

> None of [the black jazz bands] are as good as the best white bands,
> and very rarely are their best players as good as the best white
> virtuosos. Their playing makes up for what it may lack in
> smoothness and finish by abandon, dash, spirit and warmth.
> There are fewer trained musicians, consequently more of the
> improvisations and variations which characterized early jazz.[5]

Paul Whiteman, writing in the same year, made only the briefest
mention of the role of blacks in the development of jazz:

> Jazz, given its start in life by the righteous old Dutch [slave]
> traders, had been biding its time among the black laborers in the
> cotton fields of the lordly Southern planters and the negroes
> lounging in the sunshine along the New Orleans levees. It had lost
> none of its primitive African swing through mingling with the
> changing of machinery, the broken crashing rhythm of Whitman's
> poetry, the gigantic steel and stone of the sky-scrapers. It was at
> once barbarous and sophisticated – the wilderness tamed to the
> ballroom.[6]

[5] Henry O. Osgood, *So This Is Jazz* (Boston, 1926), p. 103.
[6] Paul Whiteman and Mary Margaret McBride, *Jazz* (New York, 1926), p. 9.

He later moved to his chief concern, the present and future of jazz in white America:

> Will it be possible eventually to establish chairs of jazz in Universities? I do not see why not. My conception of a college is a place which teaches its students that which will be useful and pleasant for them to know. Jazz music is certainly useful. Players who have worked their way through college blowing a saxophone or twanging a banjo can often step into jobs that pay $75 or $100 a week. I mean jazz banding jobs. Tell me any other occupation that starts the June graduate off at any such salary.[7]

And Isaac Goldberg, Gershwin's first biographer, admits that while jazz "is traceable in part to the Negro" and while like ragtime "it traces its ancestry back to roustabouts, black trash, white trash, dives and brothels," it has been "developed, commercially and artistically, by the Jew" – that is, in New York.[8]

In Gershwin's world, New York was the jazz capital; the songs of Irving Berlin and the music of the bands of Roger Wolfe Kahn, Ted Lewis, and Paul Whiteman were the highest manifestations of jazz; Al Jolson was the supreme jazz singer; and jazz was thought to be progressing steadily up the artistic scale. Whiteman dreamed of compositions "written around the great natural and geographical features of American life – written in the jazz idiom. I believe this would help Americans to appreciate their own country. . . . Jazz can help by catching our national themes fast in composition."[9]

It is also important in understanding this view of jazz to remember what was missing from it. Paul Whiteman insisted in his book that New Yorkers had not heard jazz until the Original Dixieland Jazz Band played at Reisenweber's Cafe in 1917. There is no evidence that white New Yorkers who were busily playing "jazz" in the early and mid-1920s, convinced that they were doing it better than earlier black performers, knew the music of Louis Armstrong, Sidney Bechet, Freddie Keppard, Jelly Roll Morton, King Oliver, Kid Ory, or Clarence Williams. And Whiteman, Berlin, and Al Jolson had almost certainly never heard country blues singers, and probably not even Mamie Smith, Ma Rainey, or Ida Cox.

What blues did Gershwin know, then, when he set out to enshrine the genre in a "serious" form of music in the second movement of his piano concerto? Gershwin folklore holds that George had many contacts with black musicians in the 1920s, but specific information

---

[7] *Ibid.*, p. 279. [8] Goldberg, *George Gershwin*, p. 278.
[9] Whiteman and McBride, *Jazz*, p. 287.

is elusive. Carl Van Vechten remembered that "my interest in the Negro began in 1924–25 and . . . George's interest grew up parallel with mine. We met many of the same people together, attended many of the same parties, concerts, and other events in Harlem together, and were equally cognizant of the same phenomena."[10] Van Vechten's diaries tell us that Gershwin met Paul Robeson, James Weldon Johnson, and other blacks at his parties, and on at least one occasion Bessie Smith was present and sang for the guests; but most of these contacts took place after the composition of the *Concerto in F.* Unless new evidence comes to light, we must conclude that Gershwin's knowledge of the blues in 1925 came from performances and recordings by dance bands of a standard blues repertory built around pieces by W. C. Handy, who autographed a copy of *Blues: An Anthology* (1926) owned by Gershwin. Popular recordings of pieces by Handy that Gershwin might have known include "Memphis Blues" (Columbia 5591, 1914), "St. Louis Blues" (Columbia 5772, 1916), and "Beale Street Blues" (Columbia 2327, 1917) by Prince's Orchestra; "Beale Street Blues" as recorded by Earl Fuller's Novelty Orchestra, with Ted Lewis on clarinet (Victor 18369, 1917); the Original Dixieland Jazz Band's version of "St. Louis Blues" (Victor 18772, 1921), and Marion Harris's hit recording of the same piece (Columbia 2944, 1920); and possibly Handy's own performance of "St. Louis Blues" (Okeh 4896, 1923).

Handy's blues were widely disseminated in the 1910s as dance music, accompanying the fox-trot popularized in the mid-1910s by Irene and Vernon Castle. In an interview published in the *New York Tribune* of 22 November 1914, James Reese Europe in fact equated Handy's blues with that dance: "The fox trot was created by a young negro of Memphis, Tenn., Mr. W. C. Handy, who five years ago wrote 'The Memphis Blues'." Unlike folk and vocal blues, which usually consist of a string of 12-bar choruses, Handy's blues and others like them contain several contrasting strains. Both "Memphis Blues" and "St. Louis Blues" begin with a brief introduction, then contrast a strain in 12-bar-blues form with another in the more standard 16-bar shape. To put it another way, commercialized blues of the 1910s and early 20s tend to have a 12-bar chorus embedded in a larger, multistrain structure. Even the most random sampling will underline the persistence of this pattern. "Immigration Blues," recorded by Duke Ellington and his Orchestra in 1926, begins with a 4-bar introduction, continues with a first strain shaped into 4 + 4

10 Jablonski and Stewart, *The Gershwin Years*, p. 24.

phrases, and ends with a second strain of four 12-bar-blues choruses. "Blue Devil Blues," recorded by Walter Page's Blue Devils in Kansas City in 1929,[11] is shaped in almost precisely the same way: a 4-bar introduction; a first strain of two 4 + 4 phrases; a second strain of four 12-bar-blues choruses.

Some of these pieces were recorded after Gershwin had composed his Concerto in F. But the point is to situate Gershwin's knowledge of the blues in a well-defined tradition of pieces played by dance bands, beginning with Handy, rather than in the more traditional vocal pieces that come to mind today with mention of the word "blues."

In the second movement of *Concerto in F* we can see Gershwin's references to the blues that he knew, and also his determination to shape the genre into a more "serious" and thus more lasting piece of music. As reference to Table 14.1 will show, the second movement is indeed a multistrain piece, ABACA, launched by a brief introduction, which Wayne Shirley has shown was an afterthought.[12] But Gershwin makes this formal structure more complex by embedding melodic material from one strain in another, by using transitional and developmental sections, and by extending tonal and harmonic patterns beyond what one would find in most dance-band blues of the time. The movement begins and ends in D-flat major, a major third below the concerto's principal key of F major, and the A theme is always stated in this key: but the extended C section is in E major, an augmented second away from the tonic. The final statement of A shifts directly from the preceding E major to D-flat major, with no preparation or modulation, and other abrupt tonal shifts occur within each section, as with the movement from D-flat major to D major in the second strain (See Table 14.1).

Again following his models, Gershwin contrasts strains built on 12-bar-blues patterns (A and B) with another (C) having no trace of this structure. And true to his intention of building on (rather than merely imitating) these models, he treats the 12-bar-blues form freely and flexibly. The first statement of A is built on the formulaic blues harmonic structure of I I I I/IV IV I I/V V I I, which Gershwin immediately transforms into a 16-bar structure by the simple expedient of repeating the last four bars. A[1] condenses the second and third 4-bar phrases into a single 6-bar unit, then adds another four bars unrelated to the usual 12-bar harmonic pattern; and the

[11] Frank Driggs, liner notes for *Sweet and Low Blues: Big Bands and Territory Bands of the 20s* (New World Records NW 256, 1977).
[12] Wayne Shirley, "Scoring the Concerto in F: George Gershwin's first orchestration," *American Music* 3/3 (Fall 1985), p. 291.

Table 14.1 *George Gershwin*, Concerto in F, *Second Movement*

Rehearsal no.	No. of bars	Theme or function	Key
0	3	introduction	D$^\flat$
0(+3)–1	16	A [4+4+4+4]	D$^\flat$
1–2	14	A' [4+6+4]	B minor
2–3	14	A [4+4+6]	D$^\flat$
3–4	20	B [8+8+4]	D$^\flat$–B$^\flat$
4–5	13	development	–
5–7	9+12	B [1+8+8+4]	D–B
7–8	9	transition [A]	A$^\flat$ pedal
8–9	8	A [4+4]	D$^\flat$
9–10	4+18	A [4], cadenza	B pedal
10–12	17+4	C [1+8+8], extension	E
12–13	12	B [4+4+4]	E
13–14	12	C [8+4]	E
14–17	6+8+11	development [C]	E
17–18	12	A [4+4+4]	D$^\flat$

Note: Underlined phrases are based on 12-bar-blues harmonic patterns.

final A extends the last four bars to six (4 + 4 + 6). In fact, even though harmonic references to the 12-bar-blues form are present in all statements of A and B, Gershwin never once writes a straightforward 4 + 4 + 4 blues pattern.

Structural matters aside, Gershwin set out to capture something of the expressive content of the blues in his piece, and in order to judge how well he succeeded, we must again try to deal with this genre as it was understood in New York in the mid-1920s.

Virtually every writer on jazz, from the 1920s until today, has emphasized the role played by "blue notes" in giving this music its distinctive sound and character. Edward Abbe Niles, in his preface to W. C. Handy's anthology, describes "the tendency of the untrained Negro voice when singing [the third of the tonic chord] at an important point, to *worry* it, slurring or wavering between flat and natural."[13] The same thing is said to happen on the seventh scale degree and also, though rarely, on the fifth. When jazz and blues musicians began to make use of instruments such as the piano which allowed no such pitch inflection, and when white people began to play this music, these "worried" notes were merely hinted at

[13] W. C. Handy and Edward Abbe Niles, *A Treasury of the Blues* (New York, 1926), p. 14.

Ex. 14.1 George Gershwin, *Concerto in F*, Second movement, bars 4–6

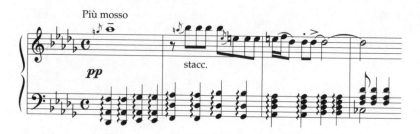

Ex. 14.2 George Gershwin, *Concerto in F*, Second movement, bars 48–51

Ex. 14.3 George Gershwin, *Concerto in F*, Second movement, bars 141–3

through the expedient of introducing flat thirds and sevenths in the context of a major scale; they appeared as false relations or even simultaneously with the major forms of these intervals. All three themes in this movement make prominent use of these "blue" notes. Both the flatted third and seventh are introduced at the end of the very first bar of theme A (Ex. 14.1). The flat seventh appears in the bass in the fourth bar of B (Ex. 14.2) and as the first stressed note of theme C (Ex. 14.3).

These prominent blue notes near the beginnings of the three chief themes are merely the starting point in Gershwin's use of this device, which occurs throughout the piece, sometimes as a false relation (Ex.

Ex. 14.4 George Gershwin, *Concerto in F*, Second movement, bars 122–5

14.4). In addition, the tonal structure of the movement stresses both the importance and instability of the third: the chief secondary tonal center, for the extended C section, is E major, enharmonically a minor third in the scale of D-flat; and the B section surrounds the temporary tonicization of B-flat with sections in D-flat and D.

Niles also points out that blues performers end each phrase "with the first beat, third bar, of its corresponding four bars of music, leaving seven quick beats or three slow ones before the melody proper resumes its motion."[14] In other words, blues singers and instrumentalists shape melodic phrases cadencing in the third bar of each 4-bar section, leaving space for an obbligato passage by either the lead performer or a member of the accompanying group at the end of each phrase. Some scholars see this as a survival of the call-and-response patterns of traditional African music. Gershwin follows this pattern with themes A and B, bringing the melody to a cadence in the third bar and writing an obbligato passage as a bridge to the phrase in Example 14.5.

Even though the *Concerto in F* is scored for full symphony orchestra, Gershwin's instrumentation often suggests the sound of a mid-1920s dance band in its prominent use of the trumpet as a solo

[14] *Ibid.*

Ex. 14.5 George Gershwin, *Concerto in F*, Second movement, bars 34–7

and obbligato instrument, its scoring for a reed section, and its piano sound. Only theme C, the least "bluesy" of the three, is introduced by strings.

Gershwin himself told us that the second movement of the *Concerto in F* was intended to have something to do with the blues. When we compare it to the music most likely known to the composer, rather than to some abstraction of "the blues," it becomes possible to see just how he proceeded in transforming a popular or folk style into a "serious form." Unlike some of his contemporaries, he did not merely abstract characteristic rhythms, scales, and melodic patterns from jazz and the blues for use in a composition otherwise constructed along classical lines. Gershwin's piece is not a concerto movement spiced up with references to popular styles. It *is* a band blues, but with structure, harmony, and instrumentation expanded and made much more complex. Thus it has much more to do with the music of Duke Ellington, for instance, than with that of Ravel, Milhaud, and Stravinsky.

Judging by its subsequent history of performance and recording, the *Concerto in F* fully realized Gershwin's hope of writing a "larger and more serious" piece in "purer form" that would remain "very much alive" after his popular songs had been forgotten. What he did not predict, though, was that the latter would also live on and, in time, be given "serious" consideration.

15

GRACELAND REVISITED

Around the time of my last visit to South Africa, some of the music I'd been studying there was in the process of being "discovered" by the outside world. Ladysmith Black Mambazo, Juluka, and other South African groups began receiving air play in Europe and North America; independent record companies such as Shanachie in the United States and Rough Trade in the UK released discs by other South African performers; rock journalists, from the *Village Voice* to *The New York Times*, displayed a sudden expertise in "African pop," including South African varieties; long-time expatriate musicians Miriam Makeba and Hugh Masekela, who had performed in international jazz and pop styles since leaving South Africa, began reintroducing traditional African elements into their music; and Paul Simon released his *Graceland* album with backing tracks by South African musicians, some of them recorded during a furtive visit to Johannesburg.

As an acoustical phenomenon, the infusion of rhythmic vitality and clean sonorities from South African popular styles had a salutary, if temporary, impact on Western pop. Social meaning was more problematic, though. In Europe and North America, this music was incorporated into existing social structures, as a new variety of dance music. But many in the West also insisted on linking it with the black struggle for freedom in South Africa, using it in anti-apartheid rallies. One doesn't minimize the role of external, international pressure on the South African government in the 1980s in pointing out that the demise of the apartheid policies of Separate Development came about largely as a result of unrelenting, heroic opposition and resistance within South Africa, mostly by blacks but also by a few whites.

This brief essay attempts to bring historical context to the prolonged debate over Simon's *Graceland*, by tying it to the ideology of the

336

so-called folk revival of the 1960s and 70s. Dave Laing, in an angry response to "the Hamm attack on Paul Simon, Miriam Makeba and Harry Belafonte," finds it curious that my article doesn't discuss Johnny Clegg, the "white South African who performed [in South Africa] with a mixed-race band but now is in exile in Europe" and who "wants the women and men of his country to hear his songs, but does not want to give aid and comfort to apartheid."[1] However, Clegg is an "exile" by choice, not political necessity, who performed and recorded his music in his home country without interference from the government until leaving to pursue his career abroad. Though his early music enjoyed some popularity among blacks when his first band, Juluka, performed in the townships, the "men and women of his country" who listen to his more recent recordings, produced abroad, are mostly white.

Laing's remarks epitomize a modernist inability to grasp that music removed from the context of its own community, and put to a different use, will take on a quite different meaning in the process. It was this mindset that led to Paul Simon's ill-fated tour of South Africa, undertaken with the erroneous expectation that the music of "Graceland" would be favorably received by South African blacks.

* * *

Does more need to be said about Paul Simon's *Graceland*? Yes, in my opinion, for two reasons: discourse to date has focused on the reception of the album in America and Western Europe; and this discourse has been largely innocent of historical perspective.

To deflect criticism of his apparent defiance of UNESCO's cultural boycott, and the absence of political content in the *Graceland* songs, Simon and his apologists have repeatedly insisted that:

- *Graceland* has focused attention on South Africa, and South African music.

- South African musicians have benefited from the enterprise. Simon allegedly paid triple union wages to his backing musicians, and many of them, particularly Ladysmith Black Mambazo, have realized even greater subsequent profits from live and television performances, and from recordings released outside of South Africa.

[1] Dave Laing, "Call and response," *Popular Music* 9/1 (January 1990), pp. 137–8. Laing does correct one mistake in my essay: contrary to my assertion, Harry Belafonte did bring out one album between 1970 and 1988, *Loving You Is Where I Belong* in 1981. But this oversight hardly invalidates my point that his "last commercially successful LP . . . was produced as long ago as 1962."

- the careers of the South African musicians involved with *Graceland* would have been endangered had the songs been political in nature.

- the mixed-racial character of *Graceland*, as recorded and performed live on the *Graceland* tour, particularly in Zimbabwe, represents a highly visible public rebuttal to the South African government's racial policies.

The reception of *Graceland* in South Africa itself is a first suggestion that the venture had nothing to do with the on-going struggle for liberation in that country. Simon's album quickly became one of the great commercial successes of the South African recording industry. Less than a year after its release, it had gone "triple platinum" by selling 100,000 copies three times over. While there is no way to break down sales between black and white consumers, there are many clues. *Graceland* was priced substantially higher than LPs and cassettes by black musicians produced for black consumers, and was sold and prominently displayed in retail outlets catering to whites. Some idea of black reaction to the venture may be gained from the fact that several participating musicians were asked to apologise for their involvement before performing again for the black community. And the *Graceland* songs were given substantial air play on the "white" services of the South African Broadcasting Corporation (SABC). The latter fact tells us something else: if the South African government had objected to *Graceland*, on any grounds, the Publications Board could have banned it – making it a crime to sell, own, or play the record within the country – or SABC censorship committees could have ruled against air play. Neither happened.

Nor has the international attention focused on Ladysmith Black Mambazo caused discomfort in Pretoria. Founded by Joseph Shabalala in the mid-1960s, the group first performed on the SABC's Radio Zulu, one of the Radio Bantu services established in 1960 to promote the neo-apartheid ideology of Separate Development, by stressing the tribal identity of each black ethnic group within the country as a deterrent to black unity. Under contract to Gallo Ltd, the largest commercial record company in South Africa, the group had released dozens of singles and eighteen highly successful LPs, with a total sale of more than four million record units, before Simon "discovered" them in 1987. Muff Andersson wrote in 1981 that "they own properties, and they all have cars." Shabalala was "very happy because he's rich; because he owns two houses, one with 16 rooms and the other with nine."[1] When asked why the lyrics of their songs

---

[1] Muff Andersson, *Music in the Mix: the Story of South African Popular Music* (Johannesburg, 1981), p. 126.

never touched on political issues, Shabalala explained that "we keep the radio in mind when we compose. If something is contentious they [the SABC] don't play it, and then it wouldn't be known to the public anyway."[2] And as Zulus they are identified with Gatsha Buthelezi's politically conservative Inkatha movement, which in recent years has clashed with other black South Africans, particularly those associated with the United Democratic Front or sympathetic to the African National Congress. Even young Zulu-speakers relate the music of Ladysmith Black Mambazo to "the culture and politics of our parents," as one of them put it to me recently.

In a recent interview Shabalala admitted that "at home they're starting to scold us because we're away all of the time." He also reported that "the next album may have as many as five [songs in English]," and that "some people are afraid we will lose our harmony if we sing in English."[3] Both fears are well grounded, if one considers the curiously similar history of an earlier black South African vocal group, the Manhattan Brothers.

This vocal jive group was also "discovered" by the SABC, in the late 1930s, and then produced a series of commercially successful 78 rpm discs for Gallo. Persuaded that they could become international stars, they defected while in London in 1961 as members of the cast of the musical play *King Kong* and performed for the next two decades in the UK and Western Europe, in a vocal jazz style that had progressively less and less to do with South African music. Voluntary exiles, they were not involved in the political and musical life of their own country; as a result, their music gradually lost all meaning for the new generation of black South Africans strongly politicized by the events at Sharpeville and Soweto, and drawn to Mbaqanga and other new musical styles of the 1960s and 70s. Today they are remembered only by a handful of elderly people.

Thus: Ladysmith Black Mambazo had a long pre-*Graceland* history, during which time they benefited handsomely from collaboration with the SABC and South Africa's internal domestic recording industry; they are aligned musically and politically with conservative black elements within South Africa; and they appear willing to remain abroad as long as it is financially advantageous. Simon's patronage has helped them accumulate even more wealth, but it is difficult to imagine that either the group or its music will have any positive impact on the black struggle for liberation.

On another point, it is simply not true that racially mixed

---

[2] *Ibid.*, p. 87.
[3] Steve Morse, "The gates are opening for Ladysmith Black Mambazo," *Boston Globe*, 16 November 1988.

performances and audiences are prohibited in South Africa. As part of a carefully plotted strategy to soften the outside world's image of the country's racial politics by abandoning certain highly visible aspects of "petty apartheid," the government has sanctioned racially mixed audiences at popular music events for over a decade, beginning with Doby Gray's tour in 1976. Multi-racial jazz, pop, and rock groups have become common the the 1980s, performing first on college campuses and small clubs and then in larger and more visible venues. The Market Theatre in Johannesburg has offered theatrical and musical events by multi-racial casts for integrated audiences for more than a decade. By 1985 large outdoor pop/rock concerts featuring both black and white performers, with racially mixed audiences, were becoming common in Johannesburg and elsewhere. Far from challenging the government's policies, Paul Simon's visit to South Africa in 1985 and the subsequent release of *Graceland* were widely covered in the pro-government press and praised as acts of "constructive engagement" between a famous American pop star and the South African music industry.

On a more abstract level, South African ethnomusicologist Andrew Tracey wrote recently that

> [*Graceland* contributes to] the perpetuation of popular stereotypes, e.g. that Africa provides the rhythm section, the body of the pop music world, while Europe provides the melody, the head. Another is that it is the Black man's job to help the White man do his thing. History repeats itself; musically and artistically nothing has changed. Is African music only good for backings, not frontings?[4]

The commercial success of *Graceland* has spawned a number of clones, such as Harry Belafonte's *Paradise in Gazankulu*. In direct imitation of Simon, Belafonte sings over the backing of black South African pop stars: the Soul Brothers, Brenda Fassie, Theta, the Makgona Tshole Band, West Nkosi. Unlike Simon, Belafonte did not go to South Africa. His backing tracks were laid down in the Powerhouse Studios in Johannesburg, under the supervision of Hilton Rosenthal, Johnny Clegg's manager, then sent to New York for overdubbing and to Los Angeles for final mixing. Some of the songs, written by Jake Holmes, are obliquely critical of South Africa's racial policies; this has had no adverse effect on the careers and lives of the backing musicians, giving lie to Simon's claim that he avoided political texts to protect his black collaborators.

Belafonte has a long history of appropriating musical styles from

---

[4] Andrew Tracey, "A word from the editor," *African Music* 6 (1987), p. 3.

other cultures: "his interpretations of Trinidadian calypso music between 1957 and 1959 won him his greatest success and marked the pinnacle of his career."[5] Jamaica's Prime Minister, Edward Seaga, charged in 1983 that "there's no question about it that a number of our folk songs have made a very few people rich – one of them an international so-to-speak calypso singer." Belafonte has described himself as "a person of great social consciousness, a very political person, involved in the liberation movements of peoples all over the world." In an interview with Dermot Hussey of Jamaican Television he denied having pirated songs copyrighted by Caribbean musicians, and insisted that he popularized the calypso music of the West Indies in order to show "the people of the world . . . who we are, as a people."[6] It is far from clear that Belafonte's commercialization of calypso has ever benefited Caribbean music, musicians, or culture. It *is* clear, however, that Belafonte's last commercially successful LP, *The Midnight Special*, was produced as long ago as 1962, and he had not released an LP of any sort between 1970 and last year's *Paradise in Gazankulu*.

Miriam Makeba's recent LP, *Sangoma*, contains a collection of "the timeless melodies of my people . . . handed down [in my home, from which I have been exiled for almost thirty years now] from generation to generation like precious stones." Through the magic of contemporary technology, Makeba is able to sing both the lead ("call") and backing ("response") parts of traditional African choral style, with vocal help from Brenda Fassie, Linda Tshabalala, and Hugh Masekela, and some occasional backing percussion. The style resembles that of the syncretic "freedom songs" heard at black funerals, protest gatherings, and labor rallies throughout South Africa. Like Simon, Makeba has been praised for "calling attention to South African music," and unlike Simon she has a long history of anti-apartheid activity, dating back to a dramatic appearance before the UN in 1963.

Her recent autobiography[7] details the circumstances under which she left South Africa. Her singing in the musical *King Kong* in Johannesburg led to a cameo performance in the film *Come Back, Africa*, directed by Lionel Rogosin, who brought her to Europe for the Venice film festival of 1959. In London she met Harry Belafonte,

[5] Ronald Radano, "Harry Belafonte," in *The New Grove Dictionary of American Music*, ed. H. Wiley Hitchcock and Stanley Sadie (London and New York, 1986), vol. 1, p. 181.
[6] Roger Wallis and Krister Malm, *Big Sounds from Small Peoples: The Music Industry in Small Countries* (New York, 1984), pp. 195–7.
[7] Miriam Makeba with James Hall, *Makeba: My Story* (New York and Scarborough, 1987).

who arranged for her to go to the United States, and she abandoned plans to return to South Africa, where she had no record of political activity, to pursue what she hoped would be a lucrative career.

With the help of "Big Brother" Belafonte ["his entire organization was mobilized to help me"],[8] she appeared on the Steve Allen show, was featured at the Village Vanguard, toured college campuses with the Chad Mitchell Trio and Belafonte himself, and brought out her first LP for RCA, *Miriam Makeba*, backed by the Belafonte Folk Singers. The peak of her commercial success came in 1967, when her *Pata Pata* LP showed up on the *Billboard* charts for twenty-two weeks. Her repertory included both commercial arrangements of "folk" tunes from different lands, including South Africa, and Broadway show tunes. It was not until her recent, post-*Graceland Sangoma* that she drew on the *style* of traditional African music.

The picture emerging from this ramble through one corner of pop music history: *Graceland* offshoots are being produced by musicians who enjoyed their greatest success during the "Folk Music Revival" of the late 1950s and early 60s, but whose careers have been in relative decline since. One further example is Joan Baez's version of Johny Clegg's "Asimbonanga" from her latest LP, *Recently*. Though she sings the piece in her usual tight-vibrato, semi-operatic, inflexible vocal style, the background vocals, arranged by Ciaphus Semenya, draw on the sound of traditional South African music – or, more accurately, this sound as recently popularized by Simon, Belafonte, and others.

To close the circle, it must be recalled that Paul Simon himself was a product of the tag end of American pop's constructive commercial engagement with "folk" music in the 1950s and 60s, and throughout his career he has been more than willing to draw on the melodies, sounds, and rhythms of various ethnic musics – traditional Anglo-American, black gospel, Peruvian, reggae, Cajun – to revitalize his style and to give rhythmic punch to his music. And though he had continued to be much more commercially successful in the 1970s and 80s than Belafonte, Makeba, and Baez, sales of his pre-*Graceland* albums had been in a relative slump.

Situating the *Graceland* phenomenon as a late-blooming product of the "Folk Revival" suggests new interpretations. Many "folk" performers of the 1950s and 60s were supporters of causes espoused by liberal humanists of the era: Civil Rights; voter registration for America's minorities; the feminist movement; opposition to the war

---

[8] *Ibid.*, p. 83.

in Vietnam. They drew on "folk" tunes from around the world, performing them in harmonic, rhythmic, and instrumental arrangements consonant with the style of mainstream American pop. The beneficiaries were first of all the performers themselves, whose careers as entertainers were launched or enhanced, and the record industry, which saw soaring sales as the popularity of "folk" music spread from college campuses and folk clubs to a larger audience. It could be argued that there was some social impact within the USA, for instance in popularizing anti-war sentiment. But it has never been argued, successfully, that the "folk" movement benefited social causes (or musicians) within the various cultures from which tunes were borrowed.

I suggest that *Graceland* and its offshoots continue this tradition. South African music is borrowed and brought in line with contemporary American and British pop styles, now through technological procedures – overdubbing and mixing. The success of *Graceland* may have focused attention on South Africa, and some performances have taken place in the context of anti-apartheid rallies. But the chief beneficiaries have been the record companies, and the performers – Simon, Belafonte, Makeba, Baez, and others who have seen flagging careers boosted; and a handful of already privileged black South African musicians.

This is not to denigrate the anti-apartheid activity of Makeba, Baez, and Belafonte outside of South Africa. But I suspect that once that country has freed itself from white minority rule, black people will remember which musicians played and sang for the direct benefit of the liberation movement, and which ones drew on South African music and the media attention focused on that country as a means to enhance their own careers as entertainers.

Discography

Baez, Joan. 1987. *Recently*, Gold Castle Records, 171 004–1
Belafonte, Harry. 1988. *Paradise in Gazankulu*, EMI-Manhattan Records, E1–46971
Makeba, Miriam. 1988. *Miriam Makeba: Sangoma*, Warner Bros, 9 25673–1
Simon, Paul. 1986. *Graceland*, Warner Bros, 9 25447–1

16

DVOŘÁK IN AMERICA: NATIONALISM, RACISM, AND NATIONAL RACE

This essay originated as a paper delivered at the Dvořák Sesquicentennial Conference and Festival held in New Orleans on 14–20 February 1991. Most of the participants were historical musicologists from the United States and what was then Czechoslovakia. The notion that Dvořák drew on American "folk" material in several of his extended pieces written in America and had urged American composers to do the same, first put forward by journalists in the last decade of the nineteenth century, is still widely accepted, though the nature and source of this "folk" material and the meaning of the term "folk" at that time are not questioned. As a result, Dvořák's knowledge of and admiration for the plantation songs of Stephen Foster and other American songwriters has been overlooked, as has the complex interaction at the turn of the century among several genres – classical music, "national song," popular music – and the ideology embedded in these genres and their labels.

* * *

Style is ultimately national.
Hubert Parry,
inaugural address to the Folk Song Society
of England, 1898

I

Nationalism in music is defined by *The New Harvard Dictionary of Music* as:

344

the use in art music of materials that are identifiably national . . .
in character. These may include actual folk music, melodies or
rhythms that merely recall folk music, and nonmusical programmatic
elements drawn from national folklore, myth, or literature. This
concept of musical nationalism has most often been employed [for]
music of the later 19th and early 20th centuries.[1]

This concept of national style emerged at a time when powerful new
nation-states were taking shape in Europe. King Wilhelm I of Prussia
was proclaimed Emperor of Germany on 18 January 1871, ruling a
new German reich made up of twenty-five states including the
former kingdoms of Prussia, Bavaria, Saxony, and Württemberg. A
similar unification occurred almost simultaneously in Italy, and
other European countries were solidifying their political structures
and boundaries as well.

In the process, once-autonomous regions, city-states, and even
entire kingdoms and countries were swallowed up by these new
modern nation-states. For ideological reasons it became expedient to
develop a new mythology of "national race," according to which the
population of a given nation-state was asserted to have a common
language, religion, history, and cultural heritage, across class lines.
I'm using Barthes' concept of mythology as a process whereby
ideologically based arguments and cultural products function to
"overturn culture into nature," that is, to make a contrived situation
seem natural, self-evident, commonsensical.[2]

Folk song, folk sagas, and folk myths were taken to be prime
markers of the character and soul of a given "national race."

> Folk song is essentially a communal as well as racial product. There
> is no music so characteristic of the German people as German folk
> song, so characteristic of the Russian people as Russian folk music.
> . . . English folk song is distinctively national and English, and,
> therefore, inherently different from that of every other nation in
> the world.[3]

> "Deutsch" is the title given to those Germanic races which, upon
> their natal soil, retained their speech and customs. . . . In rugged
> woods, throughout the lengthy winter, by the warm hearth fire of
> his turret chamber soaring high into the clouds, for generations

---

[1] *The New Harvard Dictionary of Music*, ed. Don Michael Randel (Cambridge, MA, and
London, 1986), p. 527.

[2] Roland Barthes, *Mythologies*, trans. Annette Lavers (New York, 1972), pp. 109–59.

[3] Cecil Sharp, *English Folk Song. Some Conclusions* (Belmont, CA, 1965), pp. 164–5. Fourth
edition, first published in 1907.

[the German] kept alive the deeds of his forefathers; the myths of native gods he weaves into an endless web of sagas.[4]

The greatest artist belongs inevitably to his country as much as the humblest singer in a remote village – they and all those who come between them are links in the same chain, manifestations on their different levels of the same desire for artistic expression, and, moreover, the same nature of artistic expression.[5]

It seemed evident, then, that if a national style of art music were to emerge within a given nation-state, reflecting its national character and its soul, this music could do no better than to draw on the folk music of the "national race" of that country.

The dark side of the developing ideology of "national race" was its necessary marginalization of individuals or groups within a nation-state who did not belong to that country's dominant "race." Richard Wagner's concept of "German" left no room for the Jew, for instance:

The Jew speaks the language of the country in which he has lived from generation to generation, but he always speaks it like a foreigner. . . . [This] makes it impossible for him ever to speak colloquially, authoritatively or from the depths of his being. A language, its expression and its evolution are not separate elements but part of an historical community, and only he who has unconsciously matured in this community can take any part in what it creates. . . . Our entire German civilisation and art have remained foreign to the Jew; for he has taken no part in the evolution of either. . . . The cultured Jew stands alien and alienated in the midst of a society he does not understand, with whose tastes and aspirations he is not in sympathy, and to whose history and evolution he is indifferent.[6]

II

In a series of *fasciculi* published in Göttingen between 1790 and 1828, Johann Friedrich Blumenbach proposed, on the basis of measurements of skulls, that there were five principal varieties of humankind – Caucasian (white), Mongolian (yellow), Ethiopian

---

[4] Richard Wagner, "What is German?" in *Richard Wagner: Stories and Essays*, trans. W. Ashton Ellis and Charles Osborne (London, 1973), p. 48. Written in 1865, first published in the *Bayreuter Blätter*, for February 1878 as "Was ist Deutsch?"

[5] Ralph Vaughan Williams, *National Music and Other Essays* (Oxford, 1987), p. 7. From lectures at Bryn Mawr, 1932.

[6] Richard Wagner, "Judaism in Music," in *Richard Wagner: Stories and Essays*, pp. 26–30. Originally published in *Neue Zeitschrift für Musik* (1850), as "Das Judentum in der Musik."

(black), American (red), and Malay (brown) – and throughout the modern era various branches of science continued to devise and refine systems of classifying the various "races" of man. Anthropologists and ethnographers studied and catalogued skin pigmentation, color and texture of hair, eye color and form, shape of nose, body stature, and other anatomical features. Linguists argued for classification by families of language. Geographers and paleontologists tried to reconstruct historical movements of entire populations, hoping to determine their places of origin. Biologists attempted to apply Darwinian theory to the evolution of humankind, searching for clues to help understand the bewildering varieties of *homo sapiens*. Various alternatives to Blumenbach's five basic groups were put forward, including a simplified threefold division into Caucasoid (white), Mongoloid (yellow), and Negroid (black), and such large groups were in turn subjected to endless subdivision.

But nowhere in this vast scientific literature does one encounter the term "national race" or the suggestion that political boundaries correspond to physically or socially homogeneous populations. Furthermore, scientists reject the notion that any "pure" racial stock has ever existed, anywhere.

The theory of national race was put forward by persons with little or no training in science; we would call it "pop science" today. It was inextricably connected, from its beginning, with the proposition that the races of humankind are not only different from one another, but are also unequal. The seminal text of this pseudo-science came from the pen of Comte de Gobineau,[7] and even though this aristocratic author may have been motivated more by anti-democratic sentiment than by racial paranoia, his book became a central document for later writers whose concern was more clearly racist. The 1956 edition of the *Encyclopaedia Brittanica*, published in the twilight of the British Empire when the theory of racial inequality had not yet been fully abandoned as a justification of empire, gives a sympathetic summary of Gobineau's "earliest, strongest, most characteristic work":

> [It] propounded the doctrine that the different races of human-kind are innately unequal in talent, worth and ability to absorb and create culture, and change their innate character only through crossing with alien strains. The genius of a race depends but little on conditions of climate, surroundings and period; it is therefore absurd to maintain that all men are capable of an equal degree of

---

[7] *Essai sur l'inégalité des races humaines* (Paris, 1853–5).

perfection. Only the white races are creative of culture, but are exhausted today because their racial composition is no longer pure.[8]

True scientists acknowledged the theory of "national race" only to distinguish it from their own work, to discredit it, and to warn of its dangers. Franz Boas wrote in 1914:

> Scientific investigation does not countenance the assumption that in any one part of Europe a people of pure descent or of a pure racial type is found, and careful inquiry has failed completely to reveal any inferiority of mixed European types. In our imagination the local racial types of Europe have been identified with the modern nations, and thus the supposedly hereditary characteristics of the races have been confused with national characteristics. An identification of racial type, of language, and of nationality has been made, that has gained an exceedingly strong hold on our imagination. In vain sober scientific thought has remonstrated against this identification; the idea is too firmly rooted.[9]

And Friedrich Hertz, writing in Vienna on the eve of the ascendency of National Socialism, warned:

> There are no principles more antagonistic to one another than those of race and nation. Modern nationalism, it is true, mostly has recourse to race theories for the support of its ideas. . . . All nations, however, are composed of the most manifold racial elements and we even see that the most mixed stand in the foremost ranks of civilization. Whenever in history different races were welded together into one nation, we see the rising up of strong national states.[10]

"National race" is an ideological rather than a scientific construct. What is one to make, then, of the fact that so many composers of classical music in the modern era apparently failed to distinguish between nationalism and racism?

III

When Antonín Dvořák arrived in the United States in 1892 to direct the National Conservatory of Music in New York, a debate over the nature of America's national character and culture, that would reach a climax in the first two decades of the new century, was in its early stages.

[8] Vol. 10, p. 459.   [9] Franz Boas, *Race and Democratic Society* (New York, 1945), pp. 106–7.
[10] Friedrich Hertz, *Race and Civilization*, trans. A. S. Levetus and W. Entz (New York, 1928), pp. 320–1.

On the one hand, some argued for a new American interpretation of the concept of "national race." The United States was a melting pot, the "Crucible of God," a stirring and seething cauldron in which "Celt and Latin, Slav and Teuton, Greek and Syrian – black and yellow – Jew and Gentile – East and West, and North and South, the palm and the pine, the pole and the equator, the crescent and the cross" would be "melted and fused in the purging flame" into "the Republic of Man . . . where all races and nations come to labour and look forward!"[11] That is, a new national race would emerge, the American race, unified neither by ethnic and national origin nor by physical characteristics, but by common social cause.

But this utopian vision was resisted by others. Since it was manifestly impossible to pretend that the United States was peopled chiefly by a single racial stock at this time, the argument of those who insisted on the existence of an American "national race" rested on the premise that a single one of the many "races" making up the American population was historically dominant and superior, and should remain so. Since "the language of the new nation, its laws, its institutions, its political ideas, its literature, its customs, its precepts, its prayers" had been shaped by the "white Anglo-Saxon Protestant tradition,"[12] this "race" remained the best possible basis for America's national character and national culture, they insisted.

> The only possible root upon which we can engraft our [national] culture is the Anglo-Saxon root . . . because those ideals upon which our republic was based are characteristically and distinctively Anglo-Saxon. The Anglo-Saxon spirit of good sportsmanship and sense of fair play and justice have been, up to this time, the basis of everything that is fine, that is liberal, that is progressive in our past and in our present. Our only hope for a nation in America lies in grafting the stock of our culture on the Anglo-Saxon root. . . . In this way, not only will our racial heritage be used to give us a national music, but the resulting music will become one of the most important means towards the end of achieving a national consciousness.[13]

> The reserve, the dislike of ostentation, the repressed but strong emotion masked by dry humor, that belong to our New England type – this Anglo-Saxon element in our heterogeneous national character is of crucial significance in determining what we call American temper.[14]

11 Israel Zangwill, *The Melting-Pot* (New York, 1909), pp. 198–9.
12 Arthur M. Schlesinger, Jr., *The Disuniting of America* (New York, 1992), pp. 27–8.
13 John Powell, "Lectures on music," *The Rice Institute Pamphlet* 10/3 (July 1923), p. 127.
14 Daniel Gregory Mason, *Tune In, America* (New York, 1931), p. 159.

Among the most articulate proponents of an American national identity and culture growing from Anglo-Saxon roots was a group of composers from New England, labelled "humanist Victorians" by MacDonald Smith Moore, who says of them:

> [They] rationalized their musical calling on the basis of redemptive culture: the doctrine that musical culture could redeem the American spirit. . . . [They] portrayed redemptive culture primarily as a potential American civil religion. As Yankees, they considered themselves leaders of a progressive movement peculiarly American and, therefore, universal. By directly experiencing the ordering principles of redemptive culture, audiences could understand the meaning of their identity as Americans.[15]

In the New World as in the Old, then, some people – including composers of classical music – argued that persons of ethnic stock other than that of the "national race" could not be expected or allowed to share in, or help shape, the country's character and culture.

> Can the Negro and the Jew stand in the relation of a folk to our nation? And if not, can the music they create be the national music? There is this possibility: that as the American winds himself around layer after layer of civilization, he diminishes the vigour of his specific characteristics.[16]

> We Americans are no more black Africans than we are red Indians; and it is absurd to imagine that the negro idiom could ever give adequate expression to the soul of our race.[17]

> The insidiousness of the Jewish menace to our artistic integrity is due to the speciousness, the superficial charm and persuasiveness of Hebrew art, its violently juxtaposed extremes of passion, its poignant eroticism and pessimism. . . . For how shall a public accustomed by prevailing fashion to the exaggeration, the constant running to extremes, of eastern expression, divine the poignant beauty of Anglo-Saxon sobriety and restraint? . . . How shall it value as it deserves the balance, the sense of proportion, which is the finest of Anglo-Saxon qualities, and to which, like the sense of humor to which it is akin, nothing is more alien than the Oriental abandonment to excess? Our public taste is in danger of being permanently debauched, made lastingly insensitive to qualities most subtly and quintessentially our own, by the intoxication of what is, after all, an alien art.[18]

---

[15] MacDonald Smith Moore, *Yankee Blues: Musical Culture and American Identity* (Bloomington, 1985), p. 44.   [16] Gilbert Seldes, "The Negro's songs," *Dial* (March 1924), p. 249.
[17] Powell, "Lectures," p. 162.
[18] Daniel Gregory Mason, "Is American music growing up? Our emancipation from alien influences," in *Arts and Decoration* (November 1920).

IV

When Dvořák arrived in America in 1892, debate over the American character and a "national" musical style was in its first stages. He is commonly supposed to have suggested that a national American music might emerge out of elements of Indian (Native American) and Negro (black) music, and *The New York Herald* for 21 May 1893 quoted him as saying "I am now satisfied that the future music of this country must be founded upon what are called the Negro melodies." But all evidence suggests that the "Negro melodies" he heard in New York were of two types, arrangements of spirituals in the harmonic style of British–American hymnody and the "plantation" songs of Stephen Foster and other white commercial songwriters, and that he had no contact with, and probably no knowledge of, more "authentic" black music.[19] The central document putting forward his views on music in America is an extended essay published in *Harper's Magazine* in 1895. After an initial disclaimer of his right to speak to the subject:

> It would ill become me . . . to express my views on so general and all-embracing a subject as music in America, were I not pressed to do so, for I have neither travelled extensively, nor have I been here long enough to gain an intimate knowledge of American affairs. I can only judge it from what I have observed during my limited experience as a musician and teacher in America, and from what those whom I know here tell me about their own country.[20]

Dvořák nevertheless proceeded to argue that:

> The music of America will soon become more national in its character. This, my conviction, I know is not shared by many who can justly claim to know this country better than I do. Because the population of the United States is composed of many different races, in which the Teutonic element predominates, and because, owing to the improved methods of transmission of the present day, the music of all the world is quickly absorbed by this country, they argue that nothing specially original or national can come forth.
>
> All races have their distinctively national songs, which they at once recognize as their own. . . . It is a proper question to ask,

---

[19] Spirituals sung for Dvořák by Henry Burleigh and African-American "folksongs" described and transcribed by Henry Edward Krehbiel, which he may have known, had been heavily mediated by white musicians and stripped of their most important link with African music, their performance style.

[20] Antonín Dvořák, "Music in America," *Harper's New Monthly Magazine*, 90 (February 1895), p. 429.

what songs, then, belong to the American and appeal more strongly to him than any others? . . . The most potent as well as the most beautiful among them, according to my estimate, are certain of the so-called plantation and slave songs. . . . The point has been urged that many of these touching songs, like those of Foster, have not been composed by the Negroes themselves, but are the work of white men, while others did not originate on the plantations, but were imported from Africa. It seems to me that this matters but little. . . . Whether the original songs which must have inspired the composers came from Africa or originated on the plantations matters as little as whether Shakespeare invented his own plots or borrowed them from others. The thing to rejoice over is that such lovely songs exist and are sung at the present day. . . . Just so it matters little whether the inspiration for the coming folk-songs of America is derived from the Negro melodies, the songs of the Creoles, the red man's chant, or the plaintive ditties of the homesick German or Norwegian. Undoubtedly the germs for the best of music lie hidden among all the races that are commingled in this great country.[21]

Though Dvořák expressed himself with perfect clarity, let me summarize what he said, since it has so often been misinterpreted:

- There is no such thing as an American race, since the country's population is made up of the "commingling" of many different nationalities.

- Modern communications systems make music from elsewhere in the world readily available in the United States.

- As a consequence of these two factors, the music of no single national or ethnic group can be considered "American."

- Nevertheless, a national song can emerge from the "commingling" of the musics of the various peoples living there.

- Such a style in fact exists in the "plantation songs" of Stephen Foster and other songwriters, which Dvořák clearly understood to be contemporary products of white, professional songwriters, not the "folk songs" of Southern blacks.

- The future will bring other types of American national song, derived from the music of other national or ethnic groups.

The truly radical aspect of these comments lies in the suggestion that American national song is the product of commercial songwriters, reflecting and at the same time shaping the complex, multicultural life of the United States, rather than folk songs dredged up from the mists of the past, mystically invoking some allegedly unitary American culture or spirit.

[21] *Ibid.*, pp. 432–3.

V

Dvořák, then, did not urge a national school of American composition drawing self-consciously on one strain or another of folk song. In fact, his comments are not concerned with "folk song" at all, as the term is understood today. Arthur Farwell's "Navajo War Dance," Henry Gilbert's "Negro Rhapsody," and John Powell's "Natchez-on-the-Hill" were not what he had in mind for the future of America's music. Rather, he predicted a succession of schools of national song, each drawing on different elements of the country's diverse population, and possibly a classical music growing out of – not drawing on – this American song.

What he proposed did in fact come about, within a generation. And it was the Anglophiles' worst nightmare: music by immigrant and first-generation Jewish composers with names like Irving Berlin and George Gershwin and Aaron Copland, drawing on black, Jewish, and Irish materials, and accepted both at home and abroad as the most distinctive and distinguished American music of its time.

Dvořák did not embrace the myth of "national race." His foresight and audacity in suggesting that contemporary, commercially produced popular music might be the "national song" of a multicultural United States was in striking contrast to the attitudes of many of his American peers, who were blinded by the modernist afflictions of racist attitudes and a disdain for popular culture.

17

THE LAST MINSTREL SHOW?

First given as a paper at a joint conference of the American Musicological Society, the Society for Ethnomusicology, and the American branch of the International Association for the Study of Popular Music, held in Chicago in the fall of 1991, this essay brings my work back home. After years of trying to understand the context of popular music from the past, and in such remote parts of the world (for me) as South Africa and the People's Republic of China, I set out to examine the meaning of a contemporary musical event in a small village near my home in Vermont.

* * *

Even though the minstrel show is thought to have died out by the middle of the twentieth century, the Civic Club of Tunbridge, a small town in central Vermont, has produced one every year for the last four decades. It may be the last minstrel show.[1]

Why has even one minstrel show survived to the present day? Why here, in a village in northern New England? How is this show related, dramatically and musically, to the nineteenth-century minstrel stage? What is its meaning in the contemporary world? These are questions to be explored in this paper, based on an analysis of the 39th annual show given in March of 1991.

Description of the show

The Tunbridge minstrel show is held in late winter in the auditorium of the town hall, seating some 200 people. The audience, thoroughly

---

[1] Since finishing this paper, I've been told that a similar minstrel show is performed in East Bethel, only some ten miles from Tunbridge, and that one or more towns in eastern upstate New York may also still stage such shows.

mixed in age, is local. The performers, all from Tunbridge, included (in 1991) farmers, loggers, school teachers, the road commissioner, and the justice of the peace. A front line included Mr. Interlocutor, in formal dress and top hat, flanked by two women in party outfits and six endmen in blackface, named after their occupations: Mr. Moonbeams, Mr. Rugrat, Mr. Roots, Mr. Eightball, Mr. Gumdrop, and Mr. Veg. The chorus sits behind in two ranks, and a pianist accompanies from audience level.

The show is in two acts, each beginning and ending with an ensemble number by the entire company. Solo and ensemble songs, instrumental pieces, dances, skits, and recitations succeed one another in apparently random order, each event framed by jokes from the endmen. There's little trace of the three-part structure of the nineteenth-century minstrel show: a first section of ballads and "plantation" songs; an "olio" of miscellaneous songs and dances; and a finale of either a walk-around or a comic skit.[2] If anything, the format of the Tunbridge show resembles vaudeville's succession of unrelated acts, though unified by the presence of the entire cast on stage throughout. The finale of the first act, with the entire front line dancing and singing, does bear some resemblance to the minstrel walk-around, however.

There's horseplay and drinking on stage, which combines with the presence of blackface "masks" to give a hint of Carnival. The majority of the jokes have to do with sex or excrement, though a few concern misadventures in the daily life of a New England villager or the ignorance of "flatlanders," the local name for outsiders. There's some verbal interplay between stage and audience, and well-known residents of the town are often the butt of jokes. This particular show took place near the end of the short-lived Gulf War, an event celebrated by a profusion of "Eye-racky" jokes and a flag-waving patriotic finale.

To tackle the question of why a minstrel show has survived in Tunbridge, one must first know something about the community.

History of Tunbridge

Governor Benning Wentworth of the Colony of New Hampshire authorized the establishment in 1761 of several new towns in

---

[2] The most useful histories of the minstrel show are Robert C. Toll, *Blacking Up: The Minstrel Show in Nineteenth-Century America* (New York, 1974), and Carl Wittke, *Tambo and Bones: A History of the American Minstrel Stage* (Durham, 1930). Eric Lott, *Love and Theft: Blackface Minstrelsy and the American Working Class* (New York and Oxford, 1993), an important new study, was published after the present article was written.

Vermont on land previously uninhabited by European colonists. On 3 September of that year he granted 23,040 acres for a six-square-mile township, to be called Tunbridge – probably after William Zulestein de Nassau, 4th Earl of Rockford, Viscount Tunbridge – to sixty-five grantees, with the stipulation that "every Grantee . . . shall plant and cultivate 5 acres of land within the term of 5 years."

Most of these grantees were land speculators from Connecticut and Massachusetts with no intention of settling on the land themselves. Nevertheless, within a decade a community began to form, of families who bought plots from the original grantees and others who simply took possession of unoccupied land. The first permanent settler was probably Moses Ordway, in 1776; Abijah Hutchinson, another early inhabitant, left the first written narrative of the town.

Settlement was slowed by war. On 16 October 1780 a raiding party of some 300 Native Americans under British command, sweeping down from Canada, "destroyed 28 houses, 32 barns full of grain, 1 Saw and 1 Grist mill, killed cattle, sheep, pigs," forcing most inhabitants to take refuge in a fort some distance away. But there were no more incidents of this sort, and by 21 March 1786, when the town was chartered, it numbered some fifty families.[3]

A small river had created a narrow but fertile valley among the surrounding hills and provided power for mills, and the community prospered. The census of 1791 counted 487 people, and by 1820 the population numbered 2,003. Sawmills and grist mills were in operation, a sulphur spring was discovered in 1806, and Methodist and Congregational churches were built. There was a rake factory, a foundry, a cider mill, and eventually the Gay Brothers Woolen Mill employed some twenty-five people.

But the town couldn't sustain even this modest growth. The growing season was short and the soil, though fertile, was rocky; the river proved to be an unreliable source of power for mills, with frequent spring floods and low summer water levels; the nearest railroad line was eight miles to the south, along the White River. The population, declining steadily as individuals and entire families left for urban centers or for more fertile farming land to the west, dipped below a thousand at mid-century and reached a low of 743 in 1960 (see the population table, Appendix I). Today the town is completely

---

[3] This information is abstracted and quoted from Robert O'Brien, *On the Beginnings of Tunbridge* (Tunbridge, 1961).

agricultural and residential. Its center, dominated by a monument to the 150 men who went off to fight in the Civil War, consists of a church, an administrative building, and a town hall; a small general store on the main street is the only commercial enterprise. In addition to the minstrel show, community activities include an annual agricultural fair dating back to 1867 (advertised as the "Tunbridge World's Fair"), a contra dance club that performs for the pleasure of its members and for local fairs and festivals and was featured at the New York World's Fair in 1940,[4] and a clogging group.

Ethnic profile of population

The demographic history of the region suggests that the first settlers of Tunbridge and those who joined them during the following three decades were of British descent, and family names in cemeteries and various historical documents verify this. The pattern of a steadily declining population after 1820 suggests that there were few newcomers to the town after this time.[5] One would expect, then, that the vast majority of the people living in Tunbridge today trace their ancestry to British-descended families settling there many generations ago, and when one examines various documents – rosters of school children over the years; lists of soldiers who served in various wars and of participants in civic events; records of births, deaths, and marriages – one sees the same family names over and over again, and these names are indeed British: Farnham, Howe, Hutchinson, Camp, Young, Larkin, Bradford, Belknap, Durkee, Pierce, Swan, Woodward, Tucker, Folsom, Alexander.

There are no German, Scandinavian, Italian, Slavic, or Greek names on these lists, nor was there historical reason for people with such names to be in Tunbridge. By the 1840s, when millions of immigrants began coming to the United States from Northern and Central Europe, Tunbridge was already socially stable and in economic decline. By the 1880s, when other millions of immigrants began arriving from Mediterranean lands and from Central and Eastern Europe, the town had nothing to offer them: no large factories or mills, no expanding agricultural opportunities, no

---

[4] See Ruth Sher, "And Everyone Would Sashay": The Remembrances of the Ed Larkin Contra Dancers (West Topsham, 1989).

[5] According to Professor Jere Daniell, Class of 1915 Professor of History at Dartmouth College and an authority on small-town culture in New England, the pattern of a declining population after the first decades of the nineteenth century links with homogeneity of ethnic origin in present-day population.

resident ethnic populations to cushion their arrival. As Oscar Handlin characterizes New England in the decades after the Civil War:

> [It] steadily lost national influence. [New Englanders] blamed their own loss of vitality upon demographic changes. The original stock [of the country] had given way to a degenerate foreign population, crowded into great cities and divorced by heredity and environment from the true sources of New England's strength. Hence the strong emphasis on the necessity for maintaining the old virtues through the discipline of strict family life and through . . . access to voluntary societies, and other [traditional] social activities.[6]

The minstrel show in Vermont

Barnstorming minstrel troupes from New York and Boston began making their way to villages in northern New England by the middle of the nineteenth century. As one writer put it, "for the comic ballad singer and minstrels, almost any village with a hotel and a printer was worth a try."[7] The Ethiopian Serenaders, Dandy Jim, Pell & Mulligan, and That Comical Brown are among minstrel performers known to have performed in this part of New England.[8] And soon Vermont had its own companies: Whitmore & Clark's Minstrel Troupe, for instance, was formed in Reading by George M. Clark, a native of Clarendon; Hank White, born in Weathersfield, performed for more than two decades in such towns as Woodstock, Rutland, and Proctorsville.[9]

After the decline of the professional minstrel show in the first decades of the twentieth century, the genre was kept alive in amateur performances mounted by churches, fraternal organizations, Boy Scout troupes, and civic clubs.[10] Local minstrel shows were performed until recently in an entire cluster of towns in this region of central Vermont. Though the Tunbridge show of 1991 was advertised as the 39th annual production, older residents recall earlier series of shows as well, including several with all-female casts during World War II.

[6] Oscar Handlin, "Yankees," in *Harvard Encyclopedia of American Ethnic Groups*, ed. Stephan Thernstrom (Cambridge, MA, and London, 1980), p. 1029.
[7] T. D. Seymour Bassett, "Minstrels, musicians, and melodeons: a study in the social history of music in Vermont, 1848–1872," *New England Quarterly* 19/1 (March 1946), p. 33.
[8] Information gleaned from various programs and local newspapers in the Vermont Historical Society, Montpelier.
[9] Mary S. Fay, "Reading's musicians of 1906 and earlier," *Vermonter* 48 (August 1943), p. 149.
[10] The Vermont Historical Society has a program of a show put on by the Lions Club of Castleton, for instance. Wittke, *Tambo and Bones*, pp. 126 ff., gives a brief history of the minstrel show in the early twentieth century.

Repertory

The nineteenth-century minstrel show had a musically homogeneous repertory only in its first decade or so.[11] By the 1850s, accretions such as Stephen Foster's plantation songs and other pieces not originally conceived for the minstrel stage were common. After the Civil War the minstrel show offered an increasingly heterogeneous mix of popular ballads, songs from the British musical stage, arias and ensembles from Italian operas, novelty songs with ethnic protagonists other than black Americans, spirituals, and various social dances.

In drawing its musical numbers from a considerable range of styles, genres, and time periods (see Appendix 2) the Tunbridge minstrel show of 1991 was thus situated solidly in the tradition of the genre. Even so, this repertory is more homogeneous than might appear at first glance.

Not surprisingly, given the ethnic background of the community, many pieces are related in one way or another to traditional Anglo-American music: the fiddle tunes; the minstrel songs; the country-western songs; some of the Irish pieces; the white gospel music. But how does one account for the fact that Tin Pan Alley songs make up the largest group? This was the popular music of the formative years of many members of the cast and audience, of course; but there's more to it than that.

Irving Berlin's "When The Midnight Choo-Choo Leaves For Alabam'" is a so-called "coon" song, with a black protagonist. The melody of the chorus has both the "Scottish snap" and the gapped scale characteristic of many traditional Anglo-Celtic tunes and imitated in many nineteenth-century minstrel songs. The same is true of Gershwin's "Swanee," which in addition quotes an older minstrel song, Stephen Foster's "Old Folks At Home." Other Tin Pan Alley pieces in the show make similar musical or textual reference to minstrel songs or their successors on the vaudeville stage, "coon" and "Mammy" songs.

These songs draw not on African-American music itself, but on the image of black music imprinted on the American consciousness by the minstrel show. Contrary to the contention by some writers that Tin Pan Alley songwriters made considerable use of elements

---

[11] See Hans Nathan, *Dan Emmett and the Rise of Early Negro Minstrelsy* (Norman, 1962) and Charles Hamm, *Yesterdays: Popular Song in America* (New York and London, 1979), pp. 122–38, for a description of this style.

from black music,[12] African-American stylistic elements didn't figure importantly in "mainstream" American popular music until the 1950s, with rock 'n' roll. Even though most Tin Pan Alley composers were immigrant or first-generation Americans living in New York City, they wanted their songs to reach the widest possible audience throughout the United States. They made it their business to become familiar with both contemporary and earlier American popular styles, and their songs, extending and expanding these styles rather than breaking with them, are compatible with Anglo-American styles.

One must distinguish between composition and performance in discussing this issue. African-American performance elements are present in Bessie Smith's recording of "Alexander's Ragtime Band," but not in Al Jolson's recording of "Swanee" or the performance of this song by the cast of the Tunbridge minstrel show.

In this connection, the only three pieces from the rock era performed in the Tunbridge minstrel show, "Rockin' Robin" and "Beep, Beep" from 1958, and "Tie A Yellow Ribbon" from 1973, have minimal stylistic links with black music, and none of the three enjoyed popularity with black audiences.

Whatever their origin, the various pieces performed in this show form a stylistic cluster, unified by their relationship to or compatibility with nineteenth-century Anglo-American styles and the absence of African-American elements.

Ideology of the minstrel show

The early minstrel show communicated pro-slavery images to Antebellum audiences. As Robert Toll puts it:

> With its images of Negroes shaped by white expectations and desires and not by black realities, minstrelsy . . . deeply embedded caricatures of blacks into popular American culture. From the outset, [it] unequivocally branded [them] as inferiors. [It] presented the plantation as a predominantly happy place, [and] repeatedly acted out images which illustrated that there was no need to fight a war over slavery, no need to accept Negroes as equals in the North,

[12] Alec Wilder, in *American Popular Song: The Great Innovators, 1900–1950* (New York, 1972), says that the songs of Irving Berlin and his peers are indebted to the music of "the early anonymous Negroes" who "had managed to create the beginnings of an entirely new music" (p. 28). Richard Middleton, in *Studying Popular Music* (Milton Keynes and Philadelphia, 1990), sees "Tin Pan Alley's incorporation of musematic repetition," which became "endemic" during the jazz age, as evidence of the impact of African-American styles (p. 276).

and no need to feel guilty for contradictions between slavery and the American Creed.[13]

After Emancipation, there was little change in the portrayal of blacks on the minstrel stage, and the message that blacks were inferior and child-like continued to be well received both in the South, which was resisting social and political equality for blacks, and in the North, which had little desire to absorb the ex-slave population.

But Toll sees the post-War minstrel show as a more complex phenomenon than this. He argues that "in folk societies verbal arts taught values and norms, invoked sanctions against transgressors, and provided vehicles for fantasy and outlets for social criticism."[14] The minstrel show, an urban product, became a modern substitute for the vanishing oral tradition, "replac[ing] rural folk culture with symbols that white 'common men' could all unite around." As "immigration, urbanization, and modernization forced the American public to undergo fundamental institutional, social, and moral changes," the minstrel show "devoted much less attention to Southern blacks and much more to national developments." In the process, various ethnic groups, and then women, joined and even supplanted African-Americans as targets of ridicule on the minstrel stage.[15]

Analysis and conclusions

In continuing to produce a grotesque stage representation of black people, in the context of a theatrical genre with a long history of obstructing the social acceptance of blacks and other marginalized groups, the villagers of Tunbridge are out of step with American public morality of the late twentieth century.

They're well aware that the minstrel show as a means of cultural expression is viewed with disfavor elsewhere, though they see the problem as lying with the rest of the country, not with themselves. They know that competitive "cakewalk" dancing by student couples in blackface, a decades-long tradition at the nearby University of Vermont during the midwinter social weekend, was discontinued several years ago after being attacked in the press and by campus activists, and they fear a similar fate will overtake their minstrel show, sooner or later.

The Tunbridge minstrel show is replete with apparent contradictions. The performers are in blackface, but the music they sing and

---

[13] Toll, *Blacking Up*, pp. v–vi.   [14] *Ibid.*, p. 5.   [15] *Ibid.*, pp. 160, 270.

play has nothing to do with the music of black people, and not a single joke in the show of 1991 was directed at African-Americans. It's performed in a community that has never had a black inhabitant, in a state in which the non-white population is only 2.5 per cent of the whole. The town sent hundreds of its men off to the Civil War to help preserve the Union and free the slaves, yet today many of its own residents display Confederate flags as a symbol of solidarity with people in the South and elsewhere who reject the multiculturalism of present-day America.

When I've discussed the show with other people, including former colleagues at Dartmouth College, the most common reactions have been: "How can you attend such a racist event?" and "How can we close it down?"

Concerning the latter: our Constitution still protects the right of the people in Tunbridge to put on such a show, and trying to force its cancellation would be the equivalent of storming an abortion clinic. No matter how distasteful the show may be to some people, it has the same protection under the First Amendment as Andrew Dice Clay, Guns 'n' Roses, Howard Stern, and Public Enemy.

But there's a more important response to these questions.

In recent decades, a central theme in ethnomusicology and popular music studies has been the use of music by national, ethnic, regional, religious, economic, and other self-defining groups to assert and strengthen group identity in the face of attempted cultural domination by central governments or other institutions with a stake in controlling public thought. This dynamic has been identified and analyzed in the townships of South Africa, the cities and towns of the Baltic States, the black ghettos of Los Angeles and New York, the college campuses of the People's Republic of China, the working-class neighborhoods of the UK, the villages of Indonesia, and the Native American reservations of the USA and Canada.

The so-called Birmingham School of cultural studies has defined a subculture as a "meaning system [or] mode of expression or lifestyle developed by groups in subordinated structural positions in response to dominant meaning systems . . . which reflect their attempt to solve structural contradictions arising from the wider societal context."[16] According to this definition, the various groups mentioned in the preceding paragraph, all of which are in "subordinated structural positions," comprise subcultures, and so do the people of Tunbridge. They're culturally homogeneous, and they see themselves

---

[16] Michael Brake, *Comparative Youth Culture: The Sociology of Youth Culture and Youth Subcultures in America, Britain, and Canada* (London and New York, 1985), p. 8.

in a "subordinated structural position" in relation to the country as a whole. Their minstrel show and its music function as an important part of a "meaning system or mode of expression or lifestyle" developed "in response to [a] dominant meaning system," in this case the multiculturalism of contemporary American life, at least as they understand it from the media, their most important link to the rest of the country.[17]

Summary

To return now to the question posed at the beginning of this paper:

- Why has the minstrel show survived to the present day in northern New England? Because the genre was a product of nineteenth-century mentality and morality, and identification with the past is an important cultural factor among rural people in this part of the country.

- How is the Tunbridge show related to nineteenth-century prototypes? It maintains their basic format, in simplified form, and continues a tradition of adding pieces in newer styles and genres to a core repertory.

- What is the meaning of the minstrel show in the contemporary world? The same as it was in the late nineteenth-century. To paraphrase Toll, it's a vehicle for fantasy and an outlet for social criticism, offering symbols that the Anglo-Saxon white "common man" can unite around. Like the later nineteenth-century minstrel show, it's a symbolic response to a collection of threatening Others – not merely blacks.

If other minstrel shows still exist, they're to be found in places like Tunbridge: small, isolated agricultural towns with homogeneous populations descended chiefly from settlers of the eighteenth and nineteenth centuries which reject the multiculturalism of contemporary American life, towns too small and isolated for the country at large to care what goes on in them.

---

[17] Regional newspapers, as well as others published in Boston, New York, Burlington, and Manchester, are available at the local general store, as are rental videos. Most homes have television sets, and some jokes in the show referred to network shows, "Jeopardy" for instance.

Appendix 1 Population of Tunbridge

year	population	year	population
1791	487	1900	885
1800	1324	1910	918
1810	1640	1920	907
1820	2003	1930	903
1830	1920	1940	882
1850	1786	1950	774
1860	1546	1960	743
1870	1405	1970	791
1880	1252	1980	916
1890	1011		

(*Source: US Bureau of Census*)

Appendix 2 Program of the 39th Annual Tunbridge Minstrel Show

selection	genre
(1) Swanee Irving Caesar & George Gershwin, 1919	Tin Pan Alley
(2) Are You From Dixie? Jack Yellen & George M. Cobb, 1915	Tin Pan Alley
(3) Sentimental Journey Bud Green, Les Brown, & Ben Homer, 1944	Tin Pan Alley
(4) Kiss An Angel Good Morning Charley Pride, 1971	country-western
(5) Music, Music, Music Stephen Weiss & Bernie Baum, 1950	Tin Pan Alley
(6) Fiddlin' Around (fiddle solo) medley of fiddle tunes	traditional
(7) One Day At A Time Marilyn Sellars, 1974	country-western/ white gospel
(8) A Little Bit of Vermont Poetry (recitation) Elaine Howe	poetry
(9) Duelin' Banjos (tap dance to recorded music) Eric Weissberg & Steve Mandell, from *Deliverance*, 1972	pseudo-folk
(10) When The Midnight Choo-Choo	

Leaves for Alabam' Irving Berlin, 1912		Tin Pan Alley
(11) Rockin' Robin J. Thomas, 1958 (popularized by Bobby Day)		rock
(12) Moonglow Will Hudson, Eddie DeLange, & Irving Mills, 1934		Tin Pan Alley
(13) Just A-Ridin' In The Rain (Goin' to Arizona)		country-western
(14) Beer Barrel Polka [Skoda Lasky] Vasek Zeman, Wladimir A. Tim, & Jaromir Vejvoda, 1934. English words by Lew Brown.		Czech/World War II song

intermission

(15) Row, Row, Row Jimmy V. Monaco & William Jerome, 1912		Tin Pan Alley
(16) Rock-a-Bye Your Baby With A Dixie Melody Jean Schwartz, Sam Lewis, & Joe Young, 1918		Tin Pan Alley
(17) Ragtime Medley (piano solo) medley		piano ragtime
(18) Shenandoah anonymous, nineteenth century		traditional
(19) Yes! We Have No Bananas Frank Silver & Irving Cohn, 1923		Tin Pan Alley
(20) Mexican Hat Dance (speciality dance)		
(21) Irish Medley (a) When Irish Eyes Are Smiling Chauncey Olcott & George Graff, Jr., Ernest R. Ball, 1912 (b) Too-ra-loo-ra-loo-ral, That's an Irish Lullabye J. R. Shannon, 1914 (c) Oh Me Clancy traditional (d) Danny Boy adapted by Fred E. Weatherly, 1913		traditional/Tin Pan Alley

(22) Beep, Beep   rock
C. Cicchetti & D. Clapps (popularized
by The Playmates)
(23) Oh Susanna   minstrel song
Stephen Foster, 1848
(24) Star Spangled Banner (clog dance to
recorded music)   country swing
Francis Scott Key, 1814, arranged as
country swing
(25) A Winner Leads The Way   pop
(26) Tie A Yellow Ribbon Round The Old
Oak Tree   pop
Irwin Levine & L. Russell Brown, 1973
(popularized by Dawn/Tony Orlando)
(27) (a) You're A Grand Old Flag   Tin Pan Alley
George M. Cohan, 1906
(b) Till We Meet Again   Tin Pan Alley
Richard A. Whiting & Raymond B.
Egan, 1918

18

THE ROLE OF ROCK,
A REVIEW*

The writings of religious fundamentalists tend to privilege one belief system over all others and to establish a hierarchy of values based on assumptions that are neither stated nor questioned. When this literature addresses music, particularly popular music, its content tends to become indistinguishable from that of critical and historical writing grounded in the modernist narratives of musical autonomy and authenticity.

* * *

The author of this book is an ordained pastor in the Christian Assembly of God sect. Like all fundamentalists, whether Christian, Muslim, Jewish, Catholic, Marxist, Constitutional, or whatever, he believes that "truth" is to be found only in the literal reading of a certain text, in this instance the Bible. Unfortunately for John Muncy, the Bible has nothing to say about rock music, but this does not deter him. Pointing out that "Jesus was called, 'The Rock,' a long time before anybody even heard of rock and roll music! Rock music is just a counterfeit for the real Rock . . . Jesus Christ!" (p. 387), Muncy proceeds to "prove" that the Bible does in fact speak to the issue of rock music by asserting that: (1) through its lyrics and with the aid of subliminal messages, rock entices its fans to engage in rebellion, sex without morals, alcohol, drugs, false religions, violence, sexual perversions, suicide, and occult practices; (2) the Bible forbids each of these practices; (3) therefore, the Bible forbids rock music.

In support of these assertions, Muncy offers quotations from rock

* The book under review is John Muncy, *The Role of Rock: Harmless Entertainment or Destructive Influence* (Canton, 1989).

367

lyrics, lurid press accounts of the antics of rock musicians and of crimes committed by troubled teenagers, and numerous biblical passages. There is no evidence that he has heard any of the music that he writes about, nor that he has read any of the large and growing body of scholarly literature or responsible professional journalism dealing with popular music.

None of this originates with Muncy. Christian fundamentalists Dan and Steve Peters, Bob Larson, and Steve Lawhead, not to forget Tipper Gore, Joe Stuessey, and Carl A. Rischke, have made identical assertions and offered the same "evidence" in their attacks on rock music. Muncy acknowledges none of these people, whose work he surely knows. One must assume that there are no biblical injunctions against plagiarism.

Muncy drags out the now-familiar accusations concerning rock's techniques of subliminal persuasion, including "backward masking"; the same descriptions of a handful of gory incidents involving troubled teenagers who happened to be fans of rock music; the same highly selective snippets from interviews with rock stars and fans. He does manage to add a few new wrinkles, though. After citing biblical passages forbidding child sacrifice, he suggests that abortion is a modern form of this practice and is thus forbidden in the Bible, though he offers no link between rock music and abortion. And he contributes some intriguing, though undocumented, bits of information that are new to me, at least: "Representatives of 500 of the nation's largest Corporations, including IBM, AT&T, and General Motors, meet regularly to discuss how metaphysics, Hindu mysticism, and the occult can help their executives to compete in the market place" (p. 143), and "Leaders [of Transcendental Meditation] plan for the elimination of 25% of earth's inhabitants" (p. 143).

The most telling rebuttal of this body of "literature" is found in Robert Walser's "Running With the Devil: Power, Gender, and Madness in Heavy Metal Music" (Ph.D. dissertation, University of Minnesota, 1991). Among Walser's arguments one finds the points that contemporary America is replete with violence – domestic, corporate, military. In addition, the country now ranks nineteenth worldwide in quality of life, according to a United Nations survey, and any chance that most young people will achieve the same affluence as their parents is fading. Heavy metal and other forms of rock did not create these situations, and in fact this music helps its fans "make sense of their own situation" by "healing the hurts of history [and] creating communal bonds that will help [them] weather the strains of modernity" (pp. 193–4). Walser also remarks that "violence is no more common at [rock] concerts than at sports events

– or at the opera in nineteenth century Paris, or at performances of Shakespeare in nineteenth-century New York" (p. 181). And further, the literary "terrorism" of writers who attack rock music depends wholly on anecdote and insinuation, and "none of these critics can cite any statistics supporting a link between [rock] and suicide, Satanism, or crime" (p. 180). Only a small fraction of the lyrics of heavy metal or other rock songs deal with such issues, and when they do, it is in ways "more complex and sophisticated than [critics] recognize" (p. 176). Moreover, a study by a group of sociologists of religion finds that there is "not a shred of evidence" that Satanism, which rock music allegedly promotes, is a problem in America (p. 179).

Why should a book such as Muncy's even be mentioned in *Notes*, then? Because the not-so-subliminal messages invariably present in fundamentalist Christian criticisms of rock music are reaching millions of people, and these messages are so inimical to what most of us are trying to do as educators and scholars that one must not ignore them. Since it is in the very nature of fundamentalism that ideological positions are simply announced to the faithful, who are expected to accept them without thought or question, it must fall to outsiders to challenge and contradict these pronouncements if they run contrary to rational discourse, scholarly objectivity, or the constitutionally protected rights of American citizens. Someone needs to point out, for example, that the present book's explicit condemnation of Mormonism, Jehovah's Witnesses, Rastafarianism, the Baha'i faith, Taoism, Buddhism, Yoga, Transcendental Meditation, and New Age as "false religions" spread by rock music, and its implicit condemnation of the Catholic, Jewish, and Muslim religions, is in contradiction to a key provision of the First Amendment. Someone needs to alert others that Muncy makes explicit what he envisions as the Final Solution to the Rock Problem: "Tens of thousands of dollars of records, tapes, posters, occult books, etc. have been destroyed as a result of people getting their hearts right with God!" (p. 15).

I respectfully suggest to fundamentalist Christian authors that future books of this sort should bear a label on the cover, reading: "Warning. This book is devoid of educational or scholarly content, and in addition it constitutes an attack on secular education and the Constitution of the United States of America." Such labels might save librarians from buying books of this sort on account of their respectable titles, unless of course they wish to bolster their fundamentalist Christian dogma collections and not their music collections.

19

GENRE, PERFORMANCE, AND IDEOLOGY IN THE EARLY SONGS OF IRVING BERLIN*

This paper was read on 5 November 1993 at the annual meeting of the American Musicological Society in Montreal. It seemed to me, at the moment, that I had articulated in the simplest possible terms the concept I'd been struggling towards for many years: that the meaning of a piece of popular music is shaped most importantly at the moment of performance; that this meaning can change from performance to performance; therefore one must either be present at a given performance, or reconstruct it, in order to understand this meaning.

* * *

Irving Berlin's 200-odd songs written between 1907, the date of the first one, and late 1914, when his first complete show for the musical stage ("Watch Your Step") opened at New York's Globe Theatre, are virtually identical to one another in their published piano–vocal format. Like other Tin Pan Alley songs of the early twentieth century, most of them consist of a brief piano introduction, a few bars of vamp, then several verses, each followed by a chorus. All are in major keys and most have a tempo marking of *Moderato*. Piano introductions are drawn from either the first or last phrase of the chorus, the vamp anticipates the melodic beginnings of the verse, and both verse and chorus are usually made up of four 4-bar phrases in C or four 8-bar phrases in other meters.

This essay is dedicated to my friend and onetime colleague Wilfrid Mellers. Though he has not yet written at length about Irving Berlin, his remarks in *Music in a New Found Land: Themes and Developments in the History of American Music* (London, 1964), including the observation that "[Berlin's] lyrics and tunes went straight to the hearts of the millions who were like him, except that they lacked his talent" (p. 383), capture the essence of Berlin and his world better than any subsequent literature.

But despite this apparent homogeneity, publishers advertised these songs under different rubrics and we know from comments by songwriters, journalists, and audiences that one song could be perceived in one way and another in quite another way. In other words, various kinds – or genres – of songs were recognized at this time.

Genre and music

Genre has been a major fascination of literary criticism for much of the twentieth century. The construction of taxonomies based on close textual analysis occupied many scholars of the modern era, while postmodern criticism has tended to deconstruct the process of genre construction itself – that is, to ask why the exercise is undertaken, not how – or to emphasize the flexibility and overlap of genres. As Jorge Luis Borges parodies genre construction:

> Animals are divided into: (a) belonging to the Emperor, (b) the embalmed, (c) tame, (d) suckling pigs, (e) sirens, (f) fabulous, (g) stray dogs, (h) included in the present classification, (i) frenzied, (j) innumerable, (k) drawn with a very fine camelhair brush, (l) *et cetera*, (m) having just broken the water pitcher, (n) that from a long way off look like flies.[1]

British and American historical and critical writing on music has tended to ignore genre, though, at least until recently. There is not even an entry for the term in *The New Grove Dictionary of Music and Musicians*, the *New Harvard Dictionary of Music* or *The New Grove Dictionary of American Music*. But German scholars have been much more concerned with the topic. Carl Dahlhaus, for instance, insists that genre must be approached from the intersection of occasion and technique, or context and text; and since he sees a general weakening of the social role of music from the late nineteenth century onwards, he argues that genre becomes progressively less important in the modern era.[2] Adorno, representing another German intellectual tradition, sees genre formation as a dialectic between Universal and Particular, with deviations generating new forms;

[1] As quoted in Marjorie Perloff, ed., *Postmodern Genres* (Norman and London, 1989), p. vii.
[2] See Carl Dahlhaus, *Musikästhetik* (Cologne, 1967) and *Foundations of Music History*, trans. J. B. Robinson (Cambridge, 1983). For an exhaustive bibliography on genre by Dahlhaus and other German scholars, see Jeffrey Kallberg, "The rhetoric of genre: Chopin's Nocturne in G Minor," *19th Century Music* 11/3 (Spring 1988), pp. 238–61.

"Universals such as genres . . . are true to the extent that they are subject to a countervailing dynamic," he argues.[3]

More recent musicological literature agrees that genre should not be defined by description or analysis of stylistic features alone. In a study of Chopin's Nocturne in G minor, Jeffrey Kallberg contends that while musical analysis may succeed in "provid[ing] factual information about a term, classify[ing] it, [it] does not explain its meaning . . . [which] must emerge from the context of the term." Defining genre as a "communicative concept" through "the reconstruction of contexts and traditions, and the perceptions of composers and their audiences, both historical and modern," he puts forward the notion of a "generic contract" between composer and listener. The composer signals his choice of genre by means of title, meter, tempo, or characteristic opening gesture, establishing a context in which "[he] agrees to use some of the conventions, patterns, and gestures of a genre, and the listener consents to interpret some aspects of the piece in a way conditioned by this genre."[4] Robert Pascall, discussing the final movement of Brahms's Fourth Symphony, takes four categories of "generic difference and development" to be "fundamental and unalienable"; in addition to description and analysis of the music itself ("its diachronic structure, with continuity and development"), one must also take into account performance site, performing forces (the "instrumentarium") and a definable expressive code.[5] Jim Samson, exploring the relationships and differences among genre, style, and form, posits that "the repetition units that define a genre, as opposed to a stylistic norm or a formal schema, extend beyond musical materials into the social domain so that a genre is dependent for its definition on context, function and community validation and not simply on formal and technical regulations."[6]

Underlying most musicological writing on genre is the assumption that both composer and listener have a technical understanding of the genre in question, and a knowledge of relevant social and historical issues, equal to that of the scholar. While it's not my intention here to agree or disagree with this assumption, I will suggest that it's of limited use in dealing with genre in popular music.

Most of the literature on genre in popular music distances itself even more vigorously from dependence on musical factors alone.

---

[3] Theodor W. Adorno, *Aesthetic Theory*, ed. Gretel Adorno and Rolf Tiedemann, trans. Christian Lenhardt (London, 1984), p. 242. See also Jim Samson, "Chopin and genre," *Music Analysis* 8/3 (October 1989), p. 214.   [4] Kallberg, "The rhetoric of genre," p. 243.
[5] Robert Pascall, "Genre and the Finale of Brahms's Fourth Symphony," *Music Analysis* 8/3 (October 1989), pp. 234–5.   [6] Samson, "Chopin and genre," p. 213.

Franco Fabbri, after objecting that "in most musicological literature which has tackled the problem of genres . . . formal and technical rules seem to be the only ones taken into consideration, to the point where genre, style and form become synonomous," then offers a definition of genre as "a set of musical events (real or possible) whose course is governed by a definite set of socially accepted rules" and suggests that semiotic, behavioral, social, ideological, economic, and juridicial dimensions must be considered as well.[7] Robert Walser argues that "musical meanings are always grounded socially and historically, and they operate on an ideological field of conflicting interests, institutions, and memories. . . . This is a poststructural view of music in that it sees all signification as provisional, and it seeks for no essential truths inherent in structures, regarding all meanings as produced through the interaction of texts and readers. . . . Ultimately, musical analysis can be considered credible only if it helps explain the significance of musical activities in particular social contexts." Or, even more bluntly: "the purpose of a genre is to organize the reproduction of a particular ideology."[8]

The flexibility of genre

Many recent critics emphasize the flexibility of genre. As Jacques Derrida puts it, "every text participates in one or several genres, there is no genre-less text; there is always a genre and genres, yet such participation never amounts to belonging,"[9] and Frederic Jameson agrees: "*Pure* textual exemplifications of a single genre do not exist; and this, not merely because pure manifestations of anything are rare, but . . . because texts always come into being at the intersection of several genres and emerge from the tensions in the latter's multiple force fields."[10] Robert Walser extends this view to popular music: "Nowhere are genre boundaries more fluid than in popular music. Just as it is impossible to point to a perfectly exemplary Haydn symphony, one that fulfils the 'norms' in every respect, pieces within a popular genre rarely correspond slavishly to general criteria. Moreover, musicians are ceaselessly creating new fusions and extensions of popular genres."[11]

7 Franco Fabbri, "A theory of musical genres: two applications," in *Popular Music Perspectives* [1] (Gothenburg and Exeter, 1982), pp. 55–9.
8 Robert Walser, *Running with the Devil: Power, Gender, and Madness in Heavy Metal Music* (Hanover and London, 1993), pp. 29, 31, 34.
9 Jacques Derrida, "The law of genre," *Critical Inquiry* 7 (Autumn 1980), p. 65.
10 Frederic Jameson, "Towards a new awareness of genre," *Science Fiction Studies* 28 (1982), p. 322.
11 Walser, *Running with the Devil*, p. 27.

In setting out to construct a taxonomy of Berlin's early songs,[12] not as an abstract intellectual exercise but as a way of getting at their meaning, I soon found that a given song could be perceived as belonging to two or more genres, or as lying between several of them. It also became clear that genre was defined more importantly by a song's intended and received meaning than by its compositional style and structure, and that two factors previously disregarded in the literature could be crucial in defining meaning and therefore genre – the identity of a song's protagonist, and performance style.

Genre, meaning, and ideology in "coon" songs

Berlin wrote each of his early songs as the expression of some protagonist, whose identity was encoded into the text and music, then projected, clarified, or even changed in the act of performance. To take the most obvious example, any song with an African-American protagonist was immediately recognized by its audience as a "coon" song. This identity could be established in the text by proper names already associated in popular culture with black characters (Alexander or Liza, for instance), by dialect purporting to represent black speech patterns and usage, by code words ("honey" or "baby"), or by turns of speech thought to reflect black practice; it could be suggested in the music by syncopated rhythmic patterns or melodic contours supposedly derived from African-American music. This racial identity was further ensured in performance by the singer's use of dialect, whether or not already present in the written text, by the interpolation of spoken dialogue clarifying the ethnicity of the song's characters, and sometimes by makeup, costume, and stage deportment.

The African-American identity of a song's protagonist would then be a key factor in the perception of its meaning. For instance, both text and music of Berlin's "When The Midnight Choo Choo Leaves For Alabam'" (1912) imply a black protagonist:

> When the midnight choo-choo leaves for Alabam',
> I'll be right there, I've got my fare.
> When I see that rusty-haired conductor-man,
> I'll grab him by the collar and I'll holler "Alabam'! Alabam'!"
> That's where you stop your train, that brings me back again.

---

[12] This taxonomy was undertaken in connection with my complete, critical edition of Berlin's early songs, scheduled for publication in 1994 as the second item of the series *Music of the United States* (MUSA), under the auspices of the American Musicological Society.

Down home where I'll remain,
Where my honey lamb am.
I will be right there with bells, when that old conductor yells,
"All aboard! All aboard! All aboard for Alabam'!"

Hints of "black" dialect in the text ("honey lamb" and the elision of Alabama) and passing suggestions of syncopation in the music may seem subtle clues today, but would have conveyed a clearer message in 1912. Beyond that, this vignette of a black man who has decided to return to his home in the South, and to stay there, takes on a more specific meaning when placed in the context of a racial issue of the day with relevance to the patrons of vaudeville houses in the urban North: resistance to the first mass migration of African-Americans from the South, where they "belonged" and where they had been happy, at least according to minstrel and "coon" songs by white songwriters.

"Midnight Choo Choo" is not an isolated song of its sort. Together with dozens of similar pieces, it forms a "back-to-Dixie" sub-genre of the "coon song," with black protagonists, often identified by even more overt references to their race than in Berlin's song, happily headed South.[13] Any possible ambiguity of racial identity is dispelled by period recordings, for instance the performance of Berlin's "Midnight Choo Choo" by Arthur Collins and Byron Harlan (Indestructible Columbia Cylinder 3289, recorded in September of 1912) in which the two singers assume broad "Negro" accents and interpolate comic dialogue unequivocally intended to depict African-American characters.[14]

However, if "Midnight Choo Choo" is performed in such a way that the race of the protagonist is changed or obscured, as in the performance by Fred Astaire and Judy Garland in the film *Easter Parade* (1958) or as recorded by Max Morath,[15] the song's meaning and thus its genre is altered. No longer a "coon" song, it now shares characteristics of two other genres, the ragtime song and the rustic

[13] For instance, the sheet music cover of another song of this type, "All Aboard for Alabam'" (George Mann and Walter Esberger, 1912), shows a black man astride a toy train. Other songs in this sub-genre, which traces its origins all the way back to such mid-nineteenth-century minstrel songs as Dan Emmett's "Dixie's Land" and Stephen Foster's "Old Folks At Home," include "I Want To Be In Dixie" (Irving Berlin and Ted Snyder, 1912), "All Aboard For Dixie Land" (Jack Yellen and George L. Cobb, 1913), "I'm Going Back To Carolina (Here Comes My Train, Ding Dong, Toot Toot)" by Billy Davis and Ernie Erdmann, 1913, and "I Guess I'll Soon Be Back In Dixieland (Hear The Whistle, Hear The Bell)" by Jack Rogers and Will Rossiter, 1915.

[14] "Gee, I'm Glad That I'm From Dixie" from the revue *Shuffle Along* by Noble Sissle and Eubie Blake, available on *Shuffle Along* (New World Records NW 260, 1976), is a recent reissue of a "back-to-Dixie" song.   [15] *Irving Berlin: The Ragtime Years* (Nonesuch Records).

ballad, the latter a favorite of such songwriters as Charles K. Harris
and Paul Dresser, featuring a protagonist who is nostalgic for his or
her childhood home in Indiana or Virginia or Michigan or New
Hampshire or wherever.

In a tradition of the popular stage going back to the early
nineteenth century, textual references to "serious" literature or
musical references to the classical repertory can be comical touches if
the protagonist of a song is lower class and ethnic. The resulting
satire is double edged: the protagonist is mocked for his or her
pretensions to elite culture, which is itself mocked for the benefit of
the working-class audiences of the popular theater through its
parody by an unlettered protagonist. The intended meaning of
Berlin's "That Mesmerizing Mendelssohn Tune" (1909) revolves
around the appropriation of the melody of Mendelssohn's "Spring
Song" by a black protagonist:

> Don't you stand there, honey, can't you hear me sighin'?
> Is you gwine to wait until I'm almost dyin'?
> Ummm! Ummm! Oh, that Mendelssohn Spring Song tune;
> Get yourself acquainted with some real live wooin',
> Make some funny noises like there's something doin',
> Ummm! Ummm! Oh, that Mendelssohn tune . . .

The identity of the protagonist is unequivocal in a period recording
by Arthur Collins and Byron Harlan.[16] But this point is lost and the
meaning, genre, and ideology of the song is changed if performed so
that "black" dialect disappears, sections of the text with overt
reference to the racial identity of the protagonist are omitted, and
voice production invokes only white performing traditions.[17] The
song becomes a romantic ballad, with the quotation from Mendelssohn
serving to suggest a "refined" protagonist.

The "suggestive song": performance and ideology

In a number of Berlin's early songs, protagonists are members of the
bourgeoisie or elite classes, and they engage in drinking, smoking,
gambling, adultery, pre-marital sex, and other acts contrary to the
dominant public morality of the day. The identification of these
protagonists as white and privileged, made clear by their British-
American names, their activities and occupations, their manner of

[16] Columbia A801, Mx. 4328–2 (January 1910).
[17] As in Joan Morris and William Bolcom, *Blue Skies: Songs by Irving Berlin* (Nonesuch Digital 9
79120–1 F, 1985).

speech, and the absence of ethnic tinges in the music, is crucial to their meaning.

In the Victorian era, songs dealing with socially unacceptable behavior followed one of two scenarios: either the moral transgression was condemned and punished, as in "A Bird In A Gilded Cage" (1902) by Arthur J. Lamb and Harry Von Tilzer, in which a young woman's greed in marrying a much older man for his money, rather than for love, brings her isolation and death; or the protagonist was a member of a lower-class, ethnic group, as in Hughie Cannon's "Bill Bailey, Won't You Please Come Home" (1902), a tale of marital strife and separation in an African-American family. But Berlin's protagonists in the songs in question, as noted above, belong to America's privileged classes, and these songs, humorous rather than tragic, become socially subversive.

Most popular songs of the Victorian era, written to be sung in the bourgeois parlor, had a didactic as well as an artistic function: their texts urged their well-to-do performers and listeners "to work hard, to postpone gratification, to repress themselves sexually, to 'improve' themselves, to be sober [and] conscientious."[18] But Berlin was not a product of American Victorianism. A member of an immigrant family struggling to rise above poverty, forced to take to the streets to earn pennies while still a child, he began singing ribald parodies of popular songs in bars and restaurants. When he began writing his own songs, it was from the perspective of the people he had known in New York's streets and working-class places of amusement, for whom the privileged classes were a fair target.

In "Call Me Up Some Rainy Afternoon" (1910), for instance, Nellie Green meets Harry Lee at a masquerade party and invites him to drop by her house for a "quiet little spoon." When he shows up one afternoon, he overhears her giving an even warmer invitation to another man, and also learns that promiscuity is a way of life in her family and by implication in her social circle:

> Call me up some rainy afternoon,
> Then again, how's the evening for a spoon?
> Call around tomorrow night,
> We can then put out that fire in the furnace.
> My Mama will sure be out of town,
> She'll be entertained by Mr. Brown,
> My Papa won't be round,
> He will call on Mrs. Brown . . .

[18] Daniel Walker Howe, "Victorian culture in America," in *Victorian America*, ed. Daniel Walker Howe (Philadelphia, 1976), p. 17.

The singer has a double task in projecting the intended meaning of this song: to make it clear through diction, voice quality, and demeanor that Nellie is white and from a privileged class, and also to leave no doubt about the nature of the "fire in the furnace" she intends to put out.[19]

Publishers, songwriters, and audiences recognized a genre known as the high-class ballad, exemplified by such classics as "The Rosary" (1898) by Ethelbert Nevin and "I Love You Truly" (1906) by Carry Jacobs-Bond. Berlin wrote a handful of these songs, marked by sentimental and chaste texts and somewhat pretentious harmonic and melodic language. As with other genres, the high-class ballad was defined not only by its text and music, but in performance, through "cultured" diction, vocal production stressing precise pitch, and a voice quality invoking the concert or recital rather than the vaudeville stage.[20] But many of Berlin's other ballads, among them "Stop, Stop, Stop (Come Over And Love Me Some More)" of 1910, were teasing, playful, and provocative, and in fact belong among his "suggestive" songs.

> Cuddle and squeeze me honey,
> Lead me right to cupid's door,
> Take me out upon that ocean called the "Lovable Sea,"
> Fry each kiss in honey, then present it to me –
> Cuddle and please me honey,
> Anchor at this kissing shore;
> My honey stop, stop, stop, don't dare to stop,
> Come over and love me some more.

The challenge for the singer is to make it clear that this song is neither a sentimental ballad nor an ethnic song, by projecting a protagonist who has more in mind than cuddling and kissing, yet is white and privileged. Elida Morris does this by singing with considerable rhythmic and melodic freedom, though still in a somewhat "cultivated" style, and speaking the key words "Stop, stop, stop . . ." in a transparently provocative way.[21]

The subversive nature of such songs didn't go unnoticed by public defenders of America's morals, who attacked them in the press and from the pulpit, and succeeded in getting them banned in Boston. As one journalist indignantly put it,

[19] Ada Jones succeeds in doing this in a recording of the song made in June of 1910, released as Victor 16058–B.

[20] Henry Burr's recording of Berlin's "When I Lost You" (Victor 17313–B, 1912) illustrates this style of "high-class" performance.

[21] Victor 17787–A (9146), recorded 13 September 1910.

[suggestive songs] laugh openly at the sacred institutions of marriage [and] frankly praise and encourage the faithlessness and deceit practiced by . . . friend, husband or wife. What has come over us anyhow? Decent women and girls with their men folk sit in theatres and applaud vociferously, amid their boisterous laughter, some singer who with well-studied indecency proceeds to gush forth songs of the most vulgar and immoral character. . . . If I had my way I would appoint a rigorous censorship upon all so-called "popular song," and make it a criminal offense to publish such songs as I have mentioned.[22]

Performance and genre in ragtime songs

The role of the performer was also crucial in shaping the genre of ragtime song. One writer remarked in 1916 that "now, everything that carries the jerky meter, or an irregular meter that possesses a pleasing lilt, is called ragtime."[23] Ragtime manuals demonstrate how popular and classical pieces could be played in ragtime style, and Wickes observes that "a clever pianist can 'rag' the most sacred song ever published."[24]

Many of Berlin's songs with no hint of syncopated rhythms in their music and no mention of ragtime in their titles or texts, "I Want To Be In Dixie" and "When The Midnight Choo-Choo Leaves For Alabam'," for instance, were perceived as ragtime songs because of the style in which they were sung and played on stage and recorded on phonograph discs and cylinders. British journalists referred to the former as one of Berlin's most popular rag songs when he performed it in London, and Berlin himself includes both in his ragtime medley "They've Got Me Doin' It Now" (1913). Almost any song, then, might be perceived by audiences as a ragtime song if performed in a "jerky" style.

Conclusions

Though the performer plays little or no role in genre formation in the classical repertory, in Berlin's early songs, as in much popular music, the performer shapes, reinforces, and even changes genre. In this repertory, genre is defined most importantly neither by formal structure nor by fixed elements of style such as melody and

---

[22] Alexander Blume, in an unidentified newspaper article from 1913 included in a scrapbook kept by Irving Berlin, now in the Irving Berlin Collection in the Library of Congress, Washington.

[23] E. M. Wickes, *Writing the Popular Song* (Springfield, 1916), p. 33.   [24] *Ibid.*

harmony, but by audience perception of the meaning of a song, shaped at the moment of performance by the singer's vocal quality, diction, and other nuances of delivery.

Thus flexibility of genre in popular music extends beyond the fact that a given piece can belong to two or more genres, or fall in the intersection of several of them; genre can change from performance to performance.

20

EPILOGUE: JOHN CAGE REVISITED

In the late winter of 1992, Northwestern University, which houses a large collection of John Cage's manuscripts, papers, art works, and programs, celebrated his approaching eightieth birthday with a week-long series of concerts, lectures, workshops, panels, and exhibits. The following remarks opened the first concert on the evening of 3 March. Afterwards, Cage and I walked back to the hotel where we were both staying. As we were saying goodbye at the elevator – I was leaving the next morning – I asked him, "What do you think about all this fuss people have been making over postmodernism?" In his usual style, he thought for a while, before answering, "I think it's wonderful when people make a fuss over anything." That was the last time I saw him; he died of a stroke several months later, a few weeks short of his eightieth birthday.

* * *

From the late 1950s through the 70s I was involved with John Cage in various ways: at the bridge and poker table; listening to and occasionally performing in his compositions; and trying to write about him. I thought I had an intuitive grasp of what he was doing and why he was doing it, but when it came to putting things into words,[1] I felt that something was eluding me.

Though I continued to pay attention to "new music" in a general way after that, I became involved chiefly with the study of popular music. Because of this, I suppose, it was suggested that my remarks might focus on Cage's relationship to popular culture.

---

[1] As, for instance, in my entry for Cage in *The New Grove Dictionary of Music and Musicians*, ed. Stanley Sadie (London, 1980), vol. 3, pp. 597–603.

Since none of his records has been listed on the *Billboard* charts recently, and I haven't seen any of his music videos on MTV for some time, it might seem that I could stop right here. But there is, in fact, something to be said.

Back in the 1960s and 70s, most musicologists and critics were under the impression that American culture was still in the midst of a stylistic/intellectual period which had begun around the turn of the century and had been most clearly defined between 1911 and 1914. John Cage and Milton Babbitt were thought to be the leaders of two important branches of the second generation of this new music. To my knowledge, Leonard Meyer and I were the only two musicologists to challenge this view, at least in print: I insisted that most music of the first half of the twentieth century could be understood as a continuation of nineteenth-century theory and practice;[2] and Meyer suggested in a brilliant essay that the "radical empiricism" of Cage represented the most dramatic conceptual and stylistic break in Western music for more than three centuries.[3]

Now, fifteen years later, there's agreement among cultural theorists and philosophers, if not yet musicologists, that a major breaking point in American culture came shortly after mid-century, perhaps in the early 1970s, and there are even labels for this new partitioning: "modernism" for the first two-thirds of the century, "postmodernism" for the past two decades or so.

Distinctions in both style and substance have been made between modernism and postmodernism in the arts, in architecture, aesthetics, philosophy, criticism, economics, and even political theory.

Concerning style, one writer has listed a number of oppositions between modernism and postmodernism: purpose vs. play; closed, conjunctive forms vs. open, disjunctive forms; design vs. chance; hierarchy vs. anarchy; determinacy vs. indeterminacy; finished art objects vs. process or performance; presence vs. absence; master code vs. idiolect; genital/phallic vs. polymorphous/androgynous; mastery vs. silence; and so on.[4] Another critic, David Harvey, argues that postmodernity has totally and affirmatively embraced ephemerality, fragmentation, discontinuity, and chaos.[5] And here's a typical description of a postmodern work of art: "One is confronted not with a unified text, much less by the presence of a distinct

[2] Charles Hamm, "Not yet," *Arts in Society* 4/3 (Fall–Winter 1967), pp. 554–60.

[3] Leonard Meyer, "The end of the Renaissance?" in *Music, The Arts and Ideas: Patterns and Predictions in Twentieth-Century Culture* (Chicago and London, 1967), pp. 68–84. Meyer's essay first appeared in *The Hudson Review* 6/2 (Summer 1963).

[4] Ihab Hassan, "The culture of postmodernity," *Theory, Culture and Society* 2/3 (1985), pp. 124–4.

[5] David Harvey, *The Condition of Postmodernity* (Cambridge, MA, and Oxford, 1990).

personality and sensibility, but by a discontinuous terrain of heterogeneous discourses uttered by anonymous, unplaceable tongues."[6]

At the level of substance, the overriding distinction between modernism and postmodernism seems to boil down to the issue of control, or power. To take the instance of architecture: modernism gave us Le Corbusier, urban renewal and public housing in both capitalist and socialist countries, the Rockefeller Center, Tiananmen Square in Beijing, the shopping mall – all instances of large spaces designed in ways to impact on everyone who inhabits them. In economics, modernity climaxed with Henry Ford's scheme for capturing, maintaining, and standardizing control over industrial production on the largest scale ever conceived. In social and political thought, modernity brought the era of the meta-narrative, with Marx and Freud, among others, offering broad, all-encompassing interpretative schemes. In the arts, the great figures of modernism were concerned with "finding some special mode of representation of eternal truth."[7] Schoenberg, and then Webern and Babbitt, came up with self-referential compositional techniques to produce music beyond criticism, because of its adherence to the meta-narrative of serialism; and Schenker proposed an analytical meta-narrative to yield the underlying structural truth about all music.

But as Terry Eagleton puts it, "We are now in the process of awakening from the nightmare of modernity. . . . Post-modernism signals the death of such 'meta-narratives' whose secretly terroristic function was to ground and legitimate the illusion of a 'universal' human history."[8]

Jonathan Raban's *Soft City* offers a vision of postmodern architecture which allows urban space to be "a theatre, a series of stages upon which individuals could work their own distinctive magic while performing a multiplicity of roles," a "labyrinth, honeycombed with diverse networks of social interaction," a "maniacal scrapbook filled with colourful entries which have no relation to each other, no determining, rational scheme."[9] Economists speak of a complex global network of "flexible modes of capital accumulation."[10] In aesthetics and the arts, we have John Cage telling us "Here we are. Let us say Yes to our presence together in Chaos."[11]

---

[6] F. Pfeil, "Postmodernism as a 'structure of feeling'," in *Marxism and the Interpretation of Culture*, ed. C. Nelson and L. Grossberg (Urbana, 1988), p. 384. The reference is to the film *Wings of Desire* by Wim Wenders.   [7] Harvey, *The Condition of Postmodernity*, p. 20.
[8] Terry Eagleton, "Awakening from modernity," *Times Literary Supplement*, 20 February 1987.
[9] J. Raban, *Soft City* (London, 1974).   [10] Harvey, *The Condition of Postmodernity*.
[11] John Cage, *Silence* (Middletown, CT, 1961), p. 195.

Cage once remarked that only the present is fixed, while the past is constantly changing. Revisiting the new music of the 1950s and 60s after not thinking much about it for a decade or so, and equipped with a new conceptual framework and a new vocabulary, I find that things have become quite different and in some ways much simpler. Now one can just say that despite the fact that Milton Babbitt and John Cage happened to have been born within a few years of one another, the music and aesthetics of Babbitt were classic examples of unrelenting modernism, while the music and aesthetics of John Cage are thoroughly postmodern.

I'd go further, and say that I've experienced nothing in postmodern art that wasn't anticipated in the music of John Cage, and I've read nothing in postmodern theory and criticism that I haven't already read in his writings.

Postmodern criticism has given us a lovely set of words to associate with the style of Cage's music: open, play, disjunctive, anarchy, chance, silence, process, participation, dispersal, anti-narrative, mutant, polymorphous – qualities present in Cage's music long before postmodern critics developed their vocabulary. Concerning substance, Cage was absolutely clear on the subject of power, long before postmodern critics focused on this as a defining issue. At a time when Babbitt and his peers were boasting that they had finally achieved total control over the notes of a composition, Cage was "compos[ing] parts but not scores, [which] may be combined in any unthought ways. This means that each performance of such a piece of music is unique, as interesting to its composer as to other listeners,"[12] and soon he would give up composing even the parts. At a time when Babbitt was insisting that his pieces could be appreciated only by those who fully understood his compositional methods, Cage was telling us that "now structure is not put into a work, but comes up in the person who perceives it in himself. There is therefore no problem of understanding, but the possibility of awareness."[13]

This exchange took place with a somewhat hostile European interviewer:

> D: Would you say something about black people's culture. . . .
> Cage: Well, when I began to be interested in noise, it was because noise was free of the laws of harmony and counterpoint. Now the exciting thing about blacks is that they are going to be free of laws which were made by whites to protect themselves from blacks,

---

[12] *Ibid.*, p. 11.   [13] *Ibid.*, p. 259.

among other things, and to keep blacks in slavery and to keep white people more powerful. Now, it won't be good for blacks to become powerful like whites, any more than it would be good for noise to become as harmonious and as devoted to counterpoint as musical sounds. . . .

D: Would you explain that once more?

Cage: Power is not the question. That was the question in harmony and counterpoint, where you have good things and bad things and you make the rules. That is what white people did to blacks: they made rules. We need a situation in which we don't have rules, in which things are not more powerful than other things, but in which each thing is what it is. Which we already have in music.[14]

But what of Cage's connection with popular culture, which I promised would be the focus of these remarks?

Some years ago Gordon Mumma and I manned radio No. 7 in a performance of Cage's *Imaginary Landscape No. 4* in the then-new Great Hall in Krannert Center on the Champaign-Urbana campus of the University of Illinois. When the time came for Cage's piece, the only radio station with a powerful enough signal to penetrate that massive structure happened to be playing Peter, Paul, and Mary's version of John Denver's "Leaving on a Jet Plane"; so the performance consisted of a hauntingly fragmented version of that piece of popular music.

Cage's aesthetic didn't prescribe this, but it didn't exclude it when it happened.

John Cage probably doesn't pay much attention to popular music, except when it turns up by chance in one of his own compositions. But that's not the issue. In its insistence that "each thing is what it is," postmodern art and criticism has challenged modernity's desperate determination to maintain all barriers between so-called high art and such products of popular culture as rock music, film, and music videos. As a pioneering postmodern artist and theorist, and in my opinion the leader of the pack, Cage has been a major force in an intellectual movement that not only has had a liberating effect on composers of new music, but has insisted on the legitimacy of the popular arts as well.

[14] "Interview mit John Cage," in *Dissonanz* (Zurich), no. 6 (September 1970).

INDEX

abolition of slavery, and popular music, 101–6

acculturation in music, 140–3, 167–8, 172, 174, 192, 202–3

Adorno, Theodor, 4 n.10, 25, 40 n.104, 43, 371–2

African–American music and culture, 11–17, 27, 37–8, 134, 196, 205, 252, 310–12, 327–30, 351, 360, 374–6; in South Africa, 146, 148–9, 157–8, 161–4, 170–209

African elements in popular music, 176–7, 184, 190, 198–9, 204–5, 235, 240, 333

African National Congress, 169, 179, 186–7, 194, 210, 220, 247, 266, 339

Andersson, Muff, 140, 145, 204, 231 n.24, 232 n.28, 236 n.36, 245, 338

apartheid, 144–5, 152, 194, 212, 218, 261, 340, 343

Arbitron Corporation, 122–3

Attali, Jacques, 188, 256, 261, 319, 320

Austin, William, 251

authenticity, in music, 11–21, 23–7, 32, 311

autonomy, musical, 2, 4–5, 18, 56–7, 71, 73–5, 317–19, 321

Babbitt, Milton, 40 n.104, 72–6, 383–4

Baez, Joan, 51, 342–3

Baker, Laverne, in South Africa, 201

Ballantine, Chris, 140, 236 n.38

Barthes, Roland, 218 n.58, 345

BBC, 214, 224, 285, 294

Belafonte, Harry, 164, 337, 340–3·

Berlin, Edward, 12 n.28, 18 n.43

Berlin, Irving, 5, 12, 183, 217, 310, 328, 353, 359, 370, 374–80; songs: "Call Me Up Some Rainy Afternoon," 377–8; "Stop, Stop, Stop (Come Over And Love Me Some More)," 378; "When The Midnight Choo-Choo Leaves For Alabam'," 374–6

Berry, Venise, 39

Billboard, 45, 48, 52, 120–2, 187, 191, 196, 205

Black Conciousness, in South Africa, 203–4, 206

Blesh, Rudi, 11, 18

Bloom, Allan, 10, 256

Bloomfield, Terry, 26

blues, 31, 34–5, 44–5, 183–4, 310, 327, 329–30, 331–3; and Gershwin, 327–35

Blumenbach, Johann Friedrich, 346–7

Borges, Jorge Luis, 371

Broederband, 220–1

Brooks, William, 99–100

Byrnside, Ronald, 56

Cage, John, 78, 89–93, 96–7, 262, 381–5; aesthetic of, xi–xii, 90, 99, 384–5; works, *Concert for Piano and Orchestra*, 90; *HPSCHD*, 92–3; *Imaginary Landscape No. 4*, 78, 385

canon in music, 18–19, 41, 56, 99, 256

capitalism and music, 1, 9, 22, 25–6, 100, 167, 182, 211, 225, 240, 261, 273, 313

Carson, Rachel, *Silent Spring*, 85–6

cassette tapes, in China, 300–1, 303

Cele, Willard, 237

Central People's Broadcasting Station (China), 270–304; music programing, 276–92; National Programs, 272, 284, 288, 292, 298–9; organizational structure, 271–2, 305

Chase, Gilbert, 11–12, 43–4

Checker, Chubby, 162, 191–3

Chernoff, John, 193

Chinese Opera, 282–3, 301

choral music in South Africa, 216–17, 232–4, 235–6

class and music, 22–3, 25–6, 33, 137, 167,

213–14, 217–18, 228, 234–6, 240, 277, 345, 376–8
"classic" popular music, 17–21, 324
classical music, Chinese, 283–4, 291–2
classical music, Western, 2–3, 17; aesthetics of, 7, 89, 268, 285, 322–4, 346, 379; by American composers, 68–76, 88, 306–24; in contemporary China, 284–5, 295, 299
Clegg, Johnny, 337
Cockrell, Dale, 147, 170, 175
Cohen, Sarah, 38–9
Coleman, Ornette, 94–5
"commercialism" in popular music, 19, 27–8, 32–4, 43, 288
"coon" songs, 359, 374–6
Coplan, David, 150, 161–2, 170, 178–9, 184, 211, 216 n.9, 218 n.10, 234 n.32, 236
Copland, Aaron, 76, 314, 323, 353
country-western music, 31–4, 52, 127, 129, 136, 288
Cui Jian, 287, 296, 301, 304
Cultural Revolution in China, 275, 283, 286, 292–3, 303

Dahlhaus, Carl, 4, 262 n.17, 268 n.24, 371
Dene, Terry, 155
Derrida, Jacques, 373
DeVeaux, Scott, 20 n.52, 40 n.104
disco, 204–5, 206–7, 245, 286; as interracial music, 205; in South Africa, 206
Douglass, Frederick, 102–3
Drum, 157–61, 163–4, 189–90, 198, 200
Dube, John, 179, 186
Dvořák, Antonin, 344, 348, 351–3
Dylan, Bob, 34–5, 47, 51, 56, 253

Eagleton, Terry, 383
Ellington, Duke, 14, 20, 163, 231, 311, 329–30, 334
Erlmann, Veit, 150, 170–1, 175–6, 181, 235 nn.33–5, 239–40
ethnicity and music, 11–17, 50, 124, 290–1, 321–2, 357–60

Fabbri, Franco, 373
Fang Kun, 281, 291
Feng Bingyou, 295–6
film and music, 301, 320–1
Fiori, Umberto, 141, 251 n.4
folk music, see traditional music
folk revival, 223, 342–3
Foster, Stephen, 116, 127, 172, 182, 251, 281, 344, 351–2, 359
"freedom songs" in South Africa, 204, 210, 341

Gay, Leslie, 39

geming gequ, see "mass song"
genre in popular music, 370–80
Gershwin, George, 306–24, 325–35, 353, 359; blues and jazz, 309–12, 315, 325–35; and "folk" music, 314–15; family of, 312–17; Concerto in F, 12, 309, 316, 325–35; Porgy and Bess, 314–17, 321, 326; Rhapsody in Blue, 311, 315–16, 326
Gillett, Charlie, 22 n.57, 30–1
Gobineau, Comte de, 347–8
Goepp, Philip, 7–8
Goldberg, Isaac, 12–13, 27–30, 310, 325 n.1, 328
Goldman, Albert, 131–8
Goodman, Paul, 81–2
gospel music in South Africa, 175, 182, 196
Graceland, see Simon, Paul
Gray, Dobie, 146, 203, 340
Green, Archie, 31–3

Haley, Bill, 134–5, 151, 158–9, 161, 187–90, 251, 266
Hamm, Marilyse, 249–50
Han Yidan, 282 n.25, 285–7
Handy, W. C., 329, 331
Harvey, David, 1 n.2, 382–3
Hassan, Ihab, 382
Hayakawa, S. I., 44–6, 52–3
Hayman, Graham, 213, 214 n.6, 216 n.8, 222 n.14, 225–6, 243 n.45
heavy metal music, 40, 367–9
Hersey, John, 81
Hodeir, André, 13
"homelands" in South Africa, 194, 219–20, 226, 228, 245; in Namibia, 241–2
Hosokawa, Shuhei, 256–7
Hou Dejien, 303–4
Huang Bingqi, 276, 285–7
Huskisson, Yvonne, 230 n.22, 232 n.37, 233–4, 239 n.43
Hutchinson Family, 100–15

Ideology and music, 35–6, 99, 129–30, 166, 194–6, 216, 229–30, 246, 280, 287, 293, 336–43, 357, 360–1, 367–9, 374–9
immigration into the United States, 7–8, 321–2
Ink Spots, 176, 236, 238
International Association for the Study of Popular Music (IASPM), 23–4, 117, 250
isicathamiya, 235
Ives, Charles, 9, 58, 308–9, 321–3

Jackson, Michael, 209, 295–6
Jackson, Millie, 144, 202
Jay, Gideon, 158–9, 162–3

389